T0336522

Unstructured
Data Analytics

Unstructured Data Analytics

*How to Improve Customer Acquisition,
Customer Retention, and Fraud
Detection and Prevention*

Jean Paul Isson

WILEY

Published by John Wiley & Sons, Inc., Hoboken, New Jersey.

Published simultaneously in Canada.

For general information on our other products and services or for technical support, please contact our Customer Care Department within the United States at (800) 762–2974, outside the United States at (317) 572–3993, or fax (317) 572–4002.

Wiley publishes in a variety of print and electronic formats and by print-on-demand. Some material included with standard print versions of this book may not be included in e-books or in print-on-demand. If this book refers to media such as a CD or DVD that is not included in the version you purchased, you may download this material at http://booksupport.wiley.com. For more information about Wiley products, visit www.wiley.com.

Library of Congress Cataloging-in-Publication Data is Available:

ISBN 9781119129752 (Hardcover)
ISBN 9781119325505 (ePDF)
ISBN 9781119325499 (ePub)

Cover Design: Wiley
Cover Images: Polygonal background © Hamster3d/iStockphoto;
Abstract Background © imagy/iStockphoto

Printed in the United States of America.

10 9 8 7 6 5 4 3 2 1

I dedicate this book to my daughters Roxane and Sofia who are my inspiring muse for writing books and for so many great things I do. Daddy is finished writing and is no longer hiding in the basement sitting in front of his computer. I hope when you will read this book, you will be proud of your patience and understanding.

A special Thanks to my wife Marjolaine for her love and support adjusting family's activities to accommodate my writing schedule.

Contents

Foreword

Undoubtedly, we've all seen some infographic showcasing how the amount of data in our digitally connected world, if represented as books, would circle the globe a number of times. We've all heard the mind-boggling amount of data created every minute of every day. Each minute generates ~456,000 tweets, ~46,000 Uber trips, ~4,150,000 YouTube videos watched, and more. How did we get here? It's simple: in 1964, 1TB of memory would have cost about $3.5 billion. Today? $27...and it fits into your shirt pocket. (Keep in mind all of these numbers were out of date the minute they were stated.)

Now consider the impact of technologies such as blockchain and the Internet of Things (IoT) on the velocity of data that's currently being collected. Data collection rates are set to go into turbo mode (if they aren't already there). If I was to grade the world on data collection, I'd give it an A+. 24/7, the world stores more and more data. Nice job, world!

What about grading the world on how much of that data it understands? C− (at best). Why? Most of the world's data is unstructured—in other words, it doesn't fit nicely into the rows and columns upon which most analytics is performed. Add to this the fact that most of the world's data can't even be "Googled" (which means your company is stuck with it)...and opportunity has been missed.

The growing importance of unstructured data is evidenced by the recognition of Big Data industry leaders and academics that unstructured data has become a critical aspect of developing and using all the types of data intelligences that organizations, governments, and businesses have at their disposal. Efficiently harnessing unstructured data helps them to better manage their entire data asset and create additional value to compete and win.

So, regardless of the industry you are in, if you are struggling to move beyond unstructured data collection or basic reporting and want to create *actionable intelligence* from your internal and external unstructured data, this book will help you achieve that goal. It will help you capture the value hidden in the abyss and open up new opportunities for top-line growth, better customer acquisition and retention, better fraud detection and prevention, better safety, better product and service, better healthcare services (saving and improving lives), and so on.

Since unstructured data is the dominant type in the data collection rates for which an A+ grade was assigned, this book serves as a magnificent guide, helping you fully leverage your data and create actionable value for your organization.

Unstructured Data Analytics takes you through a framework for putting unstructured data to work in your organization (with examples across a multitude of industries and cross-industry use cases that inspire "the art of the possible" thinking), and it's done in an easy-to-read manner. I found a number of embedded "Aha" moments throughout the book that even seasoned analytic professionals will benefit from, a tribute to the talent and experience that Jean Paul Isson brings to all of his work.

Unstructured data is the lift, shift, rift, or cliff for any business today. Those who take the right path will find themselves with top-line growth, as disruptors with new business models to profit from, with a sound defense mechanism (data) against would-be disruptors. *Unstructured Data Analytics* is a must-read for not just data professionals, but businesspeople in general, across all industries. I hope you enjoy the read as much as I did.

Paul Zikopoulos, IBM Vice President Cognitive Systems
@BigData_paulz

Preface

Over the past few years, we've witnessed a lot of hype and blandishment around Big Data, the Internet of Things, and artificial intelligence such as machine learning, deep learning, and cognitive analytics. The news constantly showcases how technological and analytical advancements change our lives and the way we do business. Transforming Big Data and the Internet of Things into actionable intelligence is the next frontier of innovation in this augmented age of analytics and is a top priority for leading data-driven executives.

Have you ever wondered how job boards like Monster match resumes to job descriptions without relying on an army of resources? How Google understands text in queries to provide pertinent articles, videos, images, and the like? How Spotify recommends a personalized Weekly Playlist that matches your musical tastes? How Twitter or Facebook derive user sentiment from millions of daily tweets and updates? How companies leverage the voices of their customers to improve client acquisition and retention or to develop new products? How IBM Watson assists physicians in diagnosing some diseases and recommends the best treatment? How national security organizations tap into billions of online communications to detect and prevent threats? How machines can find legal information to assist lawyers to defend cases? If your answer is "yes," then unstructured data analytics (UDA) is the door to open for clues.

This book is about the analysis of unstructured data. Unstructured data does not fit a conventional relational database. It flows in a variety of formats—text, voice, images, bitmap, audio, and video—at an unprecedented speed and volume. It is propelled by the underpinning growth in technology and advances in computing power. Unstructured data makes up more than 80 percent of Big Data.

Today, companies can capture and store a lot of data, structured and unstructured, thanks to the low cost of storage. Many companies have done a great job in analyzing traditional structured data. However, they struggle to find actionable knowledge buried in texts, voice recordings, audio, video, images, and pictures. They consider themselves data rich but insight poor. In a worldwide competitive environment, executives are under extreme pressure to analyze this new type of data to create actionable business value and differentiate their company from the competition.

From increasing strategies to acquire or retain customer or talent to improving fraud detection and prevention, from human resources and human capital management, legal services, sports performance, healthcare and medical research, national security, and social media management, to product and services development, UDA will make a tangible impact across all industries and fields.

I wrote this book to be different from available books on text analytics, and I am glad you have chosen to read it. The motivation for writing this book comes, in part, from key learning from my previous books on data analytics and people analytics. This book fills a gap of knowledge on how to deal with unstructured data coming from Big Data. During my interviews for my previous books, *Win with Advanced Business Analytics* and *People Analytics in the Era of Big Data*, I learned from the leaders with whom I spoke that the biggest hurdle in the era of Big Data was taming unstructured data. Most leaders were convinced this new type of data had huge potential, but they didn't know where to start. Since most books do not really provide business-oriented insights and frontline stories while covering this topic, I decided to address the gap the executives felt by providing a how-to framework that any leader could use.

The concepts and approaches presented here are a combination of my own practical analytical leadership experiences in more than 50 countries and insights I gathered throughout my research. As such, the book is not written in an ivory tower. I have been through what I write in this book, have overcome the pitfalls I outline, and have created successful analytical solutions for a wide variety of global business solutions.

This book focuses on practical approaches that can help businesses create value from their data and make the most of the organization's analytical assets. Also, unlike other books, I outline how unstructured data analytics can be applied in several industries, along with an actionable framework and some frontline case studies from industry leaders in different organizations. What is working and what should you avoid? This book will help you evaluate the effectiveness of your UDA strategy and implementation, and will provide you with a framework to take your efforts to the next level, creating business value for your organization in the process.

This book is for leaders who want to learn about the power of UDA to optimize their data analytics strategy and practices. It provides an easy-to-implement framework and real-world case studies and interviews from leading organizations that are harnessing their structured and unstructured data to address their key business challenges. Managers and graduate students will also find the book useful, as it provides tactical information to support their roles. Although this is not a technical book, it is written to be relevant to someone with no analytical experience as well as to the person with a great deal of analytical experience. I have included an appendix section called Tech Corner Details to provide some fundamental techniques from linear algebra that are commonly used in UDA, such as text analysis and image analysis. Of course, there is a lot of software that performs text analytics and natural language processing, but I believe it is worth looking under the hood to better understand how things work.

I recommend reading the book from cover to cover; however, every chapter can stand on its own. If you are interested in using UDA to detect and prevent fraud, you can jump right to Chapter 5 (The Power of UDA to Improve Fraud Detection and Prevention). Likewise, if you are interested in understanding how NBA teams like the Houston Rockets use analytics to drive team performance, you can go to Chapter 11 (The Power of UDA in Sports). And if you are interested in understanding how you can improve your product development, you can Go to Chapter 9 (The Power of UDA in Product and Service Development). However, you will get the most from the book if you first read Chapters 1 (The Age of Advanced Business Analytics) through 3 (The Framework to Put UDA to Work). Readers not interested in understanding some technical details can skip the appendix A section.

To support the UDA framework proposed, I have included interviews and frontline stories from leading UDA organizations including: IBM, SAS Institute, Manulife, AXA, Monster Worldwide, LinkedIn, Google, Amazon, Facebook, Spotify, Pfizer, Under Armour, The Container Store, Dell, JPMorgan Chase & Co, Citi, Toronto Raptors, and the Houston Rockets.

Over a 22-month period of research for this book, I spoke to 253 business leaders across several industries and regions. Many of these interviews are found in the book, and for the majority of them, I gathered my interviewees' input to validate the framework I propose and to underscore what is needed to leverage the untapped data. I engaged with leaders from businesses in several industries that are using UDA solutions, as well as with leading solutions providers to understand why they invested resources in developing UDA tools and solutions and, more important, what they foresee as the Next Big Thing.

The accuracy of text analysis to identify emotion or sentiment still sparks heated debate. Don't wait to get the perfect solution. With this framework, you can start your UDA journey today to stay current and remain competitive while you learn and improve based on the data you have. You will be able to create business value from both your structured and your unstructured data to ultimately compete and win.

Acknowledgments

I engaged with hundreds of leaders to write this book, whether through interviews, formal contribution, or informal collaboration. I am indebted to many for helping me to complete this book.

I would like to thank Elise Amyot, who reviewed all chapters and case studies contained in this book. Elise's insightful, constructive, and invaluable feedback helped make the book easier to understand for all readers.

I would also like to thank Kim Lascelles, who reviewed my two previous books and helped by reviewing the first proposal of this book as well as some early chapters. Kim is a key pillar for the writing of my books.

Writing a book with a full-time job is a big undertaking. It would not have been possible without the support and input of other professionals, the hundreds of industry leaders and experts who generously participated in my research and shared their unstructured data analytics (UDA) journeys. You will see contributions and great insights throughout the book, in the form of quotes and concrete examples of how they make UDA work. I would like to thank all of them. The following list identifies many to whom I am indebted:

Foreword to the Book

- Paul Zikopoulos, Vice President Big Data and Cognitive Systems—IBM

Interviews and Case Studies

- Wayne Thompson, Chief Data Scientist, SAS Data Science Technologies—SAS
- Fiona McNeill, Global Technology Product Marketing Manager—SAS
- Suzanne Sprajcar Beldyck, Head of Content and Communications—SAS Canada

- Heather Johnson, Manager, Analytics, Assets, Market Development and Insights—IBM
- Eugen Wen, Vice President, Group Advanced Analytics— Manulife. Thanks a lot for your continuing support.
- Stephani E. Kingsmill, Executive Vice President, Human Resources—Manulife Financial
- Cindy Forbes, Executive Vice President and Chief Analytics Officer—Manulife Financial
- Vishwa Kolla, Assistant Vice President, Head of Advanced Analytics—John Hancock Financial Services
- Winston Lin, Director, Strategy and Analytics—Houston Rockets
- Tommy Balcetis, Director of Basketball Strategy and Analytics— Denver Nuggets
- Keith Boyarsky Director of Analytics—Toronto Raptors
- Yongzheng (Tiger) Zhang, Senior Manager, Data Analytics/Data Mining—LinkedIn
- François Laviolette, Director, Laval University Big Data Research Centre—Université Laval
- Seth Grimes, President and Principal Consultant—Alta Plana Corporation; Founding Chair—Sentiment Analysis Symposium
- Greta Roberts, Chief Executive Officer and Cofounder—Talent Analytics, Corp.
- Pasha Roberts, Chief Scientist and Cofounder—Talent Analytics, Corp.
- Diane Deperrois, General Manager South-East & Oversea Regions—AXA France
- Mateo Cavasotto, Cofounder and Chief Executive Officer—Emi Labs
- Doug Klinger, Chief Executive Officer and Member, Board of Directors—Zelis Healthcare
- Mark Stoever, Chief Executive Officer—2020 Inc. former CEO Monster Worldwide Inc.
- Arun Chidambaram, Global Head Talent Analytics—Pfizer

- Troy Barnette, Customer Engagement Executive SAP; former Sr Director Corporate Service Business Relationship Lead at Under Armour

- Rell B. Robinson, Senior HRIS and HR Analytics Professional—Bloomberg

- Ian Bailie, former: Senior Director, People Planning, Analytics, and Tools—CISCO; current: Cofounder—270 degrees

- Dawn Klinghoffer, General Manager, HR Business Insights—Microsoft

- Joanie Courtney, President and Chief Operating Officer, Professional Division—EmployBridge

- Bruno Aziza, Chief Marketing Officer—AtScale

- Louis Gagnon, Chief Executive Officer—MyBrainSolutions

- Art Papas, Chief Executive Officer and Cofounder—Bullhorn

- Gregory Piatetsky-Shapiro, President and Editor— KDnuggets

- Ian O'Keefe, Managing Director, Global Head of Workforce Analytics— JPMorgan Chase & Co.

- Vasu Nagalingam, Director, Personal Wealth & Retirement—Merrill Lynch

- Hugues Bertin, Chief Financial and Risk Officer, head of Digital Transformation—BNP Parisbas Cardif

- Stéphane Brutus, Ph.D., RBC Professor in Motivation and Employee Performance—Concordia University

- Jennifer Priestley, Ph.D., Associate Dean, Graduate College—Kennesaw State University

- Paul Mason, Senior Manager, Corporate Education—University of California, Berkeley

- Chantal Czerednikow, Dentist—Centre for Innovation, Montreal Children's Hospital, McGill University

- John Houston, Principal and US Data Science Offering Leader—Deloitte

- Amel Arhab, Senior Business Analytics Leader and Strategist, Senior Manager—Deloitte Consulting

- Abby Mehta, Ph.D, Senior Vice President, Marketing Insights and Media Analytics—Bank of America
- James Gallman, People Analytics Director—Boeing
- Fanta Berete, Responsable Pôle Devp. Ressources Humaines et Formation—CCI France
- Bryan Richardson, Global Practice Manager, Risk Advanced Analytics—McKinsey & Company
- Paul Fletcher, Senior Vice President Marketing—Aviva Canada
- Edmund Balogun, Project Director—IQPC
- Eric Siegel, Founder—Predictive Analytics World Conference Series
- All members of APM (Association pour le Progres du Management), a French CEO association with more than 6,500 members. Thanks for your useful insights, contribution with interviews, and business challenges you provided during our executive workshops that inspired some adjustments to the book.

Thanks to the members of the **Monster Worldwide team**: Matt O'Connor, John McLaughlin, Claude Yama, Meredith Hanrahan, Pat Manzo, Javid Muhammedali, Steve LeClair, and the Monster product team for their support and assistance with some content for this book.

I am also grateful for the support of the **Manulife executive team**, who found some time for my interviews despite their busy schedule. And special thanks to Eugene Wen for his continuing support and insightful inputs that help to reshape some parts of this book. And Angela Costa for helping to set up all interviews with some executives at Manulife. And Eugene Wen-Eugene your support and insightful inputs were extremely invaluable and helped to reshape some parts of this book.

I would like to thank my friends for their support: Nathalie de Repentigny for the continuing support for all of my major projects, Ryan Jung, Alejandro Del Moral, Eugene Wen, Eric de Larminat(for your support to find creative solutions to successfully address unplanned challenges), Kim Vu, Oumar Mbaye, Alfonso Troisi, Karima

Ahrab, Marc Bienstock, Ezana Raswork, Sean Dalton, Karim Salabi, Diawo Diallo, Eugene Robitaille, Mario Bottone, Mr and Mrs Guy, Siroux, and Guy François (my personal Abs coach at YMCA) and his colleague Rick Padmore.

I would also like to thank my family for their support: my parents, my mom Martha and my dad Samuel, for nurturing my passion for mathematics and teaching me the value of hard work at an early age; my brother Faustin (Moise), my sister Betty, my cousin David, my niece Marthe, my aunt Marie Christine, and my uncle Jackson (Isaac).

Special thanks to my two daughters, Roxane and Sofia, and my wife Marjolaine for their patience and understanding while I was robbing family time to research and write this book, hiding in the basement. Your love and support are key pillars to this achievement.

CHAPTER 1

The Age of Advanced Business Analytics

In God we trust; all others must bring data.
—Attributed to W. Edwards Deming

INTRODUCTION

If you believe that the data analytics revolution has already happened, think again. After the steam engine, mass production, and Internet technology, the Internet of Things and artificial intelligence make up the fourth industrial revolution. However, the motor of this fourth revolution is *analytics*. The impact of analytics in our societies, our communities, and the business world has just begun. In fact, knowledge gained from analytics in the recent years has already reshaped the marketplace, changing the way we shop, buy, think, vote, hire, play, choose, date, and live. With more than 20 billion connected devices by 2020[1] and more than 5 billion people with IP addresses sharing information and intelligence by 2025, the pace of upcoming changes resulting from analytics is mind boggling. The Internet of Things was the genesis of the *Analytics of Things* and *Analytics of Apps*. In the Analytics of Things era, new knowledge, resulting from artificial intelligence, like machine learning, deep learning and cognitive analytics, and blockchain, will be gathered from complex information networks flowing from billions of connected devices and from humans interfacing with their intelligent devices such as machines, apps, and wearables of all kinds.

Today, companies are under extreme pressure to dig deeper into and connect all information and pieces of data at their disposal to find new differentiators from their competition. They need to better understand their market, customers, competitors, and talent pool. They also need to think laterally and look for creative ideas and innovations in other fields. Think of all the new information layers that are at their disposal to help them achieve this goal. Exhibit 1.01 showcases the five layers of new information that are being generated and helping organizations to create business value.

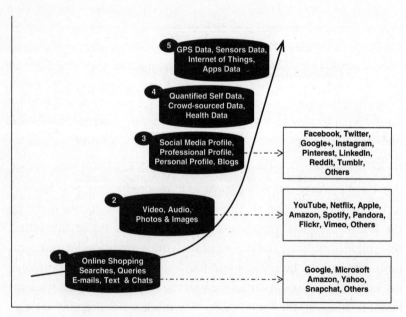

Exhibit 1.01   The Exponential Growth of New Information: The Five Layers

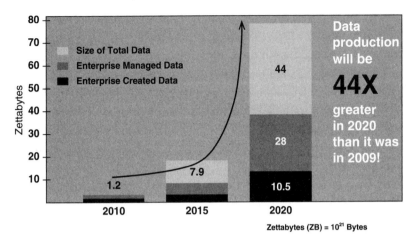

Exhibit 1.02 Data Production Evolution
Source: CSC IDC Estimate

Exhibit 1.02 showcases the exponential growth of digital information. According to International Data Corporation (IDC) estimates, by 2020, data production will balloon to 44 times what it was in 2009.

Customers and users have become more technology-savvy and are expecting more from their service providers or product manufacturers. They are very fickle and can switch to the competition with a single click. They have options and a lot of choices. They expect their service provider to know their habits, wants, and needs and even to anticipate their next move or transaction. Therefore, for any leading organizations poised to play in this digitized data economy where consumers and users are empowered, selective, and highly informed, analytics is key.

Analytics enables organizations of all sizes to meet and exceed customers' expectations by becoming data-driven to play in the new digital economy, where customers and market deep knowledge are front and center. However, to harness and create actionable insights from the complex user- and machine-generated data, organizations need to apply science to that data. Yes, science. In *data science*, specialists play with unorganized or "messy" data[2] to distill the intelligence differentiator.

Data Scientist: The Sexiest Job of the Twenty-First Century

You probably came across this concept if you read *Harvard Business Review* in October 2012. In their article,[3] Thomas H. Davenport and D. J. Patil provided a comprehensive overview of the prominent job occupation for Big Data tamers. They underscored the sudden rise of data science in the business scene.

For those of us with a math and computer science background, being labeled as *sexy* was a shock. When I was a graduate in mathematics and statistics, most of my class was made up of men. We were referred to as "those guys" or "those geeks," and we were mostly left alone by others. Our program was perceived as difficult to understand or too theoretical. This made our field of study very hermetic and unappealing to many. At that time, none of us could see a real-life application resulting from linear algebra. How did all the theorems and concepts we were learning apply to the business world? Our ideal career pathways in those days were math teacher or researcher, not data scientist. The term was not sexy at that time.

Studying the theory of vector space along with the concept of singular value decomposition (SVD) in algebra, we manually decomposed a matrix into a product of three matrices. We understood SVD was useful in dimension reduction: It helped to transform any matrix with a universe of n vectors into a smaller number of vectors that contained all the information of the original complex matrix. For high-dimension matrices, the process was manually tedious, starting with finding eigenvalues and then building eigenvectors. While we became adept in SVD, we had no clue as to where this skill-set could be applied in real life. At that time, we didn't know that SVD would be used to analyze text. We didn't know that counting terms weights and using SVD dimension reduction would provide clean separation of customer opinion or text categorization and sentiment analysis. Now computers are proficient in running complex computations like SVD (see Chapter 3). It was when I entered the workforce that I finally came across the first application of SVD, embedded in a software program designed for text analytics. There it was, hidden in the technical section of the software: The theory of vectors space reduction power of SVD was leveraged. The text content was placed into a matrix, and a quantitative representation of the content matrix was then created. Eigenvalues and -vectors were found to reduce the content into a smaller number of vectors while retaining the essence of the original content. It turns out that the vectors space reduction and SVD I had learned in algebra were the foundations of most text analysis.

It is uncertain whether our professors had envisioned the real-life applications for the math theories they were teaching then. Only visionaries could have foreseen such an explosion of applications in our lives, today and in the future, given the new information layers I mentioned. Such foresight would have changed the evolution of the data science for sure. However, it is the explosion of technologies, the new information layers, and the empowerment of the consumers and users that have shed light on analytics and propelled it into a new science.

WHY THE ANALYTICS HYPE TODAY?

Analytics is now part of the bottom line of leading organizations and industries of all sizes and types. Some companies have used analytics to power growth and to move into new sectors. In today's global competitive landscape, where data never stops flowing and challenges and opportunities keep changing, a lot of hype surrounds advanced business analytics. Your company is probably constantly exhorted to build and implement strategies to collect, process, manage, and analyze data (big and small) and to create business value from it. And you are warned about the potential risk of falling behind your competition by not doing so.

The *data scientist* job title has been around for a few years; it was coined in 2008 by D.J. Patil and Jeff Hammebacher, data analytics leaders at (respectively) LinkedIn and Facebook. In fact, a lot of data scientists were working in leading companies long before the recent traction around data science. The rapid appearance of data analytics in the business arena came from Silicon Valley's online giant companies, such as Google, eBay, LinkedIn, Amazon, Facebook, and Yahoo!, all of which surged to prominence during the Y2K dot.com boom. These online firms started to amass and analyze the gigantic volume of data generated by the clickstreams generated through user searches. They pioneered the data economy by building data products, and Big Data invaded the business world. A new data economy was created;

companies were inundated with information flowing from different sources, in varieties, volumes, velocity, and veracity that they wanted to harness to create actionable business value. The emergence of Big Data has triggered the overall traction around advanced business analytics, which was propelled by the consortium of the following pillars:

1. Costs to store and process information have reduced

2. Interactive devices and censors have increased

3. Data analytics infrastructures and software have increased

4. User-friendly and invisible data analytics tools have emerged

5. Data analytics have become mainstream, and it means a lot to our economy and world

6. Major leading tech companies have pioneered the data economy

7. Big Data analytics has become a big market opportunity

8. The number of data science university programs and MOOCs has intensified

1. Costs to Store and Process Information Have Reduced

The cost of storing information has significantly dropped: $600 will buy a disk drive that can store the entire world's music.[4] In 1990, it cost $11,000 to buy 1 GB of disk space; today, 1 GB disk space costs less than 1 cent.[5] Data storage and data processing have grown tremendously. The smartphones we all carry have more storage and computer power than a mainframe did in the 1980s. And large amounts of complex and unorganized data, such as audio, video, graphic, e-mail, chat, and text data, are widely available across infinite networks of computing environments at very low cost. In parallel, the cost of censors, photovoltaic cells, and all kinds of high-technology data-driven products has also decreased, enabling more people to use them—and generating more data to store and process.

2. Interactive Devices and Censors Have Increased

There are countless interactive devices such as smartphones, tablets sensors, surveillance cameras, and wearable devices that can capture, store, and send information, including everything we see, touch, hear, feel, and smell. This information no longer resides on an offline siloed desktop. It is instantly sent online via Internet Protocol (IP) and shared, transformed, and enriched by millions of users. Data is pumping in from a growing universe of connected sensors and machines.

3. Data Analytics Infrastructures and Software Have Increased

Over the past few years, there has been a rapid increase of data analytics tools and software that process and analyze data with unprecedented speed. Technologies such as artificial intelligence, machine learning, and deep learning are advancing more quickly than anyone anticipated.

The recent enthusiasm was propelled by the emergence of technology that makes taming Big Data possible, including Hadoop, the highly used framework for data file systems processing. Nowadays data scientists turn to Spark (and other tools) as a more efficient data processing framework. Open source cloud computing and data visualization capabilities are commonplace. A self-driving car, for example, can collect nearly 1 GB of data every second—it needs that granularity to find patterns to make reliable decisions. It also needs the computing power to make those decisions in a timely manner. As far as the computing power goes, we have moved from the central processing unit (CPU) to the graphics processing unit (GPU), and more recently, Google has developed the Tensor Processing Unit (TPU). During Google's 2017 I/O Conference, Google chief executive officer (CEO) Sundar Pichai discussed how Google is rethinking its computational architecture and building artificial intelligence and machine learning first data centers. He introduced Google's TPU, which supports Google's new artificial intelligence computational architecture, because, according to Google, TPUs are not only 15 to 30 times faster than CPUs and GPUs but also 30 to 80 percent more powerful. TPUs are now used across all Google products. In 2016, the TPU powered DeepMind AlphaGo during its historic 4–1 victory against Lee Sedol, the Go grandmaster. Machines can diagnose diseases, navigate roads, and understand and respond in natural language.

4. User-Friendly and Invisible Data Analytics Tools Have Emerged

There is an emergence of easy-to-use software that enables the processing and creation of actionable business value from the raw data. These user-friendly tools do not necessarily require technical background from the end user. Data analytics is becoming pervasive because the volume of data generated by embedded systems increases, and vast pools of structured and unstructured data inside and outside the enterprise are now being analyzed. According to David Cearley, vice president and Gartner fellow, "Every app now needs to be an analytics app."[6] Organizations need to manage how best to filter the huge amounts of data coming from the Internet of Things, social media, and wearable devices, and then deliver exactly the right information to the right person at the right time. He continues, "Analytics will become deeply, but invisibly embedded everywhere." Big Data is the enabler and catalyst for this trend, but the focus needs to shift from Big Data to Big Analytics, because the value is in the answers, not the data.

5. Data Analytics Is Becoming Mainstream, and It Means a Lot to Our Economy and World

There has been a significant proliferation of analytics benefits from a variety of sectors and industries. Cases demonstrating how organizations and businesses are winning with analytics are more and more available and accessible to everyone. Marketing has been extremely powerful in sharing those success stories everywhere, from business magazines to traditional media. Depending on their level of analytical maturity and their most pressing business objectives, companies and organizations across different industries and business functions have embraced analytics to create business value and develop competitive differentiators. Following are examples where advanced analytics are impacting today's world:

Politics

- Politicians have been leveraging data analytics to be more successful at winning elections.

- Politicians use social media analytics to determine where they must campaign the hardest to win states, provinces, and cities in the next election.

- During the 2012 presidential election, President Obama's team tactically leveraged Big Data analytics to target fundraising messaging to voters by location, age, group, occupation, and interest. For instance, according to their models, women from 35 to 49 years old were more likely to respond to messages such as "Dinner with the president and George Clooney." Data-driven targeted fund activities helped the Obama team raise more than $1 billion (an all-time record in any presidential campaign in modern history). The team optimized their campaign ad spend and, more importantly, targeted undecided voters in swing states to register and persuaded them to vote for Obama.

- Following the unexpected results of the 2016 election between Clinton and Trump, analysts attributed the discrepancy to five factors that traditional polling data could not capture: (1) A nontraditional candidate (no previous political history that resonated with traditional nonvoters); (2) An unprecedented investigation by the FBI during the final few days of the election; (3) The alleged influence of a foreign state; (4) The miscalculation in the distribution of voters (turnout) among different demographic groups; and (5) The impact of the "digital disruption of media," which allowed so many new channels of conflicting information to spring up. The 2016 election is likely going to change how political analytics is conducted in the future.

- It is important to note that the Trump campaign also leveraged Big Data insights from a U.K.-based Big Data analytics company called Cambridge Analytica, the same company that helped the Brexit leaders to win. Cambridge Analytica crunched data for Donald Trump, building psychological profiles of American voters. They leveraged more than 5,000 pieces of data about every adult American from sources such as personality tests on social media, voting history, personality type, shopping history, and television and cable viewing history. Insights from this analysis helped the Trump campaign tailor its message and strategy in battleground states and win.

Sport & Entertainment

- Forward-looking companies use machine learning to analyze video content and identify key information aspects from it. Machine-learning technique is also helping them to uncover actionable insights from video content. These insights are helping their digital marketers to align their advertisements with the right videos and drive customer engagement.

- Companies such as New York-based Dataminr, which provides a market monitoring platform for Brand, help businesses monitor and track their brand and immediately take appropriate actions. For instance, the platform can identify tweets related to stock trading and monitor discussion threads and communications to identify relevance and urgency. News organizations such as CNN and BBC use similar unstructured data analysis (UDA) technology to quickly identify news stories and have reporters deployed or engaged to cover them in a timely manner.

- Video analytics and sensor data of tennis, baseball, and football games are used to improve the performances of players and teams. You can now buy a baseball with more than 200 sensors in it that will give you detailed feedback on how to improve your game.

- Augmented reality technology is used to overlay supplemental information, such as scores and other statistics, over a live video field in sporting events to enhance the viewers' experience.

- The Oakland Athletics (an American professional baseball team based in Oakland, California) pioneered analytics in sports, and now all teams use analytics. Today information and statistics about players are a prerequisite for recruitment.

- Spotify uses unstructured data analytics to provide its popular Discover Weekly playlists, which are personalized to our musical tastes. The company leverages collaborative filtering, convolutional neural networks, and natural language processing to scan music blogs, build microgenres, analyze the contents of playlists, and detect and eliminate outliers to find songs that fit our profile, but that we haven't yet listened to.

■ Artists such as Lady Gaga are using data about our listening preferences and sequences to determine the most popular playlists for live performances.

Business

■ Amazon uses analytics to recommend what books to buy; more than 35 percent of their sales are generated from these recommendations: "People who bought this book also bought ... "

■ Netflix leverages analytics to recommend movies you are more likely to watch. More than 70 percent of Netflix movie choices arise from its online recommendations.

■ Pinterest leverages UDA to provide a personalized experience on its home feed by surfacing content each user would be more interested in seeing.

■ Companies use sentiment analysis from Facebook and Twitter posts to determine and predict sales volume and brand equity.

■ Target (a large retailer) predicts when a pregnant woman is due based on products she purchases. The company simply combines her loyalty card data with social media information, hence detecting and leveraging changing buying patterns. As a result, the company can target pregnant women with promotions for baby-related products. The company increased revenue 15 to 20 percent by targeting direct mail with product choice models.

■ Google's self-driving car analyzes a gigantic amount of data from sensors and cameras in real time to stay safe on the road.

■ The global positioning system (GPS) in our phones provides location and speed information for live traffic updates. Location-based data has generated billions of dollars for companies and even more value for users.

Healthcare

■ Pediatric hospitals apply data analytics to livestreamed heartbeats to identify patterns. Based on the analysis, the system can now detect infections 24 hours before the baby would normally begin to show any symptoms, which enables early intervention and treatment.

■ After winning the TV show *Jeopardy*, Watson the IBM supercomputer now assists physicians to better diagnose and cure aggressive diseases such as cancers. Watson is being enlisted to help doctors predict cancer in patients. Watson has greatly speeded diagnosis of acute myeloid leukemia, a type of blood cancer, as well as glioblastoma multiform, an aggressive brain cancer.

■ DNA sequencing: It took 10 years to sequence the DNA of one person, at a cost of more than $100 million. Today, DNA sequencing is done very quickly for less than $99. This availability leads to personalized medicine and drug prescriptions. Genomic precision medicine is becoming a game changer.

■ Natera can predict Trisomy 21 disease without the risk of miscarriage from an amniocentesis test just by testing blood from the mother-to-be. The results of that blood test have a 99 percent accuracy rate, similar to those from the traditional amniocentesis test.

Government, Security, and Police

■ The FBI combines data from social media, closed-circuit television (CCTV) cameras, phone calls, and texts to track down criminals and predict terrorist attacks.

■ JPMorgan Chase & Co. invested $837 million in people analytics to anticipate rogue employee behavior that has cost the bank more $36 billion since the end of the 2008 financial crisis.

Human Capital Management

■ HR analytics companies are now using people analytics to optimize talent management. Big Data analytics help to attract, acquire, develop, and retain talent. Google, Cisco, Microsoft, GE, Xerox, Bloomberg, Deloitte, and Pfizer have been accumulating success stories and benefits from people analytics to optimize their talent equation.

6. Major Leading Tech Companies Have Pioneered the Data Economy

Major tech companies such as Google, Facebook, eBay, Amazon, LinkedIn, and Yahoo began to monetize their data. As a result, their entire businesses reside on their ability to harness the data at their disposal. Most recently, some of these companies shared Big Data analytics algorithms they pioneered with the public: open source, Hadoop, and Spark. As a result, entire businesses that stem from data analytics and raw data have been developed. A new digital economy was born, in which data is the currency and analytics sets the trading rules. Data analytics has become pervasive and omnipresent. Social media, cloud, mobile, and Big Data provide disruptive ways to capture, process, analyze, and communicate data analytics findings and recommendations.

7. Big Data Analytics Has Become a Big Market Opportunity

Big Data analytics has a big market opportunity: The research firm IDC forecast that the market opportunity for Big Data and business analytics software, hardware, and services will grow by 50 percent from 2015 to 2019. This means that the market size will reach 187 billion by 2019. Services accounting for the largest portion of the revenue with manufacturing and banking poised to lead the spend.[7]

8. The Number of Data Science University Programs and MOOCs Has Intensified

Before Big Data, there were no university data science programs or degrees. The need to harness the complex volume of so-called "messy" data such as images, text, audio, video, chat, graphics, and pictures forced universities to adapt. The article "Big Data: The Next Frontier for Innovation, Competition, and Productivity" from McKinsey&Company[8] has played a key role in raising the awareness of the eminent data scientist labor shortage. According to the article, in 2018, there will be 140,000 to 190,000 data scientists and 1.5 million data-savvy managers. This headline has pulled the alarm signal, creating awareness among organizations eager to join the new data economy.

A variety of business schools and universities now offer data mining and data science programs and degrees. In the United States alone, there are more than 20 universities offering data science programs,[9] as well as a panoply of executive programs covering data analytics either locally from universities' classrooms or via the Internet and videos. This has led to the multiplication of massive open online courses (MOOCs). MOOC distance education was first introduced in 2008 and emerged as a popular mode of learning in 2012,[10] and offers a lot of data science modules and programs.

The top of the list includes MOOCs in Exhibit 1.03, organized based upon the date of inception.[11]

Other MOOCs include Future Learn Open Education Europe and The Open University Classroom.

At Harvard University, more people signed on in one year to the online courses than had graduated from the university in its 377 years of existence.

In addition, communities' and analytics groups' niche sites have been proliferating. The ever-growing data volume has put more pressure on companies to hire data scientists. This job occupation has been a hard-to-fill position, a situation that is not poised to change. How did we get here? What is the timeline that led to the Analytics Age?

MOOC Name	Inception Date	Founders	MOC Summary/Value Proposition
Khan Academy	2006	Salman Khan	Khan Academy is a nonprofit educational organization that produces YouTube videos of short lectures on specific topics within many subject areas to supplement classroom learning. It uses online tools to provide meaningful educational content to students
Udemy	2010	Eren Bali, Octay Caglar, and Gagan Biyani	Udemy is an online learning platform that does not focus on traditional college courses. Instead it enables instructors to build online courses aimed at professional adults and offer those courses to the public.
Udacity	2011	Sebastian Thrun, David Stavens, and Mike Sokolsky	Udacity is a for-profit educational organization that originally offered traditional university courses, but in 2013, it shifted focus to vocational courses for adult professionals
edX	2012	Harvard University and the Massachusetts Institute of Technology (MIT)	edX provides interactive online classes in a wide number of subjects, ranging from biology, chemistry, and engineering to law, literature, and philosophy from partner organizations including university MOOC.
Coursera	2012	Andrew Ng and Daphne Koller (Stanford University computer professors)	Coursera partners with universities to offer online courses in a wide range of subjects. Its student users can even pursue specializations and degrees as well as a comprehensive list for data science programs.

Exhibit 1.03   MOOCs

A SHORT HISTORY OF DATA ANALYTICS

Modern UDA has been 58 years in the making. In 1958, IBM engineer H. P. Luhn wrote an article in which he indicated that business intelligence is the analysis of structured and unstructured text documents. In that article, he defined business intelligence as a system that will:

> utilize data-processing machines for auto-abstracting and auto-encoding of documents and for creating interest profiles for each of the "action points" in an organization. Both incoming and internally generated documents are automatically abstracted, characterized by a word pattern, and sent automatically to appropriate action points.[12]

However, the first representation of data in rows and columns can be traced back in the second century in Egypt! With today's fast evolution and revolution of technology (software and hardware), data mining, business intelligence, and UDA have evolved rapidly since 1958. Past unresolved analytics problems are now being addressed, thanks to the sophistication of tools and software. Consider Siri, Apple's voice recognition technology for the iPhone. Siri's origins go back to a Pentagon research project that was spun off as a Silicon Valley start-up. Apple bought Siri in 2010 and has been feeding it data ever since. Now, with people supplying millions of questions, Siri is becoming an increasingly adept personal assistant, offering reminders, weather reports, restaurant suggestions, and answers to an expanding universe of questions.

From a historical perspective, consider the following timeline, which outlines key milestones leading to the current state of UDA:

- *Second century*: In Egypt, the first table with data represented in rows and columns.

- *Seventeenth century*: The two-dimensional graph is invented by René Descartes (French philosopher and mathematician).

- *1756–1806*: The line graph, line chart, line bar chart, and pie chart were invented by William Playfair.

- *1856–1915*: Frederick Winslow is credited for applying engineering principles to factory work, which was instrumental in the creation and development of industrial engineering.

- *Eighteenth and nineteenth centuries*: Modern statistics emerged, with A. Fisher and Karl Spearman introducing factor analysis and principal components analysis (PCA). Spearman introduced PCA in 1901.

- *1958*: The first definition of *business intelligence* as text analytics or document analysis appeared. H. P. Luhn, an engineer from IBM, introduced the idea of basic stats analysis on text terms. He also introduced the concept of text summarization, but the software and the tools were not ready to support it.

- *1960–1980*: The focus was on database technology and relational databases.

- *1970–1980*: Analytics became mainstream. John Tukey published *Exploratory Data Analysis* in 1977.

- *1980–1990*: Business intelligence emerged as software categories and a field of expertise, but the focus was on numeric-coded data and relational databases.

- *1990*: Scott Deerwester, Susan T. Dumais, George W. Furnas, Thomas K. Landauer, and Richard Harshman introduced the first application of SVD to text mining in their article, "Indexing by Latent Semantic Analysis," in the *Journal of the Association for Information Science and Technology*.

- *1990*: The World Wide Web became global with its influx of data clickstreams and searches.

- *1990–2010*: Text analytics and data mining rose in prominence. Companies such as AltaVista and Teragram focused their efforts on search and text mining.

- *1995–1998*: Online giant firms came to life: in 1995, Amazon and eBay, and in 1998, Google, Hotmail, and PayPal.

- *2010–Present*: Currently, there are advances in advanced text analytics and semantics. Social media analytics, human resources (HR) analytics, healthcare analytics ... the current trend is the Analytics of Things.

The last step in Exhibit 1.04 illustrates how semantics really is the future in the analysis of unstructured data:

- *2000*: Social media giants came to life: in 2003 LinkedIn and Skype, in 2004 Facebook, and in 2006 Twitter.

- *Late 2010*: A variety of UDA solutions providers, vendors, and open sources were available: more than 70 commercial and 30 open source.

Analytics Genesis Era

1. **3000 BCE: Babylonians** strive to gather a national head count.
2. **2nd century: Egyptians** have first representation of data in rows and columns.
3. **1663: John Graunt**, the founder of demography, carries out the first recorded experiment in statistical data analysis.
4. **17th century: Rene Descartes** invents Cartesian coordinates, as the well as two-dimensional table.
5. **1736: Leonhard Euler** publishes the first paper in the graph theory.
6. **1786: William Playfair** invents several types of diagrams: line graph, circle graph, area, bar chart, and pie chart of economic data.
7. **19th century:** Emergence of modern statistics; **Ronald A. Fisher and Charles Spearman** introduce factor analysis and principal components analysis.
8. **1865:** The term *business intelligence* is used by **Richard Millar Devens** in his *Encyclopedia of Commercial and Business Anecdotes.*

Advent of Computer Era

1. **1837: Charles Babbage** proposes the first general mechanical computer, the Analytical Engine.
2. **1890: Herman Hollerith** invents the Tabulating Machine.
3. **1928: Fritz Pfleumer** invents the magnetic tape.
4. **1936–1938:** The first programmable computer, the Z1, is created by German Konrad Zuse.
5. **1936: Alan Turing** creates the first concept modern computer.
6. **1958:** IBM engineer **Hans Peter Luhn** provides the first definition of business intelligence as analysis of documents and text.
7. **1960:** The **U.S. National Security Agency (NSA)** starts collecting and processing signal intelligence automatically.
8. **1962:** IBM engineer **William C. Dersch** works on the beginnings of speech recognition.

Relational Database & Business Intelligence Era

1. **1970: Edgar F. Codd** presents his framework for a relational database.
2. **1972: John Tukey** publishes *Exploratory Data Analysis*
3. **1976: Anthony James Barr, James Goodnight, John Sall, and Jane Helwig** found SAS, a statistical analysis software.
4. **1980s:** Relational databases emerge, based on **Jon Von Neumann's** architecture, which allowed users to write (SQL) to retrieve data from a database.
5. **1980–1990:** Business intelligence emerges as a software category and a field of expertise, but focus is on numeric coded data and relational databases.
6. **Late 1980s: William H. Inmon** proposes a data warehouse.
7. **1990:** Data mining emerges.
8. **1996: Usama Fayyad, Gregory Piatetsky-Shapiro, and Padhraic Smyth** published "From Data Mining to Knowledge Discovery in Databases."

Big Data Era

1. **1990: NASA** researchers use the term "Big Data" for the first time to describe supercomputers generating massive amounts of information that cannot be processed and visualized.
2. **1991: Tim Berners-Lee** announces the birth of what would become the World Wide Web of today.
3. **1994–1998: Tech giants** come to life: (Amazon-1994, eBay-1995), 1998 (Google, Hotmail, PayPal).
4. **2000: Social media networks giants** came to life (LinkedIn, Skype, Facebook, Twitter). Tech blogger and user-generated content exploded, solidifying the foundation of Big Data.
5. **1990–2010: Text analytics and data mining companies,** such as Alta Vista and Teragram, focused on search capabilities.
6. **Late 2000s: High-speed processing and distributed computing leverage frameworks** such as Hadoop and Spark emerge. Production version of R language for analytics.
7. **2008: D.J. Patil and Jeff Hammebacher** invent the term *data scientist.*
8. **2010: Amazon Redshift and Google BigQuery** are released, providing web based data optimization and high performance data analysis in memory and on the cloud.

Internet of Things Era and Augmented Age

1. **1999:** The term *Internet of Things (IoT)* is created by **Kevin Ashton,** executive director of the Auto ID Center MIT.
2. **2004: Neil Gershenfeld, Raffi Krikorian, and Danny Cohen** write in "The Internet of Things" in *Scientific American:* "Giving everyday objects the ability to connect to a data network would have a range of benefits."
3. **2008–2009:** Birth of the Internet of Things. According to CISCO report, between 2008 and 2009 for the first time more "things or objects" were connected to the Internet than people.
4. **2008: U.S. National Intelligence Council** lists the Internet of Things as one of the 6 Disruptive Civil Technologies with potential impacts on U.S. interests out to 2025.
5. **2010:** Chinese Premier **Wen Jiabao** calls the IOT a key industry for China and plans to make a major investment in it.
6. **2010: Cisco, IBM, and Ericsson** produce large educational and marketing initiatives on the topic.
7. **2011:** The Internet of Things is added to the **annual Gartner Hype Cycle,** which tracks technology trends and life cycles.
8. **2015:** The research firm **Gartner** predicts that by 2020, there will be 20.8 billion connected devices. According to **IDC,** by 2025 there will be more than 80 billion connected devices.
9. **2016: Google DeepMind's** Go-playing AI defeats legendary Go master Lee Sedol.

Exhibit 1.04 Analytics Evolution

Early Adopters: Insurance and Finance

To best navigate today's globally connected competitive marketplace, which has been propelled by the explosion of digital information, companies have been embracing analytics at different paces to derive strategic insights.

From an industry perspective, some early adopters pioneered the integration of analytics into their business processes, then the late adopters followed, and finally the laggards trailed far behind. While most businesses have heard about the benefits of analytics, some struggle to move beyond basic reporting. However, the majority of leaders are requesting their analytics team to deliver on Big Data promises, monetizing their data by creating new data products and services to truly compete on analytics—as one CEO told me, "to rethink our analytics journey."

In *Win With Advanced Business Analytics*,[13] I described how the insurance and financial service industries have been pioneers in collecting, managing, and leveraging predictive analytics to create actionable insight from their data. Given the mandatory reporting environment of these fields, not to mention the direct correlation between accurate data and revenue, these industries first began using analytics in the 1800s to price life insurance and underwrite marine insurance. They have since continued innovating, undergoing many waves of improvement, including the use of neural networks[14] to optimize premiums, the introduction of credit scores in evaluating a customer's financial position, and the use of various behavioral, third-party, and social media datasets to supplement their forecasts and future predictions.

Over the years, the success stories have been numerous, and financial institutions that are not currently using predictive analytics in product pricing and underwriting are seen as obsolete and doomed to failure. As a result, these companies are now developing new applications and expanding their analytics into different business units. For instance, *safety analytics* is the science of using information about a company's current state and other geodemographic data to prevent accidents from happening and avoid the associated insurance costs by creating a safer workplace. Similarly, *claims analytics* is a discipline in which claim severity (amount of loss) is scrutinized for drivers of high-dollar claims by injury type. It aims at understanding and predicting probable losses (damages, litigation costs, etc.) based on frequency, severity, and other characteristics of the claims. Claims analysis is also used for early identification of litigious claims, efficient claims settlement, adequate loss reserving, and claims predicting, among other activities.

Fraud analytics is also a hot topic. It is estimated that fraud claims cost the insurance industry between $5 and $7 billion every year. Complex predictive models designed to find intricate patterns of unusual behavior to uncover fraudulent schemes are being used by various insurance organizations and state agencies throughout the United States. Models that use machine-learning techniques to adapt to new schemes are being built and put into production to pinpoint which incoming claims are likely to be fraudulent, prompting an investigation.

Today, major players in the data economy are monetizing their data to create new products and services, making their data the most powerful currency in this digital world.

The evolution of analytics can be summarized in three major eras:

1. *Analytics before Big Data*

   This analytics era was characterized by relational databases, data warehouses (DWHs), statistical analyses performed on samples, and numeric-based analytics. The advent of computers and the growth of personal computers have helped to increase adoption.

2. *Analytics in the Big Data era*

   The advent of Internet (World Wide Web) and the birth of Silicon Valley's online business behemoths such as Google, LinkedIn, Facebook, Amazon, and Yahoo! pioneered the digital economy and promoted the analysis of new types of complex and messy user-generated data. This enabled the development of infrastructures and tools powered by Hadoop and Spark cloud computing mobile, with computing power that made data processing, analysis, and distribution more efficient and effective than ever before. This analytics era is also defined by the emergence of computing power that enabled the realization of artificial intelligence (AI), machine learning, representation learning, and deep learning. The Big Data era fed those algorithms with endless data to learn by experience and to understand the world in terms of hierarchy of concepts. It also provided new solutions to previously unsolved problems, such as computer recognition of images and video.

3. *Post–Big Data analytics era*: The Analytics of Things and Apps, cognitive analytics, and the Augmented Age

As demonstrated in Exhibit 1.04, we are just at the beginning of the Analytics of Things era, and disruptive changes are coming within the next decade. Billions of connected devices and intelligent machines interacting with human beings will generate a tsunami of data that organizations and companies will have to analyze to play in the data economy. The post–Big Data era will also be defined by cognitive analytics and the real-time integration of AI, machine learning, representation learning, and deep learning algorithms to address business and societal challenges coming from billions of connected objects. More importantly, these algorithms will build a dynamic intelligence based on the interaction between human censors and computers, using natural language to communicate with computers and devices for the most part.

We are now heading into the augmented age, where Big Data, Internet of Things, intelligent apps, and AI will provide additional insights at our fingertips. Think about what we do today when somebody asks you a question and you don't know the answer. Your smartphones automatically come to your rescue, enabling you to Google the information needed. As Maurice Conti, chief innovation officer at Telefónica, eloquently put it:

> Welcome to the Augmented
> Age. In this new era, your natural human capabilities
> are going to be augmented by computational
> systems that help you think, robotic systems that help
> you make, and a digital nervous system that connects
> you to the world far beyond your natural senses.[15]

Where does your organization sit on this scale?

WHAT IS THE ANALYTICS AGE?

The Analytics Age is simply a data-driven, intelligence-driven environment. It is an era in which questions related to business, people management, and consumer behaviors are addressed using data intelligence. A period in which data intelligence for decision making is the new norm. Where best-in-class, data-driven companies are using machine learning and a deep analytics arsenal to understand customers/consumers, voters, players, talent, court rulings, patents, and markets, and to develop new products in response. Whether in sports, politics, entertainment, healthcare, HR, legal services, research, security, or government, the usage of analytics is pervasive. In this Analytics Age, complacent companies and organizations not using analytics are considered laggards and risk being left behind.

The speed at which technology has evolved, enabling the capture, storage, and rapid processing of information without limit, has set the foundation for the Analytics Age. Gone are the days where part of the web log data had to be purged for lack of space, and where building models was limited to running cumbersome samples and queries on the entire customer base. In the Analytics Age, data is the currency, and decisions are made in real time or near-real time. This new era is a playground for artificial intelligence, machine learning, and deep learning.

In the Analytics Age, companies can now address business questions that were previously ignored or omitted because there was no software robust enough to process and analyze the data. Physicians can make better diagnoses of some diseases by leveraging image recognition software powered with deep learning algorithms. Even though the mathematic formulae used in today's analytics were developed a while ago, the interest in applying analytics to business and real world questions is a new phenomenon. Previously, data intelligence and applied analytics were mostly living in research labs. In marketing, analytics climaxed with the emergence of the World Wide Web and its influx of clickstream and search data. Marketers were even praised for their intuition and creativity in developing and executing campaigns. They started asking questions such as:

- Which customers should we retain?
- Which prospects should we acquire?

- Which customers should we win back?
- Which customers should we upsell?
- To whom should we market?

As a result, marketing analytics became a must-have department in every respected data-driven organization.

In 2009, Hal Varian, chief economist at Google, said, "I keep saying the sexy job in the next ten years will be statisticians."[16] When people laughed, he argued that marketers could gain a 360-degree understanding of their customers, given that they had access to resources and could interpret them with statistics and mathematics. Such resources could transform data from multiple sources into actionable insights to address business challenges.

There is an intensifying demand for science, technology, engineering, and math (STEM) occupations, as the world is becoming an economy of service. A service economy requires a full understanding of customers' needs, preferences, habits, and more importantly customer satisfaction drivers. A happy customer is a customer who does not need to ask, one who has a great experience when doing business with you. Companies should follow the footsteps of the Silicon Valley giants: monetize their data in all capacities by creating data services and data products that will help them achieve a 360-degree understanding of their customers.

INTERVIEW WITH WAYNE THOMPSON, CHIEF DATA SCIENTIST AT SAS INSTITUTE

I had the opportunity to discuss the state of analytics, UDA, UDA best practices, and the future of analytics with Wayne Thompson, chief data scientist at SAS Institute, the leading software analytics solutions provider.

Isson: *The majority of organizations I've spoken with have told me we are living in the Data Analytics Age. Would you agree? And, if so, could you describe analytics evolution at SAS? What has been the major data analytics disruption at SAS?*

Thompson: *Yes, I totally agree. There have been some major disruptions at SAS.*

I was a data mining product manager of SAS Enterprise Miner (EM) back in 2002. For a very long time, SPSS Clementine and SAS were both chasing the same goal: to build process flow to make data mining more repeatable and more consumable to people who might not program.

In 2002, I worked on a program to incorporate text analytics into EM, called Text Miner. And that became disruptive at SAS, because then customers had a wonderful, market-leading data-mining software platform, but didn't have a way to integrate textual data into predefined format. Being able to add textual data as candidate predictors in a predictive model was disruptive. Essentially we introduced three steps:

- Parse the text
- Create a term by document matrix
- Term by frequencies

Four major applications of the Text Analytics Node include:

- Insurance (Fraud)
- Product Taxonomy at HP
- Healthcare System
- Manufacturing

The first Application was related to fraud for an insurance company, where getting good information in warranty claims about very rare events was critical to success.

For Hewlett Packard (HP), I worked with Randy Kalika. At HP, they have different business units and a huge taxonomy of products. At that time, there were no blueprints for this. It was essential to develop a blueprint to better understand the line of products and business opportunities. Randy used text analytics to provide a SKU number hierarchy across HP's portfolio.

The third example involves the late Patricia Serito from University of Louisville. Patricia did a lot of work with IDC9 and ID10 Codes, which are international codes for diagnosis and diseases. She worked to accelerate clinical trials. She used kernel density estimation (KDE) to understand things like symptoms, diagnoses, and patients' characteristics at emergency (in the health system or ambulance). At that time, in the health emergency system, CPR would not be administered for a period exceeding 20 minutes, as the person would be deemed brain dead. After analyzing structured and text data and verbatim information from medical providers, it was found that CPR administered well beyond 40 to 60 minutes could still save the *lives of individuals who suffered heart attacks or strokes. Patricia also found some correlation and causation between admission to emergency and proximity to pollutants for manufacturing processes. She used mapping with a geographic information system (GIS) coupled with text analytics to understand proximity to heavy manufacturing processes and hospital admission.*

Ford was an early adopter, as they used the customer feedback text scenario to understand how to build the next best car. Procter & Gamble (P&G) also did some great use of text analytics. P&G analyzed consumer feedback to create the best shampoo.

Isson: *In the era of Big Data, what do you see as the next frontiers of data analytics innovation?*

Thompson: *Cognitive computing.*

Cognitive computing is where we are in the Big Data era. We are not only dealing with text or structured data; we are dealing with images, voice, audio, video, and speech. Cognitive computing is the Holy Grail that we are all chasing. And what makes it possible is natural language processing (NLP). But machine learning has got much better with deep learning. Deep learning is a subset of machine learning that enables the building of neural networks that have eight or more hidden layers. Now with images analysis, for example, you can detect images with less than 6 percent error rate.

At the core, cognitive computing is a combination of NLP and deep learning. You use NLP to respond to a request made to a computer. It has to go beyond Siri, Cortana, or Alexa. All these understand what you are saying and do a very good job for retrieving and searching. They have elementary text analytics built into them. But the ability to look at the machine learning library and understand things that are more complicated involves deeper learning. For instance:

- *What are the factors affecting cancer among these patients?*

- *What factors affect the graduation rate among these students in the greater Chicago area?*

You can ask more analytical questions to cognitive computing, and the machine can automatically reason on inputs and provide you with the insights, and they do things like natural language generation (NLG). That is where text analytics is going. With NLP, we can understand inputs. NLG enables storytelling or writing verbatim about what the results mean. That is a function of text analytics and machine learning.

Isson: What are the major impacts of such innovations for businesses and societies?

Thompson: The next frontier of analytics innovation is cognitive computing and artificial intelligence (AI). Cognitive computing and AI boundaries can get fuzzy. But in terms of AI, we are trying to get to something called artificial general intelligence (AGI). AGI is where the computer can have a human-like conversation and provide insights just like a human.

And UDA will have a broad range of impacts across all functions in business and communities.

In marketing, it can help for:

- Churn analysis
- Voice of customer analysis
- Social media analysis
- Market research
- Competitive intelligence

In business, it can help for:

- HR management
- Fraud detection and prevention
- Finance and accounting
- Product development
- Customer service, call center management: Optimizing customer service

In societies and communities, it can support:

- National security
- Sport analysis
- Legal systems

Isson: What is the biggest hurdle you will face when implementing UDA?

Thompson: The biggest hurdle I see is getting actionable insight from unstructured data, such as text, audio, and video data. Most companies, even if they have textual data, have not made the leap to Big Text Data. We always talk about Big Data, but I don't think we think enough about text and having systems in place to manage and process text. It is a very intensive process to parse all this information, standardize it, and integrate it so you can start making decisions from it. So I think companies are gradually putting together a Big Data strategy that will be scalable; I just don't think that they are there *yet. They are still in data warehousing, ingesting data, lacking data prepro-cessing capabilities that are necessary for UDA. When you do text analytics, people forget it, just like machine learning, where you have to replicate all of the process to get insights from text to actually deploying the scoring. And that is even harder.*

And with text you have to read it first in machine-readable format; you have to make it structured. Structured data like age, income, length of service, all structured data are already in direct machine-readable format. It is not hard to get text data assembled in machine-readable format; however, when you apply that to incoming data, I found people have a hard time doing that. Implementation or scoring of text analytics is the biggest challenge.

Another big problem with text analytics is the timing element associ-ated with it, just like in the recommendation engine. People are continually changing their attitudes and opinions. To my knowledge, there is little to no incorporation of time series elements into text analytics. And there is very lit-tle monitoring of the text analytics models and understanding when to refresh those models. People in credit scorecarding, in marketing, and in campaign management have understood this for decades. Most of the time, the models you develop could be two to three months old. The longevity of text analytics models could be very short, two to three weeks, before they stall and need to be rebuilt. For text analytics to become more cognitive, it will have to incor-porate the time series element. Having text analytics become cognitive is the Holy Grail.

Isson: *What advice would you give to a company trying to implement UDA and stay ahead of data analytics innovation?*

Thompson: *UDA is a little softer than machine learning; in terms of resource, we should have type A and type B people working together. I want somebody who understands analytics even if text analytics is predominant. You first need to count, then you do dimension reduction.*

You count terms across documents and you get a table with counts. But that table is extremely spared and extremely Big. That is why you need scala-bility. But you have to decompose that into latent factors that mean something in human language . . .

If you have someone who is analytical in nature, that helps. But you need builders—builders who can take raw text data from multiple sources and develop data analytics products. This is what I call type B; and data scientists are in this category. They can bring text analytics to the next level, as they can use text analytics to build text products. You need a mix of those two types. You need someone who is not uncomfortable with Big Text or any unstructured data. Someone who is constantly asking: How I can leverage it, make it, build it from the data I have?

Isson: *What will be the state of UDA ten to fifteen years from now?*

Thompson: *Ten to fifteen years is a long time to project to. I do see it having major impact five years from now in:*

- *Robotics*

- *Autonomous cars*

- *Thinking machines (as where we need to go)*

- *Being able to remove the language obstacle, manage all those languages concurrently as one corpus*

- *Expanding of algorithms and apps capable of driving autonomous-type behaviors across several fields*

    All these progresses will remove the language obstacle. We should be able to manage and process all languages in the next five years. Just five years from now, many things that we do should be automated because of the ability we will have to do UDA; think about what happened in 2000. Some of these changes may happen in five years, others in ten. Fifteen is too long.

 KEY TAKEAWAYS

Analytics has been used since 1800, but started to emerge in late 2000s. It gained some traction and attention in the late 1960s when computers were used in decision support systems. Since then, analytics has exploded with the introduction of cloud computing, Big Data, and mobile. Changes in data management processing and computing power have brought analytics to a new level, with an endless universe of applications and opportunities.

The Analytics Age has also been driven by the following:

- Silicon Valley online firms such as Google, Facebook, LinkedIn, Amazon, eBay, and Yahoo! emerged and pioneered the data economy, enabling development of data services and data products that best fit their users, consumers, and the overall market.

- Technologies such as deep learning are advancing more quickly than anyone anticipated. Machines can now diagnose diseases, navigate roads, understand and respond using natural language.

- There is increased awareness in businesses and societies regarding the benefits of fact-based decisions, where success stories of applied data intelligences and data analytics have been broadly shared from business magazines to traditional media outlets. Big Data analytics have been successful in politics (such as U.S. presidential elections), sports, healthcare, medicine, HR, consumer recommendations for products, such as the Amazon recommendations model, the LinkedIn data services suggesting connected people or potential jobs, and Google's search results and traffic analysis. Tapping in those sectors and industries has helped to spread the analytics impact to people from all spectrums of our societies.

- Usage of interactive devices has increased as well, including smartphone sensors, wearables, and computing power that streamlines the process of capturing, storing, integrating, managing, and analyzing internal and external data, Big Data, and complex data such as unstructured data. The advent of disruptive software enabled companies to harness the ongoing information flow. Computing power has made it fast and scalable to perform advanced analytics like machine learning and deep learning, with no limitation on computer time thanks to new computational architectures powered by GPUs and TPUs.

- Data science has been around for while (it appeared in mid-1950s) but data analytics frameworks, such as Hadoop and Spark, made data processing much easier and faster, enabling users to perform robust and efficient analytics on any kind of data in real or near-real time.

- The advent of the Internet (World Wide Web), with its influx of data (from clickstreams and searches), and of the Internet of Things has opened a new universe of data analytics by generating a tsunami of data to be harnessed to provide strategic insights to businesses.

NOTES

1. Rob van der Meulen, "Gartner Says 8.4 Billion Connected 'Things' Will Be in Use in 2017, Up 31 Percent from 2016," Gartner Newsroom (February 7, 2017): www .gartner.com/newsroom/id/3598917

2. The term *messy data*, coined by D. E. Johnson and G. A. Milliken in 2006, refers to data that require nonstandard statistical methodologies and approaches. By opposition, *dirty data* refers to data that is inaccurate, incomplete, or erroneous.

3. Thomas H. Davenport and D. J. Patil, "The Sexiest Job of the 21st Century," *Harvard Business Review*, October 2012: hbr.org/2012/10/data-scientist-the-sexiest-job-of-the-21st-century

4. James Manyika, Michael Chui, Brad Brown, Jacques Bughin, Richard Dobbs, Charles Roxburgh, and Angela Hung Byers, "Big Data: The Next Frontier for Innovation, Competition, and Productivity," McKinsey & Company (May 2011): www.mckinsey.com/business-functions/digital-mckinsey/our-insights/big-data-the-next-frontier-for-innovation

5. Matthew Komorowski, "A History of Storage Cost," mkomo.com (September 8, 2009): www.mkomo.com/cost-per-gigabyte

6. Janessa Rivera, "Gartner Identifies the Top 10 Strategic Technology Trends for 2015," Gartner Newsroom (October 8, 2014): www.gartner.com/newsroom/id/2867917

7. Jessica Davis, "Big Data, Analytics Sales Will Reach $187 Billion by 2019," InformationWeek (May 24, 2016): www.informationweek.com/big-data/big-data-analytics/big-data-analytics-sales-will-reach-$187-billion-by-2019/d/d-id/1325631

8. Manyika et al., "Big Data: The Next Frontier."

9. Usama Fayyad, Gregory Piatetsky-Shapiro, and Padhraic Smyth, "From Data Mining to Knowledge Discovery in Databases" *AI Magazine* 17, no. 3 (Fall 1996): www.csd.uwo.ca/faculty/ling/cs435/fayyad.pdf

10. Tamar Lewin, "Universities Abroad Join Partnership on the Web," *New York Times*, February 20, 2013: www.nytimes.com/2013/02/21/education/universities-abroad-join-mooc-course-projects.html?_r=0

11. Wikipedia.

12. H. P. Luhn, "Auto-Encoding of Documents for Information Retrieval Systems," in M. Boaz, *Modern Trends in Documentation* (London: Pergamon Press, 1959): 45–58.

13. Jean-Paul Isson and Jesse Harriotts, *Win with Advanced Business Analytics* (Hoboken, NJ: Wiley & Sons, 2012).

14. Isson and Harriotts, *Win with Advanced Business Analytics.*

15. Maurice Conti, "The Incredible Inventions of Intuitive AI," TEDxPortland Talk (April 2016): www.ted.com/talks/maurice_conti_the_incredible_inventions_of_intuitive_ai/transcript

16. "Hal Varian on How the Web Challenges Managers," *McKinsey Quarterly*, January 2009: www.mckinsey.com/industries/high-tech/our-insights/hal-varian-on-how-the-web-challenges-managers

FURTHER READING

Natalino Busa, "The Evolution of Data Analytics," SlideShare.net, May 12, 2015: www.slideshare.net/natalinobusa/the-evolution-of-data-analytics-48033452

Bloomberg Technology video, "Why Big Data Failed to Predict the U.S. Election," Bloomberg.com, November 9, 2016: www.bloomberg.com/news/videos/2016-11-10/why-big-data-failed-to-predict-the-u-s-election

Cray, Infographic: "The Evolution of Data Analytics." www.cray.com/sites/default/files/resources/evolution-of-data-analytics-infographic.pdf

Thomas H. Davenport, "Analytics 3.0," *Harvard Business Review*, December 2013: https://hbr.org/2013/12/analytics-30

Robert Handfield, "A Brief History of Big Data Analytics," International Institute for Analytics (September 26, 2013): http://iianalytics.com/research/a-brief-history-of-big-data-analytics

Mathew Ingram, "Here's Why the Media Failed to Predict a Donald Trump Victory," *Fortune*, November 9, 2016: http://fortune.com/2016/11/09/media-trump-failure/

Alex Jones, "Data Analytics for Business Leaders Explained," KDnuggets.com (September 2014): www.kdnuggets.com/2014/09/data-analytics-business-leaders-explained.html

Masashi Miyazaki, "A Brief History of Data Analysis," FlyData.com (March 11, 2015): www.flydata.com/blog/a-brief-history-of-data-analysis/

Reuters, "Decoded: Why the Opinion Polls Failed to Predict the Trump Win," DNAIndia.com, November 10, 2016: www.dnaindia.com/world/report-decoded-why-the-opinion-polls-failed-to-predict-the-trump-win-2272109

Ira Simon, "The Evolution of Analytics: Then and Now," Industry Perspectives, *The VAR Guy* guest blog, June 10, 2014: http://thevarguy.com/blog/evolution-analytics-then-and-now

"Wise after the Event, or Why Big Data Failed to Predict President-Elect Trump," Cyber Security Intelligence, November 29, 2016: www.cyber securityintelligence.com/blog/wise-after-the-event-or-why-big-data-failed-to-president-elect-trump-1892.html

CHAPTER 2

Unstructured Data Analytics

The Next Frontier of Analytics Innovation

Change is the law of life. And those who look only to the past or present are certain to miss the future.

—John F. Kennedy

INTRODUCTION

Today we are living in a world of digital power propelled by an unprecedented increase of interactive devices such as smartphones, tablets, wearables, sensor networks, and global positioning system (GPS) sensors that create new data from everything we see, hear, touch, and feel. This new data, of various formats and content, is in turn shared in real time or near-real time with other users, sometimes even by avatars and humanoids! The Internet of Things (IoT), or the Internet of Everything, describes exchanges of data between objects (e.g., devices, vehicles, buildings) via embedded electronics, software, sensors, actuators, and Internet connectivity. The IoT creates opportunities for smart environments (homes, transportation, cities, factories, retail, worksites, and offices) that interface with humans. Businesses, organizations, and governments can now capture, store, process, and analyze this new goldmine of people and machine data, which flows in huge volume at exponential speed to derive actionable insights. In this digital world, structured and unstructured data commingle and complement each other. Examples of structured data include customer ID, financial information, and demographic characteristics like gender. Unstructured data might be voice records of a customer's interaction with a support center, survey verbatim, social media content, or search query text. Analytics of structured data has been around for several decades; however, unstructured data analytics (UDA) is a new challenge. Modern analytics methods work strategically with both types of data.

In this globally connected arena powered by the explosion of the Internet, social media, mobile, cloud computing, and Big Data, UDA is no longer a choice for any forward-looking company or organization; it is a must. As discussed in Chapter 1, The Age of Advanced Business Analytics, companies need to leverage intelligence from multiple data sources and multiple data types to stay current, gain path-breaking insights on customers, and gain knowledge of market growth possibilities. This approach will allow them to successfully operate in a highly competitive marketplace and challenging world. Organizations and governments are also leveraging data to anticipate threats, and detect and combat fraud.

Gartner Research estimated data recorded an increase 800 percent from 2012 to 2017, and more than 80 percent of the business data is unstructured.[1] According to IDC research, only 0.5 percent of the world's data has been analyzed.[2] In a study, IBM determined that 90 percent of the data we have today was created during the past two years.[3] The overwhelming volume of unstructured data comes from various sources, such as social media, chat, e-mail, Web logs, product reviews, market research, customer-care conversations, location stream, voice of customer, insurance claims, consumer feedback, and employee narrative through performance review. The challenge is to derive reliable and relevant insights from the ever-increasing stream of data and maximize the business value buried in the unstructured data. This means uncovering complex patterns, trends, and sentiments that will lead to strategic business actions. Companies that currently do this have a competitive advantage. However, in the future, success in getting business value from UDA will be a survival race for businesses.

In this chapter, we will explore the evolving discipline of UDA and examine the goals of business analytics in the current environment, as well as the strategies and techniques being deployed to extract, transform, load, analyze, and impart meaning from unstructured data.

Within the sections of this chapter, we will address the following:

- What Is UDA?
- Why UDA Today?
- The UDA Industry
- Uses of UDA
- How UDA Works
- Why UDA Is the Next Business Frontier of innovation?
- UDA Success Stories
- Interview with Seth Grimes, Pioneer in Text Analytics and founding chair of the Text Analytics Summit and the Sentiment Analysis Symposium
- The Golden Age of UDA
- Key Takeaways

WHAT IS UDA?

Before we discuss UDA in more detail, let's first define what is meant by *unstructured data*. The term refers to data that does not have a predefined data model and/or does not fit well into traditional relational database tables. Unstructured data typically has no identifiable structure and may include bitmap images/objects, text, audio, video, and other data types. Unstructured data is frequently text-heavy, but may contain data such as dates, numbers, and facts as well. Traditional analytical programs deal with data stored in fielded forms in relational databases or annotated (semantically tagged) in documents. However, the various formats of unstructured data create irregularities and ambiguities that are problematic to traditional analytics techniques.

UDA first emerged in the late 1990s as *text mining*. Early approaches treated and analyzed text as a bag of words. Text mining evolved early to use basic shallow linguistics to handle variant word forms, such as abbreviations, plurals, synonyms, and conjugations, as well as multiword terms known as *n*-grams. *N*-grams are a contiguous sequence of items from a sequence of text or speech. The items in question can be phonemes, syllables, letters, or words, depending on the application. An *n*-gram text analytics model is a type of probabilistic language model for predicting the next item in such a sequence. Basic text analysis might also count frequencies of words and terms to carry out elementary functions, such as attempting to classify a document by topic. Yet at that time, there was little ability to understand the semantics or meanings of the words in the context contained within a given document, as we will discuss in the next sections.

Contemporary UDA addresses issues that arise from unstructured content by applying statistical methods and linguistic rules to automatically assess, analyze, and act on the insights buried in unstructured text, such as e-mail and social media content, Web and call center logs, survey data, insurance or warranty claims, and loan applications.

As mentioned previously, the variety, volume, and velocity of Big Data is growing exponentially. Globally, more people communicate, in various languages, on the Internet. Many are using smaller, voice-enabled mobile devices and, thus, are communicating more frequently in a larger, richer data environment than ever before. However, business interests have remained invariant for many years: Who are my customers? How do they make their purchase decisions? What do they want? What could they need? How are we doing? How are our competitors doing? What should we do in the future to remain competitive? What should we do to retain our most valuable customers? What should we do to grow our business?

Organizations are using modern predictive analytics to address, in real time, the evolving needs and trends of their customers. *Big Data*, an overused buzzword, is today's business reality. However, what we need to talk about is Big Analytics! In the 2010 *IBM Global CEO Study*, a survey of more than 1,500 business leaders in 60 countries, chief executive officers (CEOs) described their companies as "data rich but insight poor."[4] The number of worldwide e-mail users is projected to increase from more than 2.6 billion in 2016 to more than 3.0 billion by 2020.[5] In 2016, the number of business and consumer e-mails sent and received per day totaled more than 215.3 billion, and that number is expected to grow at an average annual rate of 4.6 percent over the next four years, reaching more than 257.7 billion by the end of 2020.

Most of the data contained in e-mail and on websites is unstructured; this offers an untapped opportunity to get insight into consumers' attitudes, behaviors, and preferences.

Premier websites such as Amazon, Facebook, and Google are constantly improving their offerings by anticipating their customers' wants and needs. These changes are the result of advanced business analytics, which are turning data into actionable information through predictive models. New approaches in parallel processing are enabling novel solutions, many of which could not be done even a few years ago. Smaller mobile devices are also increasingly being driven by voice interaction. As mobile devices shrink and become highly featured, voice command/control with audible response becomes a requirement. With it comes the challenge not only to do what was asked, but also to track the interaction for billing, reporting, quality control, and potential buying behavior. Also, increasingly, the application fulfillment is in the cloud, complicating the unification of data for analysis. For example, a typical smartphone user may consult his or her mobile device's search engine for a service nearby, such as a restaurant. Then, the individual might follow GPS directions to it, tweet for preferred menu items, tweet comments, and then pay for the meal, all using a mobile device. Each of the Internet services is interested in the complete details of its part of the interaction. In this example, most of the "work" is performed by software that resides on the Internet rather than on the person's low-powered device. Much of this transaction's data is unstructured.

In addition, legal requirements (HIPAA, Sarbanes-Oxley) vary across borders for and against data capture and data retention, presenting additional challenges to unstructured data management, as the laws continue to evolve to protect the right to privacy. Thus, it is necessary to determine the value and accessibility of the data and whether it can be used for analysis.

In a more formal way, I define **UDA** as a method for extracting usable knowledge from unstructured data, leveraging statistics/mathematic techniques and linguistics to derive meaning from the data to address a business question.

In the case of text analytics, the knowledge extraction concerns the identification of similarities, differences, core concepts, sentiments, and trends, and then using this knowledge to support decision making.

Exhibit 2.01 summarizes some major unstructured data types and their sources.

Unstructured Data Types	Sources
Text	■ E-mails
	■ Web logs
	■ Chats
	■ Tweets
	■ Facebook posts and updates
	■ LinkedIn updates
	■ Other social media
	■ Customer feedback
	■ Product reviews
	■ Book reviews
	■ Customer narratives
	■ Customer feedback
	■ Voice of customer (speech to text)
	■ Open-ended questions (satisfaction survey/survey verbatim)
	■ Employee narrative from performance appraisal
	■ Vaccine adverse reaction
	■ Job seeker resumes
	■ Job posting description
	■ Intensive Care Unit verbatim
	■ Emergency Healthcare Center verbatim
	■ Insurance claim narratives verbatim
	■ Document (Microsoft Word and other)
	■ PowerPoint presentation
Images	■ Pictures (JPEG and other)
	■ Magnetic Resonance Image (MRI)
	■ Bitmap
Audio	■ MP3 and other formats
	■ Voice of customer (call center log): phone call
	■ Voice recognition: semantics search: Apple's Siri, Microsoft's Cortana, Amazon's Alexa, Google Assistant
Video	■ Eye tracking system
	■ Candidate video presentation and interview
	■ Sport video streaming
	■ Surveillance video
	■ Weather videos

Exhibit 2.01 UDA and Sources

Today's businesses also need to develop and maintain demographic and behavioral customer profiles to personalize the customers' experience and anticipate their interests, wants, needs, and opportunities in real time while the customer is engaged. Businesses need to provide personalized information, actionable immediately, but at the same time not seem "creepy" to customers. For example, in a couple of well-known incidents, a popular vendor anticipated customers' product needs correctly by providing online recommendations while inadvertently missing the sensitivity of the personal nature of the information, causing a consumer backlash.

WHY UDA TODAY?

In this era of digital information explosion from Big Data, humans cannot possibly process and understand all the unstructured data available today. Making sense of this data is beyond the capacity of the human brain and so, by necessity, much of it has been ignored.

Leveraging statistical and mathematical algorithms combined with linguistics rules to automatically harness this new data has become vital for companies and organizations to increase their efficiency, effectiveness, and productivity.

While speaking at a data analytics conference early this year in Las Vegas on the topic of people analytics in the era of Big Data, I had provided a definition of Big Data when someone asked: "Why do we have Big Data today?" I responded that Big Data exists today because of three major reasons:

1. The first reason is the drop in storage costs. According to McKinsey Global Institute, with $600 you can buy a disk drive to store the entire world's music.[6] Back in 1990, 1 GB of space cost more than $11,000; today, 1 GB of space costs less than 1 cent.

2. The second reason is the increase of interactive devices: sensors, smartphones, tablets, and GPS navigation systems that help us capture everything we see, hear, feel, and touch. And all that information, once captured, no longer resides only on our desktop; it is shared online with other users.

3. The third reason is the increase of infrastructures and tools that help us manage, process, and analyze data in parallel and in the cloud—data that we used to ignore due to its volume, velocity, and variety. The power of the computing infrastructure, parallel processing in cloud and in memory computing, enables the use of statistical and mathematical techniques and algorithms to process and analyze this new type of data. Even though most of the mathematical and statistical procedures and techniques that we use today to mine unstructured data have been around for quite some time, the lack of computing power had held back implementation in practice.

Big Data as a Catalyst

Big Data is a term that is very ill-defined and could mean many things. Big Data is simply the term that is used to describe the exponential growth of digital information (structured and unstructured), information that we were not able to process or analyze due to its volume, velocity, variety, and veracity. Most (80%) of Big Data is unstructured. It used to be ignored by businesses due to the inability to properly analyze it. However, today it is seen as a goldmine, providing relevant insight about customer needs, wants, preference, and feedbacks. Companies and organizations can now store, analyze, and gain insight from that massive volume of data by leveraging tools and software that perform advanced analytics. Those mathematical and statistical techniques have been around for quite some time but were not easily applied to unstructured data. The advent of computing power propelled by the emergence of UDA software solutions enables the analysis of unstructured data of different types. Though most software focuses on text, audio, and image data, tech giants have developed and created data products that leverage UDA, machine learning, representation learning, deep learning, artificial intelligence (AI), natural language processing, and cognitive analytics. Thus, the emergence of Big Data was the catalyst of an unprecedented increase of AI, machine learning, and deep learning applications across a variety of industries and sectors. It was not surprising to see machine learning top the Gartner Technology Adoption Hype Cycle in 2016.

Mainstream examples of artificial intelligence were seen in games such as chess when in May 1997 IBM's chess-playing computer Deep Blue defeated chess grandmaster Garry Kasparov. In a *Jeopardy!* quiz show exhibition match in 2010, IBM's question answering system, Watson, defeated the two greatest Jeopardy champions, Brad Rutter and Ken Jennings, by a significant margin. In 2016, Google DeepMind's AlphaGo program defeated South Korean Go grandmaster Lee Sedol in the board game Go. AlphaGo's victory put AI, machine learning, and deep learning on the front page of media networks. This news added traction to Google's self-driving car, Facebook's intelligent content management and delivery, and Amazon's and Netflix's recommendations algorithms. In August 2017 Elon Musk claimed on twitter: "OpenAI first ever to defeat world's best players in competitive eSports (Dota 2). Vastly more complex than traditional board games like chess & Go."

The potential for the development of the AI sector is immense, and its global value may reach $36 billion by 2025. The greater part of this market will probably be taken by the tech giants such as Amazon, Google, Facebook, Apple IBM, and Microsoft, which have been investing in this sector for many years. Smaller segments of the machine learning market, usually focused on specific, individual solutions such as in healthcare, might be picked up by technological start-ups. Advances in computing power and technology are revolutionizing businesses, governments, and communities. In the following sections we will go over some key analytics topics useful for UDA.

Artificial Intelligence (AI)

In 1956, at the Dartmouth Artificial Intelligence Conference, AI was first described as: "Every aspect of learning or any other feature of intelligence can in principle be so precisely described that a machine can be made to simulate it."[7] So what is AI today?

AI is defined as the intelligence exhibited by machines.[8] It concerns the development of computer algorithms and systems that can perform a variety of tasks that usually would require human intelligence: computer systems that mimic human intelligence, such as: understanding human speech, autonomously driving cars, perception and reasoning, competing at a high level in a strategic game (such as Go and Chess), following intelligent routines in content delivery network, and decision making that leverages complex data or information.

AI is the overarching concept in advanced computing power and computer intelligence. It is important to note that there are three types of AI:

1. *Narrow artificial intelligence (Narrow AI)*. As its name implies, this refers to AI that is skilled in a specific task. For instance, IBM's Deep Blue was skilled in playing chess only while Google DeepMind's AlphaGo was skilled in playing Go.

2. *Artificial general intelligence (AGI)* is different from Narrow AI, as it concerns AI that is considered human-level intelligence and can handle multiple intelligent tasks.

3. *Super-intelligent artificial intelligence* is considered to be smarter than AI and is concerned with an intellect that some experts described as "smarter than the best human brain in every field, including general wisdom, scientific social skills, and creativity." Super-intelligent AI really exists when computers outpace in all types of intelligences.

See Exhibits 2.02 through 2.04.

Machine Learning

Coined in 1959 by Arthur Samuel, a pioneer in the field of computer gaming and artificial intelligence, machine learning is about providing computers with the ability to learn by themselves. Instead of programming everything they should do, we just train them to learn for themselves and apply their learning to new data. Machine learning evolved from AI.

It is important to note that machine learning is a subfield of AI that takes a large dataset, analyzes it, and learns from it. Machine learning systems can then make predictions based on a new set of data without being explicitly preprogrammed to perform predefined tasks.

IBM's chess-playing computer Deep Blue, which defeated Kasparov in 1997, was not a machine learning system, as it was only programmed to play chess. Examples of machine learning include spam filtering, detection of network intruders or malicious insiders, optical character recognition, search engines, and computer vision.

Machine learning is becoming more and more pervasive and part of our day-to-day life. In 2015, Google CEO Sundar Pichai announced that Google will have machine learning in all their products.

See Exhibits 2.02 through 2.04.

Deep Learning

Deep learning (also known as deep structured learning, hierarchical learning, or deep machine learning[9]) is a branch of machine learning based on a set of algorithms that attempt to model high-level abstractions in data. Deep learning leverages a subset of machine learning techniques and tools to solve a variety of problems that would normally require human intelligence or AI. In deep learning, the computer ingests massive amounts of data and creates a subset of networks of binary decisions to uncover patterns and anticipate trends and outcomes. Goodfellow, Bengio, and Courville, in their book *Deep Learning*, define deep learning as "a solution to allow computers to learn from experience and understand the world in terms of a hierarchy of concept."[10] The more data the system ingests, the more accurate, precise, and intelligent it becomes.

Deep learning systems feed data into a neural network that learns the characteristics of something such as an object or an image. Facial and video recognition algorithms use deep learning to figure out who is in your photos or video. Google Photo leverages deep learning to classify and organize its 1.2 billion daily uploaded photos. When you watch a video on YouTube and instantly receive a list of recommended videos you may like, it's because YouTube uses deep learning algorithms behind the scenes to make those recommendations.

Deep learning can be applied to a variety of data formats and sources, including audio, video, speech, written word, documents, PowerPoint and other presentations, images, and pictures. Deep learning can process, analyze, and interpret data like a human mind would do, but with high accuracy, high speed, and high volume. Intelligent personal assistants such as Apple's Siri, Amazon's Alexa, Google Assistant, and Microsoft's Cortana leverage deep learning. Other examples of deep learning application include Amazon recommendations for products to purchase, Netflix recommendations for movies, and autonomous cars.

Google also reported that deep learning enabled its DeepMind's AlphaGo to defeat the Go master Lee Sedol in 2016. According to Google, AlphaGo studied 30 million human moves in Go and learned by playing against itself to finally win the highly anticipated match.

Today, forward-looking companies have embraced DL and made it part of their business model. In fact, Google, Facebook, Twitter, Amazon, Netflix, IBM, Microsoft, and Apple—and all tech giants dealing with massive amounts of data from different formats and sources—have been leveraging AI, machine learning, and deep learning to optimize their productivity, user experience, and product offering.

See Exhibits 2.02 through 2.04.

Representation Learning or Feature Learning

In machine learning, representation learning, or feature learning is a set of techniques that learn a feature: a transformation of raw data input to a representation that can be effectively exploited in machine learning tasks. This obviates manual feature engineering, which is otherwise necessary, and allows a machine to both learn at a specific task (using the features) and learn the features themselves.

Feature learning is motivated by the fact that machine learning tasks such as classification often require input that is mathematically and computationally convenient to process. However, real-world data such as images, video, and sensor measurement are usually complex, redundant, and highly variable. Thus, it is necessary to discover useful features or representations from raw data. Traditional handcrafted features often require expensive human labor and often rely on expert knowledge. Also, they normally do not generalize well. This motivates the design of efficient feature learning techniques, to automate and generalize this.

Feature learning can be divided into two categories: supervised and unsupervised feature learning, analogous to these categories in machine learning.

See Exhibits 2.02 through 2.04.

Natural Language Processing

Natural language processing is an area of computer science and AI that assesses human language and a variety of computer science techniques to analyze and automatically organize, process, interpret, and understand the human language.

See Exhibits 2.02 through 2.04.

Cognitive Computing/Analytics

Cognitive computing is about teaching the computer to mimic the way the human brain works, leveraging computing science, deep learning, neural network, artificial intelligence, and cognitive science to provide thoughtful answers to natural language questions. IBM-Watson Analytics has been the leader in cognitive computing, with the application expanding in various industries. With guided data discovery, automated predictive analytics, and cognitive capabilities such as natural language dialogue, one can interact with data conversationally. We will broadly discuss cognitive computing in Chapter 12, The Future of Analytics.

See Exhibits 2.02 through 2.04.

Neural Network

The neural network, also called the artificial neural network, was defined by the inventor of one of the first neurocomputers, Dr. Robert Hecht-Nielsen, as " ... a computing system made up of a number of simple, highly interconnected processing elements, which process

Artificial Intelligence (AI)

AI is the development of a set of algorithms and systems to perform tasks that would usually require human intelligence.
AI is the science of programming machines to do things that would be considered intelligent if they were done by a human.

Examples:

- Google's self-driving cars
- Understanding speech
- Content delivery network

Machine Learning

Machine learning is a subset of AI that is concerned with teaching the computers to learn by themselves and apply that learning to new data.
The fundamental difference with basic AI is that in machine learning computers are *not preprogrammed to perform a given task.* They take the data and learn for themselves, then apply that knowledge and training from a huge dataset to recognize patterns and make predictions, such as facial and object recognition, translation, speech recognition, and more.

Examples:

- Logistic regression
- Naïve Bayes
- Spam filtering
- Security threats
- Detection of network intruders
- Search engine

Deep Learning

Deep learning, a subset of machine learning, uses some machine learning techniques and neural network to replicate the human decision-making process to answer real-world questions or problems. In deep learning, the computer ingests a lot of data and performs decisions that would usually require human intelligence. Deep learning is concerned with computers that learn from experience and understand the world in terms of a hierarchy of concepts. They can read and interpret data in different formats.

Examples:

- Audio, images, video recognition
- Facial recognition
- Personal assistant: Google Assistant, Cortana, Alexa, Siri

Cognitive Analytics

Cognitive analytics is about teaching the computer to mimic the way the human brain works, leveraging computer science, deep learning, and artificial intelligence to provide thoughtful answers to natural language questions by searching through massive amounts of information.

Examples:

- IBM-Watson
- Natural dialogue questions
- Health Care: A doctor can use cognitive analytics to quickly comb through medical journals, clinician notes, patient history, and other documents to find highly relevant information to improve a diagnosis or treatment plan.

Exhibit 2.02 AI, Machine Learning, Deep Learning, and Cognitive Computing/Analytics Overview

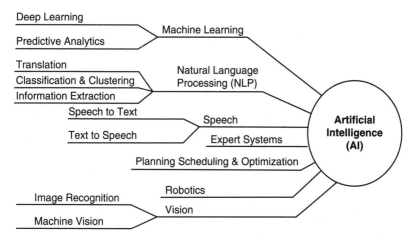

Exhibit 2.03 AI, Machine Learning, and Deep Learning Explained
Source: Alex Castrounis, "Artificial Intelligence, Deep Learning, and Neural Networks Explained," KDnuggets, October 2016. www.kdnuggets.com/2016/10/artificial-intelligence-deep-learning-neural-networks-explained.html

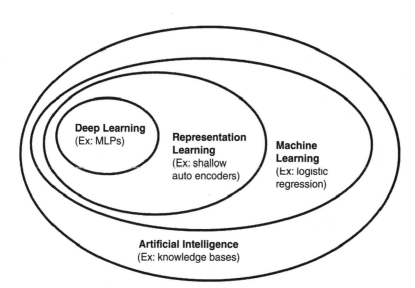

Exhibit 2.04 Venn Diagram of AI, Machine Learning, Representation Learning, and Deep Learning
Source: Adapted from Ian Goodfellow, Yoshua Bengio, and Aaron Courville, Deep Learning *(Boston, MA: MIT Press, November 2016).*

information by their dynamic state response to external inputs."[11] Simply stated, neural network computer programs analyze and classify information such as pictures, images, audio, video, and text in the same way or close to the same way our human brain would. These systems are self-learning and trained, rather than explicitly programmed, and excel in areas where the solution or feature detection is difficult to express in a traditional computer program.

In summary, the convergence of an information explosion (Big Data) with the availability of affordable devices, infrastructure technologies, advanced analytics, and consumer empowerment has created the perfect condition (a Big Bang) for UDA. The mission is to scout, explore, research, and use the new technologies to uncover the insight from a multitude of data sources to design a more consumer-focused, participatory, and sustainable business system that is location-independent.

See Exhibits 2.02 through 2.04.

Exhibit 2.04 is a Venn diagram that illustrates how deep learning is a kind of representation learning, which is in turn a type of machine learning, which is used for many but not all approaches to AI.[12] Each section of the Venn diagram includes an example of AI technology.

In examining Exhibits 2.02 through 2.04, it is important to understand the difference between these useful concepts, as it may be confusing. It all starts with AI as the foundation. Then we have machine learning, which is a subset of AI. Representation learning and deep learning are both subsets of machine learning.

THE UDA INDUSTRY

Industry consolidation of UDA providers is ongoing, as key technologies and even more precious patents and skilled engineers are acquired by companies with an interest in unstructured data technologies. In the search engine arena, numerous well-known vendors have been assimilated—AltaVista, Autonomy, Endeca, and FAST. Record-linking technology companies (technology to de-duplicate different forms of people and place names, such as IBM / International Business Machine) have also been absorbed by larger vendors. Taxonomy and information retrieval companies (for example, InXight, Teragram) have similarly been snapped up. Statistical software vendors with text analytics solutions have also been acquired. Today, UDA is very crowded with vendors and open sources.

IBM's Watson debuted as a fine example of the promise of question-answering technology. Now IBM Watson has been expanded to other areas, such as healthcare, where it assists physicians to better diagnose some diseases and provides relevant recommendations for treatments; customer service agent support, including customer service and sentiment analysis; and sports, in which it can analyze some physical sports aspects, such as a tennis serve.

Apple's Siri is an intelligent personal assistant and knowledge navigator that is part of Apple's operating systems. The feature uses a natural language user interface to answer questions, make recommendations, and perform actions by delegating requests to a set of Web services.

Amazon's Alexa is an intelligent personal assistant developed by Amazon Lab126 and made popular through the Amazon Echo. It is capable of voice interaction, music playback, making to-do lists, setting alarms, streaming podcasts, playing audiobooks, and providing weather and traffic reports and other real-time information.

Microsoft's Cortana is an intelligent personal assistant and knowledge navigator created by Microsoft for Windows 10 users. It leverages the semantic search and unstructured data to provide administrative support or respond to queries.

Google Assistant is an intelligent personal assistant developed by Google. Google Assistant can engage in two-way conversations. The Assistant is currently integrated into the Google Home device, Allo app, Google Pixel, and Android Wear.

Attivio, a premier independent vendor of hybrid structured and unstructured data management, offers a solution that seamlessly integrates traditional relational database technology with the capabilities of a full-text search engine.

At the consumer level, it is possible with a small and talented staff to conduct hybrid structured and unstructured analytics, using a blend of

Open Source Software	Commercial Software
■ TM: Text mining infrastructure in R	■ IBM Text Analytics
■ Gensim: Python library for Text mining	■ SAS Text Analytics
■ PERL	■ Lexalytics Text Analytics
■ Kmine	■ SmartLogic
■ QDA Miner Lite	■ Provalis
■ KH Coder	■ OpenText
■ TAMS Analyzer	■ Alchemy API
■ Carrot2	■ Attensity
■ CAT	■ OdinText
■ GATE (General Architecture for Text Engineering)	■ Clarabridge
■ Natural Language Toolkit (NLTLK)	■ Content Analysts
■ RapidMiner	■ Oracle Social Cloud
■ Unstructured Information Management	■ Angoss Text Analytics
■ OpenNLP	■ Discover Text
■ Apache Mahout	■ NetOwl
■ LPU	■ Oracle Endeca
■ LingPipe	■ Satssoft
■ S-EM	■ Verint System
■ LibShort Text	■ Ascribe
■ Twinword	■ Forest Rim's Textual ETL
■ Datumbox API	■ muTextMu Sigma
■ Aika	■ Text 2data
■ Distributed Machine Learning Toolkit	■ SAP Text Analytics
■ Coh-Metrix	■ HP Autonomy
■ VisualText	■ Loop Cognitive Computing
■ Pattern	■ Luminoso
■ Orange TextTable	■ Google Cloud API
■ MathLab	■ Aylien
■ Natural Language Toolkit	■ Loop Cognitive
■ Voyant Tools	■ VisualText
■ Baleen	■ Buzzlogix
■ The PLOS	

Exhibit 2.05 Text Analytics Text Mining Software
Source: Adapted from Forrester, "Vendor Landscape: Big Data Text Analytics," Forrester, November 10, 2015: www.forrester.com/report/Vendor+Landscape+Big+Data+Text+ Analytics/-/E-RES122598

open source and commercial software. Open source solutions include Python, R, a statistics package, and Apache Lucene/Solr, a full-text search engine. However, the choice of implementation technology and the degree of sophistication are driven by budget, staffing, and opportunity. The solution spectrum ranges from custom, highly configured, distributed collection and automated analysis and reporting solutions on the high end to modest, limited processing for key metrics on the low end. Open source technology can also be a viable option at all scales.

Against this competitive backdrop, the traditional business intelligence technologies of database and statistical analysis converge and merge with younger analytical technologies such as text analytics, computational linguistics, natural language processing, and machine learning. As these solutions mature and are proven, often by small start-ups, established companies are expected to develop or continue to acquire them.

Exhibit 2.05 provides a list of UDA vendors and open sources. Notice this is a very crowded market.

USES OF UDA

Whether it is for companies, research groups, public service, or government organizations, UDA provides tangible benefits through an infinite variety of uses. Examples of the uses of UDA include:

- Increasing competitive intelligence from analyzing documents, blogs, and reports from the competition
- Providing voice-of-customer analysis from open-ended survey questions, call center logs, e-mails, blogs, or opinion sites, a skill that can also be used to increase customer satisfaction, customer acquisition, customer retention, and customer loyalty by reaching out to customers proactively
- Helping to maximize a company's customer relationship management (CRM) efforts by leveraging customers' feedback analysis and considering customer needs and preferences.
- Increasing effectiveness of customer retention efforts by providing enhanced insights from unstructured data to enrich traditional predictive retention models

- Driving product development and adoption by analyzing early customer feedback on a product and/or analyzing warranty claims

- Enhancing government investigation procedures to uncover security threats and criminal actions and to detect terrorist activities

- Detecting patterns of fraudulent behavior; as, for example, Monster Worldwide does, using UDA to detect fraudulent actions and activities on its sites

- Influencing financial investment strategies

- Enhancing the drug discovery processes for pharmaceutical research companies, which can explore articles, journals, patents, and other research material related to existing drugs

- Enhancing emergency procedure and saving lives by analyzing verbatim at emergency centers and ICUs

- Improving drugs and vaccines by analyzing patients' feedback narrative regarding side effects

- Increasing employee satisfaction and retention by analyzing employee narratives from performance review and employee feedback

- Improving sports team performance by analyzing team practice and game videos

HOW UDA WORKS

As presented in Exhibit 2.06, UDA is a five-step process:

1. Prepare unstructured data for analysis.

2. Complete data preprocessing: Apply linguistic statistics and machine learning techniques to the unstructured document before the extraction and the modeling.

3. Extract and model the information from textual unstructured data sources using a variety of mathematical techniques, such as AI, machine learning, representation learning, deep learning, and natural language processing.

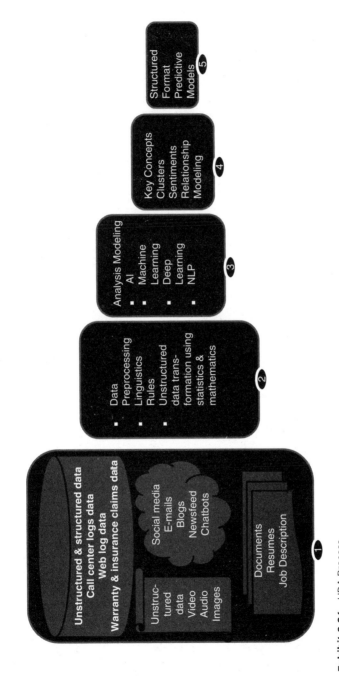

1
- Unstructured & structured data
- Call center logs data
- Web log data
- Warranty & insurance claims data

Unstructured data
Video
Audio
Images

Social media
E-mails
Blogs
Newsfeed
Chatbots

Documents
Resumes
Job Description

2
- Data Preprocessing
- Linguistics Rules
- Unstructured data transformation using statistics & mathematics

3
Analysis Modeling
- AI
- Machine Learning
- Deep Learning
- NLP

4
Key Concepts
Clusters
Sentiments
Relationship
Modeling

5
Structured
Format
Predictive
Models

Exhibit 2.06 UDA Process

4. Extract the key concepts cluster, convert unstructured text into categories, and structure the format for advanced analytics.

5. Transform the data into actionable intelligence to address business challenges, such as fraud detection, customer acquisition, customer retention, financial investment strategies, or consumer sentiment.

WHY UDA IS THE NEXT ANALYTICAL FRONTIER?

Analytics is the next business frontier due to the abundance of data generated globally by people using the Internet, social media, mobile devices, and all sorts of wearables and applications. The analysis of all this data subsequently generates even more data. As companies gather greater amounts of unstructured information regarding their customers and the market, new tools will be needed to turn this data into business value. This requires mastering new types of analytics, such as:

- Semantics analytics and search
- Sentiment analysis
- Deep learning
- Machine learning
- AI
- Cognitive analytics

We see four major drivers for the future evolution of UDA:

1. *Voice of the market.* Leveraging the voice of the market to provide innovative services, products, and technologies to the market.

2. *Voice of the consumer/customer.* Leveraging the voice of consumer/customer to increase intimacy, satisfaction, up-sell, and profitability.

3. *Scramble for semantic.* Coupling text analytics with business intelligence to create self-learning artificial intelligence. Using a human-like approach to leverage context and concept when searching for a candidate's resume from a resume database, answering user questions on the weather or on directions,

responding to patients' questions regarding their health. Recognizing images, videos, the concept and the context of the words in any unstructured text or document.

Exhibit 2.07 clearly defines *semantic* and sets it apart as today's and the future's focus for text analytics.

4. *Integration of text analytics in predictive analytics.* Coupled with predictive analytics, text analytics transforms unstructured text, such as customer e-mails, chat bots voicemail transcripts, and social media activities, into actionable intelligence to address the most imperative business problems companies could face in the future.

A case in point: Monster Worldwide has leveraged semantic searches to build its SeeMore technology and Super Search, which helps employers perform human-like resume searches by leveraging advanced matching of job titles, skills, industries, education, and other information from job seekers' professional backgrounds. The latent semantic indexing technology provides a precise match of resumes to job requirements, ranked by actual experience, including how recent a job was and the length of time the relevant skills were used in a job. SeeMore has helped Monster Worldwide's customers to reduce by 70 percent the time spent searching through resumes. Also, 68 percent of SeeMore users claimed they could find resumes they couldn't find before.

In this new field of advanced analytics, tech giants such as Google, Apple, Facebook, Intel, Twitter, and Salesforce lead the way in key takeovers. As shown in Exhibit 2.08, there has been a lot of activity in AI mergers and acquisitions over the past five years. CBInsights reports:

- In 2013, Google picked up deep learning and neural network startup DNNresearch from the computer science department at the University of Toronto. This acquisition reportedly helped Google make major upgrades to its image search feature. In 2014 Google acquired British company DeepMind Technologies for $600M. Last year, it acquired visual search startup Moodstock and bought platform Api.ai. More recently, in Q1 2017, Google acquired predictive analytics platform Kaggle.

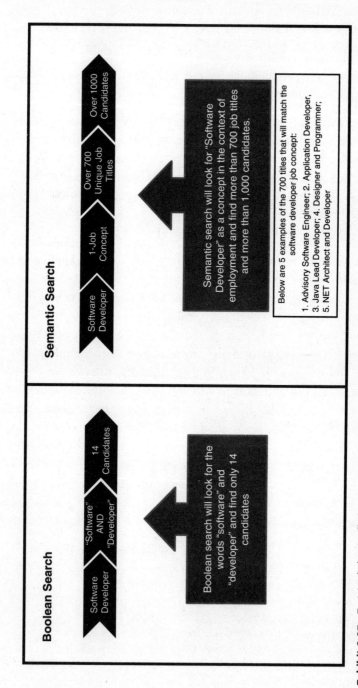

Exhibit 2.07 Text Analytics Applied to Resume Search: Boolean vs. Semantic Search Results of "Software Developer" Job Title (Output from a resumes database in medium Designated Market Area in Texas)

- Apple has been ramping up its M&A [mergers and acquisitions] activity, and ranked second with a total of 7 acquisitions. It recently acquired Tel Aviv-based RealFace, valued at $2M.

- Intel, Microsoft, and Facebook are tied for third place. Intel acquired 3 startups in 2016 alone: Itseez, Nervana Systems, and Movidius, while Facebook acquired Belarus-based Masquerade Technologies and Switzerland-based Zurich Eye. Microsoft recently acquired Genee and conversational AI startup Maluuba.

- Twitter is the next-most-active acquirer, with 4 major acquisitions, the most recent being image-processing startup Magic Pony.

- Salesforce, which joined the race in 2015 with the acquisition of Tempo AI, made two major acquisitions last year: Khosla Ventures–backed MetaMind and open source machine-learning server PredictionIO. GE made 2 acquisitions in November 2016: AI-IoT startup Bit Stew Systems, and CRM-focused Wise.io.[13]

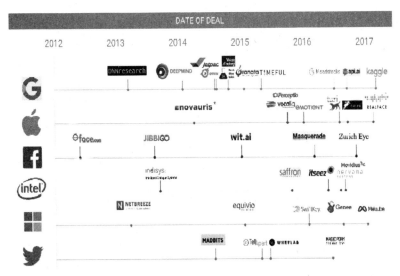

Exhibit 2.08 The Race for AI: Google, Twitter, Intel, Apple In A Rush To Grab Artificial Intelligence Start-ups

Source: CBInsights, "The Race for AI: Google, Baidu, Intel, Apple in a Rush to Grab Artificial Intelligence Startups," July 21, 2017: www.cbinsights.com/research/top-acquirers-ai-startups-ma-timeline/

INTERVIEW WITH SETH GRIMES ON ANALYTICS AS THE NEXT BUSINESS FRONTIER

I had a chance to interview Seth Grimes, a pioneering leader in the field of UDA and the founding chair of the Text Analytics Summit and the Sentiment Analysis Symposium. Here is what he had to say:

Isson: **What are the top five benefits of text analytics in today's business environment?**

Grimes*: Text analytics extends business intelligence to text sources—to e-mails, survey responses, social updates, online news, financial filings, warranty claims, and scientific papers—to sources that contain immense business value that until just a few years ago couldn't be included in enterprise, government, and scientific data-analysis efforts. Text analytics delivers many business benefits, including:*

- *An ability to extract useful information—facts, relationships, events, sentiment—from online, social, and enterprise information, including in real time. Information extraction capabilities make for richer search and findability and for more efficient text processing in realms that range from customer support to e-discovery.*

- *An ability to get at the reasons behind the numbers, at the root causes—in the customers' and stakeholders' own voices—behind the patterns that surfaced in analyzing transactional and operational data.*

- *The possibility of automating work with textual sources. I know of one company that reduced the time to analyze free-text responses of each employee survey it ran from five person-days to half of one person-day.*

- *Extended reach. Automated methods run 24/7 and are capable of ingesting and analyzing huge volumes of material, including in international languages.*

- *Data-mining capabilities that find patterns in large text volumes that are invisible to human analyses.*

Isson: **What companies or industries do you believe are really leveraging the power of text analytics?**

Grimes*: Government intelligence analysts and life sciences researchers were early text analytics adopters, with serious work that dates to the late 1990s. Text analytics is more important in those domains than ever and has also proven especially compelling for customer-experience management, risk* *management and corporate compliance, financial services, market research and competitive intelligence, media and publishing, and for just about anyone who's doing serious social media analysis. Text analytics market size is estimated to grow from US$2.65 billion in 2015 to US$5.93 billion by 2020, at a compound annual growth rate (CAGR) of 17.5 percent, and I foresee strong, sustained growth in the years to come.*

Isson: What are the key steps to implement text analytics—some dos and don'ts?

Grimes: *As with any analytics process, the number one key step is to start with business goals and work backward to understand the insights that will help you tackle those goals, the analyses that will produce those insights, and the data—from transactional and operational and text and other sources—that you'll need to feed your analyses. Best not to start with the thought "Text analytics sounds really interesting. How do I get going?" Better to start with an assessment that identifies the particular types of information, in an accessible set of text sources, that will generate high-value insights to help you optimize your business processes and decision making.*

Once you've made that assessment, experiment! The joy of working with text is that it was created for human consumption, so we're usually able to judge how accurately and effectively our text analysis systems are working. There are many free and low-cost solutions and very strong commercial implementations that are well suited for the range of business domains, information types, and analysis needs. Survey the options to find the best candidates for your particular needs.

Isson: What is the future of text analytics?

Grimes: *A recent focus for text analytics has been handling the deep and complex subjective content in social, online, and enterprise sources. The field is called sentiment analysis, the application of analytical methods to discern and decode attitudes, emotions, opinions, and intent signals in the spectrum of text sources.*

Expect text analytics to be built into text-rich mainstream business and consumer applications. We're seeing a consumerization in technologies such as Apple Siri, and we're seeing the creation of highly sophisticated text analysis systems such as IBM Watson, targeting large-scale problems in high-value domains such as healthcare. In between the extremes, text analytics will soon be pervasive for social media analyses and routine enterprise and small to medium companies' business intelligence.

UDA SUCCESS STORIES

Early successes are encouraging and compelling others to invest. Here are some examples of companies that have successfully taken advantage of UDA.

Amazon.com

Amazon is a premier online shopping destination. Started as an online bookseller in 1994, the company has expanded to become eBook publisher, tablet and smart home devices manufacturer, movie studio, Cloud computer giant and more. Its customer rating system is top-notch, providing an easy-to-use application for its customers to review and comment on products and service levels of itself and its partners. While some purveyors are not above writing glowing self-reviews, Amazon employs analytics to vet them, as well as exclude inappropriate posting content. New developments in unstructured analytics enable the detection and management of these reviews written under false pretenses.

Amazon's numeric categorical rating system allows customers to selectively review comments by satisfaction and level of interest. Amazon's authoritative and comprehensive product reviews attract repeat business and links to ratings from other sites. Through registration and login, as well as tracking cookies, Amazon can assist its customers with order status, product interest lists, possible related products and services of interest, and ease of purchase. Purchase pattern recognition using UDA enables Amazon to determine next probable purchases, such as the follow-on book by the same author in a series, service items for products purchased, and items reviewed and not retained on a wish list. And more than 35 percent of sales on Amazon are from the recommendations Engine. UDA is powered by deep learning algorithms that produce the best recommendations to consumers based upon their viewing behaviors.

Spotify

Spotify: Finds songs that fit your profile, that you haven't yet listened to.

Founded in 2006, Spotify is a music, podcast, and video-streaming service that was officially launched on October 7, 2008. The company now provides digital rights management–protected content from record labels and media companies. One of Spotify's great products, powered by UDA algorithms, is Discovery Weekly: a playlist that is personalized with recommended music for you. Chris Johnson and Edward Newett introduced Discovery Weekly at DataEngConf 2015.[14]

Like me, you probably enjoy your weekly playlist from Spotify's Discovery Weekly, with its music recommended just for you. But have you ever wondered how Spotify puts together the perfect playlist that you simply love without you ever having talked to them?

The answer is UDA! Yes, Spotify uses UDA algorithms to prepare that tailor-made weekly playlist so that it perfectly matches your musical tastes.

How Do They Do That?

It starts with the data: Spotify has a Big Data set encompassing all its users. In 2017, the company had more than 140 million users (60 million paying) in its user database and a Big Data matrix of users by artists, processing several terabytes of data every day. The data set includes all their users' listening habits and preferences.

Spotify leverages its users database to perform UDA, profiling and segmenting its users based on their listening habits and micro-genres. The company leverages the UDA results to find patterns from users' past behavior to generate recommendations via collaborative filtering models.

With that knowledge they then extrapolate to new listener and new song leveraging natural language processing and deep learning techniques. They use natural language processing to scan music news and blogs to discuss how a particular artist is mentioned and defined. The company uses deep learning methods (such as convolutional neural network or ensemble methods), natural language processing and collaborative filtering to parse music blogs to detect outliers, build micro-genres, and analyze the content of playlist.

Armed with these actionable insights from the power of Big Data and UDA, Spotify can accurately pick your next favorite song.

Facebook

The leading social network leverages UDA algorithms powered by AI and relevancy score models to optimize the experience of its more than 2 billion users when they interact with Facebook products such Facebook Messenger or Instagram. The company leverages UDA to manage photos and to distribute personalized content to its users based across the world.

Facebook creates a personalized user experience by leveraging algorithms that use more than a thousand data sources to assign relevancy scores to every piece of content a user could see in his or her newsfeed. The company then runs predictive models to anticipate content preferences and interest for every single user. Facebook regularly optimizes its relevancy score by running some surveys through which users' content and response is captured to automatically feed Facebook's relevancy score algorithms and models to improve their accuracy.

Yes, behind the personalized content you receive in your Facebook newsfeed are UDA algorithms, running behind the scenes to achieve one of Facebook's most important company goals, as stated in 2014 by its CEO Mark Zuckerberg: "Our goal is to build the perfect personalized newspaper for every person in the world. We are trying to personalize and show you the stuff that's to be most interesting to you."[15]

ITA Software

ITA Software's technology is widely used by domestic and international airlines, online and traditional travel agents, corporate and government-managed booking tools, global distribution systems (GDSs), metasearch services, leisure packaging systems, and technology providers. The software quickly, consistently, and accurately identifies the best available airfares without relying on high-cost, low-efficiency mainframe computers. The system provides a unique way to store, calculate, and distribute seat availability and flight schedule data to satisfy more than one million queries per second.[16]

This software is the epitome of what is possible with a smart investment in UDA. As Craig Stoltz described it: "For instance, ask the software to quote prices on a flight from Washington to Los Angeles. Before you start the search, it will let you open the query to any airports within a mileage range you choose (25, 50, 100 miles, or more) or to any airports you specify.... You can also ask the tool to scan for flights within a time window ranging from two hours to two days, with different specs possible for departure and return."[17] Assimilating volumes of airline data, including current seat availability, allows ITA software to offer a premier booking service through its deep analysis of flight and fare options.

Internet Search Engines: Bing.com, Google.com, and the Like

Current search engines tackle the challenge of intuiting and satisfying user intent using UDA in several ways. Since the average search text is a few words, this is a very difficult endeavor. These methods include user profiling through IP address detection, identifying interests and information needs from query text, providing a deep analysis of query context, and determining probable meaning based on the popularity of other sets of queries used by other searchers. Perhaps the greatest knowledge is gained from the aggregation and analysis of all the searches performed. Because interest in a topic rises and falls over time, detecting trends and providing options to satisfy the associated information and product need is crucial for continued business viability. Last year's top Christmas toy is this year's loss leader.

Monster Worldwide

Monster Worldwide, the global leader in online recruitment solutions, manages and analyzes structured and unstructured data from employers' job descriptions to seekers' resumes' contents. At Monster, we have leveraged UDA to analyze the voice of customer and other text-based communications, such as e-mails and call center logs, to enrich our existing customer attrition models and significantly increase the efficiency of our proactive customer retention programs.

As mentioned previously, Monster moved one step further by providing its employers with a semantic resume search technology called

Power Resume Search (PRS). PRS enables customers to match resumes from any resumes' database to their job descriptions, leveraging artificial intelligence and machine self-learning. Monster also leveraged text analytics for its content categorization for its China branch. Launched in 1997, ChinaHR.com (formerly owned by Monster) is an innovator in online talent recruitment. It was the first company to offer online recruiting services in China, and it also offers campus recruiting and recruiting process outsourcing services. ChinaHR.com needed to manually assign meaningful occupational categories to recruitment postings. To master these needs, ChinaHR.com leveraged UDA to provide content categorization, allowing clients to extract key information, assign categories to resumes and job postings, and store all the information as metadata. This content categorization led to an increase in customer satisfaction and loyalty and an increase of services representative productivity.

THE GOLDEN AGE OF UDA

We noticed from the evolution of UDA that the computing power has enabled businesses and organizations not only to collect tremendous amounts of unstructured data from their customers from multiple sources, but more importantly to analyze and better understand customer needs, wants, preferences, and feedback, thanks to the advent of text mining software processes. Knowing that 80 percent of that data is unstructured and that only 0.5 percent of the data is being analyzed today, we are really living in the golden age of UDA. With the help of tools to analyze and understand what our customers are saying, what the feedback of the overall market is, what the competition is doing, and what the businesses' reputations are on social media, we can open the vault.

The UDA market is crowded and offers a variety of solutions providers, open sources, and vendors. With mathematical algorithms and techniques provided by deep learning, machine learning, AI, and now cognitive computing, there is no excuse not to tackle or harness that 80 percent of untapped data.

UDA could be applied to a long list of industries and business challenges, including:

- Human resources
- Sports (performance analysis)
- Legal services
- National security
- Healthcare
- Service industries (customer acquisition, customer retention, sentiment analysis)
- Product development (sentiment analysis, product quality analysis)
- Banking, finance, investment, and insurance (fraud detection and prediction or gains and losses, credit risk)
- Transport industry (aviation and others)

In this book, we will first discuss the framework we recommend to implement UDA and then cover some of the various industries from the above list in designated chapters. We will also provide, when available, case studies to show and underscore the application of the concept.

 KEY TAKEAWAYS

- According to the research firm IDC, the world's data will be 44 times greater in 2020 than it was in 2009; and at least 80 percent of it will be unstructured, creating an unprecedented need to uncover buried meaning.
- In this globally connected arena, with the explosion of the Internet, social media, mobile, cloud computing, and Big Data, UDA is no longer a choice for any forward-looking company or organization; it is a must.
- In today's business environment text analytics should help companies analyze untapped information via content categorization, voice-of-customer analysis, sentiment analysis, open-ended questions analysis, e-mail and blog analysis, and the like to enrich predictive models.

■ Text analytics enables companies to address many Big Data issues that arise from unstructured content by applying linguistic rules and statistical methods to automatically assess, analyze, and act on the insights buried in electronic text—such as social media content, call center logs, survey data, e-mails, loan applications, service notes, and insurance or warranty claims.

■ Text analytics improves the precision of traditional predictive models by providing customer feedback data to enrich the models through e-mails or voice communication with services.

■ There has been a scramble for semantic search that is becoming more predominant in innovative organizations. Semantic offers the advantage of being context-, concept-, and business intelligence–driven, and will be the focus in the near future.

■ The pace of technical improvement is rapid, in keeping with the very high value that text analytics is delivering to enterprise users. Text analytics solutions have proven capable of addressing diverse challenges, and with business intelligence integration and embedding lines of business applications, text analytics is poised for a broad market adoption.

■ The power of AI, machine learning, deep learning, and cognitive analytics applied to unstructured data is enabling leading companies to compete and win in this data analytics era.

NOTES

1. Tom Groenfeldt, "Big Data—Big Money Says It Is a Paradigm Buster," *Forbes*, June 2012: www.forbes.com/sites/tomgroenfeldt/2012/01/06/big-data-big-money-says-it-is-a-paradigm-buster/#41029b70e389

2. EMC Corporation, "IDC Digital Universes Study: Big Data, Bigger Digital Shadows and Biggest Growth in the Far East," Presentation sponsored by EMC, December 2012: www.whizpr.be/upload/medialab/21/company/Media_Presentation_2012_DigiUniverseFINAL1.pdf

3. IBM, "Big Data Analytics: What is Big Data Analytics?" IBM Analytics: www.ibm.com/analytics/hadoop/big-data-analytics

4. IBM, "How Has the Nature of Leadership Changed in the New Economic Environment? Capitalizing on Complexity: Insights from the 2010 IBM Global CEO Survey," IBM c-Suite Study Series, 2011: www-935.ibm.com/services/us/ceo/ceostudy2010/index.html

5. Sara Radicati, "Emails Statistics Report, 2016–2020," Radicati Group, Inc., March 2016: www.radicati.com/wp/wp-content/uploads/2016/01/Email_Statistics_Report_2016-2020_Executive_Summary.pdf

6. James Manyika, Michael Chui, Brad Brown, Jacques Bughin, Richard Dobbs, Charles Roxburgh, and Angela Hung Byers, "Big Data: The Next Frontier for Innovation, Competition, and Productivity," McKinsey & Company (May 2011): www.mckinsey.com/business-functions/digital-mckinsey/our-insights/big-data-the-next-frontier-for-innovation

7. J. McCarthy, M. S. Minsky, N. Rochester, and C. E. Shannon, "A Proposal for the Dartmouth Summer Research Project on Artificial Intelligence," August 31, 1955. www-formal.stanford.edu/jmc/history/dartmouth/dartmouth.html

8. Wikipedia, "Artificial Intelligence," https://en.wikipedia.org/wiki/Artificial_intelligence

9. Wikipedia: "Deep Learning," https://en.wikipedia.org/wiki/Deep_learning and Ian Goodfellow, Yoshua Bengio, and Aaron Courville, *Deep Learning* (Boston, MA: MIT Press, November 2016).

10. Goodfellow, Bengio, and Courville, *Deep Learning*.

11. Maureen Caudill, "Neural Nets Primer, Part VI," *AI Expert* 4, no. 2 (February 1989): 61–67.

12. Venn diagram from Goodfellow, Bengio, and Courville, *Deep Learning*.

13. CBInsights, "The Race for AI: Google, Twitter, Intel, Apple in a Rush to Grab Artificial Intelligence Startups." CB Insights.com, July 21, 2017: www.cbinsights.com/blog/top-acquirers-ai-startups-ma-timeline/

14. Chris Johnson and Edward Newett, "From Idea to Execution: Spotify's Discover Weekly" (presentation, DataEngConf, November 2015): www.slideshare.net/MrChrisJohnson/from-idea-to-execution-spotifys-discover-weekly

15. Eugene Kim, "Mark Zuckerberg Wants to Build the 'Perfect Personalized Newspaper' for Every Person in the World," *Business Insider*, November 6, 2014: www.businessinsider.com/mark-zuckerberg-wants-to-build-a-perfect-personalized-newspaper-2014-11

16. Craig Stoltz, "The Second.coming," *Washington Post*, December 5, 1999, www.washingtonpost.com/wp-srv/travel/online/ita120599.htm

17. Stoltz, "The Second.coming."

FURTHER READING

Bolo, "A Basic Introduction to Neural Networks," Bolo's Home Page, n.d.: http://pages.cs.wisc.edu/~bolo/shipyard/neural/local.html

Maurice Conti, "The Incredible Inventions of Intuitive AI," TEDxPortland Talk (April 2016): www.ted.com/talks/maurice_conti_the_incredible_inventions_of_intuitive_ai/transcript

Michael Copeland, "What's the Difference between Artificial Intelligence, Machine Learning, and Deep Learning?" Nvidia blogs, July 29, 2016: https://blogs.nvidia.com/blog/2016/07/29/whats-difference-artificial-intelligence-machine-learning-deep-learning-ai/

Jeff Dunn, "We Put Siri, Alexa, Google Assistant, and Cortana through a Marathon of Tests to See Who's Winning the Virtual Assistant Race— Here's What We Found," *Business Insider*, November 4, 2016: www.businessinsider.com/siri-vs-google-assistant-cortana-alexa-2016-11

IBM, "TED: Cognitive Computing," YouTube, August 13, 2013: www.youtube.com/watch?v=np1sJ08Q7lw

IBM, "Welcome to the Cognitive Era: IBM CEO Ginni Rometty Describes a New Era in Technology and Business," Gartner Business Symposium: YouTube, October 12, 2015: www.youtube.com/watch?v=bMLYKhiZCVI

Bernard Marr, "What Everyone Should Know about Cognitive Computing," *Forbes*, March 23, 2016: www.forbes.com/sites/bernardmarr/2016/03/23/what-everyone-should-know-about-cognitive-computing/

Bernard Marr, "4 Mind-Blowing Ways Facebook Uses Artificial Intelligence," Forbes, December 29, 2016: www.forbes.com/sites/bernardmarr/2016/12/29/4-amazing-ways-facebook-uses-deep-learning-to-learn-everything-about-you/#6db51b432591

Matt Mills and Tamara Roukaerts, "Image Recognition That Triggers Augmented Reality," TEDGlobal 2012 Talk (June 2012): www.ted.com/talks/matt_mills_image_recognition_that_triggers_augmented_reality

CHAPTER 3

The Framework to Put UDA to Work

A woodsman was once asked, "Give me six hours to chop down a tree and I will spend the first four sharpening the axe.

—Abraham Lincoln

INTRODUCTION

Over the past decade, the explosion of digital information has provided an unprecedented opportunity for businesses and organizations to capture, store, and process different types of new data, both structured and unstructured. With the advent of computing power and the decreased cost of storing information, the real challenge that companies face today is the *variety* of the data they have at their disposal: e-mails, chats, tweets, audio, video images, and pictures.

Information such as customers' needs, feelings, and feedback, as well as employee narratives, stays buried in tweets, Facebook updates, and human resource information systems and files. These real-time insights encapsulating consumers' viewpoints about content, a product, a service, consumers' needs and preferences, or employee experience engagement or satisfaction remain untapped.

Enhancements in computing power originally propelled a variety of analyses of structured data, leveraging several statistical and mathematical techniques. However, due to computing limitations, it was only in the late 1990s that unstructured data began to be analyzed. Most recently, deep learning algorithms have been used to analyze videos and voice streams. Tech giants, such as Google, Facebook, and Amazon, and online hiring solutions, such as LinkedIn and Monster, have created entire data products and lines of business by leveraging massive amounts of data, unstructured for the most part, that they collect from their users and consumers.

Originally, Google built its entire business by understanding text on Web pages to provide the best result for consumer search queries.

Big Data continues to be touted as the next wave of technology and analytics innovations. However, the magnitude of the wave is not related to the size of the data, but rather to the task of leveraging data intelligence that drives business performance. In this chapter I will provide key components of the UDA framework that you need to distill intelligence from all your data and discuss the following:

- Why Have a Framework to Analyze UDA?

- What Are the Key Components of the IMPACT Cycle?

- Story from the Frontline: Interview with Cindy Forbes EVP Chief Analytics Officer Manulife Financial

- The Team Tool and Techniques for Successful UDA

- Text Parsing Example and Text Analytics Useful Vocabulary

- The IMPACT Cycle in Action with: Airline Case Study

- Key Takeaways

WHY HAVE A FRAMEWORK TO ANALYZE UNSTRUCTURED DATA?

As we discussed in the previous chapter, in today's globally connected digital world, we have access to more data than ever before. More than 80 percent of that data is unstructured and more importantly, only .05 percent of the data is analyzed. Companies that are not analyzing their unstructured data are missing a huge opportunity to understand their customers, their prospects, their competition, and their overall market. So how can they tackle their unstructured data?

The human mind can read and comprehend text whether it is a sentence, a paragraph, or a document; a computer can be taught to efficiently achieve the same goal. To derive meaning from text or images, unstructured data must be transformed into quantitative representations (numbers), leveraging mathematical formulas like linear algebra. The computer needs to be taught how to read, interpret, and understand the structure of a phrase, a sentence, and a paragraph. It then uses mathematical algorithms to remove the noise and redundancies from the data and retain the most meaningful information, the essence of the original data, which I call the *signal*. Making the computer understand what the text is saying can be a daunting exercise, though great progress has been made in the past decade. Think about all the connections and associations your brain is doing while you are reading this chapter. Your level of understanding of some concepts such as vector space model, which will be introduced in this chapter, would depend on your background. If you have studied linear algebra, you know that vector space model will not refer to astronautics. You will quickly think about linear algebra. Without that background, however, the concept and its meaning need to be clearly defined and explained to avoid any ambiguity.

To create business value from complex data, we need to have a framework. The framework I will present in the following section is based on the IMPACT cycle along with the T3 (team, technique, and tools) approach. Based on my experience successfully building and implementing analytics capabilities, I will explain how the IMPACT cycle and the T3 are the essential ingredients any organization needs to put data analytics to work. This approach has also been validated through interviews I conducted with industry leaders during my research for my previous books and enhanced thanks to inputs from industry leaders in unstructured data analytics (UDA) I interviewed for this book. My goal was to ensure that all types of data analytics and business lines could benefit from it.

Regardless of whether your business is insurance, human resources (HR), fraud detection, finance, marketing, telecommunications, healthcare, sports, or national security, when you are inundated with data, your goal is to create business value from it. This means harnessing all of that data to understand your market and your customers; to anticipate your customer needs and behaviors; to leverage the voice of your customer to drive business performance; and to harness consumer feedback and insights to develop better products or services.

The upcoming sections discuss a useful and easy-to-implement framework that provides the essential ingredients to harness data and drive business performance.

THE IMPACT CYCLE APPLIED TO UNSTRUCTURED DATA

Focusing on the IMPACT

During my career of more than twenty-five years building and implementing analytics centers of excellence across several organizations and industries, and advising companies in different regions of the world, and through my twelve years of experience harnessing unstructured data from job seeker resumes, employer job openings, and customer service call logs, I saw most organizations sitting on a goldmine of unstructured data. During my research for this book, I spoke with 253 industry leaders, experts, and business partners about their data assets and challenges. Consistently, I heard that organizations are drowning in data but lacking in deriving actionable insights from it to better understand their customers, their prospects, the market, and their competition. I then realized that the IMPACT cycle powered by the T3 (the right team, tools, and technique) could help guide analysts to become insightful business partners. Introduced in my first book, *Win with Advanced Business Analytics*,[2] the IMPACT cycle is a framework for creating actionable insights from structured and unstructured data.

To get analysts to pull their heads up from the data vault and focus on the business is not always an easy task. It is both an art and science. The IMPACT cycle offers the analyst the following steps, which are described in the following section:

- Identify
- Master

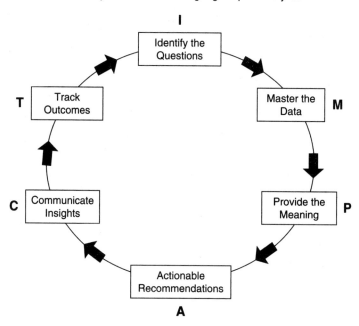

The Analyst Guide for Creating High Impact Analytics

Exhibit 3.01 The IMPACT Cycle

- Provide
- Act
- Communicate
- Track

Identify Business Questions

In a nonintrusive way, help your business partner identify the critical business questions he or she needs help to answer. Then, set a clear expectation of the time and the work involved to get the answer. In the case of unstructured data, business questions could include the following sample of thirty:

- Detect spam e-mails
- Filter and categorize e-mails

- Classify news items
- Classify job titles in a marketing database for e-mail prospecting
- Classify job seeker resumes in categories and occupations
- Classify new job openings in categories and occupations
- Cluster consumer and customer comments and complaints
- Classify and categorize documents, patents, and Web pages
- Cluster survey data (open-ended questions) to understand customer feedback
- Cluster analysis research in a database
- Cluster newsfeeds and tweets in predefined categories
- Classify and categorize research reports
- Classify research papers by topic
- Create new live-streaming movie offerings based on viewer ratings
- Create food menus and combos based upon customer feedback and ratings
- Retrieve information using search engine
- Predict customer satisfaction based on customer comments
- Predict customer attrition based on customer feedback or conversations with call centers
- Predict which resume best matches a job description
- Predict employee turnover based on social media comments and performance appraisal narratives
- Anticipate employee rogue behavior
- Predict call center cost based on call center logs
- Predict stock market price based on business news announcements
- Predict product adoption based on consumer feedback tweets
- Predict terror attacks based on social media content
- Detect and predict fraudulent transactions in banks and government
- Detect fraudulent claims in insurance companies

- Perform image detection, image recognition, and classification
- Perform facial recognition, video, and voice recognition
- Perform sentiment analysis

Master the Data

This is the data analyst's sweet spot—preparing, importing, assembling, analyzing, and synthesizing all available information that will help to answer critical business questions, and then creating simple and clear visual presentations (charts, graphs, tables, interactive data environments, and so on) of the data that are easy to comprehend.

To efficiently master unstructured data, we will leverage Exhibit 3.02: the UDA Recipe Matrix in the table below to describe what type of analytics and techniques could be used based on the type of unstructured data to be harnessed. In the upcoming sections, we will describe the analytics and techniques to be used when the type of unstructured data presented in the Recipe Matrix Table above is text.

If the unstructured data is audio, video, or pictures, we recommend using machine learning and deep learning techniques that will produce best results for recognition and classification. Techniques such as singular value decomposition (SVD) and principal component analysis could still be used for image classification and recognition; however, the latest progress in computer vision was achieved with the deep learning technique, which produces more robust and accurate results, although it requires more training data and more memory. This is no longer an issue since we moved from CPUs (central processing units) to GPUs (graphics processing units) and, most recently, to TPUs (tensor processing units), which enable effective usage of the deep neural network. Because this book is not about deep learning, for simplicity, let's discuss how to master text data using the traditional linear algebra technique.

Mastering Text Data

Mastering text data in all forms involves five steps, described in Exhibit 3.03.

Unstructured Data Type	Analytics Category	Analytics Subcategory	Techniques
Text	Text analytics/Text mining Natural language processing (NLP)	Text summarization Text /content categorization Topics extraction Text retrieval Opinion mining Sentiment/Emotion analysis	Singular value decomposition (SVD) Latent semantic analysis (LSA) Quick response (QR) factorization Artificial intelligence (AI) Machine learning Deep learning
Images and pictures	Image analytics	Image classification Face classification Face recognition Computer vision	SVD LSA QR factorization AI Machine learning Deep learning
Audio voice of customer	Voice analytics Speech-to-text	Voice recognition (NLP Text summarization and classification Topic extraction Sentiment analysis opinion mining	SVD LSA QR factorization AI Machine learning Deep learning
Video	Video analytics	Video recognition Video classification	Machine learning Deep learning

Exhibit 3.02   UDA Recipe Matrix

Exhibit 3.03   The Five Steps of Text Analysis

Step 1: Importing the Data and Preprocessing

The first step consists of identifying and defining what type of data you envision using to address your business question. Then, you integrate this data by loading your raw text data into your UDA software. It is important to note that you can access the data directly from the web via URL or point to a directory on your local machine or server. Your text document could be of any format: Adobe portable document format (PDF), rich text format (RTF), Word document, Excel file, HTML document, and the like. The output will be a dataset ready to be used by the unstructured analytics software you intend to use: Python, R, PERL, Math-lab, SAS Text Miner, IBM SPSS, or other. This process creates a working text-mining dataset that will include two important fields, one for customer identification and one generally called *text* that encompasses customer opinions or voice, as we will see later in this chapter.

Step 2: Text Parsing

Once the data is imported and preprocessed, parsing is performed. Text parsing is about decomposing the unstructured raw data (text or images) into quantitative representations that will be used for the analysis. The goal of the parsing is to normalize the raw text data and create a table with rows and columns in which rows represent the terms in the documents collection and columns represent the documents. This table is called a *term-by-documents matrix*. We will provide examples of term-by-document matrices in upcoming sections.

Below is a high-level summary of the ten major text parsing steps; if you are just seeking a high-level overview of text analytics, feel free to give this section a skim.

1. *Tokenization* involves breaking sentences, paragraphs, or sections of the documents into *terms*.

2. *Identification and extraction* of nouns, noun groups, multiword terms lists, synonymy and polysemy, and entities to consider and include in parsing (or treat as a parsed terms part of speech) that are meaningful to your application. It's helpful to work with linguists and other business partners to identify,

based on the business questions and industry, what terms should be used as parts of speech, and what synonyms or polysemy to include or exclude from the analysis. Synonyms help to link together words that do not have the same base form but share the same meaning in context.

3. *Building automatic recognition* of multiword terms and tagging parts of speech. A multiword term is a group of words that should be processed as a single term—for instance, idiomatic phrases, collections of related adjectives, compound nouns, and proper nouns.

4. *Normalization of various entities* such as names, addresses, measurements, companies, dates, currency, percentages, and years.

5. *Extraction of entities* such as organizations, products, Social Security numbers, time, titles, and the like.

6. *Stemming the data* by finding the root form or base form of words. Stemming helps to treat terms with the same root as equivalent; it also helps to reduce the number of terms in the document collection.

7. *Apply filtering to identify the Stop Word List* (list of terms to ignore) *and Start Word List* (list of terms to include). The stop word list is a collection of low information value words and terms that should be ignored during parsing.

8. *Creation of a Bag of Words*: a representation that excludes some tokens and attributes.

9. *Weighting*: Depending on the type of UDA, it is often useful to apply some weighting to terms in a document or document collection to optimize subsequent analysis results such as information retrieval and sentiment analysis.

10. *Create a term-by-document matrix*: a term-by-document matrix is a quantitative representation of the original raw unstructured text that will be used as the foundation of the document collection analysis.

Step 3: Dimension Reduction and Text Transformation

Dimension reduction transforms the quantitative representation of the raw text data into a compact and informative format. Dimension reduction takes the terms-by-documents matrix, which is generally high dimension, and creates a simplified representation of the same documents collection in a lower dimension by leveraging linear algebra concepts such as vector space model, SVD, and QR factorization. Those linear algebra techniques, which will be discussed quickly in the T3 section and in broader details in the appendix Tech Corner are powerful tools in text analytics.

Why practice dimension reduction? Since the number of terms needed to represent each document in the document collection could be extremely high (thousands or hundred thousands or more) and consequently difficult to model, dimension reduction is a critical procedure when you want to analyze text. The goal of dimension reduction is to remove redundancy and noise from the original data and thereby get an optimal representation of the original data in a lower dimension.

The power of dimension reduction really comes to light when you have to address business questions with millions of variables and observations. Without dimension reduction, it would be impossible to find any meaning in the content. Dimension reduction is also useful in experimental science, where most experimenters frequently try to understand some phenomenon by measuring various quantities, such as velocities, voltages, or spectra. However, they will usually face the dilemma of not being able to figure out what is happening, which data to keep, and what part of data is redundant, noisy, or clouded. They must distill signal from noise.

Step 4: Text Analytics

The goal of text analytics is to articulate clear and concise interpretations of the data and visuals in the context of the critical business questions that were identified. This step is about performing several types of analyses, such as clustering, classification, categorization, link analysis, and predictive modeling, on the raw data collected. Beyond getting cluster categorization and sentiment from text analysis, the output of the text categorization or clusters could also be used as inputs or independent variables for predictive models, such as customer attrition, customer acquisition, fraud prevention and detection, resume matching, or job opening categorization.

Step 5: Outcome Business Actions

In Step 5, the findings from the text analytics are put into action across the organization. For instance, negative feedback regarding your service should lead to enhanced customer touchpoint training and lead to a subsequent increase in customer satisfaction. A negative sentiment regarding your brand should trigger actions that improve your online reputation. Groups of triggers within e-mail exchanges between customers and customer service representatives should result in proactive outreach and courtesy calls to prevent customer attrition.

Provide Meaning

This step is about finding the knowledge buried in your unstructured data using text analytics techniques described in the Text Analytics Process Stage 4 and 5, explained in the previous sections. Providing meaning is about articulating clear and concise interpretations of the data and visuals in the context of the critical business questions that were identified.

This is where businesses get actionable insights from their unstructured data.

Actionable Recommendations

The fourth step in building the IMPACT cycle is concerned with actionable recommendations. At this step, you create thoughtful business recommendations based on your interpretation of the unstructured data. Even if they are off-base, it's easier to react to a suggestion than to generate one. Where possible, tie a rough dollar figure to any revenue improvement or cost saving associated with your recommendations. Some recommendations with financial impact include:

- Proactively reduce insurance claim fraud by text mining customer claim narratives. A 1 percent decrease in fraud can represent a saving of $XXXX.

- Proactively reduce customer attrition by analyzing customer feedback and call center logs. A reduction of 10 percent in attrition can represent revenue increase of $XXXX.

- Develop an attractive new product based on consumer reviews and social media feedback mining. A profit of 10 percent can represent additional revenues of $XXXX.

Communicate Insights

Focus on a multipronged communication strategy that will get your insights as far into and as wide across the organization as possible. Maybe your strategy is in the form of an interactive tool others can use, a recorded WebEx of your insights, a lunch and learn, or even just a thoughtful executive memo that can be passed around. The final output should target end users, such as customer touchpoints (customer service representatives and sales representatives), and be easy to access and available in the system for them to do their job.

Track Outcomes

Set up a way to track the impact of your insights. Make sure there is future follow-up with your business partners on the outcome of any action. What was done? What was the impact? What was the return on investment? What are the new critical questions that require help as a result?

TEXT PARSING EXAMPLE

Let's go through a simple example to explain parsing in practice. In Exhibit 3.04, you find in the left column Sentence, the original statement; in the right column are Parsed Terms, the basic terms.

Sentence	Parsed Terms
Randstad announced a buyout of Monster Worldwide Inc. on Aug 9, 2016, offering $3.40 per share in cash. The stock price surged more than 26%.	Randstad +announce a +buy of Monster Worldwide Inc. on Aug 9 2016 +offer $3.40 per share in cash The stock prize +surge more than 26%

Exhibit 3.04 Sentence and Parsed Terms

The next example will provide a broader view of text parsing that includes text normalization, stemming, and filtering. The creation of terms-by-document matrix as well as the application of some parsing steps will be shown.

Term-by-Document Matrix

One of the biggest airlines in Europe ran a food satisfaction survey for its customer satisfaction retention regarding its business-class snack salad. Exhibit 3.05 is a sample of feedback from four customers in response to an open-ended question in the survey.

Customers were asked to provide which meal they enjoyed most during their last flight. Analyzing the text embedded in the open

Original Documents/Customer Responses		Parsing	Parsed Document
Document1	Customer1: "During my flight last week, I loved the banana and kiwi salad"		+love banana kiwi
Document2	Customer2: "During my flight last week, I really enjoyed the mango and kiwi salad"	Normalize Stem Filter (remove low information words)	+enjoy mango kiwi
Document3	Customer3: "During my flight last week, I loved the broccoli and bean salad"		+love broccoli bean
Document4	Customer4: "During my flight last week, I enjoyed the broccoli and cauliflower salad"		+enjoy broccoli cauliflower

Exhibit 3.05 Analyzing the Text

question enabled the airline to launch the right new salad, helping the airline increase customer satisfaction with food as well as the overall customer flying experience. The ultimate goal was significant improvement in customer retention and loyalty.

Normalize: Identify and find noun group, noun entity part of speech word: for the above example: *During, flight, I, and*

Stem: Identify root words to be used in the parsing:

- For *loved*, the root word is *love*, parsed as *+love*
- For *enjoyed*, the root word is *enjoy*, parsed as *+enjoy*

Filter: Remove low-information words: *during my flight, last week, I, and, salad* have been removed because they are considered in this case to be low-information terms.

A term-by-document matrix table, a quantitative representation of the four documents after parsing and normalization, is represented in Exhibit 3.06.

The term-by-document matrix is a representation of how many times each term appears in each document. Sometimes we must apply weighting to impart more value on some of the terms. In this case, we

	Document 1	Document 2	Document 3	Document 4
+love	1	0	1	0
+enjoy	0	1	0	1
banana	1	0	0	0
kiwi	1	1	0	0
mango	0	1	0	0
broccoli	0	0	1	1
bean	0	0	1	0
cauliflower	0	0	0	1

Parsing transformed each sentence into a parsed sentence (broken down into words/terms).

Text normalization filtered to exclude words that are prepositions/parts of speech such as *and* or *I*, words that do not have value.

Text stemming keeps only the roots of words: +love→ loved, +enjoy-→ enjoying, enjoyed.

Exhibit 3.06   Term-by-Document Matrix Table

did not apply any weighting. The above matrix becomes the foundation for subsequent analyses of the collection of the four documents. From this matrix, we can now apply dimension reduction, which is to find a collection of terms that best describes the concepts in the documents. This helps to assess the similarity between documents and terms versus documents.

INTERVIEW WITH CINDY FORBES, CHIEF ANALYTICS OFFICER AND EXECUTIVE VICE PRESIDENT AT MANULIFE FINANCIAL

I had the opportunity to discuss UDA with Cindy Forbes, EVP chief analytics officer at Manulife

Isson: What made your company decide to invest in analytics such as UDA?

Forbes: *A few years ago, the company shifted from product-centric strategy to customer-centric strategy, with the ultimate goal of providing holistic advice and an unsurpassed customer experience. Analytics is foundational to our customer-centric strategy.*

Isson: The majority of organizations I've spoken with have told me they are overwhelmed with a lot of data, but not getting a lot of meaning from it. Would you agree?

Forbes: I do not fully agree with that. We are not overwhelmed with data. In our case our objective has been to implement an enterprise-wide analytics function, and we have created an analytics use-case roadmap. Our data strategy aligns with our roadmap ingesting the requisite data into our enterprise data lake to support our analytics workplan. We prioritize based on the value we can generate, the alignment with our strategy, and the potential positive impact on the customer experience.

Isson: Can you give me examples of business challenges you were able to address leveraging UDA? What was the benefit of your investment?

Forbes: We use unstructured data in the areas of text analytics and natural language processing (NLP).

We do quite a bit of NLP to gain insights from text. We use it with our survey data to analyze and understand customer comments. Without text analytics and NLP, it would be hard for an individual to read all comments and derive key drivers of customer satisfaction, customer sentiment, net promoter score (NPS), or feedback from employee engagement.

In fraud, we use text analytics for case notes and narrative analysis. And for our underwriting models, to analyze underwriting data and to improve our claims management or suspicious activity detection.

We also use UDA for our call center analytics to analyze voice recording to determine efficiency and drive performance and customer satisfaction.

Isson: What advice would you give to someone new to UDA? Dos and don'ts?

Forbes: I don't think that there is any specific advice when it comes to text analytics that would be different from traditional analytics. There are a lot of tools today to analyze unstructured data. Open source tools such as R, Python can be used to analyze unstructured data such as text data.

Isson: What is the top reason to invest in UDA? What is the biggest hurdle you will face?

Forbes: There already is more unstructured data than structured, and it is growing by leaps and bounds thanks to mobile devices, the Internet, and the Internet of Things (sensors and wearables). Thus, the greatest insights, given the amount of data, will come from unstructured data. The issue with unstructured data is that it is more complex to capture and store unless you have

> adopted technologies such as a data lake, and it requires a specialized skill set and tools to process.
>
> **Isson: What do you foresee as the biggest impact UDA will have in the future?**
>
> **Forbes:** Unstructured data from mobile devices and sensors will provide much greater insight into our customers and the world around us. This is the area where UDA has and will continue to have the biggest impact. For example, processing this data allows you to understand how your customers want to be contacted and what they may be interested in buying next, in real time. Digital data will be the most important game changer for insurance companies. Look at things like how the Internet of Things works in healthcare: Having coverage where you can keep people with a disability at their home with the best support will have a positive impact on people's lives.
>
> Sensor data can be used to predict when a machine will need to be repaired, enabling an informed preventative maintenance program. In property and casualty, telematics in cars also help to understand driver behavior, eventually anticipating the risk of claims and providing best practices and advice to drivers to better manage risk and reduce their spending on fuel and overall fees. Information from drones can be used to underwrite properties for insurance. The list of possible applications is endless.

In the next section, we will discuss what is needed to start your text analytics journey leveraging the IMPACT cycle.

The T3

Team

The ideal team to launch UDA includes people with a mix of business and technical backgrounds. The technical background is brought by data analysts, data scientists, statisticians, data miners, mathematicians, or computer scientists. The technical team members help import and load the data, and build algorithms to parse the data and analyze the text data through dimension reduction, clustering classification, and categorization prediction. Linguists and psychologists can help define the structure of the language, the meaning of words, and how to interpret and define some specific clusters in behavioral analysis or sentiment analysis. Their expertise is required because text analytics tools need be taught how to treat and understand the structure of the language, how sentences are formed, what words could be considered as a part of speech, idioms, polysemy, or synonymy in documents or sentence sections in a given sector or industry. Consequently, it is important that these experts work with data analysts to ensure the best understanding of the meaning of words, groups of words, concepts, topics, and text sentiment in the algorithms to be developed.

The business expertise is represented by managers who understand the business question to be addressed. They are also instrumental in explaining the business language and concepts to the technical team. People with business industry acumen are required to ensure the end results are practical and actionable.

Technique

The most frequently used technique to analyze unstructured data leverages linear algebra, vector space model, matrices decomposition, and dimension reduction techniques such as SVD or QR factorization. Once the dimensions are reduced, techniques such as clustering and classification predictive models are applied to get more insight from the text data. These techniques help to derive topics and concepts and provide answers to the original business question raised in the Identify stage of the IMPACT framework. SVD is the most important linear algebra technique used for dimension reduction in text mining or NLP. Deerwester, Dumais, Furnas, Landauer, and Harshman[3] were the first to apply SVD to term frequency matrices. This was done in the context of information retrieval called latent semantic indexing (LSI).

SVD can be found in many technical textbooks. While this book is not technical, the notion of dimension reduction is so critical that it is worth detailing. You can think of SVD as a mathematical technique that creates an optimal representation of the information contained in text data by reducing its dimension while keeping the essence of the original text. Instead of having a document represented by, as an example, eight terms, we can find an optimal way to represent documents using two concepts.

In our previous example concerning airline food satisfaction survey, the concept *fruit* would represent banana, kiwi, and mango as one dimension, while broccoli, bean, and cauliflower would be represented by the concept *vegetable* as a second dimension. SVD simplifies the hundreds of dimensions (varieties of fruits and varieties of vegetables), into two dimensions: *fruits* and *vegetables*. Looking at the document with sentences about preference for fruit or vegetable could help to understand food appeal and support the design of salads with fruits or vegetables.

Exhibit 3.07 showcases how SVD is used to decompose a document-by-terms matrix into three matrices:

The first matrix:	The document-by-concept similarity matrix
The second matrix:	The concept strength matrix
The third matrix:	The concept-by-term similarity matrix

Applying Exhibit 3.07 to our four documents, customer responses to airline satisfaction survey result in the table shown in Exhibit 3.08, a quantitative representation of the responses. Their responses were parsed, and the table showcases the terms used by each customer.

Let's call the matrix representation of the document-by-terms Table A.

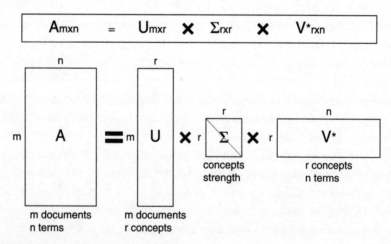

Exhibit 3.07 Singular Value Decomposition

Customer	love	enjoy	banana	kiwi	mango	broccoli	bean	cauliflower
Customer1	1	0	1	1	0	0	0	0
Customer2	0	1	0	1	1	0	0	0
Customer3	1	0	0	0	0	1	1	0
Customer4	0	1	0	0	0	1	0	1

Exhibit 3.08 Quantitative Representation of Responses

Thus: A encompasses the number of documents ($m = 4$), and the number of terms ($n = 8$). A is therefore a 4-by-8 matrix.

$$A = \begin{bmatrix} 1 & 0 & 1 & 1 & 0 & 0 & 0 & 0 \\ 0 & 1 & 0 & 1 & 1 & 0 & 0 & 0 \\ 1 & 0 & 0 & 0 & 0 & 1 & 1 & 0 \\ 0 & 1 & 0 & 0 & 0 & 1 & 0 & 1 \end{bmatrix}$$

From matrix A, we can use SVD to factorize the document-by-term matrix A into a product of three matrices, including concepts, concept strength, and term. SVD defines a small number of *concepts* that connect the rows and columns of the matrix.

The trade-off for having fewer dimensions is the accuracy of the approximation.

For text analytics, SVD provides the mathematical foundation for text mining and classification techniques generally known as LSI. In SVD, the matrix U is an entity-of-documents matrix; a way to represent the document and text to be mined in a high-dimension vector space model that is generally known as *hyperspace document representation*. By reducing the dimensional space, SVD helps to reduce redundancies and noise in the data. It provides new dimensions that capture the essence of the existing relationship.

Important note: Readers interested in the technical details behind the SVD will find additional information in the Appendix section called Tech Corner Details.

Techniques such as machine learning and deep learning provide great performance and results for UDA.

Tools

Text mining or NLP could be performed by leveraging two types of tools or software: Open source software and paid software. Exhibit 3.09 is the list of 10 open source and paid text analytics software. An exhaustive list is available from *Predictive Analytics Today*.[4]

Ranking*	Open Source	Paid Software
1	TM: Text mining infrastructure in R	SAS Text Analytics
2	Gensim: Python	IBM Text Analytics
3	MathLAbs	LExalytics Text Analytics
4	PERL	Smartlogic
5	Natural Language Toolkit	Provalis Research
6	RapidMiner	OpenText
7	KH Coder	AlchemyAPI
8	CAT	Pingar
9	Carrot2	Attensity
10	QDA Miner Lite, Gate	Clarabridge

Exhibit 3.09 Ten Open Source and Paid Text Analytics Software Packages

Exhibit 3.10 includes a summary of the T3 to support successful implementation of text analytics.

There are also powerful artificial intelligence APIs that could be leveraged to help you harness your unstructured data, whether it be text audios videos or images.

So if you don't have data scientist talent in house—positions that are currently very hard to fill—you can leverage UDA APIs provided by companies such as Microsoft, Amazon Google, IBM, Kairos, Trueface.ai, and API.ai. These APIs are pretty scalable and can help you quickly get some actionable value from your unstructured data.

CASE STUDY

This example provides a comprehensive overview of how the IMPACT cycle is applied to text mining, expanding the previous example. Readers not interested in understanding the how-to could skip this case study and go to the Key Takeaways section.

The T3	Name	Roles
Team (Talent)	Managers	Help define the business questions to address. Help to explain the business terminology and concepts.
	Computer Scientists Statisticians Mathematician Data Scientists IT	Import the raw unstructured data (documents and images). Build program to create a vector space model of the raw data. Build program to reduce dimension and analyze documents. Perform analyses such as clustering, classification, detection, and predictive model. Define the required infrastructure.
	Linguists Psychologists	Identify linguistics rules to use and help in defining parsing (term, synonymy, and polysemy) for document normalization. Help define concept definitions from clustering or topics analysis.
Techniques	Raw Text Import	Load the raw data into the text analysis tool.
	Text Parsing	Normalize and stem, and filter the original data.
	Vector Space Model	Create a quantitative representation of the data.
	Terms by Document Matrix	A row and columns table (matrix) that encompasses the frequency of each term present in documents.
	Dimension Reduction	Create a simplified representation of the original data in lower dimension.
	Singular Value Decomposition (SVD)	Linear algebra mathematical technique used to reduce the number of rows while preserving the similarity structure among columns.
	QR Decomposition (Factorization)	Linear algebra/mathematical technique for matrices decomposition.
	Similarity Measure between Documents	Provide a measure of distance or similarity among documents. For example, cosine similarity measure is used in some information retrieval.
	Clustering, Classification Predictive Model	Group and classify input raw text into categories.
Tools	Open Sources and Paid Software	Analyze text data by leveraging prebuilt algorithms or packages.

Exhibit 3.10 The T3 Summary Table

AIRLINE COMPANY CUSTOMER FOOD SATISFACTION TEXT MINING CASE STUDY: PUTTING THE FRAMEWORK IN APPLICATION

The Challenge

One of the largest European airline companies wanted to identify the best combos to launch for its newly healthy snack menu. Their ultimate goal was to increase customer satisfaction and also reduce costs and food waste.

The company tested new snacks for its Business and Premium Economy classes for six months. They wanted to launch the new menu based on insights they received from 8,420 passengers who filled out the open-ended question from the customer satisfaction survey.

The Solution

UDA: "Without text analytics software, it would have been extremely cumbersome and cost-prohibitive to have resources go reasonably through thousands of customers' feedback to derive meaning," said the chief marketing officer for the airline.

- Throughout this example we will discuss how the IMPACT cycle was applied to underscore application of our UDA framework discussed in this chapter.

- Text analysis: text clustering and topic mining were used to find topics from 8,420 customers feedback.

- Optimization models were performed to create twelve optimal healthy snack combos based on airline constraints such as budget, the maximum number of snack combos, flight season, and flight day of the week, route, and duration.

- We will also discuss the T3s (Tool, Technology, and Team) that were required to deliver the solution.

A sample of fifteen customers' responses is presented to showcase some text parsing and transformation that took place. Throughout this sample, we can see how raw text, also called terms, is transformed into numbers to be analyzed.

Following the IMPACT Cycle

The IMPACT Cycle was introduced in Exhibit 3.01.

Identify

The business challenge was identified as the need to analyze feedback from passengers regarding the snacks they had in order to launch the best health snack menu and increase customer satisfaction.

Master

Mastering the data encompasses five major steps:

1. *Import the raw text data; in this case import dataset that includes 8,420 pdf form documents along with passengers' healthy snack feedback. The ultimate goal of importing the text document is to create a text mining dataset to be normalized and parsed. The imported dataset had two fields that were relevant to the text analysis: the document number or passenger identification key, and the passenger feedback field, which contains passengers' raw text feedback to be mined.*
   Text parsing and normalization includes the remaining steps:

2. *Tokenize the documents collection by breaking each sentence phrase of the document into terms.*

3. *Identify nouns, group noun entities, synonymy, polysemy, parts of speech, and multiword nouns to normalize terms in the documents collection. Words such as During, flight, last, week, my, and I will more likely be tagged as candidates to be ignored (they provide less information).*

4. *Apply stemming: Only keep the root of the word; for instance, the root word for enjoyed and enjoyable is enjoy.*

5. *Apply filter: Create a stop word list and a start word list. The stop word list includes a list of words that will be removed from the analysis. For example, words such as During my flight last week I will be removed, as we will see in the example. Those words do not provide a lot of value.*

From the customers' responses to the open-ended question "What healthy snack did you enjoy during your last flight?" a quantitative representation of the documents collection was then created as shown with the sample of 15 customers' responses below:

- *During my flight last week I loved banana and kiwi*
- *During my flight last week I enjoyed rice and broccoli*
- *During my flight last week I enjoyed beet and broccoli*
- *During my flight last week I enjoyed broccoli potatoes and carrots*
- *During my flight last week I enjoyed banana kiwi and mango*
- *During my flight last week I loved kiwi and blueberry*
- *During my flight last week I enjoyed kiwi blueberry and banana*
- *During my flight last week I loved banana and blueberry*
- *During my flight last week I loved mango and blueberry*
- *During my flight last week I loved broccoli and beans*
- *During my flight last week I loved carrots and broccoli*
- *During my flight last week I loved cauliflower and broccoli*
- *During my flight last week I enjoyed potatoes and beet*
- *During my flight last week I enjoyed sprout and rice*
- *During my flight last week I enjoyed rice and beet*

Let us revisit how things work behind the scenes:

Exhibit 3.11 shows how text analytics algorithms parse raw text in the feedback column into parsed, normalized terms in the third column.

After the parsing, filtering, and normalization, the parsed table is then transformed into a table with quantitative representation terms and documents, called the terms-by-document matrix. Terms represent the words used by customers, and document refers to customer's feedback. As we can see in Exhibit 3.12, the rows and columns are filled with 0s and 1s, where 1 indicates that the term appears in the document and 0 otherwise.

The exhibit showcases how customer feedback is transformed into a quantitative representation derived from the text parsing, tokenization, and application of filters to exclude low-information terms. The output of this decomposition of the raw feedback data from passengers into a table with the 0 and 1 numbers is called the terms-by-document matrix M.

The next step is a statistical transformation: the dimension reduction.

Document ID	Feedback	Parsed Normalized Terms
D_1	During my flight last week I loved banana and kiwi	+love banana kiwi
D_2	During my flight last week I enjoyed rice and broccoli	+enjoy rice broccoli
D_3	During my flight last week I enjoyed beet and broccoli	+enjoy beet broccoli
D_4	During my flight last week I enjoyed broccoli potatoes and carrots	+enjoy broccoli +potato +carrot
D_5	During my flight last week I enjoyed banana kiwi and mango	+enjoy banana kiwi mango
D_6	During my flight last week I loved kiwi and blueberry	+love kiwi blueberry
D_7	During my flight last week I enjoyed kiwi blueberry and banana	+enjoy kiwi blueberry banana
D_8	During my flight last week I loved banana and blueberry	+love banana blueberry
D_9	During my flight last week I loved mango and blueberry	+love mango blueberry
D_10	During my flight last week I loved broccoli and beans	+love broccoli +bean
D_11	During my flight last week I loved carrots and broccoli	+love +carrot broccoli
D_12	During my flight last week I loved cauliflower and broccoli	+love cauliflower broccoli
D_13	During my flight last week I enjoyed potatoes and beet	+enjoy +potato beet
D_14	During my flight last week I enjoyed sprouts and rice	+enjoy sprouts rice
D_15	During my flight last week I enjoyed rice and beet	+enjoy rice beet

Exhibit 3.11 From Raw Text to Parsed, Normalized Terms

Dimension Reduction

Dimension reduction is about decomposing the terms-by-document matrix, which we called here M, into a product of three matrices that will be easy to manipulate and to perform calculations upon. The dimension reduction used here is SVD, which helps to write matrix M into lower-space matrices that keep all the essence of the matrix M while removing noise and redundancies from the raw data.

	D1	D2	D3	D4	D5	D6	D7	D8	D9	D10	D11	D12	D13	D14	D15
banana	1	0	0	0	1	0	1	1	0	0	0	0	0	0	0
+bean	0	0	0	0	0	0	0	0	0	1	0	0	0	0	0
beet	0	0	1	0	0	0	0	0	0	0	0	0	1	0	1
blueberry	0	0	0	0	0	1	1	1	1	0	0	0	0	0	0
broccoli	0	1	1	1	0	0	0	0	0	1	1	1	0	0	0
cauliflower	0	0	0	0	0	0	0	0	0	0	0	1	0	0	0
+carrot	0	0	0	1	0	0	0	0	0	0	1	0	0	0	0
+enjoy	0	1	1	1	1	0	0	0	0	0	0	0	1	1	1
kiwi	1	0	0	0	1	1	1	0	0	0	0	0	0	0	0
+love	1	0	0	0	0	1	1	1	1	1	1	1	0	0	0
mango	0	0	0	0	1	0	0	0	1	0	0	0	0	0	0
+potato	0	0	0	1	0	0	0	0	0	0	0	0	1	0	0
rice	0	1	0	0	0	0	0	0	0	0	0	0	0	1	1
sprouts	0	0	0	0	0	0	0	0	0	0	0	0	0	1	0

Exhibit 3.12 Sample of the Terms-by-Document Matrix

All text analytics software programs can provide this decomposition.

Text Analytics

LSA is a technique in NLP, in particular, distributional semantics of analyzing relationships between a set of documents and the terms they contain by producing a set of concepts related to the documents and terms. LSA assumes that words that are close in meaning will occur in similar pieces of text.

For this project, two text analytics techniques were used: text clustering and topic mining.

Text clustering, or text cluster analysis (powered by SVD), was used to create subgroups of documents that encompass most similarities. It identifies similar terms in order to derive concepts.

The outputs in Exhibit 3.13 provide three clusters derived from the 8,420 customers.

Cluster ID	Cluster Description	Frequency	Percentage
1	blueberry "kiwi blueberry " kiwi mango +love	3280	39%
2	broccoli sprouts rice +carrot beet +potato cauliflower +bean +enjoy, +love	4610	55%
3	"banana kiwi" banana kiwi mango +enjoy blueberry +love	530	6%

Exhibit 3.13   Text Clustering

A quick analysis of the clusters, cluster descriptions (terms), and frequency led us to conclude that we could reduce the number of clusters. In fact, we only needed two clusters. Cluster 1 and Cluster 3 could be combined into one cluster, because both are related to fruits. Therefore, we request the number of clusters to be 2.

Exhibit 3.14 showcases the underlying output from the merge.

Cluster ID	Cluster Description	Frequency	Percentage
1	broccoli sprouts rice +carrot beet +potato cauliflower +bean +enjoy, +love	4610	55%
2	blueberry kiwi banana mango "banana kiwi" "kiwi blueberry" +love +enjoy	3810	45%

Exhibit 3.14   Further Text Clustering

The second analysis was topic mining. Topic mining identified key topics derived from customers' feedback, as shown in Exhibit 3.15.

Exhibit 3.15   Passenger Feedback Mining (Topic Mining Output)

Exhibit 3.15 is the output of text topic analytics and showcases three topics that were derived from the customers' feedback:

- Topic 1: blueberry, mango, kiwi, banana, +love
- Topic 2: rice, sprouts, +enjoy, beet, +potato
- Topic 3:+carrot, broccoli, cauliflower, +love

Provide Meaning

Two major clusters were derived from the analysis that includes fruits and vegetables; therefore, every passenger's feedback could be represented on two dimensions: vegetables and fruits. Optimization models were performed to identify the best healthy combos to offer to the Business and Premium Economy classes. The healthy snack combo menu should only include vegetables and fruits, helping the airline to reduce food waste, reduce costs, and increase passengers' satisfaction.

Act

The airline developed an optimized healthy snack menu based upon actionable insights of the customer feedback analysis discussed in the previous section. Twelve healthy snack combos came out of the text analytics and optimization process.

On top of this, the airline was also able to leverage flight information and its passenger social media feedback by putting in place social media monitoring platform to listen, interact, and engage with customers in order to address any pain point or negative feedback and keep their customers happy and loyal.

Track the Outcome

After performing a before/after analysis (twelve months before and twelve months after), the airline registered a 27 percent reduction in food waste, a 20 percent reduction in food costs—and a 17 percent increase in customer satisfaction.

The T3

Team: *The team was made up of a data miner working with the marketing manager of the airline to go through the menu items. The IT manager was also involved to gather the data and provide some additional company data to the data miner for the analysis.*

Tool: *To perform the analysis, SAS Enterprise Miner's Text Mining Module was used, leveraging Text Cluster and Topic Nodes. It is important to note the same analysis could have been performed using open source software, such as R or Python. The airline also run the optimization models for healthy snack combos.*

Technique*: SVD and text clustering, topic mining, and optimization.*

Text Analytics Vocabulary

Let's review descriptions of each text analytics technique mentioned in the previous sections and provide useful definitions.

Important to note: If you are not interested in understand text analytics jargon used in the previous sections, feel free to skip the following section that discusses text analytics vocabulary. You can jump into the last section of this chapter, Key Takeaways, to conclude the chapter.

Clustering is concerned with grouping different objects or people that have similar characteristics (like customer wants and needs) with one another, and that are dissimilar or different from other objects or people in other groups.

Text clustering is about applying clustering to text documents. It involves measuring the similarities between documents and grouping them together. An unsupervised text analytics technique, it breaks documents into clusters by grouping together documents that have similar terms, concepts, and topics. It could also be used to group similar documents such as tweets, newsfeeds, blogs, resumes, and job openings into categories. Text clustering can be used to analyze textual data to generate topics, trends, and patterns. There are several algorithms that can be used in text clustering.

Information retrieval: Information retrieval is concerned with comparing a query with a collection of documents to locate a group of relevant documents. Google search queries are good examples of information retrieval that leverages text analysis. Some techniques, such as QR factorization or SVD, are generally used to achieve this goal. We will also discuss these techniques in the next section.

Classification or categorization helps to assign a class or category to a document based on the analysis of previous documents and their associated categories. This is a supervised process where a sample of the data with a known category is used to train the model, for instance, job postings with their respective occupations. The classification model will create a knowledge base from a sample of jobs descriptions with occupations which will enable assigning occupations to new jobs postings which have missing occupation designations.

Predictive models could be applied here to classify new documents, categorize new e-mails as spam, or detect and predict fraudulent activity.

Additional Useful Text Mining Vocabulary

The following is a list of terms useful in understanding some details of UDA.

Vector Space Model

For information retrieval, indexing, filtering, and relevancy ranking, the vector space model is an algebraic model used to represent any set of documents (text or images) as vectors of identifiers (rows and columns), where rows represent documents and columns represent document terms.

Let's illustrate vector space based on the following search queries from two documents:

Doc_1: customer loves meat

Doc_2: customer loves vegetables

	Customer	love	meat	vegetable
Doc_1	1	1	1	0
Doc_2	1	1	0	1

Exhibit 3.16 Vector Space Model

Without doing any text filtering, the vector space model of Doc1 and Doc2 is represented in the table in Exhibit 3.16. It is a binary representation of the documents and their terms, where:

- 1 means the word (term) appears in the document
- 0 means the word (term) does NOT appear in the document
- Word frequency location filtering and normalization have been applied to this representation

Term

Term refers to words, punctuation, phrases, multiword terms, expressions, or simply put, a token in any given document.

Document

A *document* is a collection of terms. It could be a title, a phrase, a sentence, a paragraph, a query, or a file. For instance, a resume, a news article, or a blog post could be considered documents in text analytics.

Corpus

A *corpus* is a collection of text data that is used to describe a language. It could be a collection of documents, writings, speeches, and conversation.

Exhibit 3.17 showcases examples of term, document, and corpus.

Stop Word List

Stop word lists are a set of commonly used words in any language that are ignored or removed during the text parsing due to their lack of relevance or value in the text analysis. For instance, articles, conjunctions, and prepositions provide little information in the context of a sentence.

Stop words are important in text analytics because they enable focus on the more important words to find pattern, trend, and meaning in text data. For instance, if we were to perform a search: "How to

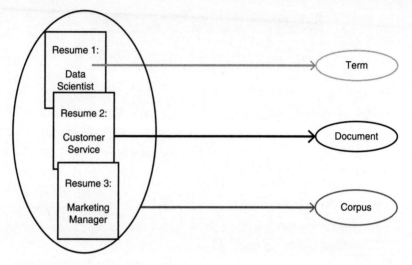

Exhibit 3.17 Term, Document, and Corpus

become a data scientist?" The search engine would find web pages that contain the terms *how, to, become, a, data,* and *scientist.* All the pages found with the terms *how, to,* and *a* would flood the search, since they are more commonly used terms in the English language, compared to *data* and *scientist.* So, by disregarding the frequent terms, the search engine can focus on retrieving pages that contain the keywords *become, data,* and *scientist* and the results will be closer to what we want.

Stop words are useful before clustering is applied. Commonly used stop words include:

- *Prepositions*: There are about 150 prepositions in English, such as *about, above, across, as, at, along, around, before, below, but, by, beyond, for, from, in, into, of, over, than, to, since, via, with, without,* and the like.

- *Determiners*: *a, an, any, another, other, the, this, that, these, those,* and the like.

- *Some adjectives*: *kind, nice, good, great, other, big, high, different, few, bad, same, able,* and the like.

It is important to note that for some analyses, such as sentiment analysis, some stop words should be included in the text mining to be able to find patterns, trends, and sentiments. When performing sentiment analysis, some information retrieval tools (search engine) will simply avoid removing those stop words to optimize the search results.

You can define and build your own stop words based on the type of analytics, domain, or industries you envision to apply text analytics. You can also define a role for your stop words and decide to include or exclude them if they are used as verbs or nouns. A good example is the word *show*. It could be excluded if it were used as a verb (display) while it would be included when it is used as a noun (spectacle). There are publicly available stop word lists that many text analytics software and open source tools use.

Start Word List

These lists enable you to control which terms are used in a text mining analysis. A start word list is a dataset that contains a list of terms to include in the parsing results. If you use a start word list, then only terms that are included in that list appear in parsing results.

Stemming

Stemming refers to the process of finding the stem or root form of a term. Like the start and stop word lists, most software uses predefined dictionary-based stemming. You can also customize your stemming dictionary to include a specific stemming technique, as in using *declar* as the stem for *declared*, *declares*, or *declaration*.

Parts of Speech

Parts of speech (POS) are the basic types of words that any language has. Each part of speech explains how the word is used. Words that are assigned the same POS have similar behaviors in terms of syntax and have similar roles within the grammatical structure of sentences in terms of morphology. In English, there are *nine parts of speech*: articles, nouns, pronouns, adjectives, verbs, adverbs, conjunctions, prepositions, and interjections.

Entity

An entity is any of the several types of information that should be distinguished from general text during text mining. Most text analytics software can identify entities and also analyze them as a unit. Entities are also normalized. You can customize the list of entities based on the domain to which you are applying text mining. Most software programs have a dictionary of normalized entities, such as company name, that will include a list of companies in a given country with all the taxonomy related to the name. An example of entity company name is: International Business Machine: IBM.

Entities that are commonly used include: person, proper noun, product, location, address, phone, time, date, company, currency, measure, organization, percent, Social Security number, code, or vehicle. You can modify this list of entities to include or exclude others based on the analysis you envision.

Noun Groups

A noun group is a group of words, nouns or pronouns, in a document collection. Noun groups are identified based on linguistic relationships that exist within sentences. Noun groups identified in text mining act as single units. You can choose, therefore, to parse them as single terms.

It is important to note that stemming noun groups will treat the group as a single term; for example, *case studies* is parsed as *case study*.

Synonymy

A *synonym* refers to a word or phrase that shares the same meaning with another word or phrase in the same language. Words that are synonyms are said to be *synonymous*, and the state of being synonymous is called *synonymy*.

Synonymy is very useful in text analytics, as it helps to reduce the redundancies by treating words with the same meaning as equivalents. A synonym list enables you to specify different words that should be processed equivalently, for instance, *vehicle* and *car*.

Polysemy

Polysemy refers to the capacity of a word term to have multiple meanings or senses: for instance, the word *show* could refer to a spectacle (noun), but it could also mean to display (verb). Polysemy is very useful in NLP and text mining, such as sentiment analysis.

N-*gram*

N-grams of texts refer to a set of co-occurring words from a given sequence or window. An *n*-gram of size 1 is referred to as a *unigram*, size 2 is a *bigram*, size 3 is a *trigram*. Larger sizes are sometimes referred to by the value of *n*, for example: *four-gram, five-gram*, and so on. When building the *n*-grams you will basically move one word forward. You can also move two or more *n* words forward. For example, consider the sentence "*The weather was really bad yesterday.*"

If $n = 2$ (known as bigrams), then the *n*-grams would be:

- the weather
- weather was
- was really
- really bad
- bad yesterday

N-grams are extensively used in text mining and NLP tasks such as type-ahead spelling, correction, text summarization, and tokenization.

Zipf's Law: Modeling the Distribution of Terms

Zipf's law refers to the power law that is used to showcase terms' distribution across documents. Zipf's law is mathematically simple; it states frequencies proportionally. The most frequent word ($i = 1$) has a frequency proportional to 1, the second most frequent word ($i = 2$) has a frequency proportional to 1/2, the third most frequent word has a frequency proportional to 1/3, and so on ($1/i$: of Cfi $\sim 1/i$).

Latent Semantic Analysis (LSA)

Latent semantic analysis (LSA)[5] is a technique in NLP, like distributional semantics, in which relationships between a set of documents and the terms they contain are analyzed by producing a set of concepts related to the documents and terms. LSA assumes that words that are close in meaning will occur in similar pieces of text. A matrix containing word counts per paragraph (rows represent unique words and columns represent each paragraph count) is constructed from a large piece of text. Then SVD is used to reduce the number of rows while preserving the similarity structure among the columns.

Words are compared by taking the cosine of the angle between the two vectors or the dot product between the normalizations of the two vectors formed by any two rows. Values close to 1 represent very similar words while values close to 0 represent very dissimilar words. LSA is used for information retrieval from search queries.

Dot Product

The dot product is a measure of a distance or angle between two vectors in each space coordinate. This operation takes two equal-length vectors (or sequence of numbers) and returns a single number. Algebraically, it is the sum of the products of the corresponding entries of the two sequences of numbers. Geometrically, it is the product of the Euclidian magnitudes of the two vectors and the cosine of the angle between them. For instance, let vectors $V1 = [1, 2, 3]$ and $V2 = [4, 5, 6]$; the dot product $(V1, V2) = 1 \times 4 + 2 \times 5 + 3 \times 6 = 32$.

Dot products and cosines are used to measure the similarity between documents. Once a quantitative representation of document is created, the cosine is used to measure the similarity between vectors that represent each term document.

 KEY TAKEAWAYS

The explosion of digital information has created a huge influx of data, mostly unstructured. Now organizations are challenged to make sense of the unstructured data found in e-mails, chats, tweets, audio, video, and pictures, which account for more than 80 percent of business data. Organizations are seeking solutions to create business value from this data.

- To successfully leverage the opportunity of the unstructured data, we recommended an easy to implement framework that encompasses the IMPACT cycle:
  - Identify the business question/challenge
  - Master your unstructured data
  - Provide meaning
  - Act
  - Communicate
  - Track the outcome

▣ Mastering unstructured data, whether it be text, images, pictures, audio, or video, leverages mathematics and statistical techniques. Text analytics includes five major steps:

1. Raw text data import and preprocessing
2. Text parsing and normalization
3. Dimension reduction
4. Text analytics clustering, classification, and predictive models
5. Text analytics outcomes and actions

▣ Text mining starts with a quantitative representation of the raw text data into a terms-by-documents collection using a vector space model.

▣ Text filters, such as a stop words list and a start words list, are defined based on the type of unstructured data analytics available.

▣ The team to successfully harness unstructured data should include technical and business members. Technical members can include data analysts (data scientists, statisticians, mathematicians, computer scientists), linguists, and psychologists. Business members can include line managers.

▣ The most frequently used techniques to analyze unstructured data leverages linear algebra, vector space model, matrices decomposition, and dimension reduction techniques such as SVD or QR factorization.

▣ Tools or software can be open source or paid. Depending on budget and resources, leading tech companies such as Microsoft, IBM, Google, Amazon, Trueface.ai, Lambda Lab, API.ai, and Kairos (just to name a few) provide unstructured data analytics APIs that could be used to perform text analysis, images, photos, and videos analysis such as face recognition, video recognition, and categorization. When the unstructured data involves image, voice, or video recognition, machine learning and deep learning techniques are best methods to efficiently find actionable insights from the raw data.

NOTES

1. C. R. Jaccard, "Increasing Understanding of Public Problems and Policies: A Group Study of Four Topics in the Field of Extension Education," *Objectives and Philosophy of Public Affairs Education* (Chicago, Illinois: Farm Foundation, 1956), 12.

2. Jean-Paul Isson and Jesse Harriotts, *Win with Advanced Business Analytics* (Hoboken, NJ: Wiley & Sons, 2012).

3. Scott Deerwester, Susan T. Dumais, George W. Furnas, Thomas K. Landauer, and Richard Harshman, "Indexing by Latent Semantic Analysis," *Journal of the Association for Information Science and Technology* 41, no. 6 (September 1990): 391–407. http://lsa3.colorado.edu/papers/JASIS.lsi.90.pdf

4. imanuel, "Top 67 Software for Text Analysis, Text Mining, Text Analytics," *Predictive Analytics Today*: www.predictiveanalyticstoday.com/top-software-for-text-analysis-text-mining-text-analytics/

5. Wikipedia, "Latent Semantic Analysis": https://en.wikipedia.org/wiki/Latent_semantic_analysis

FURTHER READING

Russ Albright, "Taming Text with the SVD," 2004: ftp://ftp.sas.com/techsup/download/EMiner/TamingTextwiththeSVD.pdf

Russell Albright, James A. Cox, and Kevin Daly, "Skinning the Cat: Comparing Alternative Text Mining Algorithms for Categorization," *Proceedings of the 2nd Data Mining Conference of DiaMondSUG*, Chicago, IL. DM Paper 113 (Cary, NC: SAS Institute), 2001: https://pdfs.semanticscholar.org/db99/a4bd20b0054975a2b4498d7e7fd7d6158c16.pdf

CHAPTER 4

How to Increase Customer Acquisition and Retention with UDA

People don't care how much you know until they know how much you care.

—Theodore Roosevelt

THE VOICE OF THE CUSTOMER: A GOLDMINE FOR UNDERSTANDING CUSTOMERS

Business survival relies on the company's ability to acquire, grow, and retain good customers. In today's global economy, companies are competing to keep their current customers and to get attention from prospects. While some are investing heavily to attract, inspire, engage, and convert prospects and successfully retain their customers, others are struggling to equate customer acquisition and retention with customer lifetime value.

Leading marketing organizations have been mining customer-generated data to understand customer behavior. They gradually embraced predictive analytics to improve precision performance, profit, and overall return on investment (ROI). According to *The CMO [Chief Marketing Officer] Survey*, companies currently spend 6.7 percent of their marketing budget on analytics and expect to spend more than 11.1 percent over the next 3 years.[1]

High-performance companies are abandoning traditional transaction-based methods such as recency, frequency, and monetary (RFM) models in favor of behavioral models to segment and conquer new markets. At stake is answering critical business questions, such as:

- Which prospect should be targeted to become a loyal customer?
- Which e-mail campaign is more likely to be opened by a customer/prospect?
- Who will buy the product and at what price?
- Who are the customers at risk of leaving?
- When and why are they at risk of leaving?

Answering these questions makes organizations more efficient and effective in targeting the best prospects and in retaining their best customers.

To have a holistic (or 360°) understanding of consumers' journeys (action and transaction patterns), leading marketers are capturing all customer interactions to acquire knowledge on their needs, wants, habits, aspirations, desires, interests, and buying patterns. It is crucial to know why a customer switched to the competition and what should have been done to prevent it. As a result, marketing has increasingly become a data-driven function.

UDA can augment product offerings, service delivery, and new product development. Powerful examples are companies like Amazon, Netflix, and Google, which create value for their customers by reading their searches and offering products for which they may have interest.

The explosion of digital information through social media and the Internet also provides consumers with the means to express their voices. Leading organizations are harnessing consumer-related data to anticipate their customers' next move. In this chapter, we will explore how UDA complements existing predictive analytics models for customer acquisition and customer retention.

WHY SHOULD YOU CARE ABOUT UDA FOR CUSTOMER ACQUISITION AND RETENTION?

The Voice of the Customer

The ecosystem of customers and businesses has changed. Interactions between customers and service providers occur online or offline. Consumers no longer directly head to your store to buy your product. They are not limited to your sales or customer service representatives for information; they search the Web, looking for references, opinions on niche sites, reviews and whitepapers, influencers in blogs and social media, forums, and the like. They compare your offerings to your competition's using their smartphones. Some eagerly provide feedback on existing products and new enhancements and developments, and perhaps more importantly, many share their experiences of doing business with you with millions of other users. Their grievances or pain points are shared with their social media community on 24/7/365 platforms, bypassing your call center service representative.

Listening to and understanding what customers say will help your organization optimize your customer acquisition and retention strategies and your overall outcome. Exhibit 4.01 showcases key components of the Voice of the Customer (VoC).

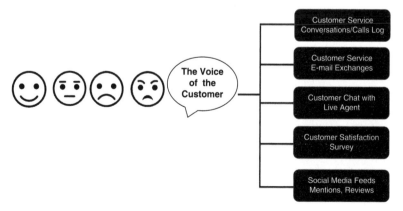

Exhibit 4.01　The Voice of the Customer (VoC)

When listened to and analyzed properly the VoC enables proactive measures to retain clients at risk of leaving. This requires tools, techniques, and resources that sift through all customer interactions to understand their state of mind. Understanding the VoC goes beyond analyzing customer purchasing and usage behaviors. It involves listening to what they say and connecting it to what they do.

The VoC is typically found in unstructured format such as e-mails, audio conversations with customer service or sales representatives, videos, open-ended questions from customer surveys, text content from review or opinion sites, and product reviews. Despite collecting all this information, most companies I have spoken to have failed to transform it into actionable insight. The perceived complexity in analyzing this raw data makes companies favor customer purchasing, or usage behaviors, or overall numeric satisfaction scales, for instance, what customers bought, how much they spent, the number of times they called customer service, or how satisfied they are on a scale of 1 to 5.

In telecommunications, for instance, our mobile phone usage behavior is constantly being tracked and stored. This data includes the number of minutes used per day (day, night, after-hours usage); minute tracking (unusual frequency usage above or below the price plan allowance); contact tracking, their sphere of influence variation (number of distinct incoming and outgoing calls); payment pattern (bills paid on time); the number of times customer service was called (for assistance, errors on bills, etc.); the type of services and plans (prepaid or postpaid); and the number of dropped calls. However, it is only from the VoC that you get the customer's state of mind and appreciation for the product or services. Often, behaviors like reducing the minutes of usage or the dollars spent are consequences which can be early warnings that the customer is unhappy. Negative actions or inactions can result from customers feeling they raised issues in vain, as companies failed to listen, understand, and act. Dissatisfied customers might have complained through satisfaction surveys, social media networks, opinion sites, call center conversation logs, chats with virtual agents, or tweets about the service or the quality of your product.

Yes, what the customer is saying is a large missing part. To gain a comprehensive view and understand your customer behavior, it is necessary to combine unstructured data from the VoC with structured data. UDA helps companies to fully understand their customers' pain points while enhancing the accuracy and effectiveness of predictive models. UDA and predictive models can be embedded into business operations to create actionable value for your business.

How can you understand what customers are saying and doing? By harnessing all pieces of data throughout your customer decision journey. UDA and predictive analytics help organizations anticipate customer buying behavior, customer responses, or outcomes by combining:

- Usage and behavior (structured) data, such as:
  - Sales data
  - Transactions
  - Services data inventory
  - Sociodemographic data
  - Firmographic data
  - Products
  - Plan
- VoC (unstructured) data, such as:
  - Website input
  - Opinion site input
  - Text, video, and audio business signals
  - Conversations with your call center (call center logs).

    Oftentimes, early warning signals of customer attrition are found in these conversations. The call center logs, a record of the interaction between customers and your customer service center, yield great information about what customers say, the reason for the call, the customer's tone of voice and choice of words (was she or he happy?). A conversation where the customer reaches out to the call center to complain about an issue usually encompasses some of the key reasons for customer attrition. Listening and understanding the content of these conversations is paramount for any business that cares properly about addressing customer pain points. Traditional structured data analytics focus on creating indications of the activities of the behavior, such as how many times a customer has called the customer service center per month. However, the most meaningful insights are discovered by analyzing what the call was about. What did the customer say? What were they complaining about? UDA practices such as text analytics help to efficiently discover knowledge buried in customer call logs as well as sales and customer service representatives' notes and narratives.

- Customer e-mails:

    UDA effectively sorts customer's e-mails, identifies junk mail, and uncovers customer pain points and sentiments. On average, there are more than 204 million e-mails sent or received every minute. It would be impossible to manually process them, and it is barely possible for any customer service center to go through the thousands of e-mails received every day to uncover customer's needs, wants, preferences, or pain points and to effectively listen and hear what customers are saying. UDA-applied text analytics can mine all customers' e-mails and derive actionable intelligence.

- Chat sessions

- Contracts or patent documents

- Customer satisfaction survey (CSAT) open-ended questions

- Social media (Twitter, Facebook, YouTube, LinkedIn, Yelp, and others)

- Event trigger data, such as:

- Marriage

- Birthday

- Relocation

- Move to College

- Business Signals
- Mergers and Acquisitions
- Earning Calls Notes, Financial Reports, and Financial News

According to a Gartner study, offers triggered by events generate response rates ranging from 4 percent to 5 percent. The number rises to between 16 and 50 percent when the system can respond to customer activities triggers.[2]

UDA such as text analytics and customer sentiment analysis will analyze the VoC and segment it into categories such as good or bad, and high, medium, or low (potential or risk), which will serve as inputs variables, along with customer usage and behavior data and event trigger data, in customer acquisition and attrition (churn) predictive models.

UDA has been shown to deliver measurable benefits to organizations in a wide range of applications, including:

- Improving customer relationship management (CRM) by providing an overall view of customers, their wishes, and their preferences, leading to more effective marketing, reduced churn, and improved customer loyalty and lifetime value.
- Catching the VoC through surveys or data from Web 2.0 interactions to improve customer loyalty and brand monitoring.
- Accelerating cycle times in the development and refinement of products, and early detecting of product issues through warranty analysis.
- Achieving a clearer view of the competitive landscape.

Exhibit 4.02 illustrates the wide range of applications of UDA.

Exhibit 4.02 demonstrates how UDA can derive actionable insights from the voice of the market and the VoC to optimize acquisition and retention strategies. Without UDA resources, companies play catch-up because they only focus on what already happened. Early warning signals captured from customer inputs can alert you to a possible loss of customers, allowing remedial action to be taken to improve the quality of the service or the quality of the product. It also helps to avoid all the ramifications of bad customer experiences shared online.

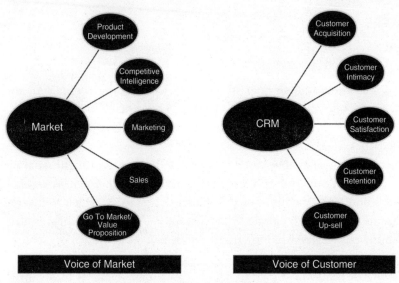

Exhibit 4.02   The VoC for Customer Acquisition and Retention

SOCIAL MEDIA LISTENING AND COMMAND CENTER: LISTEN, ENGAGE, ACT

Business Challenge:

Dell wanted to leverage the 24/7/365 Web social media platform that consumers and customers (existing or potential) have and to listen to the VoC. The company wanted to use that input to enhance its existing products and services, develop new products, and optimize its product offerings.

Solution

Back in 2007, Dell wanted to have a website that enabled them to gauge which ideas were the most important and most relevant to the public. Dell launched a website called IdeaStorm. Dell's IdeaStorm started as an online suggestion box. After registering with Dell's IdeaStorm website, users were given the ability to submit ideas, promote or demote them, and provide feedback on a variety of technology-related products and services.

Just two years after launch, more than 11,000 ideas were generated by the community, and more than 300 of these ideas were actually implemented

by Dell. In 2017, there were more than 27,058 ideas submitted, with 746,863 votes and 103,011 comments. More than 550 of these ideas were implemented by Dell. Some key implementations from IdeaStorm include:

- *Linux preinstalled*
- *Backlit keyboards*
- *Rack-mounted workstations*

The initiative was pioneered by Michael Dell (the founder and CEO), who believes, "In this globally connected digital world, where users have 24/7/365 access to digital platforms, it is critical for any business success to listen to the voice of customers. IdeaStorm is a wonderful way to augment customer listening and customer dynamic. It helps the organization to stay current." Dell believes that talking with and listening to your customers should help to shape the future of your business.

In March 2008, almost a year after Dell's IdeaStorm launch, coffee company Starbucks unveiled at its annual meeting an idea community website called MyStarbucksIdea.com. The goal was to create an IdeaStorm-style idea submission website where anyone could submit an idea to Starbucks. Five years after its launch, MyStarbucksIdea.com had registered more than 150,000 ideas submitted; 277 of these ideas were brought to life by Starbucks.

PREDICTIVE MODELS AND ONLINE MARKETING

Predictive Models

Predictive analytics help companies evaluate their risks and opportunities in customer acquisition and retention strategies. Today's predictive analytics use a variety of machine learning algorithms, such as regression, neural network, decision tree, random forest, Naïve Bayes Rules–based models, memory-based reasoning ensemble models, support vector machine (SVM), and gradient boosting, to name a few, to determine the importance and prediction power of every variable.

For simplicity, in the next sections we will use the traditional regression equation, which includes a dependent variable usually called *outcome* or *output* and independent variables or predictors. Additional details about predictive models will be provided near the end of this chapter, in the section called Predictive Models, Additional Inputs.

UDA and Online Marketing: Optimizing Your Acquisition and Customer Response Models

Do you still need a human to understand how to craft a message that will trigger a tangible call to action, such as motivating your customer (existing or new) to open your e-mail or buy your product or service? With recent progress in text analytics and machine learning, the surprising answer is "No."

Some leading companies have now automated this process using text analytics algorithms and natural language software. For instance, according to an article from Erik Sherman, firms like Persado analyze data with semantic algorithms to determine what e-mail subject lines, for example, will get the best response:

> Working for clients like Citi and Neiman Marcus, the company's systems can reach into its database of scored language, analyze all the variations of a particular message, and systematically create wording that will have the necessary emotional pull, with the ability to test thousands of permutations to find the best performing versions. Machine-generated email subject lines can sometimes double the number of messages opened compared to human-written ones.[3]

HOW DOES UDA APPLIED TO CUSTOMER ACQUISITION WORK?

From a universe of prospects, we want to answer the following questions:

Who? Which prospect will convert to a customer? / Who will buy?

Why? Why will the prospect convert / Why will she/he buy?

When? When will the prospect convert? / When will she/he buy?

What should we do to optimize conversion or buying behavior?

How do we leverage UDA to increase customer acquisition? We apply predictive analytics on the structured data (usage, behavior, and trigger events) and we include structured variables derived from the unstructured data (VoC) and market knowledge content. Exhibit 4.03 shows the main steps.

Data	Descriptive Analytics	Predictive Analytics	Prescriptive Analytics
Capture all the data: Structured & Unstructured Proceed with ▪ Data cleansing ▪ Data integration ▪ Data standardization and validation	Perform exploratory data descriptive analysis of the structured factors Assess data distribution Assess correlations between variables Correlation between inputs variables and the conversion Assess multicollinearity Replace and Impute variables Perform Text Analytics on the unstructured data	Predict Conversion Score Use Machine Learning techniques such as Logistic Regression Decision Tree, Support Vector Machine, Neural Network Gradient Boosting Random Forest and the like Build predictive models leveraging structured and unstructured data to assign a conversion probability or a probability to buy to all prospects and address questions: Who? When? Why?	Optimize Conversion Put actions (prescription) in place to maximize conversion via predictive models. What should you do to maximize conversion? Set up KPI and alerts based upon prospects conversion score and Customer Lifetime Value (CLTV) Strategic proactive prospects outreach program with success plays

Exhibit 4.03   Leveraging UDA to Increase Customer Acquisition

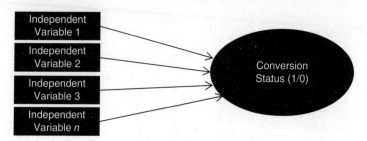

Exhibit 4.04 Customer Acquisition Predictive Model/Conversion Model

In the case of customer acquisition as described in Exhibit 4.04 above, the dependent variable could be the conversion status, with two values: Yes and No, or (1/0). Independent variables from internal, external, and third-party sources can be structured or unstructured. Because the outcome is binary or categorical, we will have a link function called a logit in the regression equation $Y = a_1X_1 + a_2X_2 + b$; where Y is the outcome or dependent variable, X_1 and X_2 are the independent variables, and b is the random error.

The success of any predictive model relies on its implementation. I recommend using the IMPACT cycle to ensure that your UDA-powered acquisition model creates value for your business. Exhibit 4.05 revisits stages of the IMPACT cycle discussed throughout this book and how these stages apply to customer acquisition.

For the Act and Communicate parts of the cycle, I recommend using the segmentation magic grid. The segmentation magic grid

Identify Your Business Challenge	Master Your Data	Provide Meaning	Act	Communicate	Track the Performance
▪ Increase number of new business ▪ Increase market share ▪ Identify which prospect will convert to customer	1. Data integration 2. Data extraction transformation and load (ETL) 3. Data cleansing 4. Text analysis 5. Predictive models	1. Who will buy/ convert? 2. Why will they buy/convert? 3. When will they buy/convert? 4. What should we do?	▪ Leverage the Magic Segment Grid and Customer Lifetime Value or Net Present Value to target most valuable prospects	▪ Make insights available in the CRM systems ▪ Sales systems that are used by customer touchpoints ▪ Represen-tatives	▪ Measure the ROI

Exhibit 4.05 The IMPACT Cycle and Customer Acquisition

crosses the customer's propensity to convert against the customer lifetime value (CLTV). The segmentation magic grid helps sales representatives and customer service representatives to prioritize their acquisition activities by focusing first on the most valuable prospects to increase the ROI and profitability. Once you identify the customer's propensity to convert from the universe of your prospects and their CLTV or net present value,[4] you can rank them into segments such as high, medium, or low. Then the grid can be used as described in Exhibit 4.06.

After getting the segmentation magic grid, it is extremely valuable to provide your customer service or sales representatives with access to a summary tab such as the one shown in Exhibit 4.07, which gives recommendations and consistent messages to support their interactions with the customers.

An industry leader I spoke with had developed and implemented an acquisition model for one of the largest financial institutions in

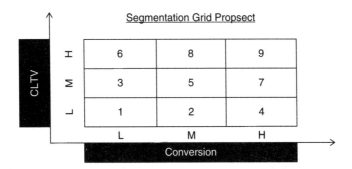

Segmentation Grid Propsect

		L	M	H
	H	6	8	9
CLTV	M	3	5	7
	L	1	2	4

Conversion

Segment Notation

The Y-axis is the CLTV: Customer Life Time Value
The X-axis is the Conversion: Propensity to convert
The letters H M L stand for

H: High
M: Medium
L: Low

Segment 9: High Conversion & High CLTV
Segment 8: Medium Conversion & High CLTV
Segment 7: High Conversion & Medium CLTV

Segment 6: Low Conversion & High CLTV
Segment 5: Medium Conversion & Medium CLTV
Segment 4: High Conversion & Low CLTV

Segment 3: Low Conversion & Medium CLTV
Segment 2: Medium Conversion & Low CLTV
Segment 1: High Conversion & Medium CLTV

Exhibit 4.06   Segmentation Grid Prospects

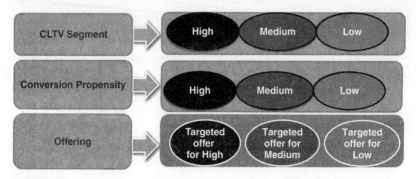

Exhibit 4.07 Customer Acquisition Insights Summary: Success Plays for Prospects

North America. Beyond regular variables such as *company size* and *industry activity*, the institution had added call center logs, social media content, e-mails, and category of service requests and business signals, which helped to augment the fit of their acquisition model by more than 23 percent. Prospects who frequently called, who received a personalized e-mail triggered by other business signals, and who had expressed the need for enhanced mortgage package or retirement plan were more likely to convert than those without those variables. Those with positive business signals who also raised their customer pain points on social media tended to convert less often than the rest of the universe of customers.

Exhibit 4.08 is an excerpt of customer acquisition model with structured variables only.

The following unstructured independent variables were added to assess their impact on new customer conversion:

■ *Customer Satisfaction CSAT Categorization*: Open-ended questions from the latest CSAT were analyzed using text mining. There were three major satisfaction issues from customer feedback:

Predictive Model without Unstructured Variables		Predicted	
Actual		0 (No)	1 (Yes)
	0 (No)	67%	33%
	1 (Yes)	40%	70%

Exhibit 4.08 Customer Acquisition Model Excerpt

Predictive Model with Structured and Unstructured Variables	Predicted	
Actual	0 (No)	1 (Yes)
0 (No)	77%	23%
1 (Yes)	15%	85%

Exhibit 4.09   Predictive Model with Structured and Unstructured Variables

1. Service and support
2. Opening hours
3. Bank monthly fees

■ *Social Media*: Company brand mentions on social media for the past six months were captured and analyzed via sentiment analysis to derive customers' sentiments.

Two negative sentiments came from social media analysis:

1. The latest change in the saving plan price appeared to upset most of the unhappy customers, driving the negative sentiment.
2. The lack of communication about a security breach also upset customers. The company had failed to inform its customers on time about phishing issues, when more than 25 percent of customers had credit card numbers and personal information stolen by hackers.

■ *Net Promoter Score (NPS)*: Text mining was also performed on the text from open-ended questions to determine why customers would not recommend the bank to their peers, which led to the identification of four key reasons.

■ *E-mails*: E-mail exchanges with customers, service center e-mails, marketing e-mails, and sales representative e-mails were analyzed and put into seven segments.

■ *Call Center*: Call center call logs were analyzed and grouped into five categories.

■ *Business Signals*: Social media business signals and newswire were analyzed for publicly traded customers of the bank.

We can see from Exhibits 4.08 and 4.09 above that the classification (Yes/Yes) increased from 70 percent to 85 percent, which indicates the model with unstructured data was more accurate in predicting who will convert or has the propensity to convert.

THE POWER OF UDA FOR E-MAIL RESPONSE AND AD OPTIMIZATION

As mentioned earlier, leading companies have now automated the e-mail composition process, using text analytics algorithms and natural language software. Some companies are already getting significant ROI through using machine-generated algorithms to increase response rate and conversion rate. UDA's artificial intelligence (AI)–driven algorithms are far more capable at performing repetitive high-volume and high-frequency tasks than humans are.

The chief marketing officer (CMO) of one the largest telecommunications companies in Europe reported that the company has recorded a double-digit increase in ROI by using machine-generated emails to reach out to new and existing customers.

The field of programming advertisement buying is also getting tremendous development. In fact, instead of having human marketing specialists choosing where to buy and place ads in magazines, advanced unstructured data analytics algorithms (powered by AI) are being used to harness billions of pieces of information about subjects and targeting ads toward the best customers and prospects in real time.

HOW TO DRIVE MORE CONVERSION AND ENGAGEMENT WITH UDA APPLIED TO CONTENT

Gone are the days where marketers had to rely on A/B testing tools to figure out the best lexical recipes for their campaigns. Today, they can leverage UDA aspects such as machine learning to perform advanced, focused semantic and lexical analyses and help digital marketers understand the words, phrases, and their conceptual and contextual usage to drive customer engagement up and increase response rate and conversion.

Forward-looking companies are now using lexical analysis to write product descriptions that drive responses and sales, e-mail bodies that drive website visits, and responses and landing page copy that drive conversions and consumer engagement.

Machine learning is helping organizations deliver the right content to the right audience at the right time, leveraging the power of UDA. It is changing the overall dynamic of storytelling marketing.

According to Paul Blamire, who pioneered the idea of machine learning in marketing, "machine learning (ML) and artificial intelligence (AI) can help marketers get the words and their structure right for more people on more devices."[5] There is more data available today than ever before, and it is too much data for humans to analyze. That's where machine learning and AI come to the marketers' rescue. Blamire claimed that machine learning and AI can help with:

- Identifying ideal topics
- Understanding your audience's reading level
- Telling you what sentiment you need to express
- Finding the ideal structure
- Identifying emotional language
- Telling you when to publish
- Identifying which screen your audiences are on and how that should affect your content

HOW UDA APPLIED TO CUSTOMER RETENTION (CHURN) WORKS

From a universe of customers, we want to answer the following questions:

Who? Which customer will leave?

Why? Why will she/he leave?

When? When will she/he leave?

What should we do to retain the customer?

How do we leverage UDA to optimize customer retention? As we described for customer acquisition, predictive analytics is applied on structured data, and we include structured variables derived from unstructured content or behavioral information.

Exhibit 4.10 shows the main steps.

Data	Descriptive Analytics	Predictive Analytics	Prescriptive Analytics
Capture all the data: Structured & Unstructured Proceed with - Data cleansing - Data integration - Data standardization and validation	Perform exploratory data descriptive analysis of the structured factors Assess data distribution Assess correlations between variables Correlation between inputs variables and the churn status Assess multicollinearity Replace and impute variables Perform Text Analytics on the unstructured data	Predict churn status using Machine Learning techniques such as Logistic Regression Decision Tree, Support Vector Machine, Neural Network Gradient Boosting Random Forest and the like Build predictive models leveraging structured and unstructured data to assign a churn probability or a probability to churn to all existing customers and address questions: Who? When? Why?	Optimize Retention Put actions (prescription) in place to maximize customer retention via predictive models. What should you do to minimize churn rate? Set up KPI and alerts based upon customer likely to churn score and Customer Lifetime Value (CLTV) Strategic proactive customers retention outreach program with success plays

Exhibit 4.10 UDA Leveraging UDA to Increase Customer Retention

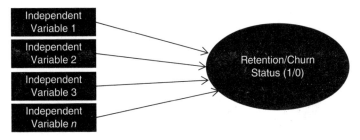

Exhibit 4.11   Customer Retention Predictive Model/Churn Model

In the case of customer retention, the dependent variable could be the status with two values: Leave (Churn) and Stay (Retain), or (1/0). Independent variables from internal, external, and third-party sources can be structured or unstructured. Because the outcome is binary or categorical, the equation $Y = a_1 X_1 + a_2 X_2 + b$ will have a link function called a logit.

The process of applying UDA to churn also follows the IMPACT Cycle, as shown in Exhibit 4.12.

As for customer acquisition, for the Act and Communication parts, I recommend using the segmentation magic grid. The segmentation magic grid crosses the propensity to churn against the CLTV. It helps sales representatives and customer service representatives prioritize

Identify Your Business Challenge	Master Your Data	Provide Meaning	Act	Communicate	Track the Performance
▪ Who are the customers more likely to churn? ▪ Why they would churn?	1. Data integration 2. Data extraction transformation and load (ETL) 3. Data cleansing 4. Text analysis 5. Predictive models	▪ Find through UDA and predictive models a list of triggers that explain churn. ▪ Anticipate who are the customers who are more likely to churn?	▪ Put in place an actionable plan to leverage UDA findings. ▪ Embed predictive and text analytics findings into business practices.	▪ Make insights available in the CRM systems ▪ Sales systems that are used by customer touchpoints ▪ Representatives	▪ Measure the ROI ▪ Demonstrate to the business the incremental value of the churn predictive model

Exhibit 4.12   The IMPACT Cycle and Customer Retention

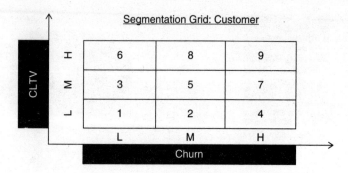

Segment Notation
The Y-axis is the CLTV: Customer Life Time Value
The X-axis is the Churn: Propensity to churn
The letters H M L stand for
H: High   Segment 9: High Churn & High CLTV
M: Medium   Segment 8: Medium Churn & High CLTV
L: Low   Segment 7: High Churn & Medium CLTV

Segment 6: Low Churn & High CLTV
Segment 5: Medium Churn & Medium CLTV
Segment 4: High Churn & Low CLTV

Segment 3: Low Churn & Medium CLTV
Segment 2: Medium Churn & Low CLTV
Segment 1: HIgh Churn & Medium CLTV

Exhibit 4.13   Segmentation Grid Insights Retention

their retention activities by focusing first on the most valuable customers, whose business increases ROI and profitability. Once you identify the propensity to churn from the universe of your existing customers and their CLTV or net present value, you can rank them into segments such as high, medium, or low for account prioritization. Then the grid can be used by your end-users as described in Exhibit 4.13.

After getting the segmentation magic grid, it is extremely valuable to provide your customer service or sales representatives with access to a summary tab such as the one shown in Exhibit 4.14, which gives recommendations and consistent messages to support their interactions with the customers.

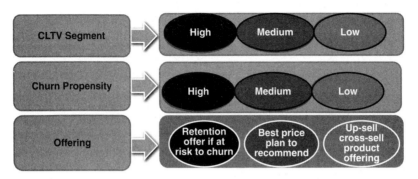

Exhibit 4.14 Customer Retention Insights Summary: Success Plays

WHAT IS UDA APPLIED TO CUSTOMER ACQUISITION?

UDA optimizes customer acquisition activities by leveraging all structured and unstructured data from every customer touchpoint. Specifically, UDA can:

1. Optimize your source of customer acquisition.

   Optimize your acquisition activities by targeting the right source or channel that will maximize conversion and minimize the cost of acquiring customer (CAC).

2. Map and optimize your customer behavior and customer outcome.

   Segment to conquer customers based on their buying habits, needs, preferences, wants, likes, and desires to optimize conversion. Text analytics help to determine the right offer and content, the right delivery channel, at the right time, to the right customer or prospect.

3. Optimize your customer decision journey knowledge.

   Map customer behavior and interactions across all touchpoints to explain and anticipate future customer behavior across every stage of their decision journey. This will be discussed further in the next section.

4. Leverage the power of Big Data.

Big Data enables us to capture, store, and analyze all types of data that are available from the digital ecosystem. Data from the VoC, the voice of the market, or any third party can enhance our customer behavior knowledge.

5. Increase the power of predictive analytics.

UDA supplements predictive analytics with unstructured data (converted into structured format) to better anticipate customer behavior.

Consumer/Customer Decision Journey

The concept of the consumer decision journey was introduced in the *McKinsey Quarterly* as a revision of the traditional consumer buying funnel.[6] The final action for a consumer through the funnel occurs when they make the purchase.

Lessons from McKinsey's Consumer Decision Journey

With today's evolving socioeconomic conditions, advances in digital platforms have changed the way consumers buy products and services. Consumers research very differently, challenging marketers to rethink the ways they approach them. The traditional marketing buying funnel begins with consumer awareness and ends at the moment of purchase/postpurchase experience.

In 2009, David Court, Dave Elzinga, Susan Mulder, and Ole Jørgen Vetvik revised this theory by including a dynamic decision-making process called the consumer decision journey (see Exhibit 4.15). Their consumer decision journey has four stages:[7]

1. Initial consideration

2. Active evaluation (information gathering)

3. Moment of purchase

4. Postpurchase experience (ongoing exposure, loyalty)

We will apply this model to the online recruitment industry by replacing *consumer* with *employer* and adapting the framework to the

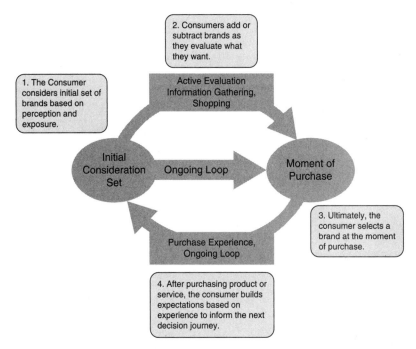

Exhibit 4.15 Consumer Decision Journey
Source: David Court, Dave Elzinga, Susan Mulder, and Ole Jørgen Vetvik, "The Consumer Decision Journey," McKinsey Quarterly, *June 2009: www.mckinsey.com/insights/ marketing_sales/the_consumer_decision_journey*

employment market. Leveraging the Employer Decision Journey provides job boards and seekers with a comprehensive map of an employer's online and offline behaviors, which can be used when seekers and employers are interacting via the various touch points throughout their journey. The Employer Decision Journey provides online recruitment solutions providers such as job board and staffing companies with relevant information on how to attract, acquire, and retain the most valuable employers as well as the ultimate best practices for leveraging your existing employers as your most important advocates to attract new recruitment business. In Exhibit 4.16, the Employer Decision Journey maps employer behavior at each stage of the consumer decision funnel.

Consumer Decision Journey	Initial Consideration	Active Consideration	Moment of purchase	Post purchase
Employer Decision -Journey/State of Mind	I consider hiring a new talent	I would like to know more	I am completely interested	I love doing business with you
Employer Triggers Or Actions	**Internal** -Business growth -Replacement of employees who left -New business opportunities and development -Meet employment market demand -Increase customer satisfaction **External** -Macroeconomic conditions: cost of hire, unemployment rate, GDP, vacancy rate, competition activity -Competition landscape branding and advertising -Connection with employer brand and value propositions	**About your company** -Visit your corporate site -Visit your social media platforms -Connect with your employer community -Visit customer review sites **About a specific job I am hiring for** -Visit supply/demand career information -Visit your career advice -Visit niche sites -Perform searches on: multiple job boards -Look for sources of hire online and offline	**Online:** -Visit your website -Evaluate various offers. Product price promotion and value. Create a profile an account and place the order **Offline** -Reach out to customers services or sales representative get more information -Product, Price Promotion -Set expectation -Place the order --Request for quote ---	**I love your company** -I love your brand -I love your services -I love your mission and value proposition -**I am engaged, happy, and loyal customer; I share my great experience,** your values with my network and peers. -**I am your advocate** -I deliver testimonials and first-hand experience to new customers, employers community -I spoke very highly about your brand, culture, and values. -I give you great rating on your NPS surveys and satisfaction survey as well as my friends.

Exhibit 4.16 From Consumer Decision Journey to Employer Decision Journey

In the *Harvard Business Review* article "Branding in Digital Age," the author identifies four major brand awareness stages:

- Consider

- Evaluate

- Buy

- Enjoy, include figure of seeker decisions journey (adapted from CDJ)[8]

We will include this categorization in the journey below.

Let's take a closer look at each of these stages and what they will mean for your company.

Stage 1: Why Is an Employer Looking to Hire a New Employee?

The Initial Evaluation or Consideration Stage is designed to uncover the hiring/recruitment motivation of your potential customer/ employer. It will provide answers to key elements that should help you optimize your acquisition strategies, tailor your sourcing activities, and seize the right opportunity to connect with your new customer/ employer when he or she is beginning to consider posting a job or buying a product. You want to be their top-of-mind, go-to service provider because they feel that you will help them find new talent.

Stage 2: Where Do Employers Turn When Seeking New Candidates or Talents?

In the Active Evaluation stage, customers/employers begin to interact with brands and companies that interest them. They start looking for different sources of hiring, online and offline. The key to this stage is finding the right channel with which to interact with them. What are their watering holes; what sites do they frequent? From there, focus your approach by listening to, connecting with, and engaging with them about job market information and candidate knowledge supply and demand, such as candidate scarcity and the best solutions.

Stage 3: How Will Employers Respond to Your Recruitment Solution Process?

This stage will force you to consider the process your customer/ employers go through as they consider hiring, posting a job, and hopefully hiring the ideal candidate. It begins with making sure your organization is equipped with the most current tools and technologies that enable user-friendly navigation, job branding, and an easy response process for interested employers.

Stage 4: How Do You Get Your Customer (Employer) Engaged and Become Brand Advocates?

Building a relationship with your current customer (employer) base is key to acquiring great customers to increase your business. This stage is dedicated to connecting with your existing customer base talent so they become your best advocates in attracting and acquiring new customers. One way to do this is through a primary focus on customer satisfaction that will lead to an increase of the net promote score and a customer community that could be a platform where customers share their experiences when doing business with you. They become your referrals and ambassadors.

UDA and the Consumer Decision Journey

UDA helps to harness all the narrative feedback that customers generate or provide through their decision journey. Leading companies are mining information from social media when customers are at their evaluation stage, and they also assess the link between brand awareness and customer actions. Is there a link between customer buying behavior and what they have seen, heard, reviewed, and read about your brand? Did your brand impact their decision to buy or do business with you? What is the correlation between your online reputation, customer feedback, and your customer acquisition metrics?

The consumer journey provides a platform for any business to listen, act, and engage with their prospective customers to increase customer acquisitions and retention.

Decision Stage	Decision Stage Data Structured and Unstructured	Analytics
Initial Consideration	Brand awareness, online ads, offline ads, TV ads, billboards, e-mails, CRM campaigns	Correlation and link analysis between brand awareness and customer actions
Active Evaluation	Competitive information, social media information narrative, sentiment, review	Sentiment analysis, opinion analysis
Moment of Purchase	Customer point of sale (POS) (people channel and the 5P: product, price, promotion, placement, people)	Text analytics: Customer interaction with POS call log analysis
Post-Purchase Experience (ongoing exposure loyalty)	CSAT open-ended question Customer community	Text analytics: Text categorization open-ended CSAT survey

Exhibit 4.17 Consumer Decision Journey

Exhibit 4.17 presents the consumer decision stage, the underlying data of the stage, and a sample of analytics we can use.

WHAT IS UDA APPLIED TO CUSTOMER RETENTION (CHURN)?

UDA optimizes customer retention activities by leveraging all structured and unstructured data from every customer touchpoint's interactions. Deep learning techniques in IVR can also assess the intonation in the customer's voice to detect courtesy or displeasure. These techniques also assess the customer service representative's efficiency and the quality of the exchange with customers. Specifically, UDA can:

1. Minimize your customer attrition / maximize your customer retention.

   UDA leverages all the inputs of customers' behavior, words, and sentiments captured through all customer touchpoints to anticipate and minimize churn. It optimizes retention activities by targeting the most valuable customers and minimizing attrition losses and win-back costs.

2. Map and optimize your customer behavior and customer outcome.

   Segment your customers based on their buying habits, behavior, needs, preferences, wants, likes, and desires to minimize attrition. Text analytics help to determine which customers are at risk so that you can intervene proactively.

3. Optimize your customer decision journey knowledge.

   Map your customers' behaviors and interactions across all touchpoints to explain and anticipate customers' behaviors across every stage of their decision journey.

4. Leverage the power of Big Data.

   Data from the VoC, the voice of the market, or any third-party data enhance our customer behavior knowledge.

5. Increase the power of predictive analytics.

   UDA supplements predictive analytics with unstructured data (converted into structured format) to better anticipate customer behavior. The categorization obtained from UDA is in turn used as independent variables or predictors in the churn predictive model. It increases the precision and goodness of fit and the lift of the model.

THE POWER OF UDA POWERED BY VIRTUAL AGENT

Welcome to the AI Customer Service Assistant

Why Have an AI Customer Service Assistant/Cognitive Computer?

According to some studies, U.S. organizations spend $112 billion on call center labor and software—yet half of the 270 billion customer service calls still go unresolved each year. This is a great opportunity to leverage cognitive computing to address call volume and call quality issues and to increase customer satisfaction by providing each customer who calls with timely and correct support to gain the information they are looking for.

We have all witnessed exchanges with customer service representatives not knowing what they are talking about or taking a while to answer a simple question regarding the company product or service.

Or in some instances, as one CEO told me, the customer feels like he is doing business with different companies while interacting with different service agents in his organization, simply because they don't have access to the same information and consequently provide different answers to the same question. Not having a consistent message or information causes customer frustration, as it has a negative impact on the customer's experience with your service and reduces his or her likelihood of doing further business with your organization. As an old adage says, "An unhappy customer is less likely to return and do business with you."

Beyond service agent knowledge, there is also a bandwidth issue. In fact, some customer services agents simply don't have the bandwidth to cover the volume of calls turning their way every day. Consequently, some leading organizations I spoke with are turning to cognitive analytics/computing that can quickly handle all calls and optimize access to the right information customers are seeking.

How an AI Customer Service Assistant Works

UDA is the foundation of cognitive computing (such as IBM Watson), and helps forward-looking organizations leverage the power of natural language processing and cognitive computing to optimize their customer services support.

Below are the four major steps involved in cognitive computing for customer service support:

1. The speech is converted to text.

2. The algorithm uses machine learning and deep learning techniques to uncover the meaning behind a customer's questions and the interactions.

3. The algorithm determines the appropriate responses and converts those responses into speech.

4. The system interacts with the caller through the cognitive agent over the phone, using natural dialogue.

Cognitive services providers like IBM Watson services are helping organizations drive conversations and provide a cognitive experience to customers by using Watson Natural Language Classifier, Watson Conversation, Watson Text to Speech, and Watson Speech to Text.

BENEFITS OF A VIRTUAL AGENT OR AI ASSISTANT FOR CUSTOMER EXPERIENCE

- Increase Customer Interaction and Engagement

  Today customers interact with your organization 24/7 across multiple channels, such as your company's website, social media network, messaging, and blog platform.

  UDA solutions such as chatbots or virtual customer service agents can help your organization interact and engage with your customers across several channels and therefore optimize their overall experience.

- Increase Customer Satisfaction and Reduce Costs

  In this globally connected world, it is imperative for organizations to provide the 24/7 support customers need. However, providing the 365/24/7 support can be cost prohibitive and barely possible to implement. Chatbots and virtual agents can help your organization improve customer service experience by shortening call-handling times, reducing agent-to-agent transfers, optimizing responses and information provided to customers, and more importantly repurposing agents to other tasks and efforts where their talent is required and better leveraged.

- Increase Customer Intimacy: Get to Know Your Customer Better

  Leveraging the power of cognitive computing provides organizations with unparalleled knowledge of their customers. And a great customer experience will more likely lead to a happy customer. The more you understand your customers, the better experience you can provide them. Cognitive solutions such as Watson provide dashboard and KPIs that include a complete history of every conversation that your virtual agent has had. You can see inquiry volume, inquiry resolution patterns, and customer pain points, to optimize your customers' experience.

▪ Reduce Costs and Increase Customer Service Productivity

Companies leveraging the power of AI have seen a sharp decrease in customer service costs and an increase in customer satisfaction due to almost all calls being efficiently processed.

According to Manoj Saxena, general manager of IBM Watson Solutions, "IBM's tests, using its own call centers and proprietary data, reported that Watson delivered a 40 percent reduction in search time for information. Watson pulls up stuff that an agent wouldn't because it is looking for semantic links, not just doing text-matching based on keywords."[9]

BENEFITS AND CASE STUDIES

The Web and social media ecosystem have provided customers with a place to share their experience with your products, services, and resources. Leading organizations are carefully listening to the VoC to enhance and improve service and product offerings, prices, and the development of new products or services. They use UDA to prioritize customer acquisition and retention strategies to engage, act, and react with customers and prospects in ways that will increase customer acquisitions, retain their most valuable customers, and improve overall customer satisfaction.

Structured (quantitative) data, such as sales, transactions, returns, pricing, spend, services plans, location, and sociodemographics or firmographics and trigger events are critical for customer predictive analytics models. However, unstructured (qualitative) data found in customer call logs, customer conversations with customer service, e-mails or voice messaging, sales representative notes and narratives, chat sessions, contract and patent documents, customer opinions from social media, and customer feedback from CSAT survey open-ended questions or survey verbatim all provide insight into the customer's state of mind and his or her pain points. Both structured and unstructured data provide input variables for predictive models to understand customer behavior and anticipate customer outcomes, such as needs, preferences, wants, habits, and next moves. Unstructured data significantly augments the predictive power of customer acquisition and retention models.

In the case study example, we will discuss how Monster Worldwide has been leveraging advanced analytics (segmentation and scoring) globally to stay on top of the competition and enrich its predictive models with UDA.

MONSTER WORLDWIDE ONLINE RECRUITMENT CASE STUDY: CUSTOMER ACQUISITION AND RETENTION

Monster Worldwide is a global online recruitment solutions company with headquarters in more than 44 countries, including Europe, North America, Latin America, and the Asia Pacific.

The Challenge

Segment and conquer the business-to-business (B2B) market in every country where Monster Worldwide operates, in order to:

- *Deepen customer knowledge*
- *Increase customer acquisition*
- *Increase customer retention*
- *Increase sales productivity*
- *Increase marketing productivity*

The Solution

Monster Worldwide has been using predictive analytics and segmentation to better understand and target both its prospects and customers. The segmentation work has helped Monster Worldwide achieve its desired results, getting high-potential customers to advertise on its site. This has a huge impact on customer intimacy, improved customer acquisitions, improved retention, and up-sell and cross-sell, to name just a few of the tangible benefits.

Monster Worldwide tackled the data challenge by looking for data in innovative places. To achieve success with predictive analytics, you often have to marry external and internal data to get a comprehensive view.

Monster Worldwide augmented their internal databases with information from third parties, including information on the entire business universe and macroeconomic data (such as gross domestic product, unemployment, turnover rates, and cost per hire). They also improved their models by including unstructured data such as business signals (customer financial reports, earning calls, mergers and acquisitions, the company's online reputation on opinion sites such as Glassdoor and Kununu, social media content, and customer online posting activity) to see how the company brand was differentiated from that of the competition. They also used their internal data, call logs, e-mail content, customer interactions with customer service representatives and sales representatives, and CRM e-mail content categorization received from potential customers. Leveraging advanced text analytics models and semantic analytics, Monster harnessed all the text inputs to augment the power of the predictive model.

Monster Worldwide used third-party data to segment the North American and European business universe into three prospect segments based on their propensity to buy and potential value. This allowed the sales force to spend time where it expected to get the best return.

The Benefits

Using segmentation and optimization techniques, Monster Worldwide calibrated the sales rep's portfolios to give everyone the same chance to reach high-value prospects. This approach allowed Monster Worldwide to understand sales performance and increase sales productivity by 33 percent. In addition, this type of success helped fuel the acceptance of advanced predictive analytics by the sales force, leading to buy-in for further initiatives.

The segmentation and optimization also helped Monster Worldwide use resources more effectively to proactively retain high-value customers. After the first year of implementation, retention was up 20 percent, thanks to the addition of text variables, and customer acquisition increased by 17 percent. The segments were not only used in sales; Monster Worldwide leveraged them when serving high-value customers and synchronized its efforts with customer service.

Monster also leveraged what it had learned to adjust advertising efforts. For example, banner advertising was adjusted to reflect where high-value segments could be found online. After the first year of adopting predictive analytics, marketing efficiency improved by 35 percent.

Exhibit 4.18 depicts Monster Worldwide's approach.

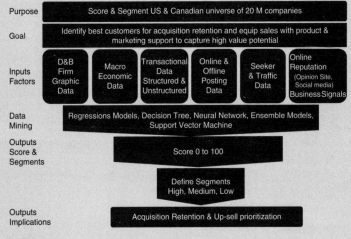

Exhibit 4.18 Business-to-Business Scoring and Segmentation Using Different Types of Data

TELECOMMUNICATION CASE STUDY: CHURN

To fully understand its growing customer attrition and put in place proactive action, one of the largest telecommunication service providers in North America (referred to as Wireless Inc. for confidentiality reasons) turned to predictive analytics, leveraging structured and unstructured data to reduce customer attrition.

The Challenge

Wireless Inc. wanted to leverage structured and unstructured customer data to predict which customers were at risk to churn (turn to the competition).

The Solution

Predictive models to identify churn were powered by UDA. Strategic interventions included a proactive outreach program, retention activities leveraging customer service representative premium team, and strategies.

The Benefit

- *Increase in customer retention in the high-value segment by 15 percent*
- *Increase in customer profitability by 27 percent*

The Process

To predict the customers who will churn, two types of data were used: the past behavior and VoC data:

- *Profile/company identity data*
- *Firmographic data*
- *Services and plans*
- *Usage data*
- *Billing data*
- *Type of handset used*
- *Call center log data (customer service representative, sales representative, interaction with live chat agent)*
- *E-mails and live chat data*
- *Sentiment from livestreaming data via social media such as Twitter, Facebook, Instagram, or LinkedIn*
- *CSAT open-ended question data*

Step 1: Data Preparation—Build a sample of past churn behavior

Look at customers who have churned between February and July 2016; track their behavior 12 months before the churn event to build and train the models. January 2015 is excluded, as it represents the month when the model was being built.

Exhibit 4.19 shows a high-level overview of the components of the churn predictive model building coming together.

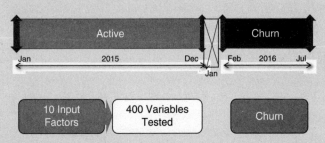

Exhibit 4.19 Churn Predictive Model Overview

Ten inputs/factors were used to build the model; those factors encompassed 400 variables that were tested to understand and predict churn status from February to July 2016. Exploratory data analysis was first performed on these variables to clean, validate, and remove outliers.

The aforementioned factors were used as inputs/variables of churn predictive models, as described in Exhibit 4.20.

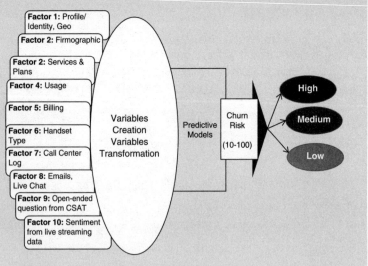

Exhibit 4.20 Churn Predictive Model Process

Factors 1 to 10: After the exploratory data analysis was completed, imputation was performed to replace missing values and variables and create new variables to be used in several machine learning models (support vector machines, naïve, bayes, logistic regression, neural network, gradient boosting, decision tree, and random forest).

First, the model was built without including factors 7, 8, 9, and 10, which encompassed text data such as customer interaction with CSRs and sales representatives, customer conversation call logs, live chats, Twitter feeds, and open-ended questions. After analyzing all the variables, machine learning techniques were used to determine the best triggers. The following were the most important structured inputs to predict churn behavior:

- *Sphere of influence*
- *Dropped calls*
- *Handset type*
- *Declining weekend minutes of usage*
- *Number of call center calls*

After running the model using only numerical and categorical data, the misclassification rate was 24.7 percent and the sensitivity was 62 percent in the validation data. A misclassification rate of 24.7 percent meant the model could correctly classify 75.3 percent of churners.

Step 2: Textual Data Inclusion

Using Text Mining, the unstructured data (raw text data) was transformed into numerical data which could then be included into the model as independent variables.

To be able to include text data, customer service call logs and customer e-mail exchanges were categorized:

- *Customer service calls were grouped into eleven topics/clusters for reason of the call.*
- *E-mail exchange categorization and topics resulted in seven clusters.*
- *Text analysis of the three open-ended questions from a CSAT survey led to six clusters.*
- *Live chat data that was captured twelve months before the attrition tracking window provided five major categories of sentiment.*

When the twenty-nine clusters from the text were included in the model, the clusters for customer service call log, e-mail exchange, and answers from open-ended questions provided the most significant insight.

The inclusion of the outcome from UDA in the predictive model helped to significantly decrease the misclassification rate of the final model from 24.7 percent to 17.3 percent.

After the predictive model was complete, the best model was chosen based on the misclassification rate using SAS model comparison. Once the final model was obtained, each customer received a score from 0 to 100, and from that score "at risk" segments were created:

- *High: Churn risk above 70*
- *Medium: Churn risk between 50 and 70*
- *Low: Churn risk below 50*

The At-Risk Predictive Model was then operationalized by defining actions and proactive retention strategies to keep and protect high-risk customers and high-value customers from churning by building strategies based on leveraged raw data from the VoC and customer behavioral data. Six months after putting the new model in place, Wireless Inc. reported a 15 percent increase in customer retention and a 27 percent increase in profitability in their medium- and high-value customer segments.

Predictive Models, Additional Inputs

Predictive models aim to address the *who, when, why,* and *what should we do* questions for business issues, such as those related to customer behavior, human behavior, likelihood to vote, date, purchase, and product usage. The list of questions we can answer with predictive models includes all aspects of today's life. In terms of customer acquisition and retention, the list includes:

- Which of my existing customers will turn to the competition?
- Why will my existing customers leave?
- When will my customers leave?
- Whom can we retain?
- Why would a new prospect convert to being a customer?

- When will a prospect convert to being a customer?
- Who will buy?
- What will they buy?
- Whom can we acquire?
- Which product and services will a customer buy next?
- Who is more likely to default on a payment?
- What are our probable costs?
- What are our liabilities?
- What are our future revenues?

Predictive models help executives to make informed strategic, operational, and tactical decisions, to prevent and predict transactions or risks, or to improve the insight into your customers'/members' behavior. Exhibit 4.21 shows the predictive model behind the scenes.

Let's describe each of the nine major steps of the predictive model that takes place behind the scenes. Exhibit 4.22 provides a high-level overview of the steps and includes some comments and examples of what each step encompasses.

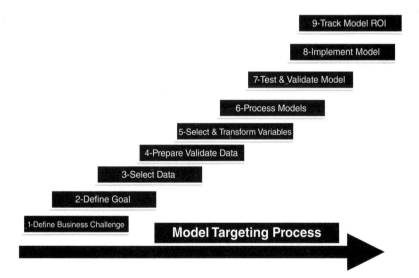

Exhibit 4.21 Churn Predictive Model Behind the Scenes

Model Steps	Overview	Comments/ Examples
Step 1: Define Business Challenge	Clearly define the business challenge the model should help to address. At this stage, it is critical to get executive sponsorship before moving forward to ensure that the model will have the support it needs for successful development and implementation.	Business challenges could include: ■ Reduce customer attrition/churn by 5 percent ■ Increase customer acquisition by 10 percent ■ Reduce employee turnover by 6 percent If you don't secure executive sponsorship, you might end up with a great model that nobody uses.
Step 2: Define Goal	Clearly explain the goal of the model. The goal of any predictive model will be to address the 4W questions: Who? When? Why? What should we do?	For instance, for churn predictive model: ■ Who are my customers at risk of churning? ■ When will they churn? ■ Why will they churn? ■ What should we do to prevent them from churning?
Step 3: Select Data	This step is concerned with identification of all sources of internal and external data that will be used to build the model, including structured data, unstructured data, publicly available data, and third-party data. This step also includes clear definition of criteria required to build the model datasets. Three datasets are required: The training dataset used to build the model, and validation and testing datasets that validate and test the model's generalization, robustness, and scalability.	For instance, for our churn and acquisition models in B2B, we look for internal data: buying behavior, transactional data, sociodemographic data, and firm graphic data. We also include unstructured data, such as social media data, call center log data, customer e-mail data, CRM contact data, business signal data (social media sentiment, buzzword and trending topics related brand), and publicly available data from social media such as reviews and recommendations from opinion sites to determine the company's online reputation.

Exhibit 4.22 Predictive Model Process: The Nine Steps Behind the Scenes

Model Steps	Overview	Comments/ Examples
Step 4: Prepare and Validate Data	This step is the most time consuming, as all different pieces of data need to be integrated, and data cleansing, data validation, outlier elimination, and standardization or normalization (when applicable) need to be performed. Some replacement or imputation of missing data may be required before proceeding with subsequent analyses, when appropriate.	The internal structured data should be cleansed. Some unstructured data, such as the customer call log data and e-mails, requires a lot of cleansing. It is also important to run some exploratory data analysis at this stage to get an overview of the dataset. Some preliminary work of normalization is usually required for the unstructured data before we include it in the model. Text mining needs to be performed on unstructured data to derive structured factors that will be used to complement the structured data in the predictive model
Step 5: Select and Transform Variables	Run descriptive analyses to assess correlations and potential multi-co-linearities. Transform some variables by creating binning or using transformation functions to increase their predictability.	There are several variables selection methods available in most of data analytics software that could be used to perform a preliminary selection of inputs variables.
Step 6: Process the Models	Once the previous steps are completed several machine learning techniques could be used including and not limited to: regression, Naïve Bayes, decision tree, random forest, SVM, neural network, rules base models, and the like. The best performing model is then selected based on the goodness of fit index and the alignment with your business goals and operational fit and risks.	At this stage, a variety of machine learning models/techniques should be run to determine the best performing model based on the fit and, more importantly, the underlying implementation efforts. What model is more actionable and more likely to have a successful implementation?
Step 7::Test and Validate the Model	Run the model against the test and validation samples to ensure it is generalizable, robust, and scalable.	Compared the goodness of fit indices of both the testing and the validation datasets before you proceed.

Exhibit 4.22 *(Continued)*

Model Steps	Overview	Comments/ Examples
Step 8: Implement the Model	Once the results are stable, meaning the training, validation, and testing datasets produce similar results, put together an implementation plan for the model. Socialize the model results and recommendations across the organization. This should be done conjointly with the business partners. Prioritization of proactive retention or acquisition activities is necessary, as you have limited resources and you want to retain or acquire only the most valuable customers. It is important to have a Target group and a Holdout group.	It is important to include business partner and end users in the beginning of the process so they can provide their input and get on board and become advocates of the predictive models. Getting business buy-in is critical for the change management and a successful implementation. The model output should be easy to access and available across all customer touchpoints and CRM system on simple clicks. The Holdout group will help to showcase the ROI of the model.
Step 9: Track the Model ROI	Measure the performance of the model versus defined ROI metrics	A couple of weeks or months after the model implementation, depending on your business, track the ROI. Measure the impact on the company's business goal and bottom line. Look at metrics such as increase in customer retention and customer conversion the lifetime value of retained customers, and the profitability of retained versus lost customers.

Exhibit 4.22   *(Continued)*

Text analytics such as text categorization, text summarization, and sentiment analysis (opinion analysis) should be performed to transform text-heavy variables into structured forms before they are included as a predictor in the model.

Predictive analytics will leverage all the data to assess correlation and causation between buying and usage behaviors, and quantitative and qualitative variables. Today, predictive analytics uses a variety of machine learning algorithms such as regression, neural network, decision tree, random forest, naïve Bayes, rules-based models, memory-based reasoning ensembles models, SVM, and gradient boosting, to just to name a few, to determine the importance of every variable as well as their prediction power.

APPLYING UDA TO YOUR SOCIAL MEDIA PRESENCE AND NATIVE ADS TO INCREASE ACQUISITIONS

Social Media Analytics

In today's globally connected market arena, it's undeniable that companies who have a social media strategy and use social media analytics in their customer acquisition and retention activities are outperforming their peers who choose to ignore or avoid them. A large body of studies provided evidence of the power of social media analytics for both B2B and business to consumer (B2C). And you probably wonder why.

Today more than 80 percent of customers research online before they buy.[10] Building and maintaining a good brand presence is no longer an option, but a necessity. It is paramount for businesses to have a great online presence and reputation in order to appeal to existing customers and attract new ones.

Studies show that more than 70 percent of B2B use at least one of the Big Four social media sites (Facebook, LinkedIn, Twitter, and YouTube) to distribute their content.[11]

At least 54 percent of B2B marketers have generated leads with social media marketing, and 40 percent of those who generated leads have generated revenue.[12] More than 77 percent of B2C and 43 percent of B2B have acquired new customers through Facebook.[13]

Given that the average American spends about three hours on social media per day, using social media provides companies with a wide window to get attention from potential customers. Today, Big Data enables companies to capture the digital footprints of their members and users. Social media service providers are putting together aggregated actionable insight information on their users, who could be your potential customers. These insights, when properly leveraged, can help you to better understand customer habits, needs, wants, and preferences. Armed with this knowledge, you can put together a tailored social media strategy to engage and interact with them directly, with relevant and appealing content. These actionable insights from social media analytics could be key drivers of your acquisition strategy to increase your market share or overall market penetration.

The Impact of UDA

Social media offers the opportunity to augment your statistics like the number of likes or followers with key performance indicators (KPIs) from behavioral data, such as buzzwords or topics related to your brand, your service, or your product.

Leading companies are using UDA to harness their social media data to listen, respond, engage, and address any potential pain points or dissatisfaction that consumers expressed regarding their product, service, or simply their overall brand. They are getting involved in social media discussions with their customers concerning their industry and their brand. They are also leveraging some brand advocates: people with strong social media presence and influence who can speak and promote the values of the brand.

Understanding the behavior of your customers should also help you to design the right messaging, the right ad, through the right channel, for the maximum impact on your company's KPIs such as customer satisfaction, net promoter score (NPS), and overall market penetration.

Social Media Analytics and Native Ads

Leveraging social media analytics can also help to better manage your brand advertising and develop native ads that are more cognizant of your customers' habits, needs, preferences, and wants. Some studies have shown that when the advertising is tied to native ads, customers begin to feel part of the experience. UDA can provide the right content, as discovered throughout their exploration of the entire customer journey. Machine learning can also help marketers to detect sentiment in their content before they publish it.

A study sponsored by Facebook found that consumers engage with native ads 20 to 60 percent more than standard banner ads.[14] Native ads are less likely to lead to user churn and ad fatigue. Native ads drive higher retention rates (up to 3×), effective cost per thousand impressions (up to 2×), and significant increase in click-through rates.

Social media analytics and native ads are essential supplements to a successful implementation of customer acquisition and retention predictive models to create business value for your organization.

KEY TAKEAWAYS

- Customers are more fickle and more technology savvy. They expect their service providers to listen to their voice and to make them part of product enhancement, services improvement, and in some cases new product development. They have high expectations from their service providers, as they are aware of what the competition is offering and can turn to it unless proactive actions take place.

- Today, consumers can openly share their overall experience with your product and services via phone conversations, e-mails, chats, satisfaction surveys, and social media platforms. They can express their grievances or satisfaction and provide insight regarding their needs, wants, preferences, and desires.

- Leading organizations are now leveraging structured and unstructured data to listen to and engage with their customers; enhance their products, improve their services, and develop their new products. They are also injecting UDA at every stage of their customer decision journey to optimize the outcome and create actionable value for their organizations and for their customers.

- With the influx of data created from user-generated data, marketing has been gradually embracing predictive analytics to better target who will buy and who will leave so they can optimize their marketing spend. Leading marketing organizations leverage key elements of VoC insights to enhance their proactive CRM activities and acquire, keep, protect, and grow their best customers.

- Big Data combined with computing power propelled machine learning and deep learning, enabling organizations to harness the VoC and create actionable value that improves not only customer retention but overall customer profitability. Social media analytics also help organizations address customer issues, such as online reputation and advocacy, in real time to protect and improve the company's brand and online reputation.

- Some leading organizations are also using UDA powered by AI and cognitive computing to provide a virtual assistant or virtual agent that can provide efficient and timely support to customers, while also freeing human service agents whose talent could be better used; the virtual assistant/agent can also reduce waiting and increase customer knowledge, customer engagement, and overall customer satisfaction.

■ Gone are the days where marketers had to rely on A/B testing tools to figure out the best lexical recipes for their campaigns. Today they can leverage UDA such as machine learning to perform advanced focused semantic and lexical analyses and help digital marketers understand the words and phrases and their conceptual and contextual usage to drive up customer engagement and increase response rate and conversion. Machine learning is also enabling forward-looking marketers to detect sentiment in their content before it gets published.

■ Predictive analytics powered by UDA help you to address the 4Ws: Who? When? Why? and What should we do? Using UDA to transform unstructured data into structured categories can improve predictive model accuracy and efficiency by double digits.

NOTES

1. The CMO Survey, February 2017: https://cmosurvey.org/results/february-2017/

2. Adam Sarner—Five Event-Triggered Marketing Steps Marketers Aren't Doing. Gartner For Marketers Blog: Gartner: https://blogs.gartner.com/adam-sarner/2013/02/05/5-event-triggered-marketing-steps-marketers-arent-doing/: Gartner study re: offers triggered by events.

3. Erik Sherman, "5 White-Collar Jobs Robots Already Have Taken," *Fortune*, February 25, 2015: http://fortune.com/2015/02/25/5-jobs-that-robots-already-are-taking/

4. Net present value is a measurement of the profitability of an undertaking that is calculated by subtracting the present values of cash outflows (including initial cost) from the present values of cash inflows over a period.

5. Paul Balmire, Machine Learning and Content Marketing: (Using Data to Turn Stale Content into Marketing Gold), presentation at Gilbane Digital Content Conference 2016; http://conferences.infotoday.com/documents/262/1330_Blamire.pdf: quote from Paul Blamire.

6. David Court, Dave Elzinga, Susan Mulder, and Ole Jorgen Vetvik, "The Consumer Decision Journey," *McKinsey Quarterly*, June 2009, www.mckinsey.com/insights/marketing_sales/the_consumer decision_journey

7. David C Edelman and Marc Singer, "Competing on Customer Journeys," *Harvard Business Review*, November 2015: https://hbr.org/2015/11/competing-on-customer-journeys

8. David C. Edelman, "Branding in the Digital Age: You're Spending Your Money in All the Wrong Places," *Harvard Business Review*, December 2010: https://hbr.org/2010/12/branding-in-the-digital-age-youre-spending-your-money-in-all-the-wrong-places

9. Ask Watson: Changing the Way Business Engage with Customers: https://storify.com/ibmevents/ask-watson-changing-the-way-business-engage-custom.html: quote from Manoj Saxena, IBM Watson Solutions.

10. Karen Kerski, "Why Diversity Your Brand Marketing?" Catalpha website: http://blog.catalpha.com/bid/323805/Why-diversify-your-brand-marketing

11. Digital Marketing Philippines, "Infographic: 10 Reasons to Diversify Your Digital Marketing Efforts," Digital Marketing Philippines website: http://digitalmarketingphilippines.com/10-reasons-to-diversify-your-digital-marketing-efforts/

12. Rick Whittington, "5 Statistics about B2B Demand Generation with Social Media That You Need to Know," Digital Marketing Trends, Whittington Consulting website: www.rickwhittington.com/blog/b2b-demand-generation-with-social-media/

13. eMerge, "Infographic: Facebook for Business," Visual.ly: https://visual.ly/community/infographic/social-media/facebook-business-0

14. Yoav Arnstein, "Native Advertising Will Be the Majority of Mobile by 2020," News and Insights, Audience Network by Facebook, April 5, 2016: www.facebook.com/audiencenetwork/news-and-insights/future-of-mobile-advertising-is-native

CHAPTER **5**

The Power of UDA to Improve Fraud Detection and Prevention

If you torture the data long enough, it will confess to anything.

—Ronald Coase, Nobel Prize winner in Economics

INTRODUCTION

In today's globally connected arena, thanks to social media, the Internet, cloud computing, mobile connectivity, and Big Data, we can instantly share who we are, where we are, what we are doing, what we will do, and with whom! We are constantly leaving digital traces that include information about our behavior, intent, needs, preferences, and likes. Everything we do in this connected ecosystem is digitized, and this digital data, when properly mined or simply linked to other data, can provide evidence to detect and prevent

157

fraudulent behavior for businesses, organizations, and government institutions.

I remember the story of Jennifer, a financial adviser at my local bank, who three years ago, got from her doctor a six-month sick leave, granting her 80 percent of her salary paid by her employer. According to her doctor, Jennifer required mandatory rest without any sports or activities. Unfortunately for Jennifer, two weeks later the human resources (HR) benefits manager discovered via her Facebook connection that Jennifer was having good time at Salt Lake City, skiing and going to the local night club several times a week. Jennifer had been posting several photos of herself skiing, drinking, and dancing late at the bar with friends. The HR department was informed and decided to take a closer look at Jennifer's files. The HR business partner discovered from Jennifer's business e-mails that she had planned her sick leave the year before, in collusion with the physician. The insurance company was informed, and discovered that the physician had a record of delivering such sick leave notes. After a comprehensive investigation, the evidence helped HR to conclude that Jennifer was on a fraudulent leave; she was subsequently terminated, and her physician faced disciplinary sanctions. This example shows how social media provided actionable insights for fraud suspicion and detection. You would probably agree there are numerous cases where a digital footprint has placed people in trouble, whether in their private or professional lives.

Most insurance companies use fraud detection models that mostly leverage information from their internal data warehouse. This means fraudulent cases like Jennifer's would go undetected. Cross-referencing internal data with other sources of data, such as unstructured data from social media like Facebook (updates or photos) or YouTube, is necessary for effective fraud detection. In this chapter, we will explore how unstructured data analysis (UDA) can help to improve fraud detection and prevention, when combined with existing models that leverage structured data. We will also provide some frontline stories from companies like JPMorgan Chase, John Hancock Financial Services, and AXA.

WHY SHOULD YOU CARE ABOUT UDA FOR FRAUD DETECTION AND PREVENTION?

Gone are the days where fraud detection was based on a sample of cases monitored and tracked for abnormal behavior trends or patterns, where a team of fraud analysts, agents, or investigators had to read warranty notes, insurance claims, consumer claims narratives, and e-mail threads, or listen to audio tape, or compare images to uncover fraudulent activities. With UDA tools and software, machine learning and deep learning solutions such as facial recognition combined with biometry data analysis, organizations and businesses can better detect and anticipate fraud while preserving a favorable digital experience for their consumers.

According to a study from the Coalition Against Insurance Fraud, more than 90 percent of insurers are using anti-fraud technology.[1] The U.S. National Insurance Crime Bureau (NICB) recorded a 24 percent increase in questionable claims for the period 2011 to 2013, noting that the full scale of insurance fraud is not known.[2] According to companies I spoke to, the following are key reasons why we should care about UDA when managing fraud.

Unstructured Data Is a Goldmine of Evidence for Fraud Detection and Prevention

Most useful information for insurance companies is buried within text-heavy data. Insurance companies collect, process, and generate mountains of text data from claimant interview notes, adjuster reports and notes, customer service call logs, and e-mails. As indicated previously, unstructured text data represents more than 85 percent of claim data. UDA will help to normalize the text data from the claim, parse it, apply filters and linguistic rules, and analyze the data to get a deeper understanding of the claims. It also offers the opportunity to analyze huge amounts of text data available within social media. Today investigators use Facebook, YouTube, and other social media to find evidence of suspicious claims.

When attorneys general, Securities and Exchange Commission (SEC) agents, regulators, or government investigators need to pursue lawsuits or other forensic financial or accounting fraud investigations, such as insider trading, stock options back dating, bribery, forgery, or money laundering, they start with information such as e-mails, phone call logs, instant messaging logs, and a variety of electronic documents and files. They look for links or correlations that might indicate fraudulent activities. Unstructured data is the starting point, as it often entails most of the behavioral inputs. Analytics of this data will not only help to detect fraud but will also speed up the process of the entire investigation, freeing up resources for other investigative actions.

Cost Savings, Productivity, and Performance Gains

To stay ahead of the curve and detect fraud at an early stage, in real time, leading companies are looking for patterns of fraudulent behavior in internal, external, and third-party data. With UDA, they can perform analysis of data in multiple formats, helping their customer touchpoints such as underwriters, customer service agents, adjusters, and call center agents make real-time, fact-based decisions and process legitimate claims efficiently. UDA increases the productivity of underwriters who would normally require days or sometimes weeks to assess a claim. UDA also helps to reduce fraud losses. Some studies suggested that in e-commerce fraud, losses as a percentage of revenue range between .85 percent and .9 percent. Since according to a Forrester study U.S. online sales will reach $414 billion by 2018,[3] this means that without improvement in fraud loss rate, U.S. e-commerce fraud will increase to approximately $3.6 billion.

Consequently, organizations that are using UDA to analyze complex data such as insurance claims, financial transactions, or healthcare claims are getting unprecedented return on investment (ROI), in processing time for legitimate claims and fraud loss minimization. Combined with structured data analytics, UDA helps organizations look for historical behavior patterns and trends of claimants to identify similarities or dissimilarities and single out atypical claims early in the process, thereby reducing the number of resources and manpower required to analyze and investigate claims.

According to the Forrester estimation, keeping fraud detection rates level, automating fraud analysis and the initial steps of investigation, companies save between 30 and 40 percent of the labor costs of analysts and investigators.[4]

Help to Fully Leverage the Power of Predictive Analytics and Big Data

UDA provides a comprehensive overview of fraud by helping organizations to address and explain the Who? Where? When? Why? and What needs to be done? including:

- Who is/was involved?
- Why does a fraud exist?
- Where is the fraud coming from?
- How did the fraud develop?
- What are the risks for the organization?
- What should the enterprise do to address and prevent fraud?

Predictive analytics powered by deep learning leverage all the data, structured and unstructured, to anticipate fraud. Companies that leverage both types of data can better detect fraud before it becomes chaos for the management team, and can act proactively in addressing fraudulent behavior.

Handling fraud manually is extremely costly for businesses such as insurance companies. The emergence of Big Data has created the growth in unstructured data, leaving room for fraud activities to go unchecked if organizations do not thoroughly analyze their data. UDA has a potential to provide a tremendous benefit by helping organizations such as insurance companies to detect, predict, and decrease attempted fraud by identifying fraudulent claims at early stages of loss, when an underwriter, adjuster, or fraud analyst would be required to evaluate the legitimacy of a claim and quickly process it. Insurance companies, banks, e-commerce businesses, financial institutions, and retailers need to balance consumer digital experience with fraud prevention; this means facing the dilemma of overweighting false positives or false negatives. For instance, if a bank blocks transactions it deems suspicious to reduce fraud losses, it might anger customers trying to complete legitimate transactions. These angered customers might turn to the competition. However, if the bank leaves those transactions unchallenged, it might increase the bank's fraud losses.

I personally experienced this dilemma with my previous bank. I was required to clear all my online flight bookings before completing a transaction; otherwise, the transaction would be blocked on my corporate credit card. After experiencing this three times in a single month, I contacted the bank and explained their fraud detection model was ineffective, but to no avail. Irritated, I switched to the competition. Good UDA that leverages all the data and historical information could have avoided this problem.

Realize the Untapped Big Data Opportunity

Most of the risk managers, fraud experts, and actuaries I spoke to during my research believe that UDA will provide huge benefits by helping to better anticipate and decrease cases of fraud. This should help organizations to reduce some losses at the early stage related to fraudulent claims.

Digital information is created every day. Every minute, more than 204 million e-mails are sent/received, 700,000 pieces of content are shared on Facebook, 20 million photos are shared with Flickr, 4 million search queries are made through Google, and 500 hours of videos are uploaded. This data has yet to be analyzed and yield meaningful behavioral insights.

For insurance companies, UDA will help identify fraudulent claims at a very early stage, such as first claims, accident reports, or notices of loss. This work is generally conducted by the insurance manager, risk manager, or underwriter. Insurance companies and financial institutions must meet customer expectations and maintain business readiness and productivity. Manual systems processing and analyzing huge amounts of complex information just can't keep up with the speed of digital transactions and meet customer expectations. UDA offers the potential to create actionable value from Big Data.

Address Weaknesses of Existing Fraud Detection Techniques

We can no longer afford to use old approaches to detect and predict fraud. Approaches based on sampling tended to focus on known fraudulent behavior. These approaches used siloed technology, and lacked governance and data integration across multiple sources, applications, and systems. For instance, companies identified a sample of data or list of customers to investigate based upon previous fraud analyses. Then a group of fraud analysts would manually review suspicious cases across multiple systems. They could request inquiries and legal action if the case ended up being a fraud. However, the detection of low incidence fraud (less than 0.001%) is essentially impossible with a sampling method.

Leveraging machine learning such as Naïve Bayes, neural network, link analysis, and deep learning new approaches enables analysis of the entire universe of transaction cases. Transactions from internal, external, and third-party sources such as e-mail, call logs, social media, chats, instant messaging, and documents are used to identify fraudulent behavior. The new approach and technique can analyze images, audio, videos, and text and can combine facial recognition and biometric data to detect and prevent fraud. Currently, the most critical unstructured information about fraud is not usually analyzed. Traditional approaches are not leveraging the power of Big Data and its unstructured content. These outdated methods only focus on internal data contained in enterprise data warehouses.

Ingesting all the untapped unstructured data and all the transactions and unleashing the power of predictive analytics would help detect and prevent fraud in an unprecedented way.

BENEFITS OF UDA

■ Improve existing approaches by supplementing them with the analysis of all the transactions to detect and predict fraud. Help to enhance existing efforts by adding an extra layer to your existing fraud detection and prevention.

■ Leverage the power of unstructured data and improve the performance and productivity of the organization.

■ Provide centralized view of customers by integrating data from a variety of sources (internal and external) to create an enterprise-wide view of the customer.

■ Identify complex patterns and behaviors that could remain unchecked due to their low incidence (e.g., less than 0.001%), and detect and prevent fraudulent activities.

■ Master all the available data: Use UDA to integrate all pieces of data—internal, external, and third-party—to create a comprehensive view of fraud patterns and behaviors.

■ Identify rogue employee behavior. Some leading companies have heavily invested in systems to predict fraud from their own employees, fraud that, even if it only involved a few employees, could cost billions of dollars.

■ Reduce costs associated with fraud (fraudulent insurance claims, fraudulent medical bills, fraudulent financial transactions).

■ Improve productivity, competitiveness, business readiness, and profitability of organizations.

■ Improve brand awareness, trust, and confidence from its shareholders and consumers.

Huge Costs If Left Unchecked/Huge Savings in Fraud Losses

Fraud costs billions of dollars to business organizations every year. Wherever there is a lot of money at stake, there is a high likelihood that fraudulent activities will emerge, and no organization or sector is spared. Insurance, healthcare, finance, banking, telecommunications, and online retail report fraudulent behaviors that have been costing them billions of dollars every year. With the speed at which the data is shared and the information is interrelated and unchecked, undetected fraud can quickly become viral and cause significant damage to organizations. Fraud brings not only a very high financial cost, but also psychological stress for businesses, organizations, governments, and society.

Let's quickly review how fraud impacts several industries today.

Banking and Finance

Theft and credit fraud activities have been on the rise. Losses reached $16 billion in the United States in 2016. According to Javelin Strategy & Research, card not present (CNP) fraud rose by 40 percent in 2016, and the number of identify fraud cases rose to 16 percent in 2016,[5] costing victims $16 billion in losses (see Exhibit 5.01).[6] By leveraging real-time data to build fraud predictive models, and by combining new data such as facial recognition data and biometric data to determine whether a transaction is fraudulent, UDA can bring value to counteract these fraud activities.

As fraudsters evolve and change the way they operate, UDA helps to better prevent financial fraud such as:

- Insider trading information used and disclosure
- Forgeries or alteration of checks, bank drafts, and financial documents
- Fraudulent and dishonest acts

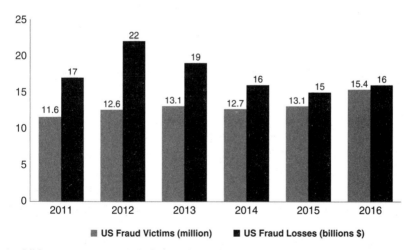

Exhibit 5.01   U.S. Fraud Victims and Fraud Losses
Source: 2017 U.S. Identity Fraud Study, *Javelin Strategy and Research*

- Misappropriation of assets
- Wrongful use of influence in business transactions to receive benefit; bribery
- Deliberately improper reporting of money
- Merger-and-acquisition fraud

Using UDA, a company tracked down a customer who, according to his Facebook update, was supposedly traveling to Sydney. He made three attempts to withdraw cash in New York while he was supposed to be on the flight to Sydney. His bank's fraud management system proactively stopped the fraudulent transaction, denied the withdrawals, and blocked the account.

In the United States, billions are spent every year on dealing with fraud. The largest investment bank, JP Morgan Chase, has spent more than $9 billion on litigation since the recession in 2008, mostly to deal with rogue employee behavior. The company decided in 2015 to invest more than $835 million to detect and prevent fraudulent behavior.

E-commerce

As discussed previously, according to several studies, e-commerce fraud loss as a percentage of revenue ranges between 0.85 percent and 0.9 percent. Forrester predicts U.S. online sales will reach $414 billion by 2018. Without improvement in fraud loss rate, U.S. e-commerce fraud will increase to approximately $3.6 billion by 2018.

Healthcare

According to Thornton, van Capelleveen, Poel, van Hillegersberg, and Mueller, every year, more than $700 billion is spent in the U.S. healthcare system due to fraud, waste, and abuse.[7] Advanced analytics approaches can help to find organizations and citizens who abuse the systems. Methods such as outliers, network analysis, and link analysis enable the connection of different pieces of data to find relationship and root cause, identifying abnormal clusters and abnormal links between clusters.

Insurance

In the United States, the FBI estimates the total cost of insurance fraud (non-health insurance) at more than $40 billion per year. That means insurance fraud costs the average U.S. family between $400 and $700 per year in the form of increased premiums.[8]

Today's fraudsters are evolving and changing their practices, becoming sophisticated in finding new ways to access customers' and decision makers' information and communication tools. Most insurance organizations have solid models to detect fraud based upon transactional data. The value added for the insurance companies is to leverage all the unstructured and semistructured data to augment their accuracy and efficiency in fraud detection and predictions. Insurance claim data can now be merged with external data found in social media such as Facebook, Twitter, and Instagram to better understand the behavior and validity of a claim request. They can power the analysis with real-time analytics software to detect and predict fraudulent behaviors. For instance, one of the insurers I spoke with mentioned that thanks to UDA, personal injuries claims based upon staged accidents, fake doctor visits, and fake medical claims could be detected. When a claimant who has been witnessed in previous claims calls in, thanks to historical data analysis and regional and alias matching, alerts can be sent to customer service. With social media analysis, images can help to detect a fraudulent claim—like the claimant who reported his motorbike was totally flooded while at the same time posting on his Facebook public profile a photo of his motorbike in a friendly race with friends.

Without UDA, it would take months for companies to process all daily transactions, billions around the world, and social media activities, internal, external, and third-party data to detect fraudulent behavior. UDA provides the analytical arsenal to harness key input variables from structured data and, more importantly, unstructured data to detect, understand, and predict future fraudulent activities from insurance claims, healthcare benefits, financial banking, and retail transactions.

WHAT IS UDA FOR FRAUD?

UDA applied to fraud answers these business-related questions:

- Is the current insurance claim fraudulent or legitimate?
- Is the medical bill fraudulent?
- Is the current online credit card transaction fraudulent?
- Is the healthcare benefit transaction illegal?
- Is the credit card payment occurring fraudulent?
- Is the merger and acquisition suspicious?
- Is the organization complying with country regulations?
- Was the timing of stock options manipulated (stock back-dating)?

Fraud UDA combines UDA techniques and technology with human interactions to better detect potential fraudulent activities, from improper transactions to rogue employee behavior like forgery, money laundering, fraud, or bribery, either before the transactions are completed or shortly after they occur.

The process of UDA applied to fraud involves gathering and integrating all relevant data and mining it for patterns, discrepancies, and anomalies and providing actionable insights to underwriters and claim adjusters to turn the insights into actions and results.

The combination of tools, techniques, and human interactions helps business to put in place a fraud management system that helps to not only detect but prevent future frauds before they happen.

Organizations I spoke with are using four major approaches to detect fraud:

- Reactive
- Proactive
- Manual
- Automated

Exhibit 5.02 summarizes the UDA for fraud detection and prevention.

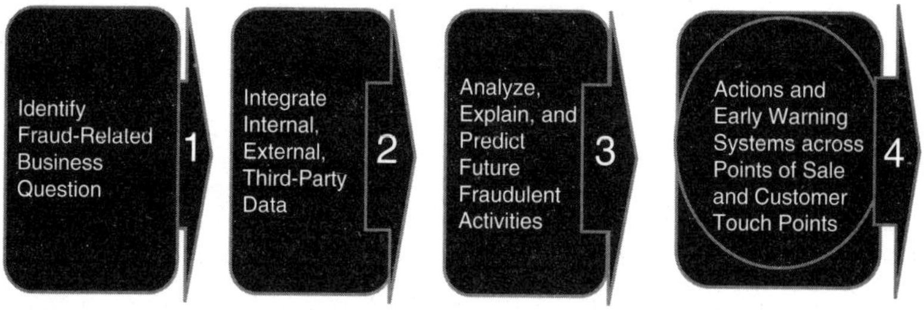

Exhibit 5.02 UDA Process for Fraud Detection and Prevention

1. *Identify* fraud-related business. Questions include:

   ■ Is the current insurance claim fraudulent?

   ■ Is the current credit card transaction illegal?

   ■ Is the credit card application form staged?

   ■ Is the healthcare medical bill illegal?

2. *Integrate* internal, external, and third-party data:

   ■ Internal data includes customer's or claimant's personal information: name, date of birth, Social Security number, mailing address, e-mail address, bank information, telephone, IP geolocation

   ■ External data includes: social media data, Facebook, Twitter, YouTube, weather data, wages

   ■ Third-party data includes: public records, liens, fraud watch list, credit bureau report, medical billing, industry consortium of claims, past claims, credit bureau records

3. *Analyze and predict* using predictive models:

   This step leverages machine learning such as logistic regression, Naïve Bayes, decision tree, neural network, text analytics, and the social media network analytics, harnessing the three sets of data to understand past fraudulent behavior and anticipate future fraud. Perhaps more importantly, the use of unsupervised algorithms can detect new types of frauds, using techniques such as the outlier detection method with deep learning techniques that combine facial recognition and biometric data. The findings are then translated into insights that enable a company to act and manage potential threats before they occur, as well as develop a proactive fraud and bribery detection environment. With the actionable insights from UDA and machine learning, adjusters, underwriters, and other fraud investigators can quickly process cases such as claims and improve the overall decision-making process, preserving the consumer experience whether online or offline.

4. *Act* or issue early warnings:

Once investigators or adjusters receive the information related to the claim, they can act based on the severity and risk it represents. The claimant could be subject to an inquiry or he/she could receive the requested payment.

HOW UDA WORKS IN FRAUD DETECTION AND PREVENTION

To fully understand how UDA works in fraud detection and prevention, it is useful to review traditional fraud detection and prevention methods. Those methods leverage mostly structured data and are based on sampling, investigation, and recommendation.

The traditional methods are based on sampling and may include reactive or proactive means of detection.

Sampling

In most enterprises and organizations, the fraud department starts by selecting a sample of transactions or customers with suspicious behavior, based upon their previous patterns. A sample of the total populations is randomly selected for further investigation. Fraud analysts and specialists will look for anomalies, trends, and patterns based upon business-defined rules. The limitations of sampling, due to the manual process, prevent all transactions from being investigated. Unfortunately, in a globally connected arena, fraud does not appear randomly, and lower incidence activities will likely remain undetected.

Reactive (hypothesis based): This approach leverages hypothesized rules to assess whether a given transaction meets the normal criteria;

the transaction may be rejected or accepted, or a flag may be raised for further investigation. This is based on Boolean logic rules (IF condition met THEN category selected).

Ongoing Analysis: Continuing analysis of fraudulent activities based on running an algorithm against incoming transactions detects those that appear to be fraudulent.

Benford's Law

Benford's law (also known as the first-digit law or Benford's distribution) is an observation about the frequency distribution of leading digits in many real-life sets of numerical data. The law states that in many naturally occurring collections of numbers, the leading significant digit is likely to be small.

For example, the first digit of:

- 178934 is 1
- 956 is 9

Benford's distribution is non-uniform, with smaller digits being more likely than larger digits. For example, in sets that obey the law, the number 1 appears as the most significant digit about 30 percent of the time, while the number 9 appears as the most significant digit less than 5 percent of the time. If the digits were distributed uniformly, they would each occur about 11.1 percent of the time. This law also makes predictions about the distribution of the other digits in the sequence, and digit combinations. Benford's law can often be used as an indicator of fraudulent data, and can assist with auditing accounting data.

Investigations: A team of analysts then performs several behavioral analyses on the target sample. If the claim is justified, no action is undertaken. If the claim or behavioral activities appear illegal, a legal action could be recommended.

Recommendations

Generally, a recommendation will be made to either provide benefit payments or engage in legal actions against the fraudster.

Internal Data	External Data + Third-Party Data
■ Demographics	■ Customer sales
■ Name	■ Inventory
■ Address	■ Labor hours
■ Date of birth	■ Accounts payable
■ Social Security number	■ Customer call logs
■ E-mail address	■ Customer claim reports
■ IP geographic location	■ E-mails, calendars, and contacts
■ Payments	■ Text messaging and instant messaging
■ Billing address	■ Voice mail
■ Shipping address	■ Encrypted files and messages
■ Payment behavior	■ Internet history files (e-mail file transmissions, website visits, system access)
■ Device	
■ Social media	■ Documents, presentations
■ Carrier model data	■ Images, audio, and video files
■ Account validation	■ Cell phone and vehicle location data
■ Call center notes	■ Social media profile (Facebook, Instagram, Google+, LinkedIn, Twitter)
■ Attorney cost	
■ Claim files	■ Niche sites (Stackoverflow, GitHub)
■ Spreadsheet	■ Social influence
■ Policy holder file	■ Expert blog forum and user forum
■ Flat file	■ Opinion sites (Glassdoor, Kununu, Amazon, ZDnet)
■ Memo and footnotes	
■ Meeting notes	■ IP location and GPS data
■ Documents and images archives	■ Newspaper articles and whitepapers
■ Phone call logs	■ Aggregated databases: government, wikis
■ Call handler notes	
■ Internal e-mails	■ Liens
■ Fraud agency report	■ Bankruptcies
■ Journal	■ Criminal records
■ Social media platform	■ Address change velocity
■ Newsfeeds	■ Judgments
■ External e-mails	■ Foreclosures
■ Graph intelligence	■ Wages
■ Voice recording	■ Weather

Exhibit 5.03 Historical and Real-Time Data to Review

The new approach with UDA is not limited to a sample of transactions. It leverages the power of Big Data analytics, data integration, and predictive analytics to analyze all transactions in real time or near-real time and make actionable recommendations to the business to detect and predict future fraudulent behaviors.

Today, thanks to UDA, insurance companies can incorporate a variety of data from social media, streaming content, and e-mails to provide real-time views of claims to their customer touchpoints, thereby helping companies quickly resolve some claims and litigations payments.

Underwriters in insurance companies cannot efficiently gather and process all the data they have available to make informed decisions. Exhibit 5.03 provides an example of the data at the disposal of companies. UDA, powered by predictive models, harnesses historical data and real-time data.

UDA FRAMEWORK FOR FRAUD DETECTION AND PREVENTION: INSURANCE

In the following section, we will describe how the fraud detection and prediction framework using UDA works to identify insurance fraud. The framework includes five steps, as depicted in Exhibit 5.04.

Step 1: Claimant Report (Narrative)

In this step, a claimant reports his/her claim over the phone talking to an insurance agent. The claim could be about a car accident involving one or several drivers, a home catastrophe such as flooding, or a medical bill from a treatment. This report is generally audio, and the underwriter will usually store all the conversation in the insurance company's claim files/reports. The claimant could also send additional files, such as photos of the car accident, photos of the flooded house, or copies of the medical bill.

Step 2: Underwriter Report (Text-Heavy)

The underwriter will then write the report from the claimant interview(s), adding some interview notes and comments. The underlying

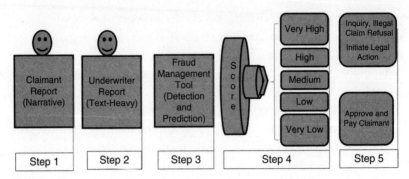

Exhibit 5.04 Fraud Detection and Prediction Framework Using UDA

report will also include all the claimants or people involved in the accident, their recounts of the event, and, more importantly, all the notes, e-mails, and interviews. The underwriter report is text-heavy, and understandably so; it is very cumbersome to manually go through thousands or millions of these reports.

Step 3: Fraud Management Tool (Detection and Prediction)

Once the underwriter's information report is entered in the insurance company datawarehouse, the fraud management system integrates the text-heavy report along with the claimant information to analyze the claim. The data is integrated with internal, external, and third-party data in this next step. Adding information about the claimant from the enterprise fraud management system can help answer questions such as:

- Does the claimant name and profile information match with internal data, including aliases, etc.?
- Has the claimant made any claims in the past?
- How many claims have been accepted or denied in the past?
- Is the claim on the hot list?
- What types of activities are associated with the claimant?
- Is the claimant on any public record, such as a fraud watch list, or medical billing data?

- What do the business rules recommend about the claims?
- Does the visualization of the distribution of claims detect outliers?
- Is the claim above or below the threshold?

If the threshold is exceeded, then an event is reported for investigation. If the transaction claim is a single outlier, this can indicate a new fraud pattern.

The text-heavy report is then mined using the *text analytics technique*. As previously noted, more than 85 percent of the most useful information for insurance organizations is buried in the text-heavy claim report, so the fraud management system processes those claims by adding additional claims information, such as claimant interviews, e-mails, and underwriter notes. This text is parsed to distill meaningful data, which is then analyzed to extract deep-dive understanding of the claim. Once the text analytics is completed, categorization and sentiment can be derived.

The analysis extends to social media data available on Facebook, Twitter, and YouTube. Fraud management systems perform social network link analysis to determine abnormal clusters as well as atypical links between clusters that will require some attention. *Social network analytics* (SNA) leverages a combination of statistical analytics, pattern analysis, network linkage, and company business rules to harness the huge amounts of data that show relationships between nodes, links, and clusters. The fraud management system can also perform social customer relationship management (CRM) analytics, combining existing CRM information with social media platforms, such as a social media listening tool, and feeding the resulting insights to the fraud management system's case management. This could trigger an alert inquiry to the investigator.

The third system embedded is *predictive analytics*, which harnesses all the data to anticipate future claim events or predict the outcomes of events. As soon as new claim data is entered in the system, the fraud management system is updated, and the claim is automatically scored according to its likelihood of being fraudulent. The underlying score is available for review. Predictive analytics is the most efficient and effective way to detect and prevent fraud, as it processes a variety of data sources and formats that would require an underwriter or fraud analyst weeks or months to manually process.

Step 3 leverages techniques and technologies such as:

- Text analytics
- Sentiment analytics
- Content categorization
- Social network link analytics
- Social CRM
- Predictive analytics

Step 4: Scoring and Classification Outputs

A fraud propensity score is then generated that is combined with company business rules. To limit the complexity of such scores, I usually recommend transforming the score into fraud likelihood segments ranging from Very High to Very Low.

Very High and High scores identify claims to report to investigators; Low and Very Low scores will lead to claim payment decisions.

Step 5: Decisions and Actions

Once investigators or adjusters receive the classification of the claim from the fraud management system, they can act based on the severity of the fraud score ranking and the underlying business rules. As mentioned, the claimant will either be subject to an inquiry or he/she will receive the requested payment.

MAJOR FRAUD DETECTION AND PREVENTION TECHNIQUES

The main techniques used to detect and prevent fraud are presented in Exhibit 5.05, along with their strengths and weaknesses.

Techniques	Examples/Definition	Strengths/Weaknesses
Machine Learning/ Predictive Analytics	Regression Neural Network Naïve Bayes Decision Tree	Analyze all the data, detect low incidence fraud. Help to detect and anticipate fraudulent activities leveraging the power of Big Data analytics with all its influx of data from various sources and formats.
Text Mining	Perform variety of analyses of data to detect and prevent fraud, such as: ■ Text Categorization ■ Text Clustering ■ Sentiment Analysis	Harness the meaning of unstructured text data buried in company claim reports.
Social Network	Leverage combination of ■ statistical analysis and pattern analysis ■ network link analysis and company business rules	Connect internal and external data. Find hidden patterns and clusters to look at and identify how those clusters are related to other data. It is very effective to analyze data from variety of sources.
Social CRM	Leverages combination of social media platform listening tool and existing CRM.	Very powerful approach that is more up-to-date to leverage a 360-degree view of customer data. When combined with social network, could help to detect and prevent fraud through internal and external data sources and maximize the outcome.
Ongoing Detection	Run the ongoing script against all the data to detect fraud instances as they occur.	Add consistencies and efficiency layer to fraud detection process.
Business Rules/Alerts	Set up some business rules and alerts based upon existing fraud occurrences.	Quickly catch existing fraud.
Sampling	Select a sample of transactions or customers with suspicious behavior based upon previous patterns.	Could be good to use when you have a lot of data in the target population and not enough bandwidth nor technical resources to analyze the data. Shortcoming: the random sampling of the population might miss low occurrence instances of fraud (which are not random).

Exhibit 5.05   Fraud Detection and Prevention Techniques

Techniques	Examples/Definition	Strengths/Weaknesses
Ad Hoc Hypothesis	Based upon some hypothesis testing to determine fraudulent behaviors or transactions; leverages some existing fraud knowledge to define hypothesis to be tested.	Is efficient in detecting existing frauds; will probably miss new forms of fraud that have not yet been observed, so there are no existing hypotheses to evaluate or catch them.
Matching Gap Duplicate	Looks for data that matches similar data from other sources and evaluates whether the match is suspicious. Assesses whether there are gaps, meaning finding cases where data sequence is suspiciously missing. Duplicate transactions might be fraudulent or due to simple errors.	Very easy to implement. Very efficient and effective approach; but will probably miss fraud instances in which multiple sources of data, such as social media data combined with internal data, are to be analyzed.
Outlier/ Anomaly Detection	Define baseline and threshold for fraud key performance indicator (KPI). If threshold is exceeded, event is reported.	Helps determine existing and new fraud. Has some weaknesses, as it does not integrate multiple sources of data to be tested.
Benford's Law	Benford's distribution is non-uniform, with smaller digits being more likely than larger digits. Benford's law can often be used as an indicator of fraudulent data and can assist with auditing accounting data.	Helps to test whether a given set of numbers or KPIs appear more frequently than they are supposed to, and classifies them as potential fraud cases for further investigation.

Exhibit 5.05   *Continued*

To better explain how UDA works for fraud detection and prevention, we will use the IMPACT cycle table showing how the cycle is applied to insurance claims (Exhibit 5.06). The UDA process could also be applied to a variety of industries and sectors beyond the insurance industry, such as healthcare, finance and banking, and retail.

Identify	Master	Provide	Act	Communicate	Track
Identify the claims or transactions to process	Master the data by integrating the claim data of transactional data with other internal, external, and third party data	Provide Meaning Leverage: ■ Machine Learning ■ Sentiment Analysis ■ Text Analytics ■ Social Network Analytics ■ Social CRM ■ Predictive Analytics to score or classify the claim/ transaction	Once the transaction is scored, have customer's touchpoint act on the findings and make recommendations Investigate Make payment or initiate a lawsuit	Communicate the results of the investigation and analytics and make them available through customer touchpoints and systems Set up alerts	Measure the early warning system performance

Exhibit 5.06 IMPACT Cycle Table: Insurance Claims

BEST PRACTICES USING UDA FOR FRAUD DETECTION AND PREVENTION

In this section we discuss the best practices for leveraging UDA to detect and prevent fraud, recommended by leading experts with whom I spoke during my research for this book.

Assess Your Current Fraud Management System

Identify and prioritize your fraud risk profile:

■ What are the key fraudulent activities or issues you would like to focus on?

■ Do you have sufficient resources?

■ Do you have an enterprise fraud management system?

■ What business rules are in place to fight fraud?

■ Are the business rules scalable? Could they be linked to external or third-party data?

■ What tools and techniques are you using?

■ How are you storing your data?

■ Do you capture unstructured data?

■ What are the strengths, weaknesses, and opportunities of your current fraud management system?

■ Can your current system keep up with the velocity of the volume and the variety of the transactions and provide actionable meanings to detect and prevent fraud?

■ Does the current system harness all the data to address risk and fraud questions?

■ Does your fraud management system meet and exceed customer expectations in a reasonable timeframe?

■ Does your current fraud management system efficiently monitor the actual fraud risk?

If you want to get more information about tools and software, Exhibit 5.07 shows Forrester's assessment of key players in fraud management.

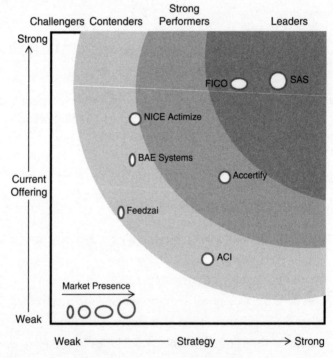

Exhibit 5.07 Forrester: Enterprise Fraud Solutions Providers
Source: Adapted from Andras Cser with Stephanie Balaouras, Alexander Spiliotes, and Peggy Dostie. The Forrester Wave™: Enterprise Fraud Management, Q1 2016: The Seven Providers That Matter Most and How They Stack Up, *Forrester: January 27, 2016*[9]

Master Your Data

Integrate all pieces of data about your customers and market (internal, external, and third-party data) to improve the efficiency and accuracy of your fraud management system and detect fraudulent activities at an early stage. This will help your organization to save time and money, ensure your key resources provide timely support to legitimate cases, and increase the satisfaction and profitability of your customers. Is there new data you need to capture? Most companies I spoke to, even if they have a fraud management system, still have very siloed data; this affects their efficiency and efficacy in detecting and preventing frauds in a timely manner.

Provide Actionable Meanings

With available data such as e-mails, call center log, social media information, customers' narratives and reviews, and social media posts and updates, the best way to leverage UDA for fraud is to build advanced analytics solutions that use predictive analytics. This includes using structured and unstructured data analytics, social analytics, social CRM analytics, social network analytics, and predictive models to uncover new opportunities to better detect and predict fraud.

Social network analytics can help connect multiple pieces of data nodes links regarding the claimant, including social media and third-party data such as public record bankruptcies, judgments, criminal records, foreclosures, address change velocity, and liens, to uncover outliers and inconsistencies and enrich the existing fraud-scoring model. Advanced analytics should help to define fraud indicators.

Company Employee Value Proposition and Culture Fit

The business culture (based upon the size, the employee policies and privacy, the region, and the demographics) and the employee value proposition of your organization should be taken into consideration to ensure the fraud management system fits. It is important to assess operational environments and address any legal concerns that could arise from the fraud management system. Identify a dream team that covers fraud with specific roles and responsibilities.

Define Policies and Confidentialities

For many organizations, and depending on the culture, privacy could be a concern. Companies are encouraged to seek legal counsel to ensure that fraud detection and prevention systems and techniques such as data monitoring are consistent with local jurisdictions.

INTERVIEW WITH VISHWA KOLLA, ASSISTANT VICE PRESIDENT ADVANCED ANALYTICS AT JOHN HANCOCK FINANCIAL SERVICES

I had the opportunity to discuss UDA for fraud detection and prevention with Vishwa Kolla, the assistant vice president, advanced analytics at John Hancock Financial Services.

Isson: What made your company decide to invest in UDA/Big Data to detect and prevent fraud?

Kolla: *Fraud detection and prevention are a common problem with big impact, and to be efficiently addressed, they require a combination of analytics, business insights, and the ability to take timely action. Fraud detection starts with suspicion. You start with, for example, one hundred suspicious cases, and only three of those could end up being fraudulent. You need to go through tons of factors to test and evaluate some business hypotheses in a time-sensitive way. Having tons of factors where only few are real drivers of fraudulent activity and analyzing them would not be possible by a person. You need a combination of person and machine intelligences to improve efficiency—to get through tons of suspicious cases. Analytics is a key component. It all starts with business hypotheses that are then turned into models leveraging current techniques.*

Isson: The majority of organizations I've spoken with have told me UDA is the next frontier of fraud advanced analytics innovation to detect and prevent fraud. Would you agree?

Kolla: *There is a lot of hype in the market today around Big Data. We are just scratching the surface. Yes, we do have a lot of data, but in our case, we have been harnessing that data, structured and unstructured, to create value for our business. If you take a call, for instance, there are elements of voice analytics where we use UDA to analyze things like the rate, the flow, and topics; the tone, the language, and the meaning. We use text analytics solutions to harness our inbound and outbound calls.*

Using UDA, we are able to define twelve patterns of behavior using deep learning. And thanks to Google's open source Tensor Flow, we are using tensor flow to run it on a cloud GPU to speed up computing power of our UDA models. We were able to leverage deep learning on call notes and call narratives. And our fraud analytics, thanks to our algorithms that harness unstructured and structured data, has led several million per month in detected and prevented fraud.

Isson: Can you give me an example of a business challenge you were able to address in the past, what you leveraged, and what was the benefit of your investment?

Kolla: *We were able to leverage Big Data machine learning and deep learning to detect and prevent fraud by applying a combination of text analytics and structured data analytics to detect patterns and see whether they mean something. As I mentioned before, our unstructured and structured data analytics efforts led to several million saved per month.*

Isson: What advice would you give to someone new to fraud detection and prevention? Any dos and don'ts?

Kolla: *I have two bits of advices in terms of dos:*

The first advice: Understand that it is all about the business problem, not the technical approach.

The second advice: You have to go in being very curious. Take the data, question it, and stand behind your model. Understand your model. Avoid the "Trust me" approach (my predictive model is perfect but I don't know how it works). And you have to work with the business to drive adoption of the model.

In terms of don'ts: Remember you don't have to be a machine learning person. You need to wear different hats. Because even if you have a great model, it means nothing if it doesn't get implemented and used. You need to be able to speak the business words on top of your technical expertise.

Isson: What are the top reasons to invest in UDA? What is the biggest hurdle you will face?

Kolla: *The number one reason to invest is that you don't want a few bad apples to destroy the entire farm or customers' base experience. You don't want to jeopardize the customer experience of your great customers while you* *are trying to detect and prevent fraud. You want to be fair with good customers, providing them with a great experience, and take care of the bad apples (real fraud cases) differently.*

Often, it can be very challenging for a company to balance both: getting the right model in place and applying its business rules to detect and prevent fraud while at the same time making sure those rules do not become a hurdle or pain point for your great customers who have never done anything wrong—and, more importantly, creating the most value for your business.

The biggest hurdle: Fraud is the most challenging behavior to anticipate, because fraudsters, when they get caught, will generally change, adapt, and adjust their behavior, and avoid repeating the same past trends and behavior.

INTERVIEW WITH DIANE DEPERROIS, GENERAL MANAGER SOUTH-EAST AND OVERSEAS REGION, AXA

I had the opportunity to discuss the impact of UDA for insurance companies with Diane Deperrois, General Manager at AXA.

Isson: What made your organization decide to invest in UDA?

Deperrois: *By the nature of our work, data analytics is mission critical. We did not really decide to invest; we were already in, because all aspects of our work require data and analytics. Today the advantage is that we can enrich our data much more with external data and especially publicly available data. Unstructured data from open data sources represents a great added value for us, and a tremendous source of insights. We have made giant strides today because we are able to capture much more data than we could even access in the past, which has made it possible to strengthen and improve our customer knowledge and market knowledge.*

Isson: The majority of organizations I've spoken with have told me they are being inundated with data, unstructured data, and reports, without enough understanding of what that data and those reports mean. Would you agree? And, if so, how is your

organization working to leverage its unstructured data to lead to a better understanding and insight (such as claim management fraud detection and prevention)?

Deperrois: *Yes, we have a lot of data from multiple sources. But we have been harnessing our data, leveraging a multidisciplinary team to create actionable insights for our organization. In fact we recruit several types of profiles: data analysts, actuaries, and computer scientists. Our actuaries used to price products in relation to a loss history; today they continue to build product pricing, but relate it to data that is more and more publicly available and accessible to better analyze customer behavior and tailor pricing models—thanks to many services and organizations that have recently opened their data, making it publicly available. Publicly available data allows us to enrich our customer behavior models, our claim management, and our pricing models.*

Isson: *Can you give me examples of business challenges your company has addressed with UDA in the past? What solutions did you leverage, and what were the benefits of your investment?*

Deperrois: *Fraud detection and prevention is a great example. We were able to scan our entire database and lift the UDA to detect fraudulent claims and false witnesses. This is thanks to the enrichment of our internal data with external data and the use of UDA models.*

These models helped us, for example, to detect that the same witnesses were used in 47 different cases of reclamation. UDA enabled us to detect this type of professional witnesses for claim files.

And it is only through UDA and the reconciliation of internal and external data that we have been able to detect these fraud cases and false witnesses. We have been leveraging these insights to detect and predict fraud for similar claims cases. Big Data analytics enabled us to lift the volume of data and easily integrate external data that could have not been accessed or processed in the past.

We are also leveraging UDA powered by machine learning models for our voice recognition and chatbots solutions. We use those solutions to assist our customers and provide the best service experience to our customer throughout several touchpoints.

The return of investment (ROI) for predicting and detecting fraud resulted in a significant increase in cost saving (millions of euros per month), a significant increase in productivity and the implementation of robust and efficient proactive fraud prevention activities.

Isson: In this Big Data era, what advice would you give to a company trying to get the most out of their unstructured data analytics capabilities? What are the Dos and Don'ts of this undertaking? What strategies are important to make the project successful?

Deperrois: *Don't try to boil the ocean; stay focused. You have to choose a business challenge or a topic and go to the end. Do not start in azimuth, because it is fairly easy to get lost.*

Think about putting together a multidisciplinary team that will work on the project. Ideally, the team should include data analysts, marketing people, actuaries, computer scientists, and data scientists. This should enable you to create solutions and products that take into account the contribution of all actors who work in the team for the best outcome.

This approach should also help you to better integrate external data with internal data and ultimately reduce the time to market.

Isson: What are the primary benefits or top reasons to invest in UDA? What is the biggest hurdle you will face when implementing?

Deperrois*: The top reasons to invest in UDA for insurance companies are: productivity of claim analysis, fraud detection and prevention, and cost reduction. It should help to increase customer and market knowledge; it can also help to build better product segmentation and insurance solutions offerings. In our case, it has also helped us to create new data products, such as a bundle of car and home insurance. We envision building future data products that leverage inputs from Internet of Things data.*

Data analytics also enabled us to anticipate customer needs, wants, and expectations. We can come up with made-to-measure insurance products and solutions in real time or near real time.

The biggest hurdle you will face is about finding the right skills set and talent to help you integrate internal and external data sources and create actionable insights from that data.

Isson: How important is UDA to companies in your industry, and how do you see UDA being used now and in the future? What

do you foresee as the single biggest impact that UDA will have on businesses?

Deperrois: *Unstructured data is mission critical for companies in our industry. It helps to create actionable value from the internal and external data insurance companies have at their disposal. Companies will be able to fully leverage data from voice recognition, chatbots, e-mails, call logs, videos, and social media to optimize their outcomes. Artificial intelligence (AI) algorithms will become pervasive, helping the industry by taking over some repetitive and high volume tasks such as some customer support; our industry is poised to undergo a revolution that will enable machines powered by AI to support human resources.*

The second biggest impact that I foresee is Internet of Things data that we will have at our disposal from more and more connected devices and APIs; this data will become pervasive and Internet-of-Things connectivity will change the way we manage risk today.

For instance, with connected devices, we will be able to better understand customer behavior such as driving habits or power consumption. This knowledge will help us to define customized products and pricing, leading to more segmented products that reflect customer habits and behavior. We're going to demutualize the insurance business. And insurance will be more and more about prevention; we will be able to empower clients with actionable insights on risks and prevention methods. For example, we will be able to tell them: "Dear customer, you have a connection in your car; we have analyzed your driving habits and we have some advice for you that will help you spend less on fuel, avoid risks, and consequently pay fewer premiums."

The biggest challenge that comes with digitalization of data and the Internet of Things is cyber-risk and analytics talent retention. Cyber risk should be the priority for any insurance company; it should be front and center to ensure that companies can securely capture, store, and analyze customer data that they will have at their disposal.

KEY TAKEAWAYS

■ Today we are living in a hyper-connected world, where the Internet, social media, mobile, and cloud offer the opportunity to create a lot of data in digital format. That digitized information often encompasses our identify, location, and behavior, leaving a window for a fraudster to get access to our data. At the same time, that information provides UDA with great opportunity to access that goldmine of data to fight and predict fraud.

■ Most businesses and organizations have done a great job putting in place traditional fraud systems; unfortunately, these traditional systems are limited to internal and transactional data, which most of the time is structured and stored in an enterprise data warehouse. The root cause of most frauds is found in unstructured data. When mined properly, such data provides invaluable information to detect and predict frauds.

■ Big Data offers the opportunity to analyze 80 to 85 percent of the data that is unstructured to predict fraud. More importantly, it can perform analysis in real-time or near-real time on all transactions.

■ As the data grows in private and public domains, opportunities exist for fraudsters' intrusion, identity theft, and other fraudulent behavior to illegally obtain access to consumer and business information and commit frauds.

■ New approaches such as facial recognition combined with biometric data are providing relevant insights to prevent financial fraud, insurance fraud, and medical health frauds.

■ Successful companies are enhancing their existing fraud management systems with Big Data and predictive analytics to harness the power of UDA to better detect and prevent fraud, therefore improving the productivity and performance of their organizations.

■ It should be front and center for every organization to develop reliable and efficient strategy to effectively detect and prevent fraud. UDA helps organizations focus on mission critical fraud cases before they produce chaos for the management team.

■ Despite all the analytics arsenal and fraud management systems in place, it is not possible to predict all future fraud trends; however, organizations that leverage UDA powered by machine learning have a better chance to detect and prevent fraud.

■ UDA is very helpful in detecting and preventing fraudulent activities and patterns; however, fraud analysts, adjusters, and underwriters will always be required to leverage the interaction between analytics solutions and human resources, turning fraud actionable insights into results.

■ Having a solid fraud detection solution helps organizations to preserve their consumer experience and limit the risk of overweighting false positives or false negatives that manual outdated fraud detection methods could create.

- The hybrid approach includes several analytical techniques that integrate data across multiple sources, create custom reports and build machine learning solutions, combined with human resources that can transform actionable insights into results; this is the best strategy to detect and prevent fraud.

NOTES

1. SAS. "Coalition against Insurance Fraud: The State of Insurance Fraud Technology." www.sas.com/content/dam/SAS/en_us/doc/whitepaper2/coalition-against-insurance-fraud-the-state-of-insurance-fraud-technology-105976.pdf

2. National Insurance Crime Bureau. "U.S. Questionable Claims Report." www.nicb .org/newsroom/news-releases/

3. Andras Cser with Stephanie Balaouras, Alexander Spiliotes, and Peggy Dostie. The Forrester Wave™: Enterprise Fraud Management, Q1 2016: The Seven Providers That Matter Most and How They Stack Up, Forrester: January 27, 2016: www .forrester.com/report/The+Forrester+Wave+Enterprise+Fraud+Management+Q1 +2016/-/E-RES113082

4. Cser et al., The Forrester Wave™.

5. Natalie Gagliordi, "Identity Theft, Credit Card Fraud Cost US Consumers $16 Billion in 2016," *ZDNet*, February 1, 2017: www.zdnet.com/article/identity-theft-credit-card-fraud-cost-us-consumers-16-billion-in-2016/

6. Nancy Ozawa, "Identity Fraud Hits Record High with 15.4 Million U.S. Victims in 2016, Up 16 Percent According to New Javelin Strategy & Research Study," Javelin Strategy via *Business Wire*, February 1, 2017: www.businesswire.com/news/home/ 20170201005166/en/Identity-Fraud-Hits-Record-High-15.4-Million

7. Dallas Thornton, Guido van Capelleveen, Mannes Poel, Jos van Hillegersberg, and Roland Mueller, "Outlier-Based Health Insurance Fraud Detection for U.S. Medicaid Data," Proceedings of the 16th International Conference on Enterprise Information Systems (ICEIS 2014) via University of Twente, April 2014. http://eprints.eemcs .utwente.nl/24984/01/49861.pdf

8. FBI, "Insurance Fraud," FBI website: www.fbi.gov/stats-services/publications/ insurance-fraud

9. Cser et al., The Forrester Wave™.

FURTHER READING

Judith Hurwitz, Alan Nugent, Fern Halper, and Marcia Kaufman, "How Big Data Analytics Can Prevent Fraud," *Dummies website*: www.dummies .com/programming/big-data/data-science/how-big-data-analytics-can-prevent-fraud/

"Some Effective Techniques of Fraud Detection Analytics," eduCBA website, July 15, 2016: www.educba.com/fraud-detection-analytics/

Scott Mongeau, "Continuous Fraud Monitoring and Detection via Advanced Analytics: State of the Art Trends and Directions," (presentation, 2014 ACFE European Fraud Conference, *Amsterdam, the Netherlands, March* 24, 2014): www.slideshare.net/smongeau1/acfe-presentation-on-fraud

CHAPTER 6

The Power of UDA in Human Capital Management

The time is always right to do the right thing.

—Martin Luther King, Jr.

WHY SHOULD YOU CARE ABOUT UDA IN HUMAN RESOURCES?

The advent of Internet, social media, and cloud offers a tremendous opportunity to capture, organize, and analyze new types of human capital data that previously were not available or accessible. While research firm IDC estimated that more than 80 percent of business data was unstructured, this proportion could reach 85 percent for human resources (HR) data. In today's globally competitive labor marketplace, the opportunity cost of ignoring HR unstructured data is overwhelming; companies simply cannot afford to disregard this differentiator in human capital management if they want to win the war on talent.

Analysis of the structured data available (only 15 to 20 percent of HR data) only provides partial insights on workforce behavior.

Unstructured data analytics (UDA) improves the predictive accuracy and power of existing HR structured data models by integrating textual, audio, and video talent- and workforce-related data.

Consider talent acquisition, for instance. Recruiters are usually showered with applicants; as a result, quality is sacrificed due to quantity. UDA approaches such as video interviews are helping leading companies to simplify their recruiting process by removing steps such as phone screens, resume reviews, and traditional assessments. Video interviews enable companies to quickly access more candidates with higher quality. Because candidates can take the interview any time at their convenience, it increases recruitment productivity and provides a better candidate and customer experience.

A key reason you need to include text data in human capital management predictive models is that it contains terms usually reflecting talent experience that could be good or bad for the organization. Experience is often consistent with employees' engagement and employees' decision to remain with your company or turn to the competition.

Leading job boards, such as Monster, Indeed, and CareerBuilder, and social medial networks, like Twitter, LinkedIn, and Facebook, have been dealing with unstructured data since their inception. Where for social media networks the main goal is to better understand habits, needs, preferences, and sentiments of the user base, for job boards the primary mandate is to connect people to job opportunities.

To achieve that ultimate goal of matching candidates to job opportunities, an understanding of the key drivers of talent management success is required. This involves a comprehensive analysis of structured and unstructured talent data across every stage of the talent life cycle.

Leading people analytics companies analyze all people data to drive business performance. When harnessed properly with the use of predictive analytics, UDA helps organizations to better understand key drivers of talent sourcing, talent acquisition, talent engagement and onboarding, talent development, lifetime value, talent retention, and talent wellness. UDA also provides actionable insights to help you optimize your human capital supply/demand equation as well as your overall talent supply chain management. UDA can also help you as an employer to assess and improve your value proposition and online reputation.

WHAT IS UDA IN HR?

HR is one of the fastest-growing industries with tremendous opportunities to analyze its untapped data, both structured and unstructured. The overall concept of analytics in HR started in 1800 during Napoleon's reign when the French and the British were using employment services to recruit for their empires. The first major disruption in HR analytics occurred in 1911, when Frederick Taylor, a mechanical engineer, began measuring workers' productivity in an effort to improve efficiency in industry. This effort served as the foundation for a new approach: the scientific management of time-and-motion studies. Taylor's methods and techniques for capturing and measuring employees' effectiveness within an organization were summed up in his book, *The Principles of Scientific Management.*

Predictive analytics in HR started in the late 2010s, as HR got more tools and software to store processes and analyze human capital data. According to a recent Deloitte study, only 8 to 10 percent of companies leverage predictive analytics in HR. Most of the HR analytics we know today is based upon typical structured data: data in rows and columns that fits in an Excel spreadsheet; data from which counts are derived and then grouped by demographic and other vertical parameters. However, simply looking at structured data provides a myopic approach to your workforce behavior, your company's online reputation, market dynamics, competition, recruitment efficiency, and overall supply-and-demand equation.

Another set of HR data, unstructured data, provides a great potential in understanding employee behavior, needs, wants, and sentiments while offering the employer insight on online branding and reputation. Unstructured data is unorganized, messy, and complex, and cannot be easily placed in a spreadsheet. But when properly harnessed by predictive models, it could yield a lot of value for HR.

Having built and implemented advanced business analytics for the past 25 years across multiple organizations, and witnessed the evolution of data analytics, I truly believe that the next innovation in data analytics will take place in HR and healthcare. Those sectors contain a gigantic amount of untapped unstructured data poised to create human capital value and drive business performance.

In the HR context, *structured data* is typically gathered from:

- Employee sociodemographics
- Name
- Age
- Gender
- Years of experience
- Job level
- Length of association
- Compensation
- Performance appraisal rating
- Performance development category
- Turnover rate

When looking at performance evaluation, the ranking of employees is often grouped into categories like: (1) Needs improvement; (2) Developing; (3) Meets expectation; (4) Exceeds expectation; and (5) Exceptional. Analysis of this type of performance appraisal data could provide insight such as correlation and/or causation between:

- Employee performance ranking and promotion
- Employee performance ranking and merit increase
- Employee performance ranking and turnover
- Employee performance ranking and performance improvement plan
- Employee performance ranking and productivity

Analytics helps, for example, to answer questions like the following: What is the turnover by career level and by job performance? Is the turnover correlated with compensation? Is the turnover correlated with years of experience?

This information can be supplemented with employee unstructured data. *Unstructured data* is being constantly generated from a variety of sources, including:

- Employee e-mails, chats, tweets, blogs, and Web documents
- Employee social media profiles, such as LinkedIn, Twitter, and Facebook, and employee updates

- Employee presence on niche sites such as Stack Overflow, GitHub, and Entelo
- Employee feedback satisfaction or complaints via open-ended questions
- Employee wearable communication devices
- Employee social badges
- Employee narrative from performance appraisal and self-appraisal
- Employee career goals
- Employee annual goals setting and achievements
- Employee self-development plan narrative
- Employer reviews on employee opinion sites such as Kununu and Glassdoor
- Customer suggestions to improve or complement service
- Customer survey response to a specific service
- Customer voice on ongoing issues
- Customer open-ended survey questionnaires
- Transcripts of complaints of customers through their call center
- Customer service call center logs
- Audio and video interview data

If you mine this content properly it could provide you with your employees' insights on training and continuing education opportunities for your overall workforce. This will have an impact on employee satisfaction, employee retention, and employee engagement. Combined with structured data, unstructured data can identify whether certain concepts are correlated to high, medium, or low employee performance and help address potential talent performance issues.

WHAT IS UDA IN HR REALLY ABOUT?

While the amount of textual data is increasing rapidly, the ability to create actionable insights for business decision making remains very challenging for many organizations. Using the IMPACT cycle introduced in Chapter 3, human capital unstructured data can be analyzed to derive actionable talent management insights to drive and improve business performance and optimize every stage of your talent life cycle.

Specifically, the application of UDA within the IMPACT cycle can address human capital business challenges, including:

- Workforce planning (How many talents your organization needs now and will need in the future to compete and win)
- Talent sourcing (Where to look for candidates)
- Talent acquisition (Whom should you hire?)
- Talent engagement and talent onboarding (What is the impact of engagement program and onboarding program on employee performance and loyalty?)
- Talent performance management and lifetime value (What drives high or low performance?)
- Talent retention (Who are the star performers at risk of leaving, and why?)
- Talent wellness and safety and health (What is the impact of wellness program on productivity and loyalty?)

In the following sections, I will discuss how UDA can impact every stage of talent life cycle management. But first let's start with the online recruitment sites that store, organize, and categorize employers' job postings as well as job seekers' resumes and profiles.

THE POWER OF UDA IN ONLINE RECRUITMENT: SUPPLY AND DEMAND EQUATION

On any given job board, employers post vacant jobs while seekers can post or create their resumes. The premise of online job boards is to connect people to job opportunities; employers find sought-after qualified talents, and job seekers find their ideal employers. To achieve that goal, job boards need to manage millions of resumes and job descriptions, in a wide variety of categories and occupations, and create perfect matches between job postings and resumes or seekers' profiles.

Manually handling millions of resumes or job descriptions is extremely cumbersome and impossible to achieve effectively. A study from Monster determined that it usually takes 90 seconds for a recruiter to go through a candidate resume. Therefore, if a recruiter receives 100,000 resumes for a customer clerk position, he or she would need 2,500 hours or more than 1.3 years to go through all resumes. Recruiters without access to resume search tools that leverage UDA algorithms just take a handful of resumes, leaving the clear majority of applicants' resumes untouched. Leading organizations are leveraging semantic search tools and solutions such as Monster SeeMore and Supersearch. Such tools perform semantic searches from a variety of resume databases in a matter of seconds. They provide context-based results and business intelligence to recruiters through the scoring of every resume in the database, based upon recruiters' criteria.

From the employers' perspective, UDA is helpful in classifying job descriptions into appropriate categories. Take, for instance, employers seeking to hire customer service representatives. Some employers use catchy job titles, such as "Come and Realize Your Dream." A typical Boolean search on the job title would not classify this job posting into the right occupational category: *customer service representative*. Leading job boards, therefore, are using text analytics to parse the job description body and find key meaning, enabling the categorization of the position into the right occupation group. From the candidates' perspective, their resumes go through text analytics parsing algorithms to be categorized into the right occupations.

In short, online recruitment sites achieve perfect matches by running parsing, indexing, and text categorization algorithms and semantic analytics to recommend the right jobs available to the right job seekers, and to present employers with the resumes and candidate profiles that best meet their job posting's requirements.

THE POWER OF UDA IN TALENT SOURCING ANALYTICS

Talent sourcing analytics uses advanced analytics to harness all the data and talent information available to optimize your sourcing results. Successfully searching for candidates in today's globally competitive talent market requires an approach that allows you to accurately identify and locate candidates, assess their potential, and efficiently engage with them in an easy way.

To enhance talent sourcing, job boards have developed text analytics algorithms that help employers parse millions of resumes, in the cloud, in a matter of seconds to find sought-after talent based upon defined criteria. These semantic search technologies use the context and concepts to score each resume according to the employer's predefined criteria. Employers and recruiters are no longer limited to traditional Boolean searches; they can leverage the power of semantic algorithms to gain efficiency, effectiveness, and productivity, and to reduce the cost of hiring.

For some "hard to fill" positions, such as occupations in science, technology, engineering, and math (STEM), leading job boards like Monster have developed state-of-the-art unstructured data algorithms such as TalentBin. These algorithms explore the entire Web, social media networks (Twitter, LinkedIn, Google+, Facebook, Pinterest, and others), and niche sites (GitHub, Entelo, and Stack Overflow) to capture the digital footprint of the talents' e-mails, photos, and social media feeds to create unique digital identifiers or digital footprints of potential candidates. They also produce aggregated profiles for recruiters, enabling them to easily reach out for those hard-to-fill positions.

Assessment and Analysis of Culture Fit Score

A bad hire is not only very costly to your company (in addition to the recruiting and training costs, there is productivity loss), it can even destroy your existing workforce (coworkers' morale) and damage your company's reputation (negative impact on client solution). UDA helps organizations develop a culture fit score from the analysis of the candidate's resume history, time between jobs, and cover letter profile. All candidates are scored in the candidate relationship management system and the applicant tracking system (ATS) to determine the best list of prospects to be met in formal job interviews.

Social Job Ad and Twitter Job

High Performing job boards have also developed creative ideas to help employers post jobs on social media networks such as Twitter and Facebook. For example, companies like Monster developed Twitter

Card postings that enable recruiters to post the full job description on a Twitter Card as an image, therefore bypassing the traditional 140-character limit of Twitter. Twitter Card helps organizations socialize their job opportunities, automatically transforming their job ads into branded, automated tweets. And those tweets appear on their Twitter network and provide relevant insights regarding positions to fill.

Employer Online Reputation: Social Media Feed and News Analysis

Employers also use UDA to assess and analyze their live Twitter feed and compare it to their competition thereby deriving the underlying sentiment: positive or negative. In a similar way, UDA can gather all news articles and blogs about your company and your competition and score and rank them into a positive or negative coverage category.

UDA is used to assess and analyze employees' input on employers' review sites such as Glassdoor and Kununu. UDA helps to compare your company's reviews to your competitors', determine whether your overall online branding and reputation are below or above the competition's, and provide historical trends (past, present, and future). In a labor market that is becoming more and more candidate driven, properly managing your online reputation and branding will become a standard to attract great talents.

Supply (Resume/Job Response) and Demand (Job Posting/Listing)

In recruitment, the supply usually refers to candidate resumes, candidate profiles or candidate applications to jobs that is usually called job response. UDA helps organizations analyze the type of resumes profile that would usually respond to the employer's job demand. By crossing job description against candidate resume or profile, UDA helps to find out if there is a way to better segment and target individuals in specific job occupation, job category and locations when hiring for some hard-to-fill positions.

UDA Applied to Candidate Resumes and Candidate Profile

A candidate's resume can be in many different formats: Word document, rich text format (RTF), upload build in, or video. To categorize a resume into a specific occupation and match it against a job description, job boards first parse and analyze resume content and create an index for the categorization. In the past, this time-consuming process required manual intervention. Today, natural language processing algorithms can map and classify resumes in given categories and occupations.

A LinkedIn social media profile provides a playground for unstructured data analytics. How do all those features (photo, update, type of update, publications, videos, background photo image, etc.) impact the visibility and performance of a given profile? Specifically:

- What is the differentiator for candidates having the same features?

- Why will one be more successful and/or productive than another?

With UDA, HR and job candidates can better understand and address the following recruitment questions:

- What makes one resume/job more appealing than another with similar content?

- What is the impact of resume format and features, such as picture, date of birth, or marital status, experience and education on resume attractiveness?

- What types of resumes will get more views?

- What is the impact of the candidate's social media profile (such as LinkedIn profile) features, such as picture, date of birth, or marital status, on a candidate's likelihood to get an interview or to get hired?

- What is the impact of video, social media feeds, updates, and type of LinkedIn profile updates on job interview requests?

- What attributes of resume or social media profile would draw recruiters' or hiring managers' attention?

Candidate Video Resume

Online recruitment talent sourcing and acquisition are no longer local processes. In certain occupations, such as those in design or customer-facing roles, candidates can send a video of themselves to potential employers, which can then be analyzed by leveraging UDA. Take a job posting position that generates, for instance, 10,000 videos; the recruiters could not possibly review all these individually. By leveraging UDA powered by deep learning algorithms to sift through the videos, the first selection can be made to focus on resumes for which the profiles and presentations best match with the employer job requirements.

Video Interview

In today's global competitive labor marketplace companies can now look for candidates in remote locations, cities, and countries for "hard to fill" roles. Companies cannot always afford to have all potential candidates come onsite for interviews; early adopters use videoconference software such as Skype, Blue Jean, Go To Meeting, and others to interview candidates. Leading organizations are also leveraging UDA by tagging all individual video interviews, then processing and analyzing all video interviews, as a whole, to identify candidates who best meet the employer's job qualifications. Subsequently, only a handful of videos are sent to hiring managers for their review to determine next steps, such as an in-person meeting. UDA is assisting candidates and employers alike by saving travel expenses and reducing costs and time commitment. Some employers I spoke with have reported tremendous benefits in cost saving, productivity, and performance from their hiring managers and recruiters.

Other leading organizations have been improving their candidate and recruiter experience using video interview technology such as HireVue. According to HireVue, when a candidate takes a video interview they create more than 25,000 unique data points, such as:

- Intonation data
- Inflexion data
- Facial expressions data
- Word choice data
- Content of each answer data

Once all these data elements are analyzed, they shape the recruiter's impression of each candidate. Video intelligence provides recruiters with the power to consistently make best decisions; they can see more candidates, in less time, and increase diversity in their talent pool. They can assess the quality of the talent pool and the fit of each candidate to meet the company business objectives. Video intelligence simplifies the overall recruiting process and modernizes candidate experience for the best talent.

Grocery delivery company Shipt decreased its candidates' application time from thirteen days to three days by using video interview intelligence—an increased efficacy of 80 percent. And thanks to the UDA video intelligence, Shipt also managed to reduce the number of recruiters from nine to five while tripling the number of interviews conducted.

UNDER ARMOUR CASE STUDY

Company Summary

Under Armour, Inc. is an American company that manufactures footwear and sports and casual apparel. From its humble beginning in the founder's basement in 1996, in less than two decades, Under Armour has grown to more than 8,500 teammates globally with more than 130 retail stores.

Since its inception, the company has been growing in revenue and resources. In 2012, a retail store was opened every other week. With a business focus on growth opportunities in footwear, women's apparel, international expansion, and retail, Under Armour shows no signs of slowing down.

Case Summary

Under Armour has reduced the time required to fill vacant position by more than 35 percent by leveraging UDA: a video analysis solution from HireVue.

Recruiting Challenges Prior to Going Digital

Overwhelming Applicant Pools

Under Armour's rapid growth is reflected in their culture. "Our culture is often referred to as 'lightning in a bottle,'" explained Troy Barnett, former director of corporate services technology at Under Armour. "We are an extremely fast-paced, high-energy, young, athletic culture. Finding the right cultural fit for our organization is key to our talent acquisition priorities."

When Barnett joined Under Armour in 2007, there were fewer than 1,000 teammates. The recruiting process at that time was in its infancy. The procedure was cumbersome; resumes and applications were not being tracked or monitored properly. Retail operations launched in 2010 with the first branded retail store in Annapolis, Maryland. In 2012, when Under Armour launched its applicant tracking system, the company was flooded with an average of 30,000 resumes each month.

Long Cycle Times Impact Store Staffing

The hiring process became drawn out because of the huge applicant pool. "To go through every application and begin the process of putting them into the pipeline to start the screening and interview process took longer than a company growing at our rate could afford. The entire process, from posting a requisition to hiring a candidate, was taking too long to effectively service our retail team," Barnett explained.

The long process to get people hired and onboarded had an impact on Under Armour's ability to have their retail stores fully staffed, ramped, and ready to operate. "The managers at our retail stores needed a way to be able to find the right talent quickly and efficiently," said Barnett.

Staffing challenges became imperative during the three peak hiring times—summer, back to school, and the holiday season—when management needed to hire several hundred associates and have them ready for crucial retail seasons.

Barnett commented, "At Under Armour, we pride ourselves on innovation. A few years ago, our recruiting process was extremely manual and our volume of applicants was overwhelming—not an innovative experience for our candidates or our hiring team."

Selection of a Digital Recruiting Solution

Barnett explained, "Like most organizations, Under Armour had all of the 'must have' HR technology in place—transactional solutions for sourcing, applying, tracking, and onboarding—but those tools didn't revolutionize and modernize our recruiting the way we needed it to. I knew there had to be a more modern and innovative way to transform our recruiting function that better matched our brand.

"We looked into digital recruiting as a way to bring innovation to our recruiting process and importantly, empower our store managers and give them a tool for finding and hiring the right talent quickly.

"We approached every level about moving to a digital process—from the C-suite to our retail managers—we implemented HireVue for both on-demand and live interviews."

On-demand interviews give managers the ability to create an interview with prerecorded questions and invite those candidates who meet the requirements to introduce themselves via video. The candidate completes the interview on their own time via a webcam or on their mobile device. "With on-demand interviews, we're empowering our retail managers to make their own hiring decisions, providing them with a tool to review their top candidates quickly and hire only the best," said Barnett.

Under Armour Revolutionizes Hiring and Modernizes the Candidate Experience with HireVue

Digital Recruiting Becomes Crucial to Retail Operations; 35 Percent Reduction in Time to Fill; Improvement in New Hire Quality

"The biggest impact we've seen since implementing digital recruiting is in our retail stores. The on-demand interviews empower the store managers to own their own store and make informed hiring decisions," said Barnett.

At Under Armour, digital recruiting isn't just a tool to replace a phone screen. The insight the company is getting into their applicants is so powerful that the in-person interviews are spent with only the best candidates.

"The manager reviews the initial resume from our ATS, sends candidates a HireVue on-demand interview with a variety of question types and when they meet with them face-to-face, it is more of an affirmation of who they've already determined will be a top-quality candidate," Barnett explains. "A resume or even a phone screen doesn't tell the full story. We found that after a phone screen, the person that shows up isn't the person you thought you were getting. Now with being able to see the candidate right away, we get a true sense of who they are and whether they'll be a cultural fit for us."

"The value is not just in the increased speed to hire, which has easily been reduced by 35 percent, but in the quality of hire as well," added Barnett.

Anywhere, Anytime Interviewing Proves Beneficial across Job Families

The corporate team of 1,400 teammates located in the Baltimore headquarters has also embraced digital recruiting as part of their process. On-demand interviews are being used in the recruiting process across all job families, and live interviews are being used to reduce travel.

THE POWER OF UDA IN TALENT ACQUISITION ANALYTICS

Whether you have a small company or manage a large organization with thousands of employees, choosing the wrong candidates can have a lethal impact on your business. Therefore, ensuring that your organization makes wise talent investments is critical to both long-term and short-term success. In acquisition analytics, advanced analytics preselects candidates for an interview. UDA also helps in optimizing the interview process by determining the best ways to vet candidates and set up interview questions. UDA also assists with creating some tests to correlate a candidate's performance during the interview and his or her performance in a particular job function.

UDA assists leading organizations to leverage all the textual data generated when hiring a new candidate. It helps to address some talent acquisition questions, including:

- What is the correlation and causation between the talent acquisition process's psychometric, open-ended questions, and talent job performance once hired?
- What is the correlation between the type of questions, candidates' feedback and answers, and their performance at work?
- What are the key drivers found in their cover letters of top performers?
- What is the impact of candidate social media presence and activities on their job performance and loyalty?

- Is there a correlation between candidate psychometric interview questions, narrative, and feedback, and their performance at work?

- What narratives do top performers provide during their job interviews?

- What makes a cover letter more attractive than others?

ARTIFICIAL INTELLIGENCE AS A HIRING ASSISTANT

Can an artificial intelligence (AI) app become your hiring assistant? With the advent of deep learning and the expansion of chatbots, the answer is yes! Leading organizations are now leveraging AI algorithms as a first-line candidate screening tool.

AI assistants are now being used to empower the conversation with candidates who apply to a job offer from various hiring sources, including: job boards, social media platforms, or the company website. These AI assistants perform human-like candidate assessments. The AI assistant assesses candidates' qualifications and also gathers useful information that a (human) hiring manager needs to be able to screen the candidate. In addition, it can schedule a candidate for an interview.

We have all witnessed how overwhelmed talent acquisition staffs are, dealing with high turnover and large numbers of applicants for roles in high demand, such as customer services clerks or retail clerks in stores like Walmart. The hiring managers and talent acquisition team cannot simply catch up with the volume of applicants they receive for these roles. This challenge is now being addressed thanks to AI. Leveraging the power of AI helps organizations free up the talent acquisition team and improve candidate experience. We all know how bad the candidates' experience could be with a talent acquisition team that is understaffed. Candidates who apply to a job will always remember the lack of decency from the hiring manager who forgot to call them back or did not provide any news to candidates who were not retained after the screening or an interview. With an AI hiring assistant, this negligence will become a thing of the past. Similarly, an AI talent acquisition assistant would provide help beyond candidate screening, including scheduling interviews and following up with the candidates and the hiring manager, reminding them of interview dates and what the candidate needs to know offhand during the interview. But more importantly, the AI application would follow up with all of the candidates who applied to inform them about the outcome of their applications, and whether they were retained or not for an interview. They will also advise unsuccessful candidates as to why they were not selected, keeping them engaged for future opportunities. Companies like TextRecruit provide a candidate engagement platform that leverages text, chat and artificial intelligence to help companies optimize their hiring funnels.

When talking to Mateo Cavasotto, CEO and cofounder of HolaEmi (a startup that provides the candidate screening chatbot app Emi) he believes that AI will completely change the way we attract and acquire talent. He claims that some customers who are using an AI assistant have already recorded some savings in talent acquisition, including:

- 70 percent reduction of recruitment team time through automating steps like screening and scheduling
- 30 percent increase in attendance to interviews
- 20 percent increase in qualified candidates who would have been rejected if evaluated only by their résumés

THE POWER OF UDA IN TALENT RETENTION

In today's complex, global, and extremely competitive world, talent is top of mind for most CEOs. While concerned with acquiring and retaining the best and brightest, executives are also worried about nurturing, engaging, and advancing their star performers. The proliferation of digital information, thanks to Internet and social media networks, offers a tremendous opportunity to mine untapped talent data that is publicly available and is mostly textual and unstructured.

Businesses have all embraced predictive models that use traditional data mining methods and techniques, which require numerical data inputs to predict dichotomous or continuous response variables—for instance, which employees are more likely to churn in the near future? However, in working with some clients, I found that along with the numerical data, the use of unstructured data such as talent profile update, talent survey responses, talent transcripts from performance evaluation and employee satisfaction, talent personal development plan narrative, talent profile photo update, talent comments, talent feedback on review sites, and talent performance appraisal narratives were very useful in improving the predictive accuracy of the talent predictive attrition model. Companies I spoke to claimed that unstructured data accounted for more than 35 percent of the predictive power in their talent retention predictive models.

The integration of textual analysis of customer call center records and publicly available external data can significantly improve the predictive ability of a numeric data model. Adding a text cluster to a numeric data model results in better performance than numeric data alone. Adding this type of unstructured data provides employers with a comprehensive knowledge of their talent pool.

CASE

INTERVIEW WITH ARUN CHIDAMBARAM, DIRECTOR OF GLOBAL WORKFORCE INTELLIGENCE, PFIZER

I had the opportunity to discuss talent retention analytics with Arun Chidambaram, Director of Global Workforce Intelligence at Pfizer.

Isson: *Can you explain how Pfizer has been leveraging Big Data analytics for talent retention?*

Chidambaram: *When we approach talent retention, we treat each market uniquely. [He explains that, with nearly 80,000 employees, the company has devised a strategy that leverages the power of HR data, publicly available information, and quantitative data to optimize and tailor its talent retention tactics for its offices throughout the world.]*

Isson: *What is the incremental value of unstructured data, such as publicly available data, for Pfizer?*

Chidambaram: *Only looking at internal data creates a limited and myopic approach toward talent retention, so Pfizer is adopting models that are dynamic and adjusted by country and region. As a result, the company is able to:*

■ *Gradually reduce employee turnover in specific areas by leveraging a proactive approach to pinpoint driving factors of talent attrition.*

> ■ *Provide a comprehensive picture of risk factors to better understand how internal and external factors impact Pfizer's talent market supply chain and identify the best actions for the company to maintain workforce stability.*
>
> ■ *Prioritize investments in programs that are working and help the company to maintain its competitive edge by keeping its most important asset—its talent.*
>
> *By implementing these new methods, each talent market is considered uniquely. When it comes to hiring and retaining the top employees, companies cannot rely on a one-size-fits-all solution.*

The Power of UDA in Employee Wellness Analytics

To be successful, organizations must create and design an environment and culture that promotes the well-being, health, and safety of their employees. This means financial and other resources need to be allocated to support endeavors that link employee health, safety, and well-being to company business performance. Best practices include proactive activities such as wellness visits, preventive checkups, and vaccinations to avoid the high cost of urgent reactive procedures. UDA in HR helps to grasp employees' perception of the overall wellness program, including potential issues, comments, complaints, or simple opinions. By leveraging textual data, UDA helps to address talent management questions such as:

- Are employees' perceptions of our wellness program bad, good, or neutral?

- What features or attributes of the wellness program do they feel bad or good about?

- What do employees think about various attributes of the wellness program, such as indoor pools, massage rooms, free lunches, flex hours, onsite physicians, onsite daycare, onsite gym or free gym membership, or healthcare insurance?

- What do employees think about the company's employee safety and health program?

- What is the overall sentiment of employees in regard to the company value proposition?

■ What is the impact of employee wearable devices data on employee wellness, safety, health, and team building?

EMPLOYEE PERFORMANCE APPRAISAL DATA REVIEW FEEDBACK

Performance management analytics helps employers to regularly assess the performance of their employees and provide frequent feedback and goals to achieve success. It can also help organizations assess how many employees they will need at each level in the coming years, which is how leading companies predict employee promotion and career pathways.

During their performance appraisals, employees usually provide a goldmine of data via their review narrative; unfortunately, though, this information is not leveraged by most organizations. The narrative and essays from employee performance appraisals and employee personal career development plans, and the text content from employee answers to open-ended questions such as self-performance appraisal, accomplishments, career development plan, and employee satisfaction survey could be harnessed to provide organizations with frontline feedback and sentiment of their employee population. Using UDA on written feedback from employers review sites such as Glassdoor and Kununu is helping leading organizations to make a difference and win against their competition by capturing, analyzing, and better understanding their employees' pain points, feedback, and overall sentiment, which is usually ignored or omitted.

UDA can help to identify positive or negative sentiment opinions and, more importantly, understand the reasons behind low levels of employee satisfaction or engagement with their jobs or their managers and their subsequent lower performance.

UDA can also reveal the most frequently used words, phrases, topics, and content that would help managers understand employee sentiments, categorize their workforce by their sentiment ranking, and put together development plans to address any latent issues.

Applied to e-mails and chats and ongoing employee performance inputs from newly adopted performance management applications, UDA can reveal employee sentiment and employee engagement.

It could also help to assess how your customer-facing employees interact with customers and with their peers and to potentially spot areas of improvement in communication or service.

Of course, there is a balancing act between employee privacy, perceived or real, and the organization's need for information to improve its performance. For employees to participate willingly and openly and provide genuine feedback, a safe culture needs to be in place within the organization.

HOW UDA WORKS

Today, the vast majority of UDA software has several text dictionaries available to organize and interpret text data, such as a recruitment dictionary, a talent acquisition and talent retention dictionary, an employee feedback dictionary, an employee satisfaction dictionary, and an employee compensation dictionary that analyze concepts, topics, and contexts that frequently appear and are used in HR.

The following are the major steps in UDA:

- Capture textual data from a variety of HR data sources.
- Prepare the unstructured HR data for analysis.
- Normalize the text data; recognize language.
- Create or update HR dictionaries (HR employee satisfaction dictionary, employee performance dictionary, talent retention dictionary, and talent engagement onboarding dictionary).
- Create a knowledge base system that includes HR-specific text and vocabulary terms, such as occupational categories, synonyms, and job concept (among others).
- Apply linguistic statistics and machine learning techniques to the unstructured data document before extraction.
- Parse the data extract and model information from textual data sources.
- Build singular value decomposition (SVD) matrices to get eigenvalues and eigenvectors or leverage other machine learning techniques.

- Convert the unstructured text into categories and structure format for advanced analytics.
- Apply the IMPACT cycle to create actionable business value.

BENEFITS OF UDA IN HR

The major benefits of UDA in HR include:

- Efficiency
- Effectiveness
- Productivity
- Cost reduction
- Business performance

UDA saves time and money by reducing the amount of effort and human hours required to manually search through resumes and sort and rank candidates by qualifications, years of experience, or skillsets. UDA recruitment solutions, such as video interview intelligence, help hiring managers and recruiters to increase their recruitment productivity and modernize candidate experience. UDA algorithms, such as semantic search and talent social media data and Web data aggregators, help recruiters reach out for hard-to-fill positions such as those in STEM fields.

UDA helps human capital managers to better understand their workforce feedback, needs, and development plan by providing a comprehensive analysis of the narrative and essay provided through employee performance appraisals and employee satisfaction surveys. UDA can sort words, sentences, and concepts that are frequently used and repeated by thousands of employees, then automatically list the concepts and sentences that frequently appear and evaluate the underlying employee sentiment. This gained insight can also help to boost individual motivation and overall engagement, increasing talent retention by tracking, analyzing, and sharing employee performance-related data. UDA also helps employers to optimize their talent life-cycle management.

CASE STUDIES

The Container Store

The Container Store, for instance, has been using wearable tech, designed to improve communication within its stores and to track employees when they're at work. Using the Theatro Wearable Computers, store management can access performance data, including how employees communicate with coworkers and customers, and where they spend the most of their time.

Applying Big Data analytics to employee performance can also help employers identify and acknowledge top performers, along with workers who may be struggling in their positions. Talent management software can assist HR professionals in gathering and analyzing the data they need to evaluate individual performance levels.

With tools like employee satisfaction surveys, team assessments, social media, exit and stay interviews, and the like, HR can essentially predict (and thus, prevent) unplanned employee attrition.

INTERVIEW WITH STEPHANI KINGSMILL, EXECUTIVE VICE PRESIDENT AND CHIEF HUMAN RESOURCE OFFICER, MANULIFE

I had the opportunity to speak with Stephanie Kingsmill to better understand how Manulife is leveraging UDA in HR.

Isson: What made your company decide to invest in HR Analytics/People Analytics?

Kingsmill: *We have been talking about HR analytics for a while because there are so many decisions in HR that can be supported with data. Most of the time leaders make decisions based on their perceptions of their employees, and this can be very subjective in various situations. For instance, the notion of gender diversity can introduce different perceptions. It would be difficult to convince people of impartiality without data. We came to the conclusion that data can help us provide a robust understanding of problems, find solutions. HR analytics helps to address the underlying struggle of differences of opinion.*

In our view, as our customer analytics evolves we also want our employee analytics to evolve. We want to think about our employee experience and employee engagement the same way we think about our customers.

Isson: The majority of HR executives I've spoken with have told me they are overwhelmed with a lot of data from disconnected sources and are not getting a lot of meaning from it. Would you agree?

Kingsmill: *That's true. We have made some progress by modernizing our technology platform, like acquiring Workday in 2011, and centralizing our HR data by creating an HR data lake.*

Isson: Can you give me an example of HR business challenges you were able to address leveraging analytics/unstructured data analytics? What was the benefit of your investment?

Kingsmill: *The main area where we've been using UDA text analytics is with our employee engagement survey. We typically get 33,000 comments from employees. We have a pretty good response rate of employees sharing their feedback on one typical question at the end of the survey: "What could we do better?" That is a pretty rich text comment/narrative from employees.*

This is where our vice president of advanced analytics, Eugene Wen, and his team have been spending a fair amount of time to help us go through the 33,000 answers using UDA, thereby saving us from a manual review. Before leveraging text analytics, every leader would have interpreted the results for their employees and drawn conclusions. With UDA, Eugene's team harnesses all that raw text data from the employee engagement survey and provides us with employee insights.

One of the insights we discovered is employee dissatisfaction with the tools they have to do their jobs; like tools we have for provisioning a computer for a new employee, reserving videoconferencing facilities or other internal collaborative tools. We haven't seen that granular an insight before because the question "I have the tools to do my job" has never been properly analyzed before using text analytics. For example, the situation of a new hire not having a computer on day one is frustrating for both the manager and the new employee. Solving the computer provisioning issue saved a lot of time, increased employee satisfaction and employee productivity, and reduced turnover.

We have also used text analytics in our performance review analysis across the organization. We looked at the core behaviors at the organizational level that drive culture change. We wanted to see the link between culture change behaviors and performance.

The application of UDA on the 33,000 performance review narratives showed differences in the extent to which various parts of the organization were embracing the culture change. We could then more specifically target further intervention. This helped us to reinforce our culture change across specific regions and countries.

Isson: What advice would you give to someone new to unstructured data analytics in HR? Dos and Don'ts?

Kingsmill: *Going back to the analysis of employee engagement, we learned that using analytical models alone could lead to unrealistic conclusions. You need to keep the human intelligence in the equation to avoid drawing strange conclusions or results. There is some subjectivity involved in the development of models. You should always have someone from HR who understands the people context when you are building your HR text analytics solutions.*

Isson: What is the top reason to invest in UDA in HR? What is the biggest hurdle you will face?

It comes down to understanding employee experience, making the right adjustments to improve that experience, and therefore driving productivity. It is also important to senior executives and the HR team to efficiently gather information and assess employee experience in order to intervene on things that are going off the rails.

How do we get assessment in real time for areas where we have real issues? We have HR business partners supporting every business area. The biggest hurdle is ensuring HR business partners know how to ask the right HR analytics question. We also need to gather clean data that the analytics team can derive insights from.

Isson: What is the biggest impact that UDA will have in the future?

Kingsmill: *Getting real-time analytics to intervene in real time or near-real time. This will help business leaders to improve productivity, engagement, and retention of our employees. It is very helpful if we are able to predict things that could go wrong and take appropriate actions. In a nutshell, employee productivity, engagement, and retention are key areas where UDA will have to play a dominant role, especially with increasing social media data.*

KEY TAKEAWAYS

In today's globally competitive labor market, propelled by the explosion of digital talent data, companies that are not analyzing their workforce unstructured data are getting a myopic view of their talent pool. Unstructured data in HR account for more than 85 percent of total data. It is being constantly generated from a variety of sources, including:

- Employees' e-mails, chat, tweets, blogs, and Web documents
- Employees' wearable devices
- Employees' performance appraisal narrative and personal development plans
- Employee satisfaction feedback from open-ended questions
- Employer online reputation
- Employer reviews on employee review sites, such as Glassdoor and Kununu
- Video interview intelligence

UDA applied to HR data helps harness structured and unstructured HR data. From matching resumes to right job postings or recruiters leveraging semantic search tools, applications and UDA social media solutions, UDA can help you optimize your recruitment efforts as well as your overall talent management analytics. Leading organizations have been enhancing their recruitment techniques and workforce behavior models by including text data and video intelligence in the equation. Terms analyzed in text data usually represent employee experience and employee sentiment that could be good or bad. That experience is often consistent with employee engagement, employee motivation, and overall employee decision to stay with your company or turn to the competition. Applying UDA to HR helps human capital and people managers optimize every stage of their talent life cycle, from talent acquisition to talent development and talent retention.

Today recruiters can no longer afford to sacrifice quality to quantity when hiring talent. UDA solutions such as video interview are helping leading organizations to simplify their recruiting process and optimize their recruitment productivity and overall candidate experience by delivering more qualified candidates in less time and increasing company talent pool.

Artificial intelligence will definitely change the talent acquisition and retention equation; it will enable companies to leverage UDA powered by AI algorithms to optimize every step of their talent life cycle management. And human capital management decisions will become more and more a combination of art (the human resource experience and intuition) and science (the data intelligences).

FURTHER READING

Alan Boyle, "AI Software Masters the Game of Go, Takes Aim at the World's Top Player," GeekWire, January 27, 2016: www.geekwire.com/2016/ai-software-masters-the-game-of-go-historic-human-vs-machine-match-awaits/

HireVue Video Intelligence: www.hirevue.com/

IBM Watson, "IBM Watson: How It Works," YouTube video, uploaded October 7, 2014. www.youtube.com/watch?v=_Xcmh1LQB9I

Jean Paul Isson, "The 7 Pillars of Successful People Analytics Implementation," *ERE Media*. May 12, 2016: www.eremedia.com/ere/the-7-pillars-of-successful-people-analytics-implementation/

Todd Raphael, "IBM Is Launching a Much-Awaited 'Watson' Recruiting Tool," ERE Recruiting, September 27, 2016: www.eremedia.com/ere/ibm-is-launching-a-much-awaited-watson-recruiting-tool/

Matt Straz, "Why You Need to Embrace the Big Data Trend in HR," *Entrepreneur*, April 6, 2015: www.entrepreneur.com/article/244326

Kaveh Waddell, "The Algorithms that Tell Bosses How Employees Are Feeling, *Atlantic Monthly*, September 29, 2016: www.theatlantic.com/technology/archive/2016/09/the-algorithms-that-tell-bosses-how-employees-feel/502064/

CHAPTER 7

The Power of UDA in the Legal Industry

If you do not know how to ask the right question, you discover nothing.

—W. Edwards Deming

WHY SHOULD YOU CARE ABOUT UDA IN LEGAL SERVICES?

Today we are living in an increasingly connected world, where more than 3.9 billion people have access to the Internet. Technology advances have recorded growth of unprecedented computing power, which enables machines to become proficient at performing high-frequency, high-volume, labor-intensive human tasks.

The demography of the workforce is changing across all industries, and the legal field is no exception. The rise of Millennials in the workplace will significantly alter the nature of talent available for law firms of the future. The majority of talent will be Millennials who, having "grown up digital," are highly adaptive to technological changes.

Throughout this book, we have discussed and demonstrated the impact of UDA, Big Data analytics, and artificial intelligence in several industries and professions. The data-driven change that we underscored elsewhere is entering the legal system, as the profession has and continues to generate an overwhelming amount of data. Every case that reaches the court is an important source of relevant data and insights that lawyers must leverage to build their cases and defend their clients.

The good news is that this data is becoming more and more digitized. It can easily feed unstructured data analytics (UDA) and artificial intelligence (AI) algorithms for legal technical applications and services. The legal system has an outstanding opportunity to tap into its data that, for the most part, has been text-heavy and generally untapped. If there is a list of industries that are fueled by unstructured data, the legal system will top it; most of its data sources come from judges' summaries, court logs, cases, statutes, regulations, contracts, witness statements, audio and video from evidences, judicial rulings, interpretation of legislature and precedents, and case discoveries. Data is found in scanned documents, e-mails, databases, legal documents, legal articles, judicial decisions, and transcripts of court hearings. To go through all this data, lawyers spend hours researching to find information pertaining to their cases.

Predictive analytics, which can help to detect and prevent fraud, to predict who will buy, who will churn, who will vote, or who will cheat, are now being used in judicial research.

Analytics systems are now capable of assisting court decisions and other judicial processes, such as using predictive modeling to determine the probability to re-offend when considering whether to grant parole to an inmate. On July 20, 2017, a group of four Nevada commissioners leveraged a statistical predictive model to grant O. J. Simpson parole as early as October 1, 2017 after nine years in prison for a Las Vegas robbery.

Whenever we have information that can be digitized, analytics can be applied to derive meaning. And in the case of law data that is text-heavy, UDA and natural language processing are game changers or disruptors for the industry. Since their inception in late 1990, online mediation services have been growing, assisting organizations and general public with e-mediation services. eBay is one of the leading organizations that has successfully implemented and leveraged an online mediation solution. In the first two weeks of its implementation, eBay's e-mediation service handled something like 150 online mediations. Today, eBay resolves more than 60 million disputes every year using its online dispute resolution system. Only a small number of those require the intervention of a mediator; nevertheless, it brings a whole new perspective to the situation. It would be impossible to imagine how such an astonishing number of disputes could be handled without a legal analytics service such as e-mediation.

According to an article from Bernard Marr, Ravel Law, a legal system service provider of search and visualization that allows researchers and developers to access, understand, and extract value from massive amounts of legal data, is working with the Harvard Law School to digitize the faculty's entire U.S. case library, the largest outside the Library of Congress, and make American case law open and free to anyone online by 2017.[1] The CEO of Ravel Law indicates that every page of every document will be scanned and converted to computer text with optical character recognition technology. This means it will be available for UDA (such as natural language processing and AI algorithms). If you still believe automation will only affect blue-collar jobs, think again! Lawyers will see an unprecedented transformation of their profession and a dramatic change in the way they deliver legal services. Change has already begun.

Several companies provide legal data information for research. LexisNexis and Westlaw are two leaders that provide these databases, making them the starting point for much legal research. According to an ALM Intelligence report, 73 percent of legal work is now performed in-house for most corporations, and only 25 percent of the market share is left to law firms, with alternative service providers (ASPs) accounting for 2 percent.[2] Even if law firms still represent the largest portion of outsourced work, this is an amazing statistic given that just two decades ago, law firms were the sole and unique legal services providers from start to finish.

The emergence of extremely capable and powerful machines and UDA algorithms has led to the development of technical applications for legal services such as E-Discovery. Technology-assisted review (TAR), also known as computer-assisted review or predictive coding, applies supervised machine learning or rule-based approaches during preliminary legal research to determine the relevance of data (responsiveness, privilege, or other categories of interest) for case preparation. According to Erik Sherman in a *Fortune* article, for high-profile lawsuits:

> ... the discovery process can involve literally millions of documents. Reviewing such materials was traditionally one of the lower-level tasks articling lawyers or paralegals could face. But now, new software systems can do that job.

> These applications use syntactic analysis and keyword recognition to comb through e-mails, texts, databases, and scanned documents to find those that one party in a lawsuit would be obliged to turn over to the other through the legal discovery process.[3]

Soon, AI-driven legal applications will be able to build a system of a comprehensive library of cases and precedents; it will even be able to create briefs.

Another example is an AI legal assistant called ROSS, developed by three students from the University of Toronto and since acquired by IBM. ROSS is being used to automate and standardize much of the same legal research, particularly the research process in bankruptcy cases. It is poised to be used in other judicial fields as well. A change is underway to use AI power to drive a more customer-centric focus to legal services.

Technology is already impacting the legal industry in various ways as it has done in other industries. A 2016 Deloitte study predicted that within the next ten years, potentially 114,000 jobs in the legal sector could be automated as the profession feels the impact of these and future "radical" changes.[4] Today, more than 31,000 legal jobs have already been eliminated by technology. However, new jobs will likely be created as well, because those labor-intense tasks will migrate to more strategic and paraprofessional roles.

The advent of computing power, UDA, and natural language processing will dramatically disrupt the legal service and create major changes, including:

- Automation of legal services and legal service delivery
- Expansion of the business of law, with more legal judicial options and services
- Generation of new legal service business models
- Fewer traditional lawyers in law firms, a growth in non-lawyer roles, and greater use of technology and alternative career options
- In-sourcing of legal services in corporations, instead of partnering with law firms
- Change in the legal system supply–demand equation, with more clients having access to legal services
- Reshaping of the legal service market, with customers having access to more affordable service providers
- Reduction of the scope and market share of law firms
- Emergence of more and more data-savvy lawyers and attorneys

In Western society, there is an alarming need for legal services and unfortunately, many simply cannot afford it. Today, many small and medium-sized businesses simply cannot afford the high cost of legal service fees of law firms. Many will turn to other providers to get legal services, reducing the amount time and money spent on traditional law firms.

New legal services providers powered by UDA, AI, and other technology will emerge, designed to deliver a more efficient, customer-focused legal service at a lower cost. The adoption of legal technology services is a global phenomenon; the market is burgeoning despite resistance from some governments to open access to investment and to non-law professionals. The legal service market is expanding across the world, driven by the overall spirit of these service providers granting access to the justice system to more people at lower costs.

In some forward-looking firms, lawyers are already teaming up with legal apps and technical tools to increase productivity and efficiency and to reduce costs. This trend will more likely become a standard when the new generation of grown-up digital native lawyers get into the marketplace, becoming the largest labor force in law firms.

WHAT IS UDA APPLIED TO LEGAL SERVICES?

UDA applied to legal services is the process of leveraging UDA (such as natural language processing, AI, machine learning, or deep learning) to address legal system business questions, including:

- Providing answers to legal search queries
- Answering legal questions
- Predicting case outcomes
- Providing explanations
- Making arguments for a case decision or against legal conclusions
- Finding applicable precedents and court judgements
- Enabling extraction of semantic information from legal text documents and assisting humans in performing legal tasks
- Finding jurisdiction and jurisprudence about previous cases and hearings
- Finding court decisions about civil or criminal cases
- Providing general legal information to average citizens

Because law articles, documents, cases, and judgments are all text-heavy, UDA is best suited to sift through and analyze the data. Today, UDA enables those in legal services to access, read, process, and harness millions of pages of legal documents in seconds. They can easily perform UDA tasks such as text clustering, classification, and categorization, as well as document classification, clustering, and ranking.

HOW DOES IT WORK?

Fundamental research and case preparation is the core of a lawyer's job, and it requires data gathering and data integration. This process is labor intensive and time consuming. Big Data has changed other industries, and the legal field has been gradually embracing this change. The legal field is poised to integrate analytics into its practice thanks to the emergence of data-savvy lawyers and other legal professionals who are eager to leverage the power of UDA and AI algorithms. The legal and medical professions are known to be some of the most conservative academic fields. However, both fields have opened to data analytics in the past few years. A new generation of lawyers who have grown up digital and witnessed the power of data analytics has high expectations from this technology. They are contributing heavily to the change that digitization and Big Data analytics will bring to the legal profession.

Legal data is mostly made up of text, images, and video data. Before applying any type of analytics, potentially relevant electronically stored information (ESI) must be extracted from its native source into a separate repository. Collecting the data requires a combination of legal and data architecture backgrounds to properly leverage all data sources and types, as well as to ensure the underlying data security.

For instance, when considering data such as an e-mail, one needs to know the following:

- Who originated the e-mail?
- When was it sent?
- Who was involved?
- Who had access to certain types of restricted information?
- Was the protocol to access the information followed?
- Was the hierarchy in the information distribution and sharing respected?

Exhibit 7.01 describes how actionable insights are created by applying UDA to legal data from a variety of sources.

The ultimate goal of the UDA bridge presented in the exhibit is to transform legal data from a variety of sources into actionable legal insights that lawyers can use to build their cases and impact court decisions.

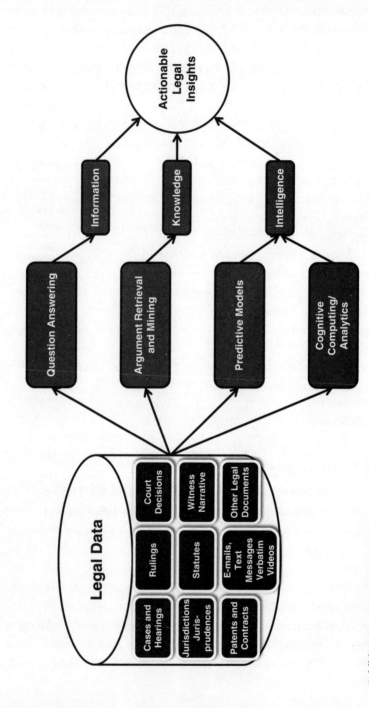

Exhibit 7.01 Unstructured Legal Data Analytics Bridge

Kevin D. Ashley, in his book, *Artificial Intelligence and Legal Analytics*, identifies several ways that UDA is used in the legal industry:

1. Question answering:

    Question answering provides the user with legal information. Question answering systems search a large text collection to locate the particular phrases or sentences that would answer a specific question; they then summarize the required information for specific documents as part of information extraction. Machine learning is applied to assist with completion of these functions.

2. Argument mining and retrieval:

    Argument retrieval or mining, as the name implies, involves specifically locating argumentative structure within texts and identifying relationships between arguments. Again, machine learning can be applied to assist in processing semantic information in the texts.[5]

3. Legal text analytics (LTA) and predictive models:

    The output of predictive models is legal intelligence. LTA enables information that is buried in legal text archives or documents to be located and identified and analyzed. Then predictive models can help to anticipate the outcome of a case, based on analysis of the historical legal data uncovered through LTA.

    The LTA process automates the knowledge representation process, leveraging text analytics techniques to automatically extract insights from cases, decisions, and statutes that will assist an attorney or any other legal resources. LTA can help to anticipate case outcomes, provides relevant answers to legal questions, and provides explanations or arguments regarding legal outcomes.

4. Cognitive computing (for argument retrieval):

    Cognitive computing in the legal industry is concerned with enabling computers to locate and identify semantic information in legal texts, providing it in a way that helps people gain answers to their legal questions. Therefore, cognitive computing also provides legal intelligence.[6]

Therefore, it is imperative that law schools address this new world of technology. Ashley points out that William Henderson endorses law schools rising to this challenge by teaching their students skills such as process engineering.[7]

It was not surprising when IBM General Counsel Robert C. Weber claimed in 2011 that cognitive computing will help and assist us in a variety of tasks (as reported by Ashley):

- Gathering facts
- Identifying ideas while in the process of constructing legal arguments
- Assisting with fact-checking in near-real time in the courtroom; for example, checking the credibility of a witness's statement
- Impacting jurisdictions' legal subject matter expert and choice of law[8]

IBM is heavily using Watson, leveraging Watson's text processing technology to perform argument mining via its cognitive solutions in a program called IBM Debater. The program, introduced in spring 2014, is trained to recognized and extract arguments from texts. IBM Debater can detect relevant information about a case and provide insights to predict the ruling, outcome, or defense strategy (the task is to detect relevant claims and return the information to predict for proclaim and conclaim).

According to many studies, legal researchers spend 20 to 30 hours to find information for lawyers to prepare their case. Imagine the potential savings of time alone that could be realized by applying a UDA solution that can leverage semantic searches and natural language processing, such as IBM's ROSS. According to ROSS chief executive officer (CEO) Andrew Arruda, their algorithm can read a million of pages per second and find the legal text the user may need. He believes that in the near future, every law firm in the world will be using ROSS to assist them. And in the spirit of justice for all, ROSS is available free for lawyers who are assisting people with low incomes who cannot afford the traditional legal fees.[9]

Let's revisit how all this works through stages:

Stage 1. A lawyer is assigned a case after meeting with a client.

Stage 2. The case is discussed with the client to get all pertinent information.

Stage 3. The information is gathered.

In this stage, the legal team needs to put together all the information necessary to prepare the case. Often, this step is very time-consuming. Most lawyers will turn to a legal research team to perform the labor-intensive manual search of all information pertaining to the case, including data like precedents, previous rulings, e-mails, patents, wills, previous court judgments and court rulings, evidence used in similar cases, judgment summaries, jurisprudences, case amendments, pictures, audio and video, and the like.

Additional information might be required based upon the nature of a case, such as:

- Accident and personal injury
- Bankruptcy
- Business and corporate
- Civil rights (human rights)
- Civil law
- Environmental law
- Family law (divorce, custody, etc.)
- Health law
- Immigration law
- Intellectual property law
- International law
- Employment/labor law
- Military law
- Real estate law
- Tax law

After the information is gathered and integrated, the research team will turn to legal database providers to acquire any complementary information.

UDA helps law firms optimize their legal information gathering process for their cases by leveraging, for instance, natural language processing–powered applications or AI algorithms to harvest the information in a matter of seconds. The lawyers can thus focus their time on strategies for bringing and defending cases in court. Some data-savvy lawyers I spoke with are also running predictive judicial judgements models to anticipate the likelihood of winning their cases and, more importantly, to gather key trigger elements that they can use to turn the court judgment to their favor.

Below is a brief description of the legal text analytics process (see Exhibit 7.02):

Step 1: *Legal Search Query Submission* (Question)

In this step, the legal search query, which is basically text from a question, is submitted to the system for analysis.

Step 2: *Query Processing*

The legal search query is reformulated, then parsed, tokenized, and analyzed to go through the text mining process.

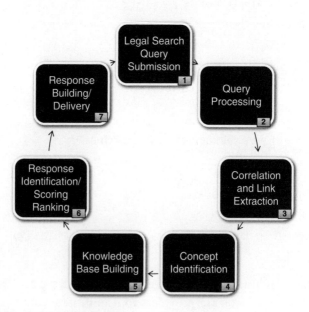

Exhibit 7.02   Text Analytics Process

Step 3: *Correlation and Link Extraction*

A semantic analysis of the submitted text is performed to extract relationship links and correlations between all the variations, called *n*-grams, of the submitted text, as well as any related information in the system that could be written differently.

Step 4: *Concept Identification*

A semantic analysis is performed to identify what concepts are derived from the text query that yield the same meaning. Within what context? The analysis provides some business intelligence metrics.

Step 5: *Concept/Knowledge Base Building*

At this step, filters are applied to define which concepts to include or exclude in the legal search query based on the semantic analysis and indexation of the search query, taking into account concepts context and analysis.

Step 6: *Candidate Identification/Scoring and Ranking*

An analysis is performed to score and rank the answers, identifying the best answers to the query. Scoring and ranking are based on their relationship with the parsed and tokenized query, taking into account the concept knowledge base, the context, and the relevance.

Step 7: *Response Building/Delivery*

After scoring and ranking all candidate responses, an optimal answer is derived by choosing the best-scored and -ranked evidence, based upon relevancy. The final response is then presented to the user who initiated the legal search query.

BENEFITS AND CHALLENGES

The implementation of UDA in the legal system will certainly deliver tremendous benefits, but it will also bring some challenges to some law firms.

The benefits will help to:

- Create easy and more user-friendly access to legal service for most people

- Make legal services more affordable by reducing costs
- Increase and diversify legal services
- Increase competition
- Empower predictive analytics and AI to optimize judicial processes and procedures
- Increase the use of technology in legal service
- Bring more transparency, efficiency, and effectiveness
- Provide equal justice for everyone
- Help reduce the time it takes a lawyer to prepare cases

Machines are now extremely capable of generating automated financial reports and sports reports, and some argue that in the near future we could witness automation of legal briefing as well. This will trigger a surgical change in the legal industry that Richard Susskind describes as a commoditization of legal service or legal work in his book *The End of Lawyers? Rethinking the Nature of Legal Services*. Susskind predicted that legal work would evolve from bespoke (or customized) to standardized systematized packaged and ultimately to a commoditized format.[10]

Most believe that machines will be able to:

- Assess legal arguments
- Pose legal hypotheses
- Make legal arguments
- Predict the outcome of legal disputes
- Settle some legal disputes, as we mentioned with the case of eBay, which is already using e-mediation to settle millions of disputes every year.

Additionally more judgments will be backed by data-driven insight, reducing error rates, mistrials, and time-consuming retrials or appeals. This should raise public trust for the legal system.

The benefits of UDA come with some challenges for the profession. Quantitative legal prediction will become pervasive. Some studies in the United States found that lawyers are highly paid to determine which arguments are most likely to win a case, to assess past court rulings, and even to discover the idiosyncrasies of a judge.

According to the article, "Using Data to Predict Supreme Court's Decisions," Daniel Martin Katz, Michael J. Bommarito, and Josh Blackman have created an algorithm that accurately predicted 70 percent of the Supreme Court overall decisions and 71 percent of the votes of individual justices, the most robust results of any other predictive study done to date.[11] Applying various techniques from machine learning, the algorithm considers dozens of variables before it makes a prediction. Being able to make predictions of legal outcomes is probably the most valuable tool lawyers can have.

Lawyers will have to adapt to the new generation of legal services delivery. It will remove repetitive, labor-intensive tasks from their desk, allowing them to focus on improving their practice. They will migrate to a service model in which they team up with computers with AI applications that will be constantly learning with them.

There will also be a reduction of legal aid lawyers. The speed with which machines can process high-frequency, repetitive, high-volume tasks will reduce workloads by scanning millions of pages per second and finding the exact parts of the texts that they are looking for.

The legal industry is not alone in this shift; we will witness similar changes in other professions such as medicine, accounting, and auditing. As Richard and Daniel Susskind, authors of the book *The Future of the Professions: How Technology Will Transform the Work of Human Experts*,[12] point out, depending on the level of capacity and the willingness to embrace change, law firms and legal systems (and others) will face three critical stages:

Stage 1: *Denial* of the impact of AI on their industry

Stage 2: *Belief* that they can simply reshuffle resource allocation for legal services

Stage 3: *Disruption*. Those who understand that disruption is coming (it is already there) will embrace it and become early adopters; they will be the leaders and potential winners

As with other industries, I believe that new rules, standards, conventions, protocols, and so forth will be embedded into the technical solutions of the legal services. Due to applications like Big Data analytics, UDA, and AI, there will be a significant decline in the traditional custom of seeking a lawyer to get professional advice.

The application of data analytics will potentially lead to the replacement of some judges and lawyers by computer algorithms in minor and noncriminal cases, where a computer algorithm can apply the judgment based solely on the rules of law, free from emotional or unconscious bias and sometimes misjudgments.

KEY TAKEAWAYS

- UDA and AI will create an unprecedented transformation in the way law firms operate and deliver services. To remain competitive, lawyers will have to team up with computer algorithms that are becoming extremely capable of performing repetitive, labor-intensive tasks quickly and efficiently, leaving more time to lawyers to strategize to defend and win cases.

- Legal systems across the world are embracing the digital transformation at various paces. While some leading firms are integrating data analytics disruption as a key component of their practice and service delivery, those who are in the denial stage or are complacent will likely become laggards and will have to play catchup.

- UDA and AI will have an impact on the legal service supply–demand equation, resulting in the automation of some legal jobs.

- The legal profession, which is considered one of the most conservative fields, will undergo major changes due to Big Data and UDA. This change will impact every aspect of the profession, the way its work is accomplished, and the way it delivers legal services to citizens. Legal service will become more accessible and user-friendly.

- The market for legal service is growing and changing, exhibiting an unprecedented increased demand for alternative or nontraditional legal service providers.

- Purchasers of legal service are evolving, being more and more data-savvy and data-inclined, leading consequently to an overhaul of the practice of law and its entire service delivery model.

- The legal profession will be radically different in the next decade, with advances in automation of tasks, a demographic change in labor force with more Millennials in senior roles, and more technology-savvy talent and clients. The talent and clients will force law firms and legal service providers to adjust their skillsets and the nature of the legal services they deliver in order to meet and exceed their higher expectations.

- The impact of UDA in legal service will be a reduction in cost, making the service more affordable; an increase in competition; and the optimization of the judicial system process and procedures, granting access to justice to more people.

■ More judgments will be backed by data-driven insight, reducing error rates, mistrials, and time-consuming retrials or appeals. This should raise public trust for the legal system.

NOTES

1. Bernard Marr, "How Big Data Is Disrupting Law Firms and the Legal Profession," Forbes, January 20, 2016: www.forbes.com/sites/bernardmarr/2016/01/20/how-big-data-is-disrupting-law-firms-and-the-legal-profession/

2. Andrew Neblett and Larren Nashelsky, General Counsel Up-at-Night Report, ALM Intelligence and Morrison Foerster, 2017: http://interactive.corpcounsel.com/Global/FileLib/Morrison_&_Foerster/FINAL_Up_at_Night_Report_6_27_17.pdf

3. Erik Sherman, "5 White-Collar Jobs Robots Already Have Taken," Fortune, February 25, 2015: http://fortune.com/2015/02/25/5-jobs-that-robots-already-are-taking/

4. Peter Saunders, Jeremy Black, Karin McNicholls, and Tutsani Lawson, "Developing Legal Talent, Stepping into the Future of Law Firm," Deloitte, 2016.

5. Kevin D. Ashley, Artificial Intelligence and Legal Analytics (New York, NY: Cambridge University Press, 2017), 5.

6. Ashley, Artificial Intelligence and Legal Analytics, 11.

7. Ashley, Artificial Intelligence and Legal Analytics, 7.

8. Ashley, Artificial Intelligence and Legal Analytics, 24–31.

9. Andrew Arruda, "The World's First AI Legal Assistant," TED@IBM, December 21, 2016: www.ted.com/watch/ted-institute/ted-ibm/the-world-s-first-ai-legal-assistant

10. Richard Susskind, The End of Lawyers? Rethinking the Nature of Legal Services (Oxford, U.K.: Oxford University Press, 2010).

11. Kim Ward and Daniel Martin Katz, "Using Data to Predict Supreme Court's Decisions," MSU Today, November 4, 2014: http://msutoday.msu.edu/news/2014/using-data-to-predict-supreme-courts-decisions/

12. Richard Susskind and Daniel Susskind, "The Future of the Professions," Talks at Google, London, October 2015: www.youtube.com/watch?v=ulXwTpW2oFI and Richard Susskind, "The Future of the Professions," Artificial Intelligence and the Law Conference at Vanderbilt Law School, April 14, 2016: www.youtube.com/watch?v=xs0iQSyBoDE

FURTHER READING

"Using E-Mediation and Online Mediation Techniques for Conflict Resolution," Program on Negotiation Daily Blog, Harvard University, October 16, 2017 (originally published 2015): www.pon.harvard.edu/daily/mediation/dispute-resolution-using-online-mediation/

CHAPTER 8

The Power of UDA in Healthcare and Medical Research

Technology is unlocking the innate compassion we have for our fellow human beings.

—Bill Gates[1]

WHY SHOULD YOU CARE ABOUT UDA IN HEALTHCARE?

Untapped Potential of Healthcare Data Goldmine

Healthcare is one of the fastest growing industries, and it is undergoing dramatic changes. The convergence of advanced technology, Big Data, cloud computing services, and machine learning is creating affordable artificial intelligence (AI)–based expert insight. We see changes in how medical service is conceived and delivered and in how medical research is done. Patients also have greater access to critical healthcare information. Insurance companies and government can leverage advanced analytics to address waste and losses in medical bills and claims. Big Data analytics is the cornerstone of healthcare transformation; it will dramatically improve patients' experience and outcome.

According to some studies, healthcare data, which is found in claims, clinical work (labs test and interpretation), doctor's notes and narratives, patient prescriptions, patients' electronic medical records (EMRs) and electronic health records (EHRs), medical journal articles, research publications, and medical images, accounts for more than 30 percent of the Big Data we have today. Most of that data is still untapped, which sets the stage for unstructured data analytics (UDA) to become the next innovation in healthcare analytics.

From the invention of the first mercury thermometer by Daniel Gabriel Fahrenheit in 1714 to today's pacemaker and smart artificial prostheses, the medical community has embraced technology to improve and save lives. Over the past few years, we have witnessed Big Data analytics applications success stories across several industries. Electronic medical record (EMR) or electronic health record (EHR) systems have democratized the access of healthcare information by the medical community. Thanks to government penalties and incentives, today 93 percent of physicians in the United States are using EHR, up from 9 percent in 2008. Healthcare costs are soaring, with global health spending projected to rise by 4.2 percent per year: from $7.1 trillion in 2015 to $8.7 trillion by 2020. The need for sustainability and affordability is forcing providers to collaborate with health system partners to apply digital technology and Big Data to lower healthcare costs, deliver safer personalized care to patients, and improve patient outcomes.

Ever-Increasing Volume of Patient Data from Internet of Things

As mentioned previously, by 2030, with the Internet of Things, more than 50 billion connected devices will be exchanging data from multiple sources. The data generated by patient wearable devices, healthcare employees' sensors, hospital room sensors, and lab equipment will create an unprecedented flow of mostly unstructured data for the medical community, patients, EMR systems, and health-care information management systems (HCIMS). Leading healthcare providers and hospitals are already leveraging data from employees' and patients' devices to provide real-time responses to patient needs, optimize services, reduce costs, and improve patient outcome.

The Internet of Things is driving more digitalization and the need for analytics of healthcare data. Remote patient-monitoring systems, sensors, smartphones, Fitbits, Bluetooth, and other wearable devices collect thousands of pieces of health data about medication intake, blood pressure, glucose levels, physical activity, heart rate, caloric expenditure, and weight, to name a few. UDA, propelled by machine learning and deep learning, is poised to dramatically disrupt medicine, in the process improving patients' safety, experiences, and outcomes.

This disruption will be apparent in the delivery of smart assistive technologies and actionable information, and it will have a huge impact on everyone in the medical system, including:

- The patient
- The physician
- The digital pathologist
- The medical researcher (through genomic analytics)
- The psychiatrist
- Public health, insurance, and government

The Patient

The patient is the main benefactor of UDA, as machine learning and deep learning algorithms applied to healthcare data will provide:

- Education, knowledge, and actionable information concerning his or her health status, diseases, and progress on the care plan. This knowledge should alleviate some stress associated with uncertainty and helplessness.
- Firsthand information about CT scan and MRI results, with comparative results and relative interpretations.

■ Empowerment to engage in his or her diagnostic and care process. This is especially possible via assistive technology. With access to the EHR, diagnostic testing results, and progress results, the patient can review for accuracy and seek better information or ask for more therapeutic options.

The Physician

It is estimated that there are 90,000 deaths per year due to errors in healthcare in the United States.[2] According to an IBM study, more than one out of five diagnoses is wrong. Common errors will result in missed, delayed, and wrong diagnoses, which can lead to unnecessary treatments, harm to the patient, and even death.[3]

An extensive body of research has examined the causes of diagnostic error at the individual clinician level. This work, informed by the field of cognitive psychology, is based on how individuals process information and subsequently develop plans.[4]

In healthcare, clinicians frequently use heuristics (shortcuts or "rules of thumb") to develop a provisional diagnosis, especially when faced with a patient with common symptoms. Researchers have used categories to classify types of errors that clinicians commonly make due to incorrect applications of heuristics: for example, availability, anchoring, framing effects, and blind obedience. In addition to cognitive errors, other human and external factors can come into play, such as:

■ Cognitive overload (humans cannot process huge amounts of information to find hidden patterns)

■ Interruptions or distractions

■ Sleep deprivation, fatigue, distraction, and emotional perturbations

■ Inadequate or defective imagery

■ Timely access to multiple and integrated data sources regarding the patient

UDA, powered by cognitive analytics like IBM-Watson, can read more than 800 million pages per second of medical research. Watson can compare millions of diagnostics and recommendations from the best physicians in the world. By using such cognitive systems, physicians could drastically correct the curve of diagnostic errors.

The Digital Pathologist

Reading and interpreting a huge number of slides and images and delivering an accurate diagnosis is an extremely complex task. To achieve this, the pathologist requires extensive training, expertise, and experience. Many hours and days can be spent on images from a single patient to ensure the quality and accuracy of the diagnostic decision. However, despite experience, expertise, and diligence, there has been significant interpathologist variability in diagnoses provided to the same patient. In their article "Assisting Pathologists in Detecting Cancer with Deep Learning," Martin Stumpe and Lily Peng pointed out:

> ...agreement in diagnosis for some forms of breast cancer can be as low as 48%, and similarly low for prostate cancer. The lack of agreement is not surprising given the massive amount of information that must be reviewed in order to make an accurate diagnosis. Pathologists are responsible for reviewing all the biological tissues visible on a slide. However, there can be many slides per patient, each of which is 10+ gigapixels when digitized at 40X magnification. Imagine having to go through a thousand 10 megapixel (MP) photos, and having to be responsible for every pixel. Needless to say, this is a lot of data to cover, and often time is limited.[5]

Leading companies have been leveraging advanced UDA to address that issue, using the power of machine learning and deep learning algorithms that can now exceed human accuracy in image recognition to optimize the digital pathology diagnoses.

Computers Are Getting Better than Humans

As Exhibit 8.01 illustrates, computer vision today has exceeded human accuracy in images and video recognition of cars, animals, or people. Computers are now being taught to identify medical diseases in medical images or videos, and the results are compelling. Computers can

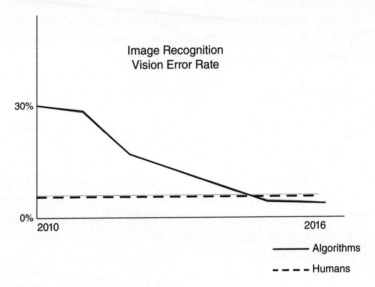

Exhibit 8.01 Computer Vision Error Rate

quickly get up to speed by reading and processing millions of medical articles regarding a specific disease or condition in seconds. The best physician in the world could not achieve a fraction of that in his or her lifetime.

Better Analyses and Diagnoses of Medical Image Texts

Multiple brain, breast, and lung MRI and CT scans are usually required to detect pathologies. A physician shared with me a story of a 40-year-old athletic and healthy man who went through several clinical tests due to a wrong interpretation of his brain MRI. The pathologist detected minor ischemic lesions in his MRI and quickly concluded the patient had had a recent stroke; the patient was placed on a stroke prevention protocol and prescribed Plavix (clopidogrel). His neurologist requested that they cross the MRI diagnosis against the patient historical EMR and brain images taken 10 years before. The neurologist discovered that the spot found in the recent MRI was already on a CT scan taken a decade before. Cross-analyses based on machine learning helped the neurologist to rule out a recent stroke. Data integration and deep learning provided more insight and relieved a lot of stress from the patient and family, as well as prevented unnecessary heavy medications.

Machine learning is not only helping pathologists to better detect brain, breast, and lung cancers; it also screens for diabetic retinopathy to prevent blindness in diabetic patients. IBM cognitive analytics tool Watson detects complicated and aggressive forms of brain cancer, such as glioblastoma, by analyzing very complex images from brain MRIs, leveraging the computing power of cognitive analytics. Google has built an automated detection algorithm to detect breast cancer in lymph node biopsies. The algorithm was designed to be highly sensitive, enabling pathologists to find even small instances of breast cancer metastases.[6]

These types of algorithms can naturally complement the pathologist's diagnostic workflow. Recent studies demonstrated that there is a double-digit improvement in diagnoses from reducing the number of false positives.

The Medical Researcher

It took almost ten years to map the DNA of one human being, at the cost of more than $100 million. Today, you can have your DNA sequenced for less than $95. Just imagine the impact this will have on medical research! Being able to cross clinical research trials data, DNA makeup, and EMR data will enable better diagnosis of some diseases and a better understanding of genetic diseases. UDA can be effectively included in genomic analytics as part of a regular medical care decision process. Another use would be to understand bacteria resistance to antibiotics and provide personalize medicine, instead of using conventional treatment based on averages. Now analytics is empowering epigenome,[7] microbiome,[8] and virome[9] sciences. UDA can help us understand what proteins of the genome change when we age, as well as what proteins change location and cause gene mutations and resistance due to environmental, physical, and psychological factors. The understanding of the microbiome and virome will provide leading indicators to help manage or cure chronic diseases.

The Psychiatrist

UDA is helping internationally acclaimed psychiatrists such as Dr. Daniel G. Amen, a distinguished fellow of the American Psychiatric Association, explore the human brain. As a pioneer in SPECT brain scanning, Dr. Amen introduced a whole new way of looking at the brain. With more than 80,000 brain images, he has the largest database of human brain images in the world. Dr. Amen underscored that analysis of brain images was paramount for psychiatric disease treatment, and added that better analysis and progress in UDA has been helping psychiatrists to better understand and address patients with psychiatric diseases by combining analysis of the brain images with the psychological pathology. His studies also demonstrated that using only a psychological approach was not sufficient, as it leaves patient brain issues unchecked. Patient brain image analytics is thus a key component of the successful treatment of psychiatric disease.

Public Health, Insurance, and Government

For public health, UDA and deep learning will not only improve patient and population health, but also lead to efficient healthcare data integration, analysis, and interpretation. Back in 2009 during the swine flu outbreak, Google leveraged text analytics of flu-related search queries to predict the propagation of the flu across states in the United States, two weeks ahead of the Centers for Disease Control (CDC) data. Such timely actionable insights can improve emergency planning and healthcare outbreak services.

As mentioned earlier, image recognition video analysis and text analytics of medical journal articles provide incremental efficiency and efficacy to physicians and healthcare researchers, to get up to speed with the latest progress and the best recommendations for diagnosis, treatment, and personalized medicine, therefore improving and saving lives. Assistive technologies can also provide access to diagnostic tests and treatments to physicians in remote locations.

For insurance and government, UDA can help analyze large amounts of claim requests to curtail medical bill fraud. By analyzing prescriptions, patients' claims, medical bills, and physicians' narratives, insurance companies can easily detect and prevent fraud.

As mentioned previously, in U.S. healthcare, more than $700 billion is lost to fraud, waste, and abuse—a huge cost for the government and society. The money saved by countering fraud activities could be reinjected into preventative and curative healthcare.

WHAT'S UDA IN HEALTHCARE?

UDA in healthcare is taking many forms. Leading healthcare organizations are now leveraging machine learning, deep learning, and cognitive analytics to drive performance and optimize their healthcare processes by creating value from digitized untapped healthcare information. Several examples of machine learning and information technology changing healthcare are found in healthcare specialties such as radiology, oncology, and dermatology.

According to Karen Taylor's article, by 2020 hospitals will be smart hospitals, enabled by innovations such as:

- *Blockchain technology*: "a shared, immutable record of peer-to-peer transactions built from linked transaction blocks and stored in a digital ledger. This allows each separate patient data source to be a 'block' part of a complete, unalterable patient data profile, which can then be shared securely with healthcare providers or research organizations."[10] It could surmount the current data security and patient privacy concerns that limit data exchange.

- *Bio-telemetry*: the use of sensors to gather "meaningful data and analytics . . . to monitor variability in vital signs throughout the day," including wearable technology either existing or in development, such as "smartwatches, eyeglass displays, and electroluminescent clothing,"[11] which can be used to monitor patients regardless of their location. Clinicians will be better able to track patient response to treatments and medications and to follow patient recovery paths.

- *Drug development/precision medicine*: the combination of genomics with Big Data to develop specific, targeted treatments. "Since the launch of the Human Genome Project, more than 1,800 disease genes have been discovered, and over 2,000 genetic tests for human conditions developed. Genomics is a major part of digital health. Computers and robotics are used to scale genomic sequencing and gene editing."[12] Oncology has benefited the most from this effort, but other specialty areas are exploring solutions in this area.

- ■ *Virtual rehabilitation in orthopedics*: To help improve success rates in physical therapy, "new sensor devices connected to a mobile app...guide patients through their daily exercise routine following orthopedic surgery, recording range-of-motion, which is key to better clinical outcomes. The data is also shared in real time so clinicians can tweak exercise protocols, and a virtual avatar can guide patients through exercises."[13]

The very notion of what constitutes a hospital is changing, with the drive to make healthcare location-independent. Walmart, Virgin Care, and CVS MinuteClinics are examples of relocalized healthcare (away from the hospital). However, the new push is for i-healthcare or virtual healthcare. In 2016, Kaiser Permanente indicated that more than half of their visits were virtual. They reported 57.5 million visits per year. Forward-looking institutions like Kaiser Permanente have integrated physical and virtual spaces to embrace patient-centricity and real-time data interpretation, while still enabling human interactions in strategic areas.

In Canada, telemedicine is also gaining a lot of momentum. Companies like GOeVisit are now challenging the free healthcare model. GOeVisit, a Canadian telemedicine subscription-based company, provides virtual consultations with medical practitioners for minor illnesses (thirty conditions) via computers, tablets, and smartphones. The GOeVisit medical team provides diagnosis, provides alternative remedies and/or prescriptions, coordinates prescriptions with the pharmacy, and arranges for their delivery. The team follows up with patients, regardless of their location.

There is a lot of effervescent development in technologies and applications to support i-healthcare. Named by Lucien Engelen in 2016, i-healthcare is defined as the practice of medicine and public health supported by AI, deep learning, and machine learning.[14] Similar concepts include e-health (supported by electronic processes and communication)[15] and m-health (supported by mobile devices).[16] Much of this development is based on everyday technology like phones and wearables and supports data sharing with peers and researchers. The following are only a few.

- **One Drop | Mobile**, from Informed Data System, Inc. (New York–based company, United States) is a cloud-based diabetes management platform delivered via mobile app. It provides real-time and historical blood glucose data and analytics to subscribers, peers, and their healthcare providers, allowing the establishment of relationships between specific health behaviors and health outcomes. It includes a fully featured Apple WatchOS app for logging and analyzing diabetes data on the go.

- **DxtER,** from Final Frontier Medical Devices (Pennsylvania-based team, United States) is an AI-based engine that learns to diagnose medical conditions by integrating learning from clinical emergency medicine with data analysis from actual patients. DxtER monitors the individual's health and autonomously diagnoses illnesses (such as anemia, urinary tract infection, Type 2 diabetes, atrial fibrillation, sleep apnea, COPD, pneumonia, otitis media, and leukocytosis). It also shares information with healthcare providers. DxtER uses noninvasive custom-designed sensors to collect data about vital signs, body chemistry, and biological functions.

- **Philips Enterprise telehealth** (worldwide) is an ambulatory telehealth program that provides daily connection between post-acute caregivers and patients, utilizing technology and clinical process to expand access, improve outcomes, and provide a better experience for patients. The program includes complex care, chronic disease management, and readmission management. Patients log their daily health status with the home tablet-based eCareCompanion app, and clinicians in the hospital can track their patients, identifying those most in need of immediate intervention to prevent a hospitalization.

- **VitalPatch**, by Vital Connect, Inc. (Campbell, California, US) is a wireless clinical-grade wearable biosensor that monitors, detects, diagnoses, and aids in directing the treatment of cardiovascular disease. The patch monitors eight vital signs continuously, in real time. Caregivers and hospital staff can access the information in a consolidated view, through one device, on a mobile platform.

- **Philips Lumify** (worldwide) is an ultrasound app that turns a compatible Android smart device into an ultrasound solution with the help of a plug-in transducer. It is designed to make ultrasound mobile and accessible.

- **IBM Watson Health** by IBM (worldwide) utilizes Watson's natural language, hypothesis generation, and evidence-based learning capabilities to support clinical decisions. When a physician queries the system, describing symptoms and related factors, Watson parses the input to identify the important pieces of information, mines patient data to find facts relevant to the patient's medical and hereditary history, examines available data sources to form and test hypotheses, and provides a list of individualized, confidence-scored recommendations. The sources of data that Watson uses for analysis includes treatment guidelines, EMR data, notes from physicians and nurses, research materials, clinical studies, journal articles, and patient information. Oncology has been an area of focus where insights to physicians and cancer patients help to identify personalized, evidence-based cancer care options.

- **HereIsMyData** by the REshape Center at Radboud umc (and Philips) is a dashboard controlled by the user (patient) that provides insights and supports health self-management. The user adds his or her own data from devices like activity trackers, weighing scales, and apps. The user can share data with peers or healthcare providers. He or she can connect apps and devices, create clinical modules with Philips, and connect services like Apple Health, Google Fit, and his or her EMR.

- **Avatars and Humanoids**
  - **Erica** and **Nadine** are female humanoids being developed in Japan with a view toward providing companionship to elderly people to help prevent mental decline and

improving communication skills among children with mental disorders.[17]

- **Molly** (Sense.ly) is a virtual nurse who provides customized monitoring and follow-up care, with a strong focus on chronic diseases. Patients interact directly with Molly using natural language.

Ultimately, UDA in healthcare helps to answer healthcare–related questions using integrated healthcare data, text, images, voice, analytics, and machine, deep, and cognitive learning. The actionable insights from UDA in healthcare systems enable patients, physicians, researchers, insurers, and all other stakeholders to detect, predict, and manage:

- Patient satisfaction
- Patient diagnosis
- Patient treatment
- Patient prognosis
- Patient risk (diseases, conditions, etc.)
- Clinical events, adverse events, and outcomes
- Population health, risks, and needs
- Medication and drug efficacy
- Costs and profitability
- Healthcare delivery efficacy (hospital readmission, staffing/ workforce needs, inventory needs)

Examples of healthcare–related questions include:

- How long will the patient stay in the intensive care unit (ICU)?
- Is the cancer present in certain tissues?
- Is the retina affected?
- Do the brain images reflect any pathology?
- Is the medical claim fraudulent?
- How resistant are specific bacteria to specific antibiotics?
- What is the best therapeutic option available for my condition?

HOW UDA WORKS

Before we address how UDA works, it is worth describing the complex reality of healthcare data.

Data Complexity

Healthcare data comes with unique data challenges related to the variety, variability, velocity, and veracity of sources, formats, standards, and definitions.

Data in healthcare comes from different source systems: different EMR or EHR software, different jurisdictions, different departments, hospitals, clinics, pharmacies, insurers, governments, and the like. Data can also be patient-generated, tracked from devices like fitness monitors, blood pressure sensors, and other health smart wearables. Healthcare data also occurs in different formats (e.g., text, numeric, paper, digital, pictures, videos, multimedia, etc.). Sometimes data related to the same event exists in different systems and is captured in different formats, like claims data versus clinical data. Such records use different nomenclatures, typologies, definitions, and coding standards—and that is assuming there is a consensus between the experts on the clinical event! That is often not the case.

The capture of information surrounding episodes of care in healthcare facilities through medical coding involves the assignment of industry-standard diagnostic, procedural, or intervention codes. In the case of patient safety incidents (or adverse events), additional data elements such as critical and contributing factors are also identified. Patient safety incidents can take place over several days, months, perhaps even years (e.g., in the case of missed diagnosis of cancer) and across multiple care episodes; they may involve numerous healthcare providers and sometimes more than one patient (e.g., a mother and baby).

Unfortunately, there is currently no universally accepted international standard for the taxonomy and definitions of clinical coding. In addition, the analysis and coding required takes significant time and the use of skilled resources, which are often not available.

Healthcare organizations can use data from other sources to monitor and measure various aspects of healthcare quality, safety, and performance:

- Electronic patient records
- Population health indicators
- Trigger tools
- Health and vital statistics
- Discharge abstracts (including ambulatory care)
- Patient safety incident reports (including sentinel events)
- Claims/complaints data
- Other relevant patient care–related registries, such as organ replacement, continuing care, hospital mental health, hospital morbidity, laboratory/imaging/radiation, prescription drug utilization, rehabilitation, trauma, etc.
- Administrative databases, such as those dealing with healthcare human resources (including physicians, nursing pharmacists, occupational and physiotherapists, and other healthcare providers), health expenditures, healthcare services, and facilities resource allocation records (e.g., staffing, budgets, equipment)
- Learning and training registries for healthcare providers
- Audit compliance reports from accreditation regulations

Some data is collected at the federal and state levels; some is collected by specialized organizations while some remains within hospitals or regions. There are also other sources of information that provide insights but are not systematically collected or measured, such as patient complaints, media reports, and findings from team meetings or discussions.

Another issue is the changing privacy, security, regulatory, and reporting requirements, which create specific issues when looking at data historically or through time. Therefore, standardizing and aggregating this data to make it accessible and actionable can be a formidable task. Such integration approaches need to handle the multiple sources of structured and unstructured data, the inconsistency and ambiguity, the variability, and the complexity within an ever-changing regulatory and reporting environment.

Aggregating Data

The common method of aggregating data from disparate source systems so it can be analyzed is to create an enterprise data warehouse (EDW). For data to be linked, unique identifier and business rules are required. This method is prevalent in manufacturing, retail, and financial services; however, it does not work very well in healthcare, because the business rule decisions required to link the data would need to be made before we know what to ask the data. In addition, healthcare is not an industry in which business rules and definitions are fixed for long periods of time. A rule set today may not be a best practice tomorrow. This implies that the data must be left "untouched" at the source and linked at a later stage of analysis. Therefore, data is aggregated quickly and business rules are made as needed to test hypotheses or search for patterns to support evidence-based decisions.

Cross-industry consensus is that approximately 80 percent of all data is unstructured. In healthcare, unstructured clinical data is often created at the point of care in the form of free-text or semistructured documentation. EMR/EHR solutions have focused on capturing clinical documentation from physicians and funnelling it into billing, decision support, predictive analytics, or population management workflows. There are billions of clinical notes written by physicians describing their clinical encounters. Those are, for the most part, excluded from analytics because they are not discrete; therefore, their insight is lost if UDA is not leveraged.

Transforming Unstructured Data into Discrete Data

To maximize the benefit of healthcare information we need to analyze the clinical narratives. Natural language processing (NLP) has been used to transform clinical narratives into discrete clinical codes. You will recall from Chapter 3 that NLP includes steps such as tokenization, sentence and structure detection, part-of-speech (POS) tagging, normalization, named entity resolution, parsing, semantics, negation and ambiguity detection, and semantics. Ultimately, the NLP application must read the text and transform it into discrete codes and classifications that are interpretable.

There are three ways NLP is applied to healthcare narratives/text data: rule-based, statistics-based, or a hybrid of both. Rule-based NLP means a group of experts write deterministic rules to implement the mappings in the NLP components. Statistical NLP means the system learns the mappings for the NLP components as statistical relationships by processing many examples. Currently, most NLP systems are adopting a hybrid approach.

Companies like 3M and SyTrue have built comprehensive smart data NLP platforms supported by core terminology servers to normalize free text into coding systems and terminologies. They also aggregate this information with discrete data from EMRs and diagnostic information systems via transformation interfaces. Those tools are designed to work in real-time to return actionable insights while the patient is being treated. The discrete clinical codes used to translate the narrative or text can be in several forms:

- SNOMED CT: a systematically organized, computer-processable collection of medical terms providing codes, terms, synonyms, and definitions used in clinical documentation and reporting. SNOMED CT provides the core general terminology for electronic health records. SNOMED CT includes clinical findings, symptoms, diagnoses, procedures, body structures, organisms and other etiologies, substances, pharmaceuticals, devices, and specimens.

- ICD: the International Statistical Classification of Diseases and Related Health Problems

- CCI: the Canadian Classification of Health Interventions is the national standard for classifying healthcare providers

- CPT: the American Medical Association standard terminology and coding used to describe medical services and procedures

- NCI: codes developed by the National Cancer Institute

As previously mentioned, none of these coding standards are internationally accepted, although the World Health Organization developed and supports ICD. Since these coding systems are not equivalent, there is a loss of information and some inaccuracy introduced when they are mapped during a data aggregation process.

Analytics

Successful implementation of healthcare analytics requires a full understanding of the healthcare environment and practices. Ideally, the data foundation would be reliable, valid, and subject to a good governance program. Given the current state of fragmentation in healthcare, this is not achievable. Despite this limitation, a properly designed analytics solution can provide insight for the healthcare organization on its progress on safety, quality, and performance goals through the monitoring of meaningful and actionable performance indicators.

Additionally, the analytics solution must be conceived in a way that allows decision makers and end-point users to access the information they require. To take full advantage of the information to guide decision making, the key performance indicators for capacity planning, performance monitoring, health trigger, or actioning should contain targets and thresholds.

The main steps of UDA in healthcare analytics are:

1. Gather all the healthcare data—structured and unstructured data—available.

2. Standardize, integrate, and centralize (if possible) the data.

3. Perform data cleansing (e.g., outlier detection, missing data, etc.).

4. Perform descriptive analysis.

5. Perform text analytics, and dimension reduction analysis like Principal Component Analysis (PCA), classification, and segmentation analysis (e.g., cluster analysis, decision trees, etc.) to reduce the dimensionality of the data and identify the key drivers.

6. Perform predictive analysis using advanced analytics software or open source or built-in algorithms.

7. Interpret the results and take proactive actions.

8. Measure; track the outcomes.

9. Optimize by putting the right strategy in place to avoid the unplanned outcome or remediate the trend.

By following the IMPACT cycle, healthcare organizations should maximize their success to implement healthcare analytics and UDA.

IMPACT Cycle

We will use the IMPACT cycle to summarize the process of applying UDA to healthcare as follows:

- *Identify healthcare–related question*: for instance, "Do the brain images reflect any pathology?"

- *Master the data*: Start with the integration of disparate data (healthcare data, EMR data, genomic data). Leverage machine learning, deep learning, and cognitive analytics to detect or make a prediction about medical health outcome.

- *Provide meaning*: Explain what's happening and why. Address what will happen so that the patient, physicians, or researcher can act.

- *Act*: Put actions in place that leverage the findings. Make recommendations or prescriptions based on machine learning models.

- *Communicate*: Make the findings accessible and available to the medical community.

- *Track the results*: Compare the results with and without UDA, and before and after UDA implementation.

BENEFITS

The use of analytics and UDA in healthcare will have a significant impact on patients, physicians, healthcare insurers, and the public health community. Some of the major benefits include:

- Help to improve patient experiences and save lives by providing personalized treatments as well as more accurate diagnosis and prognosis, thereby improving public health outcomes.

- Reduce stress for the patients and physicians; reduce healthcare disparities; engage patients and their families.

- Provide clinical innovations and cost-effective paths and care coordination for diagnostics and treatments.

- Provide enhancement in assistive healthcare technology and devices. UDA helps to provide patients with access to their healthcare data for them to manage their own healthcare.

- Enhance innovation in drug development and medical device research and development.

- Enable faster go-to-market for new drugs, new personalized treatments, and medicine based on individual DNA makeup, environmental and genetic factors, and patient behavior.

- Reduce the number of medical and diagnostic errors significantly.

- Reduce and save costs for government and insurance companies with effective and efficient approval of healthcare claims and payment of legitimate claims.

- Reduce public health waste and abuses, and provide effective ways to detect and prevent fraud in healthcare.

- Enable faster identification of disease outbreaks, and increase remote consultation platforms (video and audio) and remote monitoring with wearable sensors and mobile phone apps that monitor and track patient health conditions and symptoms.

- Improve telemedicine and alleviate some struggles that the healthcare system faces, such as lack of physicians to serve in remote location due to geographical constraints.

- Enable mobile health technologies and medication management.

- Identify and develop the next generation of healthcare treatments.

- Enhance remote patient monitoring service and improve remote/robotic clinical operations.

INTERVIEW WITH MR. FRANÇOIS LAVIOLETTE, PROFESSOR OF COMPUTER SCIENCE/DIRECTOR OF BIG DATA RESEARCH CENTRE AT LAVAL UNIVERSITY (QC) CANADA

I had the opportunity to speak with Mr. François Laviolette about the impact of Big Data and machine learning in healthcare and medical research.
Mr. Laviolette is a professor of computer science and serves as director of the Big Data Research Centre at Laval University (QC), Canada.

Isson: Why are we talking about Big Data and machine learning today in medical research?

Laviolette: Let's start with Big Data. We are talking about Big Data today for the following reasons:

1. *The computational architecture has exponentially increased. Computers today can process huge amounts of data from different sources in different formats that flow in continually. The speed of processing the data has dramatically improved; we moved from computing processing units (CPU) to graphics processing units (GPU); this migration provided computers with more speed and accuracy.*

   Last year, Google launched its cloud tensor processing unit (TPU), which is 15 to 30 times faster than CPU and GPU, to perform very complex tasks such as video recognition and voice recognition.

2. *We have seen an increase of infrastructures and tools that enable us to capture, store, integrate, and analyze a lot of data in memory. The storage and analysis of this data was previously impossible due to the volume, velocity, variety, and veracity of the data.*

3. *Machine learning algorithms that have been used in other business sectors are now being migrated and applied to healthcare and medical research, where we have a lot Big Data and Fat Data to harness.*

Isson: Where do to you see Big Data analytics having the biggest impact in healthcare?

Laviolette: The biggest impact in healthcare that I see will definitely be around machine learning and deep learning in medical research. It will enhance genomics analytics, lead to more personalized medicine, and improve the development of new drugs and treatments.

Isson: Can you give me examples of projects in healthcare/medical research where you have used machine learning?

Laviolette: Application of machine learning models to genomics data enabled us to better understand the resistance of bacteria such as M. tuberculosis, C. difficile, S. pneumoniae, and P. aeruginosa to some antibiotics. We have built machine learning algorithms, such as learning interpretable models of phenotypes from whole genome sequences, with the set covering machine models for antibiotics resistance. Our algorithms can predict antibiotics resistance using genome data with an accuracy as high as 90 percent. With such models, we expect great benefits to improve the personalization of medicine, giving patients the right antibiotics based upon the machine learning algorithm and optimizing the patient's treatment design plan. Our set covering machine models also help to address overfitting issues that usually happen with Fat Data, such as dealing with genomic data with thousands of rows and hundred millions of columns.

Isson: How do you see machine learning being used now and in the future in medical research? What do you foresee as the single biggest impact that machine learning will have on healthcare?

Laviolette: Precision medicine and personalized healthcare with better patient outcomes are the two areas where I see the biggest impact. Being able to transform billions of EMR data elements into relevant and robust health predictions and diagnostics will help to save and improve lives across the world.

INTERVIEW WITH PAUL ZIKOPOLOUS, VICE PRESIDENT BIG DATA COGNITIVE SYSTEM AT IBM

I had the opportunity to interview Paul Zikopoulos, Vice President Big Data Cognitive System at IBM.

Isson: What made IBM decide to invest in cognitive analytics/ computing?

Zikopoulos: The way I would best say is that, as an organization we are actually getting dumber. And that is a pretty profound statement. The amount of data that organizations are taking in is unprecedented, and it's going to grow even *more; think about the Internet of Things, Internet of Things sensors, block chain—companies are experts at having loads and loads of data. But the analytics on that data is getting dumber. Because if you think about the curve of the data we collect, it is exponential, but the amount of data we are analyzing (the curve) is going flat. We know less and less about what we could already know.*

A great example is in the medical area, where Cognitive and IBM had made a major investment. In areas such as an aggressive form of brain cancer called glioblastoma, there are 23 million medical research articles that have been published for that form of brain cancer. So, you could be the greatest clinician in the world, the number-one brain cancer doctor, but how could you possibly know all of the researches in 23 million medical research articles? You couldn't; the amount of data is enormous, so we are moving from the area of tabulated computing to programming. Programming computing now becomes cognitive, where machines are learning in recognizing patterns. And that's the reason why we have to pursue the virtue of analytics, and cognitive is the next step.

Isson: The majority of organizations I've spoken to have told me cognitive analytics is the next frontier of Big Data analytics innovation. Would you agree? And, if so, how is your organization working toward leveraging cognitive analytics that leads to better understanding and insight in areas like healthcare, national security, sports, and human capital management?

Zikopoulos: *Yes, I totally agree, and there are two areas;*

First, at IBM we are training Watson, our cognitive computer, around specific areas. For example, in healthcare, we've been training Watson for five or six years around cancer; and if you think about Watson, what it can do. We fed it with more than15 million pages of relevant journals and textbooks and 15,000 hours of oncologists' training every single month. So, you get professional cancer doctors who are teaching Watson about cancer. In other words, they may ask Watson a question, Watson comes back with an answer, and they say, here is the "rightest" answer. I like to say that in a year or two all of us will know someone whose life was saved or made better because of Watson.

The other thing we're doing is to try to make it for everyone. What I mean is that today, one of the biggest problems of Big Data is to be able to leverage data and analytics so it is not reserved to the privileged few—the few with a math, stats, computer science, or analytics background. We have to democratize that to the many. Make it accessible to everyday people, and the way to do that is to have a computer able to understand human requests in a natural language. You are seeing this everywhere: Amazon's Alexa, Apple's Siri and Home, the Google Assistant. The whole point of our cognitive mission is having that natural language conversation with Watson. How you get more people involved in analytics is to change the interface of the conversation. We are investing in training and access to the information.

Isson: Can you give me examples of business challenges you have addressed with cognitive analytics in the past? What solutions did you leverage and what were the benefits of your investment?

Zikopoulos: *Cancer is a great example of business challenge; a lot of information is coming in. The point Watson is addressing here is, how do we find inference in data that would never occur with a professional? Because clinicians and doctors don't have the bandwidth to go over all the data and digest that in a reasonable, timely manner.*

Isson: In this Big Data era, what advice would you give to a company trying to leverage cognitive analytics to get the most out of their unstructured data capabilities? What are the dos and don'ts of this undertaking? What strategies are important to make the project successful?

Zikopoulos*: Two big things: executive sponsor and business project, not technology-driven project.*

Get started with your analytics journey with the executive on board; go to the top and get buy-in. You have (need) a culture change. That's a do.

The don't: Don't make a dataset science project, and a lot of financial institutions did this. They created technology/data science projects. Don't create data science projects; create a business project, where the line of business sponsors the project; otherwise, you create all that and no one uses it. And the line of business is getting zero value. You need to have line of business sponsoring the project and working with IT.

Another do: Get started today. There is a Chinese saying that goes like this: The best time to plant a tree was 23 years ago; the second best time is today. You have to start this journey, and many companies haven't. You just have to get moving, otherwise the amount of data becomes bigger and bigger.

Isson: What is the number one benefit or top reason to invest in cognitive analytics? What is the biggest hurdle you will face when implementing?

Zikopoulos: *I think that cognitive analytics and data-driven decisioning is the way of the future. You are in an environment where massive companies, Standard & Poor's (S&P) companies, are getting massively disrupted by anybody. You need to get your strategy to understand customers and market strategy.*

And for the hurdles: First, culture and buy-in, and second, your data has to be curated and trusted. And most people do not have a relevant data governance strategy in their companies. My biggest fear is that we are going to train computers with non-curated and non-trusted data.

Isson: How do you see cognitive analytics being used now and in the future? What do you foresee as the single biggest impact that cognitive analytics will have on businesses and community?

Zikopoulos: *In the future, every company will be using it. At IBM we have taken Watson into 28 application programming interfaces (APIs).*

If you want vision recognition to be used by everyone: phone analysis and visual recognition. This will enable people to find inferences in data that would be very difficult to find without a computer in a variety of sectors such as healthcare, finance, sports, and national security.

Isson: Would Watson replace humans?

Zikopoulos: *That is a great question and a great debate. I don't think Watson will replace humans at all. I think we should let humans do what they're great at and computers do what they're great at. Computers are great at detecting patterns. So why would we not let computers go and detect a pattern and find a problem and then suggest to the expert who has more logical reasoning, empathy, and those types of things, to look at it? Watson will help the doctor see hidden patterns in huge amounts of data. What will be really interesting is that the doctor will see the patient and symptoms; he will be able to look at those symptoms in a cognitive computer, so he/she can look at data in the cognitive system about any emergency drop-in for the flu or flu-like symptoms in the last three weeks in the entire nation and its spread across the country, look for some similarity and draw some parallels. If I am talking to my doctor about a specific disease like Crohn's disease, and I am talking to my doctor about my diet, that doctor will have access to the impact of diet* *and food on Crohn's disease from 20 million Crohn's disease patients who love their food and the way their gut reacted that day.*

I don't think Watson will replace, but it will enhance doctors' and caregivers' impact.

It will move forward some of the stuff where people spend their time on questions that don't need an expert. As an example, I go to chat with my bank's cognitive computer. It can easily tell me how much I need to pay so I don't pay any interest.

This approach will help us to put humans on high-level tasks and give the low-level ones to computers.

CASE STUDY

CASE

GOOGLE USES DEEP LEARNING ALGORITHMS TO ASSIST PATHOLOGISTS IN DETECTING CANCER[18]

Challenges

Every year there are more than 230,000 breast cancer patients in the United States. Who looks for pathologist expertise to uncover whether the cancer has metastasized away from the breast? Metastasis detection is currently performed by pathologists reviewing large expanses of biological tissues.

Solution

To address the issues of limited time and diagnostic variability that most pathologists face, Google presents a framework to automatically detect and localize tumors as small as 100 × 100 pixels in gigapixel microscopy images sized 100,000 × 100,000 pixels. Their method leverages a convolutional neural network (CNN) architecture and obtains state-of-the-art results on the Camelyon16 dataset in the challenging lesion-level tumor detection task.

With eight false positives per image, they detect 92.4 percent of the tumors, relative to 82.7 percent by the previous best automated approach.

As a comparison, a human pathologist attempting an exhaustive search achieved 73.2 percent sensitivity. They achieve image-level AUC scores above 97 percent on both the Camelyon16 test set and an independent set of 110 slides.

With these results, Google was able to show that it was possible to train a model that either matched or exceeded the performance of a pathologist who had unlimited time to examine the slides.

KEY TAKEAWAYS

- From the invention of the thermometer to today's pacemaker and smart prosthetics, the medical community has been gradually embracing technology and analytics to save and improve lives and enhance patient care.

- The advent of EMR/EHR provides the opportunity to better integrate and harness healthcare data, leading to major benefits for every player in healthcare ecosystem: the patient, the physician, the researcher, the insurer, and the government.

- The advent of UDA computer vision, machine learning, and deep learning have leveraged EMR data to significantly improve the accuracy of diagnoses and pertinence of prescriptions and care paths.

- UDA will empower both patient and physician with actionable healthcare information, providing patients with firsthand advice about and access to their health information.

- UDA enables faster go-to-market for new drugs and new treatments and provides more personalized medicine based on individual DNA makeup.

- UDA enables faster identification of disease outbreaks.

- UDA provides regulatory agencies with evidence of drug safety and efficiency and better understanding of disease state.

- UDA improves manufacturing processes and sales and marketing efforts and helps to identify optimal strategies to commercialize treatments.

- UDA helps to leverage the power of DNA sequencing for personalized medicine, better treatment of some chronic diseases and types of cancers.

- UDA reduces costs and hurdles to access to healthcare data and information, spark innovation from health apps developers, clinics and hospital, and ultimately save and improve lives.

- UDA will transform healthcare and healthcare economy across the board by finding meaning buried in massive amounts of unstructured healthcare data.

NOTES

1. Bill Gates, "Bill Gates: Here's My Plan to Improve Our World—And How You Can Help," *Wired*, November 12, 2013: www.wired.com/2013/11/bill-gates-wired-essay/

2. L. T. Kohn, J. M. Corrigan, and M. S. Donaldson, editors. *To Err is Human: Building a Safer Health System* (Washington, DC: National Academies Press, 2000): www.ncbi.nlm.nih.gov/pubmed/25077248

3. "Watson Is Helping Doctors Fight Cancer," IBM press release: http://p3.m.ibm.com/http/www-03.ibm.com/innovation/us/watson/watson_in_healthcare.shtml

4. Justin Morgenstern, "Cognitive Errors in Medicine: The Common Errors." First10EM website, September 15, 2015: https://first10em.com/2015/09/15/cognitive-errors/

5. Martin Stumpe and Lily Peng, "Assisting Pathologists in Detecting Cancer with Deep Learning," *Google Research* Blog, March 3, 2017: https://research.googleblog.com/2017/03/assisting-pathologists-in-detecting.html

6. Katherine Chou and the Google Brain Team, "Partnering on Machine Learning in Healthcare," *The Keyword*, Google Blogs, May 17, 2017: www.blog.google/topics/machine-learning/partnering-machine-learning-healthcare/

7. Epigenome: a record of the chemical changes to DNA and histone proteins of an organism.

8. Microbiome: the microorganisms in a particular environment (including the body or a part of the body).

9. Virome: the collection of viruses in and on the human body.

10. Karen Taylor, "By 2020 Smart Hospitals Will Be a Reality," *Future Health Index*, June 13, 2017: www.futurehealthindex.com/2017/06/13/by-2020-the-smart-hospital-will-be-a-reality

11. Taylor, "By 2020 Smart Hospitals Will Be a Reality."

12. Taylor, "By 2020 Smart Hospitals Will Be a Reality."

13. Taylor, "By 2020 Smart Hospitals Will Be a Reality."

14. Lucien Engelen, "Smart Hospitals, Apple, Samsung, and Amazon Next Steps in Healthcare, and a Drone Faster than an Ambulance?" LinkedIn, June 18, 2017: www.linkedin.com/pulse/smart-hospitals-apple-samsung-amazon-next-steps-drone-lucien-engelen?trk=mp-reader-card

15. "eHealth," Wikipedia: https://en.wikipedia.org/wiki/EHealth

16. "mHealth," Wikipedia: https://en.wikipedia.org/wiki/MHealth

17. Bernadette Keefe, "Robots/Robotics in Healthcare," *Mayo Clinic* blog, May 6, 2015: http://blog.centerforinnovation.mayo.edu/2016/05/06/robotsrobotics-in-healthcare/

18. Yun Liu, Krishna Gadepalli, Mohammad Norouzi, George E. Dahl, Timo Kohlberger, Aleksey Boyko, Subhashini Venugopalan, Aleksei Timofeev, Philip Q. Nelson, Greg S. Corrado, Jason D. Hipp, Lily Peng, and Martin C. Stumpe, "Detecting Cancer Metastases on Gigapixel Pathology Images," ArXiv website, March 8, 2017: https://arxiv.org/pdf/1703.02442.pdf

FURTHER READING

"The 10 medical devices that changed the world," *Asian Scientist*, April 2015: www.asianscientist.com/2015/04/features/10-medical-devices-changed-world/

Neill K. J. Adhikari, "Patient Safety without Borders: Measuring the Global Burden of Adverse Events," *BMJ Quality and Safety* 22, no. 10, August 2013: http://qualitysafety.bmj.com/content/22/10/798

The widely cited estimate from the U.S. Institute of Medicine of 44,000–98,000 preventable deaths annually due to medical care made medical error the eighth leading cause of death in the USA.

Tom Hardy, "Significant Benefits of Big Data Analytics in Healthcare Industry," Built in Los Angeles website, January 12, 2016: www.builtinla.com/blog/significant-benefits-big-data-analytics-healthcare-industry

Esther Landhuis, "Neuroscience: Big Brain, Big Data," *Nature.com*, January 25 2017: www.nature.com/nature/journal/v541/n7638/full/541559a.html

Y. Liang and A. Kelemen, "Big Data Science and its Applications in HealthCare and Medical Research: Challenges and Opportunities," *Austin Biometric and Biostatistics*, Austin Publishing Group.

Joseph Mercola, "Most Americans Will Be Misdiagnosed at Least Once," Mercola.com, September 30, 2015: http://articles.mercola.com/sites/articles/archive/2015/09/30/diagnostic-errors.aspx

Melissa Turtinen, "Mayo Clinic Says Get a Second Opinion: First Ones Are Frequently Wrong," GoMN, April 4, 2017: www.gomn.com/news/mayo-clinic-says-get-a-second-opinion-first-ones-are-frequently-wrong/

Fritz Venter and Andrew Stein, "Images & Videos: Really Big Data," *Analytics*, November/December 2012: http://analytics-magazine.org/images-a-videos-really-big-data/

Richard Wolniewicz, "Computer-Assisted Coding and Natural Language Processing," 3M Health Information Systems whitepaper, 2015: http://multimedia.3m.com/mws/media/756879O/3m-cac-and-nlp-white-paper.pdf?&fn=3M_NLP_white_paper.pdf

CHAPTER 9

The Power of UDA in Product and Service Development

Success is a science; if you have the conditions you get the results.

—Oscar Wilde

WHY SHOULD YOU CARE ABOUT UDA FOR PRODUCT AND SERVICE DEVELOPMENT?

Today, the pace of technology development and Big Data analytics is creating disruptive mind-sets across all spectrums of industry. According to the GE Global Innovation Barometer 2016, 61 percent of executives are using Big Data and analytics to improve decisions, and 86 percent of executives believe advanced manufacturing (the use of innovative technology to improve products or processes) will radically transform the industrial sector.[1] Big Data analytics provides us with the opportunity to capture, store, process, and analyze unprecedented amounts of data from internal and external sources. The outcome of these analytics is enabling businesses to seize new data-driven innovation opportunities. Data analytics has definitely changed the way we live and do business. It has changed the way organizations operate, governments and communities function, and companies assess their disruptive ideas and develop new innovative services and products.

For some leading companies the power of Big Data insights is now their key differentiator for creating innovative products. Others who choose to ignore it will be lagging behind and playing catchup.

Several statistics remind us of some challenges companies face when trying to be disruptive: According to the *Harvard Business Review* article "Understanding the Psychology of New Product Adoption" by John T Gourville, 70 to 90 percent of new products stay on store shelves less than twelve months;[2] and Booz & Company found that 66 percent of products fail within the first two years.[3] Additionally, according to a Doblin Group study, 96 percent of all innovations fail to return the cost of capital.[4]

UDA AND BIG DATA ANALYTICS

So how can UDA help tap into the actionable, disruptive insights of Big Data analytics? In his book *The Innovator's Dilemma*, Clayton M. Christensen explained how some companies pioneered innovative products and services but later faced the challenge of generating disruptive products in a repeatable and scalable fashion.[5] That is the innovator's dilemma.

One of the major disruptions for product and service development in the era of Big Data analytics is the opportunity that leading organizations have to find new ways of extracting actionable value out of the information; and capitalizing on its volume, velocity, variety, and value. When leveraged properly, Big Data analytics can provide actionable, competitive, and differentiating insights to propel organizations in the leading group and avoid playing catchup in this evolving digital economy.

In a 2013 article titled "Analytics and Innovation" for the Journal of American Management Association, I explained how Big Data analytics coupled with innovation provides great opportunities to enhance and create new products and services.[6] In this chapter, I will use that foundation to showcase how underlying insights from UDA when crossed with key goals of innovation can lead to new products and services development.

The following are the four major drivers of UDA and their impact on product and service development:

1. *Data analytics* has become the most valuable asset of our digital economy. It has led to the creation of data analytics products and services.

2. The digital competitive world now offers a *365/24/7 platform* where customers can get and provide feedback regarding products and services.

3. The *intersection between analytics and innovation* leads to new products and services innovations.

4. The *Voice of the Customer (VoC) and the "Customer is always right" mantra* are more relevant today than they ever were as we enhance existing products and services or create new ones.

In the following sections, I will discuss these four key factors that enable the power of UDA for product and services development.

1. Data Analytics: Data Products and Services

In the late 1990s, a significant number of leading tech giants in Silicon Valley leveraged the explosion of digital information provided by the then-new Internet and used analytics to create data products and new lines of business. With the explosion of digital information, data and analytics came to the forefront of data product design and new product creation. These companies had seized the opportunity to find innovative ways to extract value from this new data and capitalize on its volume, velocity, and variety.

Today, analytics is the most valuable asset in our digital economy. A 2015 report from the Organization for Economic Co-operation and Development (OECD) stated, "Data-driven innovation forms a key pillar in 21st-century sources of growth ... large data sets are becoming a core asset in the economy, fostering new industries, processes, and products and creating significant competitive advantages."[7]

In the summer of 2016, I had the opportunity to speak at the OECD's New Approaches for Economic Challenges Forum. I was invited to present findings of my book, *People Analytics in the Era of Big Data*, and had witnessed firsthand a body of researches and publications around digital information, Big Data analytics, product innovations, and opportunities for digital economy. For instance, Google, Amazon, Facebook, LinkedIn, Twitter, and Monster created their entire businesses based upon a data-driven model.

Google was built because the founders started to understand text on Web pages. To be able to return relevant and meaningful information from text, UDA algorithms are performed behind the scenes. Understanding text on Web pages requires the capability to analyze billions of words from billions of searches and instantly provide meaning to those user searches.

Since then, Google has developed models that are capable of understanding images, videos, and more. Analyzing video or photos before making a recommendation to users of similar videos also requires advanced UDA to build the overall recommendation model. Analytics and, more importantly, UDA are part of Google's DNA and its overall value proposition.

Google manages and analyzes a lot of data. As Sundar Pichai, Google's chief executive officer (CEO), said during the Google I/O conference in 2017, every single day:

- YouTube users watch more than 1 billion hours of videos.
- More than 1.2 billion photos are uploaded to Google Photos.
- Users navigate more than 1 billion kilometers with Google Map.
- More than 1.3 billion searches are performed on Google.
- And every week, more than 3 billion objects are uploaded to Google Drive.

It is hard to imagine what this would look like without UDA, whether it be singular value decomposition (SVD), QR factorization, or machine learning and deep learning algorithms. Without these algorithms, all this data would not make any sense.

Google Translate, one of the best open source translation tools, is powered by machine translation. It has a model that uses more than

3 billion words for its training and state-of-the-art machine learning models to provide translations for a comprehensive list of languages.

Google significantly improved its translation solutions with the release of the Pixel Buds in October 2017. When paired with a Google device, the Pixel Buds (wireless earbuds) can access the Google Assistant, enabling a user to send text and give directions, check for messages, and communicate with the other device verbally. The new translation solution is better than all its predecessors, as it is powered by neural machine translation features that can translate an entire sentence instead of slicing up text and trying to match each word to a big dictionary.

All these great data products from these tech giants are built and enhanced thanks to UDA and computing power. When you watch a YouTube video, Google runs its video recognition model to provide you with immediate recommendations of similar videos that you may like.

Other examples of companies that have leveraged their user data are Spotify and LinkedIn. As discussed in Chapter 3, Spotify has moved from idea to execution with its Spotify's Discover Weekly PlayList. The Discover Weekly playlist is a Spotify product powered by UDA deep learning algorithms that leverages user-based data to accurately make perfect personalized recommendation lists of songs users will enjoy. And as we will discuss in the LinkedIn Voices case study later in this chapter, LinkedIn leverages the power of UDA to create LinkedIn Voices, which enabled the company to listen to the voice of its members and gain insights from its own database or from external data sources.

Using its LinkedIn members' data, the company has developed products including the popular:

- People You May Know
- Jobs You May Be Interested In
- Groups You May Like

Facebook also has People You May Know, while Twitter suggests People You Should Follow.

Amazon is well-known for its service and customer reviews for most products that it sells. More than 35 percent of its sales come from its recommendations model. Amazon and Netflix were major companies that pioneered the recommendations engine, making it part of the customer experience to retain and attract customers. For new product development, customer feedback and reviews on Amazon represent a powerful source of information to analyze for a better understanding of the consumer journey and overall consumer online experience.

2. 365/24/7 Platform for Customers

Today, we are living in a globally connected world where customers are technologically savvy and empowered by broadband Internet mobile social media. Before buying a new product, they can look up information and reviews, compare pricing, and consult consumer appreciation of the product. With a single click, they can place an order to buy your product; or if they are no longer happy with it, they can easily turn to your competition for better service, a better product, or a better offer.

Customers can also provide live feedback regarding your product or your service, grading the service they have received and the overall experience of doing business with you. The Internet and social media provide them with an unprecedented 365/24/7 platform to share their points of view with their community. They can share all of the experiences, good or bad, that they have had with you, providing their opinion, advice, and recommendations regarding your service, your brand, or your product. Some of them are eager to provide suggestions to enhance existing products, as well as new ideas for the development of new products.

The Internet has become a place with multidirectional conversations where consumers can seek information and share their own information and recommendations. We have seen how customer feedback can encapsulate the drivers for churn behavior or customer attrition. We also demonstrated that customer feedback is paramount, whether it is from a customer opinion satisfaction survey or from a net promoter score. One of the main reasons why we should care is because behavioral intent and actions are embedded in text data, such as consumer comments and feedback. Customers want to be heard and to participate by sharing their experience with others and by providing advice. This goldmine of information should be included in the product development process to optimize outcomes. Leading companies are formally leveraging such customer inputs to enhance their existing products and services and to develop new ones.

UDA can be used to address underlying questions around the traditional 4Ps of marketing:

- Product
- Price
- Promotion
- Place

For instance, conjoint analysis[8] helps organizations understand what attributes are most important to consumers and customers. Leading companies capture customer opinions about price, promotion, and product features from a variety of customer touchpoints. UDA enables these companies to make sense of this customer information and inject analytics across all the major steps of their product development process.

As we have discussed in Chapter 4, leading companies such as Dell and Starbucks have been leveraging social media to provide their user communities with a place where they can share their ideas and concerns, and provide suggestions regarding existing and new products.

Companies can store these ideas and quickly analyze and interpret them thanks to the power of UDA.

The whole idea here is to leverage the VoC, which is available through multiple channels, including:

- Internet/Web
- Social media
- Video
- Audio
- E-mail and text

3. Intersection between Analytics and Innovation

To succeed in today's fast-evolving, competitive marketplace, with consumers who are more informed and increasingly demanding, companies must harness advanced business analytics to meet their business challenges. To maintain their competitive edge, those companies need to analyze their data (big or small) coming from multiple sources and transform it into actionable intelligence. This intelligence not only provides a competitive edge but also enhances visibility to decision makers; it enables them to detect problems, better plan the future, and more importantly identify opportunities to develop and improve their products and services.

Data intelligences, as discussed throughout this book, help companies to understand: What happened? What is happening? What will happen? and What should be done to improve the product or service? It provides forward-looking companies with the opportunity to understand their market, the competition, and their customers while enabling them to differentiate their offers, services, and technology. Hence, it enables them to innovate.

In this era of global competition, companies need to constantly improve customer experience, services, and products, and the way to do this is through innovation. Client-facing innovation can only occur if there is synergy across departments. The ability for a company to analyze, respond, and optimize iteratively, adding new approaches to the way customer data is captured, processed, managed, integrated, and analyzed is called *customer data intelligence integration.*

Analytics and innovation are sometimes perceived as opposing concepts. Many argue that innovation cannot be reduced to a set of processes, or even worse, a set of metrics. Even if there are countless books covering innovation, very few of them mention analytics or the critical value of analytics in the innovation process.

Let's explore the intersection between analytics and innovation, and illustrate how forward-looking companies have been leveraging advanced business analytics to stoke innovation and create new products and services, and to enhance their value proposition. I will also attempt to outline the importance of innovation within analytics and identify the common traits of innovative companies.

To have all the preliminary elements to ensure a comprehensive exploration, we will discuss the following questions:

- ■ What is innovation?
- ■ What is the promise of analytics and its impact on innovation?

- What is the intersection between analytics and innovation?
- What are the common denominators of innovative companies?

What Is Innovation?

Wikipedia defines *innovation* as:

> ... the creation of better or more effective services, technologies, products, processes, or ideas that are accepted by markets, governments, and society at large.[9]

Peter Drucker adds:

> Innovation is the provision of more and better goods and services ... Innovation can consist of a new and better product, a new commodity or creation of new demand. Innovation can happen in any business area. One can innovate on design, product, sales techniques, prices, services, management, organizations or methods.[10]

After the financial crisis in 2008, the majority of companies were seeking new ways to get back to profitability, looking for ways to innovate and grow. From my experience working with innovative companies, and from what I learned through interviews with innovative leaders, I propose that the innovation process is made up of two principal factors:

- An internal factor that represents the core and the epicenter of the innovation, which includes the company (brand, value proposition, customers, product, services, and technology) and its workforce.
- An external factor that includes the market, global trends, competition, and consumer needs, preferences, and expectations.

It is the interconnectivity of these internal and external factors that makes the innovation process successful.

Often there is confusion between innovation and creativity. Creativity is about coming up with great ideas while innovation is about bringing those creative ideas to life. Louis Gagnon, the former senior vice president of product and innovation at Monster Worldwide, said, "Innovation is about execution."

It is important to underscore the process of innovation: how companies innovate, and what really drives them to do it. As discussed in the previous section, there are many descriptions of how companies innovate; but a simple and straightforward one was given by Richard Saul Wurman, the TED (Technology, Entertainment, Design) Conference founder. When he was asked to define innovation, he referred to the first TED conference he organized: "In order to innovate, one needs to add or subtract." To organize the conference, he said, "Everything I did was subtraction." He took away panels, dress code, politicians and CEOs, long speeches, silos, and podium.[11]

No discussion about innovation (subtraction and addition) would be complete without a look at Apple. In 2003, when Apple introduced the iPod with the iTunes store, the company revolutionized portable entertainment, creating a new market and transforming completely the company business model. According to an article published in the *Harvard Business Review* entitled "Reinventing Your Business Model," in just three years, the combination of iPhone and iTunes became a nearly $10 billion product, accounting for almost 50 percent of Apple's revenue. Apple market capitalization catapulted from $1 billion in early 2003 to more than $150 billion by late 2007; today the company's market value is around $1 trillion.[12] Since its debut in June 2007, Apple's iPhone has managed to move a total of 1.2 billion cumulative units globally, remaining the most popular smartphone model in the world in terms of unit sales, brand power, and influence.[13]

Although Apple's success story is well known, what is less known is that Apple was not the first to bring a digital music player to the market. A company called Diamond Multimedia introduced the Rio in 1998, and Best Data introduced the Cabo 64 in 2000. Both products worked well; they were portable and stylish. So why did the iPod succeed while the Rio and Cabo did not? Apple took a good technology and wrapped it in a great business model. Apple's true innovation was to make downloading digital music easy and convenient—the iTunes store. Apple was able to draw a line directly connecting the recording artist and consumer through the platform while providing commerce and recommendation (subtracting). More than a manufacturer of a good device, Apple became a gateway for distribution of content through podcasts, iTunes, audiobooks, and the like.

To achieve this objective, the company built a groundbreaking business model that combined hardware, software, and service via the iTunes platform (adding). The idea was a game changer for the company and for the consumers. Apple was now the leader.

With the iPod, as Steve Jobs said when introducing it, "you are able to carry your entire music library in a little box."[14] Similar changes took the industry by storm when Apple introduced its first smartphone, the iPhone. Apple recognized that the main features that really appealed to consumers were a touch screen, along with the intuitive and user-friendly high-resolution visualization and a core focus on design. A couple of years later, Apple's share in the smartphone segment outpaced RIM's BlackBerry.

What Is the Promise of Advanced Analytics and Its Impact on Innovation?

Advanced analytics include three major steps:

- Unlocking (finding meaning in structured and unstructured data)
- Prediction
- Optimization

In today's business environment, companies are inundated with data from multiple sources, including: market data, chat and e-mail data, sensor data, Web data, servicing data (warranty claims), social media, mobile data, and call center data. Unlocking converts, integrates, and streamlines these media to detect problems and opportunities, analyze strengths and weaknesses, measure performance, and track success. Advanced analytics aims to provide a complete knowledge of the market, products and services, technology, and most importantly, the overall performance level of a company vis-á-vis its competitors and the market as a whole. However, in the process, advanced analytics can also help businesses to understand, identify, and test innovations that develop new markets, new services, or new products.

To innovate, companies need to analyze their past and present performances and must anticipate the future. Basically, companies need to understand where they came from, how they are performing today, and how they plan to perform in the future. But it is not only crucial for them to understand their markets, products, customer service, and technological capabilities; companies must also understand the competition.

It is imperative when thinking of innovation to know what the competition is offering. Competitive knowledge can be provided by the competitive intelligence (CI) team. The CI team, through analytics, helps companies define their strengths and weaknesses. That team is also instrumental in identifying areas for innovative products and services, because they know what customers want and they know what the competition is offering.

UDA enables the team to process the volume and variety of competitive information. Properly leveraged, the proliferation of data coming from multiple sources provides insight that should enable companies to listen to the voices of their customers; understand their wants, needs, and preferences; and more importantly, spot areas of opportunities to improve the current business model to compete and win by creating and offering new products or services.

I outlined in the previous sections that to innovate, companies need to understand what to subtract or add to the existing products, services, and technologies, while comparing their offerings to that of the competition. I should also restate that the promise of analytics is to address fundamental business questions.

Analyzing customer feedback and the market can help distill signals from Big Data analysis. In turn, operations is where the company would synchronize their processes to execute the ideas from analytics.

What Is the Intersection between Analytics and Innovation?

My experience in working with executives in innovation from multiple industries led me to a construct of the most important factors in the intersection between analytics and operations:

- Customer base
- Product
- Service

- Technology

- Market

- Competition

Exhibit 9.01 illustrates factors that make up the intersection between analytics and innovation.

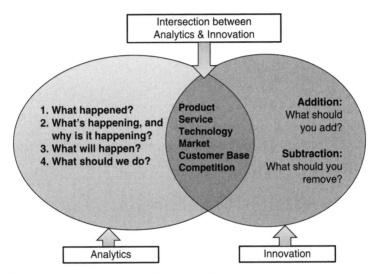

Exhibit 9.01 Analytics and Innovation Intersection

A deep understanding of the aforementioned topics can only be achieved by the use of advanced analytics, such as UDA.

Innovation, the execution of creative ideas, will only occur if we understand what is happening in the marketplace, what is missing, and what would appeal to customers. Analytics provides a blueprint to innovation by giving intelligence (dos and don'ts) while operations executes the concepts. Only by combining these two forces are organizations able to innovate.

Timing and speed to market are as critical in innovation as they are to any project in a highly competitive market environment. The market-place has no room for second chances or delays. We have witnessed this with the past "war" on tablet computers, when RIM's delayed launch undermined the company's perceived competitiveness and impacted the sale of other products. Apple, Google, and Samsung outpaced RIM in its core market, the smartphone.

Great ideas are not enough; execution is key to success. From the interviews I conducted, and based on my experience working with innovative organizations, I learned that the process of innovation can only properly take place if preliminary analytics and operations are working in tandem. Innovation requires these two key processes to occur.

What Are the Common Denominators of Innovative Companies?

In sports, we know that most professional athletes share common characteristics:

- They are extremely focused on achieving their goals.
- They have strong discipline.
- They have an excellent work ethic.

The same can be said for innovative companies. In many cases, these characteristics are what sets innovative companies apart and separates those who have creative ideas from those who bring those creative ideas promptly to execution.

They empower their strongest asset, their workforce, by enabling a culture of innovation. Google, for instance, encourages its engineers to spend 20 percent of their work time on projects that interest them as a motivational technique. Some of Google's newer services, such as Gmail, Google News, Orkut, and AdSense, originated from these independent endeavors.

Even if innovative companies have different business models, most of them are known to be analytical companies, which means that they have a data-driven decision-making process. These organizations have common denominators that drive their success:

- Strong customer focus (know the customer's wants, needs, preferences, and expectations)
- Strong product diversity (be eager to try and expand the product line and engage in new markets)
  - While every product may not be a success, innovative companies try to get ahead of the marketplace through the addition or subtraction of service delivery models.

- Strong competitive intelligence (be aware of what the competition is doing, identify their strengths and weaknesses, and know how to outpace them)
- Strong update on trends (understand business trends)

Successful and innovative companies understand that above all, business is about the customer, and focusing on customer is the core of the innovative process. Leveraging analytics and operations to develop innovative products and services for their customers is key to their success.

Here are two companies that top my list of strong innovators:

Amazon.com

Amazon is the largest online retailer in the world, with a focus on customer satisfaction that starts with their branding: the Amazon logo is an arrow leading from A to Z, representing customer satisfaction with a smile.

The company innovated by quickly focusing on diversification of products and services to seize opportunities to sustain growth and increase its value. It started as a bookstore, but soon diversified by introducing a variety of products, including DVDs, CDs, MP3s (downloadable), software, video games, video streaming, electronic apparel, toys, and jewelry. And now a giant cloud services provider an ebook and smart tablet and home manufacturer.

In September 2011, with the explosion of the tablet market, Amazon launched the Kindle Fire, which runs a customized version of the operating system Android. The aggressively low pricing of the Kindle Fire (originally $199) was largely perceived as a strategy, backed by Amazon's revenue from its content sales, to drive the adoption of the device. Amazon's American Customer Satisfaction Score Index was 86 in 2017; the company is a top performer in customer satisfaction (It has the #1 Ranking score). Amazon is one of the best examples that illustrates how analytics and operations lead to innovation. For example, Amazon is one of the pioneers of the recommendation engine, which drove incremental sales through customer recommendations. This model, along with their strategic product diversification, was based upon advanced analytics. Amazon is now the premier retail site and has expanded its business in video streaming, food and beverage, and Amazon Web services. Today all retail products are available on Amazon, and books now occupy only a small portion of their business.

Google

Google, initially the leader in search engine, defines itself as a customer-centric company:

> Larry Page, co-founder of Google and now CEO of Alphabet, says, "Serving our end users is at the heart of what we do and remains our number one priority." Despite being perhaps the only company in the world whose stated goal is to have its customers leave its website as quickly as possible, Google is no doubt committed to making those customers satisfied.
>
> "From its inception, Google has focused on providing the best user experience possible," says Page. "While many companies claim to put their customers first, few are able to resist the temptation to make small sacrifices to increase shareholder value. Google has steadfastly refused to make any change that does not offer a benefit to the users who come to the site."[15]

Google, since its incorporation, has been part of the fast-growing Fortune 1000. Google's experience is a classic example of a company committed to wowing its customers based on consistent quality and constant innovation. Google leads with analytics; they quickly understood the market trends and the crucial need to diversify their products and services.

This rapid growth has triggered a chain of new products, acquisitions, and partnerships beyond the company's core search engine. Today, they offer online solutions such as an office suite and a mobile platform, Android, for harnessing the content they generate. Google has today seven key lines of products.

In this highly competitive market, analytics and operations are the pillars of innovation. Analytics' ultimate feat in any organization is to provide the opportunity to innovate and move the organization forward as a sustainable industry leader.

With today's customer expectations, innovation has become a standard. Companies must constantly put themselves in the customer's mind and evolve their products and services to meet those expectations. In the end, advanced analytics and, more importantly, UDA, when applied to understanding customer wants, needs, and preferences, pave the way for innovation and are a must for companies that seek to grow and sustain their competitive edge.

INTERVIEW WITH FIONA MCNEILL, GLOBAL PRODUCT MARKETING MANAGER AT SAS INSTITUTE

I had the opportunity to discuss the state of analytics with Fiona McNeill, Global Product Marketing Manager at SAS Institute, the leading software analytics solutions provider.

Isson: In the era of Big Data, what do you see as the next frontiers of data analytics innovation?

McNeill: *Frontier #1: Look at analytics as being embedded with the data. We have done this by putting analytics into a car with utility data.*

Frontier #2: Cognitive applications: This has to do with AI. Machines being able to process, analyze, and interpret in human terms the human outputs. Machines being able to interpret human interactions.

The second layer of cognitive is that, as we move toward the IoT, we will have a machine talking to other machines, talking to other machines. Machines developing their own cognitive requirements.

Right now, it is more about data format and security protocol. This is where AI will come into play. AI is mimicking human behavior. In the second era of cognitive computing, we will have embedded analytics in any kind of cognitive function.

When you start to release this type of data and intelligence, you have analytics depth, as it has been greatly covered by Google.

Isson: What are the major impacts of such innovations for businesses and societies?

McNeill: *The promise of computing has always been to free humans from repetitive tasks. What we're seeing is that we're tied to our devices and never get a lot done. Computing should alleviate humans from doing mundane tasks.*

The next area is text analytics, in meeting with some philosophers who have started to do some work regarding analytics: What should we do as a society? What is the responsibility from businesses that act based upon information systems and algorithms? This will change some of the laws we have now, defining a new kind of ethics. Will we start embedding bar codes into data? Probably. More data, more dependence on machines, instead of machines depending on them.

Isson: What will be the state of analytics ten to fifteen years from now?

McNeill: *The state of analytics in ten to fifteen years is autonomous intelligent data. Multisystem self-knowledge. Data having self-awareness. Data will encompass its own knowledge. I like to think of it as a cell that has everything to live, to evolve. Data will have to know what the computation protocol is. Your cell phone knows where you are, and can find and locate your friends. For children who are in third grade today, 80 percent of jobs they will have do not exist yet, and will be invented. Some skill-sets will become obsolete. Think about Cobol, for instance. The challenge will be about understanding the business and being able to think outside the box.*

4. The Voice of the Customer (VoC)

In this globally connected 365/24/7 digital economy, the Internet, mobile social media, the cloud, Big Data, and apps have empowered the interaction between consumers and service providers.

Today's consumers are technologically savvy and are actively engaging on a 365/24/7 multidimensional channel platform. More importantly, they can share their experience and feedback with their entire social network. Their network can relay the information, creating a viral impact on the social media ecosystem. Today consumers are more and more vocal, and most know how to leverage the power and efficiency of Internet social media to ensure their voices are heard.

To compete and win in this new economy, companies need to have a successful VoC strategy. The VoC is a success criterion for product development, product enhancement, and customer relationship management (CRM) and optimization. It would be impossible without proper UDA to distill, from thousands or millions of feedback posts and suggestions, the essence of the customer voice.

So, the VoC, powered by UDA, provides the key component of today's customer experience and product development.

Why Have a VoC?

We all have at some point witnessed products being launched based upon a personal agenda as opposed to company goals; one where decision makers deliberately ignored recommendations from market research and competitive intelligence. "No-Go" recommendations suggesting not to move forward with the product may be based on several reasons, including:

- Customers don't need it.
- Customers do not see the incremental value when compared to existing competitive products.
- The new product simply does not meet the expectation of its market.
- The timing for "Go-to-Market" is unrealistic.
- The new product will be introduced too late and will have no place in the market.

Despite market research warnings reflecting the VoC, political agendas have wrongly pushed products to market, creating complete fiascos. In some cases, those bad decisions have led to massive losses of revenue and jobs and have harmed both the reputation and competitiveness of the company.

Advances in technology have provided powerful mechanisms to facilitate information gathering from a variety of sources from the globally connected marketplace. Leading companies have been leveraging these to create strategies to meet and exceed consumer expectations and stay ahead of their competition. They can leverage insights from opinion sites, multivariate online testing, existing product key performance indicators (KPIs), customer surveys (offline and online), interactive blogs, Facebook, Twitter, and other social media sources to listen to their customers and utilize these actionable insights for product development.

So, what is the VoC, and how could it be leveraged?

The slogan "The customer is always right" was coined almost 100 years ago by Marshall Fields and Harry Gordon Selfridges in the early 20th century. The motivation behind it, which showed a company's keenness to put the customer first, is still just as relevant today. Almost a century later, the customer is more in charge than ever. Whether "right" or not, customers today are certainly much more sophisticated, analytical, demanding, and savvy at comparative shopping, and able to speaking openly and loudly about the products and the services they use. Businesses that are not listening to what customers are saying and are not appropriately leveraging this input into their daily business decisions do so at their peril. There is no product that successful businesses bring to market without putting the customer first. Exhibit 9.02 showcases key components of the VoC strategy.

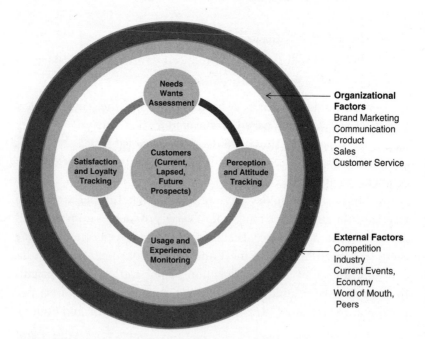

Exhibit 9.02   The VoC Strategy, Based on Customer Experience

Customer Feedback Is Invaluable

Customers today—and by *customers* I mean *current* as well as *future* customers—have choices. They will do business with you only if you are responsive to their needs. Getting feedback from your customers and turning the feedback into action that satisfies and delivers value to them is essential for your business success. Failing to do so will make you play catchup with your competitors and waste time putting out fires to help your customers get what they are looking for. Done right, putting the VoC in the business decision-making loop can provide a huge opportunity for an organization to be proactive, on target, and responsive to customers, ultimately improving loyalty, retention, and new customer acquisition and product development.

For example, Netflix had a brilliant idea and can be truly acknowledged as the pioneer that changed how entertainment is distributed. It had major success; however, a subsequent unjustifiable, haughty price increase in 2011 boomeranged badly for the company, which experienced a record downhill slide in response. Thanks to the insight provided by proper VoC analytics, the company was able to recover. Short-term profitability is certainly great, but lasting profitability is based on continued enthusiasm and patronage from customers.

Technology has changed the way businesses work today. The Internet has increased competition multiple-fold, as customers can shop far and wide, not just down the street or within driving distance. With a click on the keypad, products, and services from thousands of miles away can be compared and obtained conveniently and easily. Even people shopping at brick-and-mortar facilities typically check out what they want to buy before going to the store to make the purchase. Peer reviews, user testimonials, expert advice, consumer reports, price comparison data, and shared comments on social media are a few of the sources that have made it extremely easy to comparison shop and find the best options.

It is a complex business environment today, and you need to be relevant to your customers. This can be achieved only if you clearly understand who they are and their needs, attitudes, perceptions, and behaviors toward your own, as well as competitor products and services. You need to sift through the voices of your customers to identify where you are not meeting their expectations and find out what they like about you, and then plan appropriate actions. At the heart of understanding customers' voices, UDA helps leading businesses to focus on their strengths, pay attention to what needs fixing, and identify the areas of opportunity. Insights from the VoC support strategic, as well as tactical, decisions and help fine-tune operational processes.

Substantial evidence shows a strong relationship between positive customer experiences and loyalty to a company. Megan Burns from Forrester Research says, "Years of Forrester data confirm the strong relationship between the quality of a firm's customer experience... and loyalty measures like willingness to consider the company for another purchase, likelihood to switch business, and likelihood to recommend."[16] Burns further states that "better customer experience can be worth millions in annual revenue."[17] The increased revenue calculations are based on existing customers' incremental purchases, savings made possible by lower churn levels and the net sales driven by word of mouth. These results are not surprising; in fact, they are quite intuitive, and each of us can relate to this quite easily. Can you remember a time when you had a bad experience with a product or with customer service and still went back to do business with the company?

Customer feedback is also very valuable in explaining trends in your *behavioral* data. For example, let's assume you notice a decline in your purchase data among a specific segment of your target, but you can't understand *why* this is happening from the available sales data. Customer feedback is needed to provide answers. Talking with lapsed customers within the declining segment will help you understand why they have stopped buying, and combining this with current customer needs and satisfaction will help you identify actions that are needed to stem this declining sales trend. Connecting customer feedback with behavioral data provides comprehensive insights about *what's* going on and *why* it's going on. Decisions based on such a panoramic view are powerful. Organizations are leveraging the power of UDA to sift through multiple customer feedback data sources to enrich their customer behavior knowledge.

LINKEDIN VOICES CASE STUDY: A TEXT ANALYTICS PLATFORM FOR UNDERSTANDING MEMBER FEEDBACK

I had the opportunity to speak about LinkedIn Voices with Tiger Zhang, senior manager, data analytics and data mining. He shared with me the LinkedIn Voices success story. Voices is LinkedIn's text analytics platform for understanding member feedback.

Case Summary

Zhang and team have built a scalable text analytics platform with innovative text mining solutions via advanced machine learning and natural language processing techniques. Such a platform allows LinkedIn to listen to feedback from its community, drive actionable insights for better business decisions, and eventually create impact for its members.

The Challenges

LinkedIn wanted to understand its members' feedback, leveraging data from customer services conversations, market research survey data, and the overall voice of members across channels, from LinkedIn's social media platform and all other sources that handle LinkedIn-relevant data for better business decisions.

The Solutions

Zhang and team at LinkedIn built Voices, a text analytics platform that provides easy access to member feedback about the LinkedIn website and key products. Voices aggregates unstructured text across both internal (e.g., LinkedIn posts, customer support cases, Net Promoter Score survey results) and external (e.g., social media such as Facebook and Twitter, news, forums, and blogs) data sources. Structured member data and unstructured textual data from various channels are ingested into the Hadoop Distributed File System and passed through a suite of text mining functions. These functions allow Voices to surface relevant insights by various dimensions, such as value proposition, product, sentiment, trending insights, and many other use cases.

Voices aggregates internal data sources and purchases external data from vendors, who pull relevant information from publicly available data on social platforms and online news, blogs, and forums. Additional data attributes (e.g., geography, sentiment, and audience segment) enable deep dives into business domains. Voices also includes reviews for major LinkedIn apps from the Apple App Store and Google Play.

Text Mining in Voices

Text mining is the computational study of unstructured text to understand members' feedback and gain insights for better business decisions. It would take years for a person to read millions of text documents manually, which is infeasible for any business. Hence, effective and efficient text mining functions are in great demand to deal with enormous volumes of unstructured text.

In Voices, there are three key text mining components, as illustrated in Exhibit 9.03:

- Relevance Solution
- Classification Engine
- Topic Mining

The Benefits

Zhang and team's method works well for VOC data in natural language, such as forum discussions, group updates, blogs, etc. Topics generated by the system can be used to:

1. Facilitate understanding and use of information in VOC without manual review of the content

2. Classify and/or group the user complaints for further processing by customer service representatives

3. Identify sentiments associated with the topics

4. Facilitate searching of the user complaints

5. Generate summaries of content associated with the topics

6. Use as features for text classification to reduce feature dimension and improve efficiency

Isson: What advice would you give to people who would like to leverage Text Analytics to harness the voice of their customer members?

Zhang: While developing the Voices system, we learned many lessons we can share with the community. First, as text mining practitioners, we often face

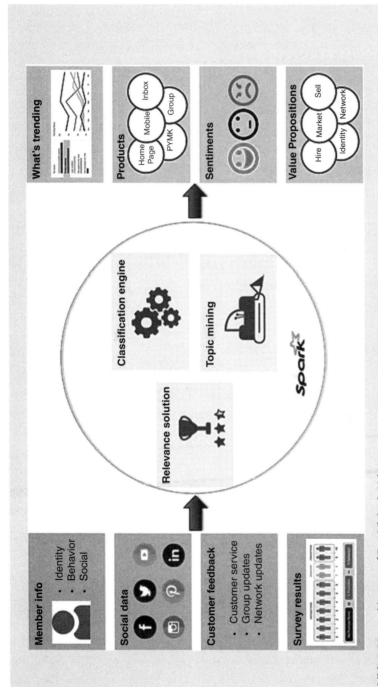

Exhibit 9.03 Architecture of Text Mining in Voices

the challenge of making a choice between vendor products, open source tools, and in-house solutions. While there is no fixed answer for all scenarios, it is important to balance the key factors, such as quality, efficiency, flexibility, scalability, and cost (including developing cost and maintenance cost). Second, we need to make tradeoffs between quality and efficiency. For example, Latent dirichlet allocation (LDA) is a state-of-the-art topic modeling method, but it is computationally expensive and hence less efficient. In practice, there are approaches that are suboptimal but much more efficient and scalable. A boost in these factors without too much loss in quality is often preferred in industry applications. Third, whenever possible, we will always strive to leverage big data infrastructures such as Hadoop and Spark to deliver truly scalable text mining functions. Last, but not least, visualization is also very important for telling stories from the results of text mining. For example, there are many options for displaying topics, such as a word cloud or topic wheel. Excellent visualization solutions can quickly and effectively tell a story for better decision-making.

The Makings of an Effective VoC Program

As described in Exhibit 9.04 many customer-centric companies have overcome the roadblocks and established effective VoC programs. They have installed centers of research and insight to manage these programs using UDA and encouraged a culture of information-based, customer-centric business decision making across the enterprise. A systematic VoC program, in its simplest form, is about being proactive in constantly capturing the customer input and incorporating this input into the key functions of the organization at the strategic, tactical, and operational levels.

Listen, Monitor, Integrate, Analyze, and Interpret

Obtaining relevant, timely, and objective customer feedback is the first step to a successful VoC program.

Online, Telephone, and Web Surveys

Well-designed survey questionnaires can be very useful in gathering customer and prospect feedback about a variety of issues that can guide business decisions. Formal surveys are typically designed to obtain feedback from large numbers of respondents. They provide

Exhibit 9.04   VoC Program Paradigm

quantitative results and can be used for high-level analytics to help companies fully understand the issues of interest. Open-ended questions or verbatim from this survey are generally very insightful, and UDA is used to distill the meaning from the raw, text-heavy data from these surveys.

In-Depth Interviews

In-depth telephone interviews are appropriate methods to gather relevant feedback in situations where a deep diagnosis of the issues of interest is needed, or when the topic of interest is in its early, exploratory stages, so that you are able to gauge the exact nature of the issue of interest. Such interviews are designed to allow the respondents to discuss the issues in detail and pontificate on their responses. After capturing customer insights from in-depth interviews, instead of manually going through hundreds or thousands of interviews, UDA is used to speed up the process of understanding the underlying customer's feedback from these interviews.

Focus Groups

Focus groups are among the most commonly used qualitative research methods today. Focus groups are cost-effective and offer good insight and feedback about what the target audience is thinking. The appeal of focus groups is further enhanced by the fact that the business sponsors of the research can sit behind a one-way mirror and observe the participants directly, which allows the sponsors to feel involved. With new technologies, online focus groups are also gaining traction, as they are more cost effective. They enable the use of UDA to efficiently process and analyze the group digital feedback.

Focus groups, however, should be used with care and caution, because there are some caveats to being effective with focus groups. One of the main disadvantages of this methodology is the group dynamics that can often occur.

Customer Service Contact and Interaction

One of the most valuable sources of customer feedback is the communication directed by customers to your customer service team. This could be positive feedback for things done well or complaints that need attention. For the latter, you probably have a system in place to address the issue in order to resolve it in a timely and appropriate fashion. However, to what extent are you using this information from a strategic perspective? From the larger perspective of gathering customer feedback for strategic use, these customer episodes of direct and proactive contact with your organization are an immensely rich source of data. Whether it is kudos or the complaints, both tell you how you are doing.

UDA solutions systematically capture and analyze this service contact data to give deep insights into what is working best and where there is critical need for improvement. The power of UDA can help organizations integrate, process, and analyze call center data in order to identify customer wants, needs, preferences, and pain points to be addressed.

Front-Line Employee Listening Systems

In addition to directly asking customers what they are thinking, learning what they tell your employees when they interact with them is another source of customer feedback that you will want to integrate in your VoC program. Your sales associates, customer service agents, call center employees, training staff, front-desk personnel, and others in similar roles should be well-trained and have access to user-friendly ways to capture customer feedback, wants, needs, and preferences and share these with your product development or innovation teams.

Ongoing UDA should be applied to this data to categorize and classify feedback and customer sentiments.

Word of Mouth and Social Media

The Internet has considerably accelerated and widened the reach of word-of-mouth communication that traditionally occurred only among relatively smaller groups of friends and family. In the past, it was hard to reliably and comprehensively gather what was being said about you, your organization, your brand, and your products among your customer network and use it in a systematic way. That has changed tremendously with the digitization of information. Social networking, blogs and microblogs, direct comments on company websites, and company pages on social networks have not only encouraged customers to openly talk about products and services and create their own content about these products and services, but the digital nature of these comments creates the unprecedented opportunity to capture this information systematically. You have probably already recognized the need to listen to this chatter and respond to it appropriately, often immediately. This scattered information, however, is precious customer feedback and needs to be integrated and channeled into your organization's VoC mechanism in a regular and systematic way, to be leveraged appropriately in planning a business strategy.

Advanced UDA solutions are now helping forward-looking organizations to analyze social media data in almost-real time to identify customer preferences, needs, wants, and overall feedback.

Customer Communities, Crowd Sourcing, Ethnography, and Diary Keeping

The new digital world offers some novel and interesting ways to engage customers and listen to them efficiently and easily, or to transform older tedious methods into a much more accessible and convenient format. *Customer communities* are online groups of passionate customers who are typically invited by an organization to take part because they want to talk to you and to one another on an ongoing basis to exchange ideas for your business. These have been successfully created and used by some companies. *Crowdsourcing* refers to an open online network of customers who post their thoughts and interact with one another to offer ideas and react to the ideas of other members. *Ethnographies and diaries* are traditional methods that have received a makeover. Previously, they were done by hand, which took huge amounts of time and expense, but now, respondents keep online diaries, and ethnographies are conducted using video cameras, making it much easier to collect and process the data. These methods can supplement the ongoing VoC efforts, as and when needed.

Analyze, Interpret, Integrate

You may have put in place many of the processes listed above to effectively collect and capture the voices of your customers, but are you *truly listening* to what is being said?

UDA turns the raw data collected from the various customer listening tools into meaningful insights that will make your VoC program successful so that it can influence business decisions, product enhancement, new product creations, and product innovations. Today, there seems to be no dearth of data within an enterprise, but managers note that there aren't enough insights. You need to make sure that you are leveraging the right UDA tools: Put in place the right talent and skills to transform the raw data into usable insights to guide your actions.

Along the same lines, verbatim comments provided by customers should also be processed and quantified to provide a clear report of what the top issues are and how these may have changed over time, or how they may differ across segments. These are quantified by coding each comment into a category and counting how often each was mentioned. You will need to develop an appropriate classification scheme to categorize the open responses into relevant topics and then compute the frequency of occurrence for each topic. Traditionally, the coding process was done manually, which required substantial resources in manpower and time to complete. Currently, excellent text-mining solutions exist to help quantify open-ended comments far more quickly and cost-effectively.

At Monster, an effective text-mining solution was conceived and developed that quantifies the ongoing survey comments regarding website satisfaction. A custom classification scheme was put in place to quantify the suggestions that job seekers, who visited the website, made, and to improve each task they performed on the site. An analysis was undertaken each month, and the product team was given a clear picture of the top issues that month, as voiced by our site visitors. In addition, this process enabled the effective tracking of the monitored issues when the site changes were made. Similar text-mining solutions are valid for open-ended questions in surveys or feedback comments in stores, on websites, or received via e-mail.

Advanced statistics and modeling may also be used as appropriate to analyze the VoC data and customer behavioral data. Several UDA techniques we discussed in this book could be leveraged.

The following questions can be answered using such advanced statistical techniques:

- What drives your customer loyalty, and how should the enterprise prioritize strategy?

- What product features are most likely to provide you with competitive advantage?

- What mix of products is most wanted by customers in your product portfolio?

- What is your best pricing strategy for each segment of interest?

- How does your brand health and brand equity compare to that of your competitors?

- Which parts of your marketing spend are providing the largest return on investment?

- Which target segments are most likely to purchase your products?

- What is your customer lifetime value for each segment of interest?

Finally, as noted previously, it is important as you analyze and interpret your VoC data to integrate the various pieces of data across the enterprise. In other words, do not simply integrate the various VoC elements that are related to one another, which certainly needs to be done, but connect the customer feedback data to the behavioral data you have collected and to the analytics you are undertaking within your enterprise.

WHAT IS UDA APPLIED TO PRODUCT DEVELOPMENT?

UDA applied to product development means leveraging UDA on product development ideas or business challenges to optimize the steps of product development so that the outcome product will be a success for your organization.

The table in Exhibit 9.05 explores how analytics and UDA could be injected at every stage of product development.

Product Stage	Stage Overview	Data Sources	Analysis
1. Identify the Need	▪ Identify consumer wants, needs, and preferences and develop your product ideas based on this consumer data. ▪ It is extremely important to keep only ideas that the market is ready to adopt and that technology can deliver. ▪ Market readiness and technology capacity are critical factors in initial idea assessment.	1. Social media such as: Twitter, Facebook 2. Blogs and forums 3. Business news 4. Intellectual propriety database 5. Geospatial database 6. Scientific articles, databases 7. E-commerce data 8. Opinion sites 9. Market research data, such as customer satisfaction surveys, conjoint analysis research, and focus groups	Perform market assessment and competitive intelligence and validate your research. Assumptions and hypotheses based on consumer wants, needs, and preferences from the nine data sources.
2. Develop the product	▪ Build Business Case and assess both technology and market readiness. ▪ Develop prototype ▪ Perform testing	The nine data sources above.	▪ Perform analysis to understand market readiness and technology readiness. ▪ Address a key question: "Is it good timing for my new product?" ▪ Use data analytics to navigate existing intellectual property, scientific articles, consumers' feedback and technology readiness to get a prototype product developed, tested and delivered. Assess how long it would take to get the product delivered. ▪ Analyze the market reaction to the prototype and competition KPIs to get actionable insights for next steps.

Exhibit 9.05 UDA and Product Development, Stage by Stage

Product Stage	Stage Overview	Data Sources	Analysis
3. Bring the product to the market. (Go-to-Market)	After completing the preliminary steps of market and technology assessments and testing the product prototype. Analyze the traditional 4Ps of marketing: ■ Product ■ Promotion: How will you promote your new product? ■ Price: What is the best pricing for your product? ■ Placement: Where are the best channels to market your new product?	■ Consumer data from internal enterprise databases. ■ Customer transaction data. ■ Competitive intelligence data. ■ Competition KPIs on similar products. ■ Marketing 4P Data gathered from the market.	■ Market response analysis ■ Consumer satisfaction survey analysis ■ Product adoption analysis ■ KPI analysis (sales, customers net present value, conversion, acquisition, net promoter score, product reviews, and consumer feedback), goals versus actual ■ Competitive intelligence analysis: How are the key competitors reacting? What products are they pushing into the market to compete against your new product?

Exhibit 9.05 *(Continued)*

UDA could also help address underlying questions around your product development, including:

■ What is the perceived value of your product or service?

■ How do you differentiate yourself from your competition?

■ How are you currently interacting with your customers?

■ How do you envision interacting with future customers?

■ What do consumers want from your product or service?

■ Does your product or service meet and exceed consumer expectations?

■ Where do potential buyers look for your particular product or service?

■ What is the journey of potential buyers of your product?

UDA allows vetting and optimizing every step of your product development. Your intuition and creativity will be augmented by advanced analytics of VoC information.

HOW IS UDA APPLIED TO PRODUCT DEVELOPMENT?

Getting all the data and information to enhance existing products or develop new products involves the use of (structured and unstructured) data analytics to understand what matters most to your customer and what matters most to the market.

Harnessing all the data from a variety of sources from the VoC (internal and external sources as well as publicly available sources) to extract the needs, preferences, wants, and key drivers of customer satisfaction and expectation regarding a product; these are the key elements that UDA leverages.

This would require that you get access to a variety of consumer data, both structured and unstructured, such as:

- Consumer feedback and opinion from social media networks
- Tweets, Facebook updates, and other livestreaming data from social media networks
- Survey data
- Open-ended questions and verbatim
- Customer feedback data
- Focus group feedback
- Opinions site
- Crowdsourcing, where great ideas regarding new products and services come in from suggestions from thousands or millions of users

The product development will also usually require using competitive intelligence and market research for clear, actionable insights regarding the state of your competition. These include:

- Offline and online market universe that should include the competition landscape, competition online presence, competition online reputation, competition firm graphic information websites, NPS, blog suppliers, and retailers.

- What exists today on the market?
- What are customers' satisfaction scores regarding those existing products: Like or hate?
- Reviews: What are they saying about existing products (which do they like the most/hate the most)? Comment note score: likes/hates.
- Manufacturer sites mined for features and pricing.
- Product association mined for business plan and market size.
- Crowdsourcing sites: Who else is out there with similar ideas or products?
- Comprehensive competitive intelligence: Have a census of all the information regarding competition products and rank them based upon features, strengths, and weaknesses.

Look at existing offers in the market that solve part of the problems and identify what they are lacking that your new product could supplement, or how your product could meet a customer's major expectations, solve existing problems, bridge existing gaps, or set new standards. What should you include to make your product better than the existing line of products? What should you remove that makes customers frustrated with the product?

Look for the features that are the key drivers of the competition product, and determine the overall sentiment of consumer regarding those drivers, what is missing, and how could you complement that.

HOW UDA APPLIED TO PRODUCT DEVELOPMENT WORKS

To understand how UDA applies to product development, let's first consider the three major product development steps that are generally used in the industry. These are:

- Identify the need
- Develop the product
- Go-to-Market with the product

Each of the above steps requires data collection, market sizing and market intelligence, competitive intelligence, and market research.

Beyond the traditional analytics that we perform to get the afore-mentioned insights, for each step we can simply use the interaction between analytics and innovation.

Let's first restate that the main business goal of analytics is to address four major business questions (see Exhibit 9.06):

- What happened?
- What's happening?
- What will happen?
- What should we do?

Analytics	Business	Product	New product
What happened?	How did we do?	How has my product(s) been doing? Why do customers hate or like about my existing products? What is missing?	How did existing similar products perform? What the market hates/likes about those products Why customers hate or like existing product What is missing?
What's happening?	How are we doing?	How is my product doing compared to the market?	How are existing similar products performing? What the market hates/likes about those products Why customers hate or like existing products What is missing
What will happen?	How are we going to do? What are we going to do?	How will my enhanced product perform? What features should my enhanced product have in order to meet and exceed market expectations? Will my product bridge existing gaps?	What features should my new product have to meet and exceed market expectations? How does my product bridge existing gaps?
What should we do?	What should we put in place?	What should I add or remove from my existing product to beat the competition?	What should I add or remove to existing competitive products that will be the key signature of my new product?

Exhibit 9.06 Address the Four Main Business Questions

KEY TAKEAWAYS

- Today, companies that once pioneered innovative products and services face "the innovator dilemma": challenges to generate disruptive products in a repeatable and scalable fashion.

- Big Data analytics and UDA help companies to address the innovator dilemma by harnessing the signals from the volume, variety, and velocity of new digital information that is flowing in from company internal and external information systems and customer touchpoints.

- The explosion of digital information powered by the advent of Big Data, cloud mobile, social media, and advances in computing power are enabling leading companies to enhance existing products and services and develop new ones.

- Leading companies are disrupting their product and services development thanks to UDA; and there were four key factors that enable the power of UDA in product and services development:
  - Intersection between analytics and innovation leads to new products and services creation.
  - The digital competitive world's 365/24/7 platform, where consumers can get (and provide their own) feedback regarding products and services.
  - Data analytics; the most valuable asset of our digital economy, where leading tech giants leverage the explosion of digital data and analytics to create data products and even entire new business lines.
  - The Voice of the Customer, even more relevant today than ever before when creating a new product.

- UDA is helping leading organizations harness all the data available to optimize every stage of product development from the ideas assessment, business case, product development, and prototype testing until the Go-to-Market analysis and post-launch analysis.

- In this highly competitive new business environment, with the proliferation of digital information, analytics and innovation are the lifeblood for successful disruptive products and services.

- To innovate one needs to "subtract" or "add" (Richard Saul Wurman). Advanced analytics is key to this process, from the macroeconomic perspective to the customer's needs perspective.

- The intersection between analytics and operations is where innovative companies simultaneously leverage and focus on ensuring that the fundamental business questions are addressed while the execution of innovation in services and products is optimized.

- Category-leading companies like Apple, Google, and Amazon lead with analytics and, more importantly, leverage analytics and operations to innovate and outpace their competition by focusing on customer experience and developing diversified products and services to meet customer and market expectations.

NOTES

1. GE Global Innovation Barometer 2016.
2. John T Gourville, "Eager Sellers and Stony Buyers: Understanding the Psychology of New-Product Adoption," *Harvard Business Review*, June 2006.
3. Booz & Company Report: Mary Meehan, "Flux: New Rules for Innovation and Growth," *Forbes*, May 2014.
4. Doblin Group, "96% of All Innovations Fail to Return Their Cost of Capital," *Fast Company*, April 4, 2012.
5. Clayton M Christensen, *The Innovator's Dilemma*, reprint edition (Boston, MA: Harvard Business Review Press: 2016).
6. Jean Paul Isson, "Analytics & Innovation," American Management Association: www.jpisson.com/wp-content/uploads/2015/04/Analytics_and_Innovation.pdf
7. Organization for Economic Co-operation and Development. *Data-Driven Innovation: Big Data for Growth and Well-Being* (Paris, France: OECD Publishing, 2015).
8. *Conjoint analysis* is a market research technique in which consumers make trade-offs between two or more features and benefits of a product on a scale ranging from "most preferred" to "least preferred." Coupled with techniques such as simulation analysis, conjoint analysis helps in evaluation of different pricing points.
9. "Innovation," Wikipedia.
10. Roy Luebe, "Peter Drucker on Innovation," *Innovation Excellence*, July 30, 2010, www. innovationexcellence.com/blog/2010/07/30/peter-drucker-on-innovation/
11. Richard Saul Wurman, Transcript of interview, *infrascape Design*, January, 11 2012: http://infrascapedesign.wordpress.com/2012/01/11/richard-saul-wurman
12. Mark W Johnson, Clayton M Christensen, and Henning Kagermann, "Reinventing Your Business Model," *Harvard Business Review*, December 2008. https://hbr.org/2008/12/reinventing-your-business-model

13. Apple: "1.2 billion iPhones Sold," August 2, 2017: www.idownloadblog.com/2017/08/02/1-2-billion-iphones-sold-to-date/

14. Steve Jobs, "Steve Jobs Introduces Original iPod—Apple Special Event (2001)," *EverySteveJobsVideo*, YouTube, January 4, 2014: www.youtube.com/watch?v=SYMTy6fchiQ

15. Evan Carmichael, "Lesson #5: Focus on the User," EvanCarmichael.com, www.evancarmichael.com/library/sergey-brin-larry-page/Lesson-5-Focus-On-the-User.html

16. Megan Burns, "The Business Impact of Customer Experience, 2011," Forrester Research, July 2011.

17. Ibid.

CHAPTER 10

The Power of UDA in National Security

The soul never thinks without a picture.

—Aristotle

NATIONAL SECURITY: PLAYGROUND FOR UDA OR CIVIL LIBERTY THREAT?

National security represents one of the fastest growing sectors that captures and processes the largest amount of people data. This sets the National Security Agency (NSA) as a leading playground for unstructured data analytics (UDA). From a public opinion perspective, the extent of people data gathered by the department, from a variety of sources, makes it the most polarizing agency. While for some the department gathers all the data and metadata to protect citizens, for others the agency represents a serious threat to citizens' civil liberties and privacy. Without getting into the pros and cons of the NSA's role and its data collection methods, we will focus on the opportunities that UDA represents for the agency's activities. First, let's look at the recent genesis of NSA's release and its underlying challenge beyond its core mission.

Edward J. Snowden, the NSA Whistle-Blower?

In 2013, the NSA found itself in disarray. The NSA took it on the chin from the mainstream media and privacy advocates because of several revelations made by one of its contractors, Edward Snowden. Snowden leaked to the entire world tons of documents about the NSA's surveillance system practices. While working as an NSA contractor through Booz Allen Hamilton (a consulting firm), Snowden copied and began releasing documents detailing NSA's secret programs that surveil communications in the United States and abroad.

Snowden claimed data from simple phone call conversations, e-mails, video calls, text messaging, chats, Internet visits, and searches were collected on every American citizen and billions of people around the world, which violated their civil liberties and privacy.

The NSA tracks the locations of hundreds of millions of cell phones every day, which enables the mapping of people's movements and relationships in detail. It reportedly has access to all communications made via Google, Microsoft, Facebook, Yahoo!, YouTube, AOL, Skype, Apple, and Paltalk, and collects hundreds of millions of contacts lists from personal e-mail and instant messaging accounts each year.

For instance, in the United States, the NSA collects and stores metadata records of phone calls, including those of more than 120 million U.S. Verizon subscribers, as well as Internet communications. The NSA justifies its activities based on a secret interpretation of the USA PATRIOT Act whereby the entirety of U.S. communications may be considered "relevant" to a terrorism investigation if it is expected that even a tiny minority may relate to terrorism. Subsequent to the Snowden leak controversy and the Senate Hearing from the Intelligence Committee, the USA PATRIOT Act was replaced by the USA Freedom Act: "a U.S. law enacted on June 2, 2015, that restored in a modified form several provisions of the USA PATRIOT Act, which had expired the day before."[1]

According to a July 2014 report in *The Washington Post*, which relied on information provided by Snowden, 90 percent of people placed under surveillance in the United States are ordinary Americans, and are not intended targets.[2] For Snowden, data collection on U.S. citizen residents (terrorists or not) based upon the principle of national security and terrorism prevention is a violation of the citizens' liberty. Beyond data collection practices, Snowden also released information on how the U.S. government's espionage services function.

What Is the NSA?

The NSA is an intelligence organization of the United States government, "responsible for global monitoring, collection, and processing of information and data for foreign intelligence and counterintelligence purposes, specializing in a discipline known as signals intelligence (SIGINT)."[3] The NSA is concurrently responsible for protecting U.S. government communications and information systems against penetration and network warfare.

> Originating as a unit to decipher coded communications during World War II, it was officially formed as the NSA by President Harry S. Truman in 1952. Since then, it has become one of the largest U.S intelligence organizations in terms of personnel and budget.[4]

The NSA operates as part of the Department of Defense and simultaneously reporting to the Director of National Intelligence. The NSA also acts as a competitive intelligence unit to protect U.S. interests in various capacities.

The advent of Big Data, with the exponential increase in computing power has enabled the agency to cull processes and analyze data from multiple sources and in multiple formats, in real time or near-real time. Over time, the NSA has improved its government espionage process by leveraging the power of Big Data and UDA. Instead of having people listening in on calls and classifying the callers into different security risk groups, the agency now uses unstructured data and advanced analytics algorithms such as machine learning and deep learning, thereby saving time and increasing productivity, efficiency, and effectiveness.

WHAT IS UDA FOR NATIONAL SECURITY?

How exactly the NSA, or any state national security agency, harnesses all the data collected is, of course, classified. But we do know that advanced analytics of unstructured data is used to create actionable intelligence. UDA leverages advanced analytics to harness all the people data to understand and predict national security threats, such as terrorism, fraud, hacking, money laundering, and other unlawful activities.

Human data for national security analysis encompasses a comprehensive list of data and information sources generated by people, whether they are online or offline, as described in Exhibit 10.01.

DATA SOURCES OF THE NSA

In the spirit of openness and transparency, here is a partial list of current and planned future data collection targets provided by the NSA on its website:

1. Internet searches
2. Websites visited
3. E-mails sent and received

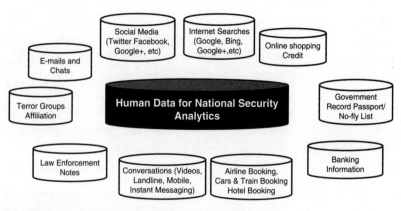

Exhibit 10.01 Human Data for National Security Analytics

4. Social media activity (Facebook, Twitter, etc.)

5. Blogging activity, including posts read and written and online comments

6. Videos watched and/or uploaded online

7. Photos viewed and/or uploaded online

8. Mobile phone GPS location data

9. Mobile phone apps downloaded

10. Phone call records

11. Text messages sent and received

12. Skype video calls

13. Online purchases and auction transactions

14. Credit card/debit card transactions

15. Financial information

16. Legal documents

17. Travel documents

18. Health records

19. Cable television shows watched and recorded

20. Commuter toll records

21. Electronic bus and subway passes/smartpasses

22. Facial recognition data from surveillance cameras

23. Educational records

24. Arrest records

25. Driver's license information

With this comprehensive data at their disposal, the NSA can perform various analyses to understand, explain, and anticipate threats, risks, and other illegal activities against the United States of America. The goal is to uncover:

- The *Past*: What happened?
- The *Present*: What is happening now, and why?
- The *Future*: What will happen?
- The *Prescription*: What should we do, knowing what will happen?

What Happened?

At this stage, the NSA sieves through all available sources of data and links all the pieces related to an event together. Past behaviors are described in terms of what people did, with whom they acted, and what went wrong. The NSA looks for a trigger for the behavior. For instance, after September 11, 2001, the police and law enforcement analyzed all the data and found that two of the 9/11 terrorists were on the government watch list and were linked to previous attacks: the bombings of the USS Cole[5] and the U.S. Embassy in Nairobi.[6]

After the Boston Marathon Terror Attack in 2013, a UDA video analysis helped to quickly find the suspects only a couple of days after the attack. UDA analyses and path analysis helped to make the links between the outcome/event and all the relevant pieces of information related to the perpetrators.

What Is Happening Now, and Why?

At this stage, the NSA is trying to determine what is happening and why it's happening. To do so, the NSA uses UDA to analyze billions of events, including: livestreaming; interaction on social media network such as tweets, Facebook posts, and updates on Instagram; and videos posted and uploaded from YouTube. The NSA creates dashboards from live data streams and derives sentiments from tweetvs, contents, updates, and text. Using UDA, the NSA analyzes structured and unstructured data on the fly. For instance, link analysis,[7] path analysis,[8] and text analysis linked to tickets purchased, chats, and ongoing posts on terror sites or niche groups help to determine what to do next.

For instance, border patrol agents could link data from existing systems to no-fly lists to determine whether a potential traveler poses a risk to the country if allowed in.

What Will Happen, and What Should We Do?

Using UDA on all the data available, predictive models can be created to anticipate unlawful behavior such as terrorist attacks and rogue behavior. These models help to anticipate who, when, how, and why:

- Who is more likely to commit a crime or become a threat to national security?
- How is the crime likely going to be committed?
- When is it more likely to happen?
- And perhaps more importantly: Why would a given behavior or an outcome/event occur?

As illustrated in Exhibit 10.2, all data sources are correlated (represented by the large oval shape), and causation between inputs data and the outcome is attempted. The model helps to determine what variables and input factors would be more useful to drive outcomes such as rogue behavior and terrorist acts. For example, one can identify at-risk people trying to travel abroad or entering the country or providing material support to terrorists or simply planning terror attacks.

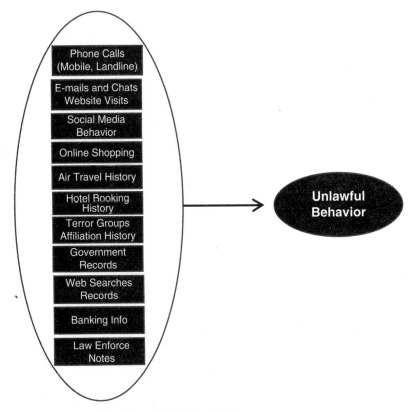

Exhibit 10.02 National Security Predictive Model

WHY UDA FOR NATIONAL SECURITY?

Government and intelligence agencies have always relied on communication surveillance to obtain information. Electronics have been part of the mix over the past decades. In today's digital information explosion, the volume, the variety, and the velocity of information gathered are no longer manually analyzed. While securities and intelligence-gathering used to rely on human intelligence, the amount of data flowing into agencies' networks in real time, needing analysis, is well beyond the scope of humans. To achieve their primary mandate to protect and anticipate threats such as terrorism, money laundering, societal unrest, and major unlawful activities, NSA performs global monitoring, collection, and processing of information and data for foreign intelligence and counterintelligence purposes. To anticipate threats, NSA leverages UDA and machine learning models to analyze all data and information that is generated from people they track or monitor. The data and information the agency captures are voluminous and varied, flowing in 24/7. The comprehensive list of data the agency collects was represented in Exhibits 10.01 and 10.02.

Before the advent of UDA, most governments across the world were using human resources to tap phone calls on a targeted number of people of interest and providing agencies with triggers on possible security threats, spying, and terrorism. Professional information agents (spies) were the major source of intelligence. This approach was time-consuming, cumbersome, and inefficient. Even if the data existed, it was impossible to comprehensively analyze it and create actionable insights for the agency to act upon. Moreover, due to the lack of resources and bandwidth to analyze all the collected data, analyses were primarily focused on a targeted group, creating weaknesses in speed to react or anticipate threats. With all the new sources of data from social media and the Web, it is now impossible for a human to link all the data sources, anticipate an imminent security threat, and make actionable impactful recommendations to prevent and avoid fraud or terror acts. NSA now has a more comprehensive, 360-degree view of risks, thanks to a unified methodology that combines different analytical techniques such as text analytics, social network analysis, predictive modeling, anomaly detection via link analysis, pattern analysis, deep learning, and machine learning. This approach has increased the NSA's productivity, efficiency, and effectiveness. And the agency can now leverage a combination of human intelligence with machine intelligence to protect its citizens, anticipate and avoid threats.

September 11, 2001: Disparate Data and Intelligence Weakness

Turning our attention back to the September 11, 2001, terrorist attack, efficient data integration across agencies and governmental bodies would have helped to prevent some of the act's perpetrators. Specifically, it has been discovered that two of the terrorists, Nawiaf Alhermir and Khalid Almihdhir, had been placed on the State Department's Watch List two weeks after President Bush heard about the planned attack. Moreover, these two men were linked to previous attacks on the USS Cole and the U.S. Embassy in Nairobi. Based on this information, these two individuals were already targets of highest priority. If the investigators had looked for them, they would have found them in the San Diego phonebook. Days after joining the watch list, the two men reserved airplane tickets using their real names. Even though the investigators could not have foreseen those aircrafts would be used as bombs, they should have seen those names pop up. By integrating all available information and analyzing it through anomaly detection pattern analysis and link analysis, the state and local national security agents would have been provided with actionable information to prevent some of the terrorists' actions. For instance, a link analysis would have helped to locate those terrorists before they went into hiding and place them on the No-Fly list.

In his book *The Numerati*, Stephen Baker describes how our everyday actions, as we communicate, travel, make purchases, can be analyzed successfully and used in early incident detection, in predicting outcomes, and even in influencing behaviors.[9] He also discusses the analytics methodology called Finding the Next Friend. This methodology allows users to follow and track people through their device(s) using GPS. This methodology also synchronizes with other applications. The next friend algorithm is being studied at Carnegie Mellon University, leveraging what they call "iffy data." It is believed the next friend algorithm would have helped to link all available information on the perpetrators and determine their current goal based upon analysis of their previous behaviors and actions.

One of the major problems in preventing terrorist acts was the lack of integration of government data across multiple sources: the NSA, the Federal Bureau of Investigation (FBI), and the Central Intelligence Agency (CIA). To minimize intelligence gaps which hamper the ability to prevent or mitigate terror attacks, the government spent $8 billion on IT in 2013. In that year, the CIA awarded a contract to Amazon AWS worth up to $600 million over a period of ten years.

The Intelligence Committee (IC) AWS cloud operates behind the IC firewall using a variety of application programming interfaces (APIs). A company official said AWS made more than 200 incremental improvements in 2013, building innovations for the Intelligence Committee cloud to keep pace with commercial advances.

UDA tools can analyze full text e-mails or scrape communication channels, looking for anomalies or patterns that indicate potential malicious actions, such as fraud or intellectual property breach. Linking communication data to airline data, social media data, and national security data across all agencies around the world could result in efficiently and effectively spotting and anticipating upcoming threats and enable proactive security actions to avoid terrorist acts. Only when the tool detects a potential issue that needs attention do the managers need to be involved. After all, organizations do want to protect their intellectual property and prevent an aggrieved employee from making sensitive data public, for example.

Social media analysis is taking an ever-increasing role in crowd control. Governments worldwide use different tools to scan and analyze tweets for security threats and will act accordingly. A good example of a tool was one developed by the Dutch government in conjunction with local police to control the crowd[10] during a large event in December 2012 in The Netherlands. The VSTEP Crowd Control Trainer, a realistic 3D virtual tool, was used to train crowd managers and police for any kind of mass events.

How the CIA Uses Big Data to Predict Social Unrest

Director Hallman said the CIA has significantly improved its "anticipatory intelligence" using a mesh of sophisticated algorithms and analytics against complex systems to better predict the flow of everything from illicit cash to extremists around the globe. Deep learning and machine learning help link seemingly disparate datasets and predict future events with national security ramifications.

According to the NextGov paper by Frank Konkel, "The reason [was] a dramatic improvement in analytics, cloud computing and deep learning."[11] The CIA can clearly picture events unfolding or about to unfold in an increasingly unclear world. At the NextTech event hosted by Government Exec and NextGov (2016), Hallman indicated that the CIA could predict societal unrest up to three to five days out.

Main data elements and variables used to predict illicit cash, extremist activities, social coups, social unrest, societal and financial instabilities include:

- CIA classified data
- Open datasets
- Sensor data
- Satellites data
- Surveillance data
- Open data repositories
- Human intelligence
- Social sciences
- Information from past six decades

Benefits of UDA

Some additional benefits of UDA range from security to investigations to intelligence and general use cases.

Security

For security, UDA benefits include:

- Incident correlation and prediction
- Epidemiology prediction
- Disaster response
- Vetting, indications, and warning
- Security incident investigation, insider threat, cyber-analysis

Investigations

For investigation, benefits include:

- Computer incident response
- Advanced persistent threat discovery
- Insider threat identification and investigation
- Disgruntled employee identification

Intelligence

For intelligence, benefits include:

- Data trend analysis
- Reputation analysis
- Military intelligence
- Counterterrorism
- Counter-fraud cyber-analysis
- Pirated software use identification
- Threat intelligence

General Use Cases

- Employee-sensitive data caching
- Asset vulnerability versus criticality comparison, threat campaign tracking
- Strategic report production for leadership
- External scanning pattern analysis
- Spear-phishing identification and impact analysis
- Integration into incidents

Return on Investment of NSA's Big Data Analytics

Meta S. Brown states that Senator Dianne Feinstein, in a 2013 *Wall Street Journal* op-ed titled: "The NSA's Watchfulness Protects America," said that we're getting a lot of actionable intelligence to protect America. She quotes Sen. Feinstein:

> Working in combination, the call-records database and other NSA programs have aided efforts by U.S. intelligence agencies to disrupt terrorism in the U.S. approximately a dozen times in recent years, according to the NSA. This summer, the agency disclosed that 54 terrorist events have been interrupted—including plots stopped and arrests made for support to terrorism. Thirteen events were stopped in the U.S. homeland and nine involved U.S. persons or facilities overseas. Twenty-five were in Europe, five in Africa and eleven in Asia.[12]

The *Wall Street Journal* article claimed, "If today's call-records program had been in place before 9/11, the terrorist attacks likely would have been prevented."[13]

UDA for National Security Challenges

In several Western countries, there is always a fine line between protection and privacy invasion, and the following are major questions that describe the concerns:

- Should the government get access to all data and metadata created by its citizens, even citizens who do not represent any risk, do not appear on any No-Fly list, nor are tied to any terrorism groups?
- How could we dichotomize people (bad/good) without analyzing the relevant data that helps to determine their 360-degree pattern?
- What if the model we are using is wrong and falsely identifies innocent citizens—for instance, putting someone on the No-Fly list by mistake?
- How does the government justify spying on its citizens, violating their human rights, to fulfill its duty to protect them?

■ What if at every national security agency there were some latent informer/whistleblower/traitor (like Edward Snowden) ready to leak government spying practices, potentially undermining the lives of people and safety of countries?

■ What if hackers get access to citizens' information and use it to their advantage? What if private citizen information is used for illegal activities?

■ Who owns all the data collected on private citizens?

These questions are the major concerns citizens have; they need to be considered by any government using Big Data and UDA to enhance their national security programs and strategies. Government security agencies need to protect their citizens and at the same time respect their civil rights, privacy, and civil liberties. The biggest challenge in our societies today is finding the right balance between national security and the protection of civil liberties and privacy.

CASE STUDIES

As is the case in other sectors, such as human resources, sports, healthcare, and marketing, security agencies use advanced UDA to answer four basic questions:

■ Who is more likely to instigate an unlawful behavior?

■ Why would that person act in such a way?

■ When is the behavior more likely to occur?

■ What should you do knowing what will likely happen?

Business Challenge

From the NSA website:

> The National Security Agency/Central Security Service (NSA/CSS) leads the U.S. Government in cryptology that encompasses both Signals Intelligence (SIGINT) and Information Assurance (IA) products and services, and enables Computer Network Operations (CNO) in order to gain a decision advantage for the Nation and our allies under all circumstances.

Inherent in their mandate, the NSA needs to identify and anticipate security threats.

Solutions

The NSA developed its own Big Data weapons systems; the major one is called Apache Accumulo. Accumulo leverages the graph theory and advanced analytics to provide the agency with a discernable picture of the world's communications, using telephone metadata and Internet traffic data collected under the PRISM program.[14]

During the wars in Iraq and Afghanistan, the NSA utilized predictive models and other Big Data tools created by the Silicon Valley company Palantir, to help connect the dots between known terrorists. According to government officials, Palantir's technology even helped the military foil suicide bomber and roadside bomber attacks. Similar tools from Palantir are now used by the NSA, FBI, and CIA, which provided monetary backing to the company.

Benefit

NSA can likely pinpoint suspicious communications activity leveraging Apache Accumulo graph theory analytics and predictive models, based on call records and Internet activity. The predictions likely use name, age, gender, and geographic location data to plot likely future locations of individuals. The system helps to clearly define relationships between different groups of people and individuals who could be on the target list of the agency. The Agency leverages advanced analytics to create inferences about how criminal organizations and terrorist groups operate. The information can be used to deduce who is or is not working together on a potential plot, where these perpetrators plan to meet, and what criminal acts they are working on. By connecting all pieces of data and information, predictive analytics and graph analytics provide national security organizations with actionable intelligence about their potential targets. More importantly, this information, not yet released or shared, is helping the agency with more insightful data than national security direct surveillance.

In his interview with InformationWeek, David Hurry, chief researcher for the NSA's computer scientist division, said "By bringing data sets together, it's allowed us to see things in the data that we didn't necessarily see from looking at the data from one point or another."[15]

THE BOSTON MARATHON AND IBM WATSON

During my interview with Paul Zikopoulos, Vice President, Big Data and Cognitive Analytics at IBM, I asked him to provide me with some insights of Video Analytics that support National Security.

Isson: *How about video analytics?*

Zikopoulos: *What is a video? A sequence of pictures—tons and tons of pictures put together. The fact that we do image analysis means we can really do video analysis. After the Boston Marathon, we teamed up with Boston's police department for a better way to do surveillance recognition of images in video. One of the suspects had a white hat, so we taught the computer what a white hat looks like. After teaching the computer what a white hat looks like, it went to video looking frame by frame for what a white hat looks like. So instead of watching five hours of video, we watched thirty-five minutes of videos where the computer detected a white hat. We were able to detect the two suspects from the video through this supervised learning: man wearing white hat.*

Let me teach Watson what snow looks like, what an alpine (downhill) ski looks like, what snowboarding looks like. Then Watson can tell you where to go and learn skiing. That's exactly how you start with video analytics. And the step after that is what we call deep machine learning.

HOW UDA WORKS

1. Gather all the people data, structured and unstructured, that is available (audio, video, text, e-mail, and social media posts).
2. Standardize, integrate, and centralize the data.
3. Perform descriptive analysis.
4. Perform event-streaming analytics of social media data and on-the-fly pattern analysis.
5. Perform predictive analysis using advanced analytics software or open source or built-in algorithms.

6. Interpret the results and take proactive actions.

7. Measure, track the outcomes, and optimize by putting the right strategy in place to avoid the unplanned outcome.

 KEY TAKEAWAYS

To keep its mission of protecting the U.S. citizens and government against penetration, network warfare, and other threats, the NSA monitors, collects, and processes information and data for foreign intelligence and counterintelligence purposes, a discipline known as SIGINT. The clear majority of data collected includes:

- Phone calls (mobile and landline)
- Video calls (Microsoft, Google, Skype, Facebook)
- E-mails
- Chats and SMS
- Social media (Facebook, Twitter, Instagram, LinkedIn, Google+)
- Online search
- Hotel booking
- GPS
- Air travel
- Online shopping
- Web behavior

The data collected by national security agencies represents a playground for UDA. Since most of the data collected is unstructured, UDA is therefore the primary analytics for security agencies monitoring and assessing the growing volume of threats incoming at great speed from social media, the Internet, mobile devices, computers, and the cloud. In particular:

- UDA helps the government to harness all the unstructured data it collects in order to understand, explain, and anticipate illegal behaviors and activities.
- UDA provides relevant benefits to other countries, ranging from national security insights to government intelligence and national and global investigations.
- UDA helps to detect and prevent terror activities and cyberthreats, and provides government agencies with actionable insights on: Who? When? Why?

And more importantly, "What should the government do with the data intelligence to mitigate risks, and detect and avoid terror plots, cybercrimes, and other unlawful activities against U.S. citizens and the government?"

Leveraging UDA for national security requires the right tradeoff between protection of citizens against threats and the protection of citizens' privacy and civil liberties and rights.

NOTES

1. "USA Freedom Act," Wikipedia: https://en.wikipedia.org/wiki/USA_Freedom_Act

2. *Washington Post*, July 2014, "How 160,000 Intercepted Communications Led to Our Latest NSA Story": https://www.washingtonpost.com/world/national-security/your -questions-answered-about-the-posts-recent-investigation-of-nsa-surveillance/ 2014/07/11/43d743e6-0908-11e4-8a6a-19355c7e870a_story.html?utm_term= .9c7f6a596585

3. "National Security Agency," Wikipedia: https://en.wikipedia.org/wiki/National _Security_Agency

4. "National Security Agency," Wikipedia: https://en.wikipedia.org/wiki/National _Security_Agency

5. "The USS Cole bombing was a terrorist attack against the United States Navy's guided-missile destroyer USS Cole on 12 October 2000, while it was being refueled in Yemen's Aden harbor. Seventeen American sailors were killed and 39 injured in the deadliest attack against a United States naval vessel since 1987." ("USS *Cole* Bombing," Wikipedia: https://en.wikipedia.org/wiki/USS_Cole_bombing)

6. "The 1998 United States embassy bombings were attacks that occurred on August 7, 1998, in which over 200 people were killed in nearly simultaneous truck bomb explosions in two East African cities, one at the United States Embassy in Dar es Salaam, Tanzania, the other at the United States Embassy in Nairobi, Kenya." ("1998 United States Embassy Bombings," Wikipedia: https://en.wikipedia .org/wiki/1998_United_States_embassy_bombings)

7. *Link analysis* is a technique used to evaluate relationships between elements (called nodes). Relationships are identified among various types of nodes, including organizations, people, and transactions. Link analysis is used for investigation of criminal activity, computer security analysis, search engine optimization, market research, medical research, and art.

8. *Path analysis* is used to describe the dependencies among a set of variables. This includes models equivalent to any form of multiple regression analysis, factor analysis, canonical correlation analysis, or discriminant analysis, as well as more general families of models in the multivariate analysis of variance and covariance analyses.

9. Stephen Baker, *The Numerati* (New York, NY: Houghton Mifflin Harcourt, 2008).

10. Mark van Rijmenam, "Crowd Control Management in the Twente Region," Datafloq, January 17, 2015: https://datafloq.com/read/crowd-control-management/519

11. Frank Konkel, "CIA Says It Can Predict Social Unrest as Early as 3 to 5 Days Out," *Defense One*, October 5, 2016: www.defenseone.com/technology/2016/10/cia-says-it-can-predict-social-unrest-early-3-5-days-out/132121/

12. Meta S. Brown, "NSA Mass Surveillance: Biggest Big Data Story," *Forbes*, August 27, 2015: www.forbes.com/sites/metabrown/2015/08/27/nsa-mass-surveillance -biggest-big-data-story/#6be193599acc

13. Dianne Feinstein, "The NSA's Watchfulness Protects America," *Wall Street Journal*, October 13, 2013: https://www.wsj.com/articles/the-nsa8217s-watchful ness-protects-americathe-nsa8217s-watchfulness-protects-america-1381688332? tesla=y

14. The NSA collects Internet communications from U.S. Internet companies in a program code-named PRISM. The NSA has demanded that under Section 702 of the FISA Amendments Act of 2008, Internet companies, such as Google Inc., must turn over any data that matched court-approved search terms. Communications that were initially encrypted can be subject to a PRISM request from the NSA, as can stored data that telecommunication filtering systems discarded earlier, as well as data that may be easier to handle, among other things. ("PRISM (surveillance program)," Wikipedia: https://en.wikipedia.org/wiki/PRISM_(surveillance_program)).

15. Doug Henschen, Defending NSA PRISM's Big Data Tools, *InformationWeek*. Data Management //Big Data. www.informationweek.com/big-data/big-data-analytics/ defending-nsaprisms-big-data-tools/d/d-id/1110318

FURTHER READING

Babak Akhgar, Gregory B. Saathoff, Hamid R. Arabnia, Richard Hill, Andrew Staniforth, and Petra Saskia Bayerl, *Application of Big Data for National Security, A Practitioner's Guide for Emerging Technologies* (Butterworth-Heinemann, 2015).

American Association for the Advancement of Science in conjunction with the Federal Bureau of Investigation and the United Nations Interregional Crime and Justice Research Institute, "National and Transnational Security Implications of Big Data in the Life Sciences," a Joint AAAS-FBI-UNICRI Project, November 10, 2014: www.aaas.org/sites/default/files/AAAS-FBI-UNICRI_Big_Data_Report_111014.pdf

James Ball, Julian Borger, and Glenn Greenwald, "Revealed: How US and UK Spy Agencies Defeat Internet Privacy and Security," *The Guardian*, September 6, 2013: www.theguardian.com/world/2013/sep/05/nsa-gchq -encryption-codes-security

Basis Technology: great text analytics software used by Amazon Microsoft Oracle and Airbnb: www.basistech.com

Clint Boulton, "How the NSA Uses Behavior Analytics to Detect Threats," *CIO Journal*, December 7, 2015: www.cio.com/article/3012322/security/how-the-nsa-uses-behavior-analytics-to-detect-threats.html

Rory Carroll, "NSA Surveillance Needed to Prevent Isis Attack, Claims Former Intelligence Chair," *The Guardian*, April 22, 2015: www.theguardian.com/us-news/2015/apr/22/mass-surveillance-needed-isis-attack-mike-rogers

Andrew Couts, "What's the NSA Picking Out of Your Phone Calls? Just 'Unvolunteered Truths.'" *Digital Trends*, August 31, 2013: www.digitaltrends.com/features/whats-the-nsa-picking-out-of-your-phone-calls-just-unvolunteered-truths/

IBM, "Intelligence Analysis and Investigations": www.ibm.com/analytics/us/en/safer-planet/threat-intelligence/

"Manage All Unstructured Data with SAS® Text Analytics" (video), SAS Software, September 15, 2011: www.youtube.com/watch?v=NHAq8jG4FX4

"The NSA Files," *The Guardian*: www.theguardian.com/us-news/the-nsa-files

Sunil Jose, "Using Big Data Analytics to Boost National Security," LinkedIn, February 11, 2016: www.linkedin.com/pulse/using-big-data-analytics-boost-national-security-sunil-jose

John R. Parkinson: "NSA: 'Over 50' Terror Plots Foiled by Data Dragnets," *ABC News*, June 18, 2013: http://abcnews.go.com/Politics/nsa-director-50-potential-terrorist-attacks-thwarted-controversial/story?id=19428148

David Sherfinski, "NSA Surveillance Prevented Terror Attacks, Most Voters Say: Poll," *The Washington Times*, June 4, 2015: www.washingtontimes.com/news/2015/jun/4/nsa-surveillance-prevented-terrorist-attacks-poll/

CHAPTER 11

The Power of UDA in Sports

War is 90 percent information.

—Napoleon Bonaparte

In the course of our lives, we have all played some sports, or have been a fan of a team or a star player in baseball, basketball, football, soccer, tennis, hockey, track and field, or golf, to name a few.

Whether you are a fan, coach, player, general manager, investor, or an owner of a team in any sports, what really matters is performance results and outcomes: wins versus losses. Did your favorite team win or lose? And why? How did your star athlete/player perform? Did she/he score? Even before the game, gathering all the information and statistics regarding players and teams has been getting a lot of traction to support team management. Predictions are made on the favored teams or players and what they need to do to secure a victory.

In most team sports, such as baseball, hockey, and basketball, star players' historical scores and performances usually drive all the prognostics that fans make around the player and the team. However, a popular player or "big name," despite poor performance results, will more likely rank higher than an undervalued unknown player. Before the advent of analytics in sports, wealthy teams were always in a race to acquire those stars because they assumed that accumulating star players would guarantee success. Most general managers and coaches have been relying on this approach that favors instinct, intuition, gut-feel, and experience in building their rosters. And not so long ago, coaches and general managers were praised for their gut-feel and instinct to find star players despite their high pay demands; fans thought it would guarantee great performance and success. This intuition-based approach ignored a great untapped pool of good, undervalued players. This was sports before Sabermetrics and *Moneyball*.

THE SHORT HISTORY OF SPORTS ANALYTICS: *MONEYBALL*

The history of how data analytics got into sports started more than 46 years ago, long before the advent of new assistive technologies, sensors, scanners, GPS, biometrics devices, and Big Data. These new technologies have been enabling forward-looking teams and sport associations to track, capture, process, and analyze player data to drive best performance results. While some sports associations have been early adopters of advanced analytics, making it a key tool for their teams, players and front office management are still skeptical of embracing it.

Below are the major milestones in the history of advanced analytics in sports:

In 1964, Earnshaw Cook, an engineer, was one of the earliest proponents of statistical and probabilistic baseball. He gathered most of his research in his book, called *Percentage Baseball*. Despite being widely criticized and ignored by baseball executives, the book got a lot of media attention.

In late 1970, Bill James, a historian and statistician, created Sabermetrics:[1] the empirical analysis of baseball that especially focused on baseball statistics that measure in-game activity. James defined Sabermetrics as "the search for objective knowledge about baseball" and envisioned addressing questions such as: Which player contributed the most to team success? How can we improve player performance by leveraging their historical game statistics? Sabermetrics produced cutting-edge statistical evaluations of player performance, starting with baseball. Baseball, with its flood of available performance data, was the first sport to adopt analytics. James and his team explored the development of statistics that could be harnessed to assess the correlation and causation between team performance outcomes (wins or losses) and individual player performance.

In the 1990s, baseball teams started to embrace Sabermetric analysis for their front office and team management. Sandy Alderson, then general manager of Oakland Athletics (Oakland A's), pioneered the use of advanced empirical analytics for player selection, player evaluation, and team management. The A's were facing major economic hurdles and insufficient financial resources to afford expensive highly valued players. Alderson understood that by leveraging Sabermetric analysis, he could build, with a very small payroll, a strong competitive team. He managed to put together a roster full of undervalued talented players with low salaries but great Sabermetric performance results.

In 1997, Billy Beane became general manager of the A's, and in 1999, Oakland became the most cost-effective Major League Baseball (MLB) team. Billy Beane brought Alderson's use of Sabermetric analysis to a higher level by hiring a Sabermetrics-inclined assistant manager named Paul Depodesta to assist in player selection and roster construction. He used Sabermetric analysis to identify undervalued players to be developed with a low budget. Using Sabermetrics, Bean effectively and efficiently managed the assets, the talent, and the resources of the team.

Billy Beane disrupted Major League Baseball by changing the way players were selected. Instead of relying on his coach's instinct and experience, as had been done for years, Beane empowered the use of analytics to build his roster. Despite his low budget and the smallest payroll in MLB, Sabermetrics propelled the A's to become one of the most successful teams in MLB, making four consecutive playoff appearances. Beane and DePodesta, bucking an ingrained system, managed to transform the A's from a team with six consecutive losing seasons into one of the winningest teams in baseball. The team's success under Billy Beane marked the genesis of data analytics in the sports arena.

In mid-1990, IBM developed Advanced Scout, a data mining knowledge management tool. Advanced Scout not only collected in-game structured stats, but also unstructured multimedia footage.

Coaches and players could use the tool to prepare for upcoming opponents using historical footage. Advanced Scout revealed hidden patterns in sports, such as NBA play-by-play data, and provided additional insights to coaches and other related organizations.

In 2001, Hawk-Eye, a complex computer system developed by Paul Hawkins, was officially used in officiating cricket games.[2] This complex computer system is now used officially in numerous sports such as cricket, tennis, Gaelic football, badminton, hurling, association football, and volleyball. The system works via six (sometimes seven) high-performance cameras, normally positioned on the underside of the stadium roof, which track the ball from different angles. The video from the six cameras is then triangulated and combined to create a three-dimensional representation of the trajectory of the ball. Hawk-Eye is not infallible; it is accurate within 5 millimeters (0.19 inch). But it is generally trusted as an impartial second opinion in sports.

Hawk-Eye has been accepted by governing bodies in tennis, cricket, and association football as a technological means of adjudication. It has been used for the Challenge System since 2006 in tennis and for the Umpire Decision Review System in cricket since 2009. The system was rolled out for the 2013–14 Premier League season as a means of goal-line technology, and in December 2014, the clubs of the first division of Bundesliga decided to adopt this system for the 2015–16 season.

In 2003, the Oakland Athletics' successful use of Sabermetrics inspired the bestseller book by Michael Lewis, *Moneyball: The Art of Winning an Unfair Game*, as well as a major motion picture. Lewis's book changed the way the average fan and the business world looked at baseball. It genuinely underscored how Billy Beane and his team challenged the MLB conventional wisdom in team roster building and player selection. It became the genesis of analytics in baseball and overall sports. A number of MLB clubs followed the example of the A's and started hiring general managers and front offices resources with analytics background to leverage statistical approach to assess player and teams.

In 2002, the Boston Red Sox hired data-driven and quantitative minds: Theo Epstein as general manager and a Sabermetrician,

Bill James, as an advisor in baseball operations. On November 25, 2002, Epstein became the youngest general manager in the history of MLB when the Boston Red Sox hired him at the age of 28. In 2004, the Red Sox won their first World Series championship in 86 years; Epstein was still general manager when the team won another championship in 2007. The Boston Red Sox used Sabermetrics and *Moneyball* to analyze player decisions. They spent smartly on overlooked stars, valuing On Base Percentage and Slugging over Batting Average, and used "rotations by milking at-bats" and raised pitch-counts to win games. The Red Sox proceeded to win the World Series in 2004, 2007, and 2013.[3]

In 1990, according to a study from Bhandari, Colet, and Parker, more than 50 percent of National Basketball Association (NBA) teams used advanced analytics to analyze games statistics and to detect nonobvious patterns in the data.[4] Coaches used this information strategically to implement game and substitution plans.

The NBA followed the MLB example by including a selection of analytics investors and statistical experts in their front offices. By the 2013–2014 season, 23 of the 30 NBA clubs used advanced statistics, and most had hired basketball analytics specialists and worked with sports analytics consultants in the field.

Small market clubs such as Baltimore Ravens, San Francisco 49ers, and big market teams like the New England Patriots are part of the forward-looking teams of the National Football League (NFL) that have embraced advanced analytics for their teams and player management.

While some teams are really leading the way in injecting data analytics for their team practices and games, others are still very skeptical or slow to embrace sports analytics. Some simply do not see the value. Exhibit 11.01, an extract of the Top 6 and Bottom 6 in major sports, gives an overview of leading and lagging teams in sports analytics, based on ESPN's *The Great Analytics Rankings*, in which a team of researchers and experts rated 122 teams on the strength of franchises' analytics staffs, the buy-in from executives and coaches, the investments in biometric data, and their analytics-based approach.[5]

According to a study by associate professors Joris Drayer and Joel Maxcey of Temple University's School of Tourism and Hospitality Management, 23 percent of the National Hockey League (NHL) teams employ analytics professionals.[6] This percentage is 56 percent for the

Major League Baseball (MLB)		
Ranking	Top 6 Ranking	Bottom 6 Ranking
1	Boston Red Sox	Miami Marlins
2	Chicago Cubs	Philadelphia Phillies
3	Cleveland Indians	Arizona Diamondbacks
4	Houston Astros	Atlanta Braves
5	New York Yankees	Cincinnati Reds
6	Oakland A's	Colorado Rockies
National Basketball Association (NBA)		
Ranking	Top 6 Ranking	Bottom 6 Ranking
1	Dallas Mavericks	Brooklyn Nets
2	Houston Rockets	Los Angeles Lakers
3	Philadelphia 76ers	New York Knicks
4	San Antonio Spurs	Chicago Bulls
5	Atlanta Hawks	Denver Nuggets
6	Boston Celtics	Los Angeles Clippers

Exhibit 11.01 Top 6 and Bottom 6 in Major Sports

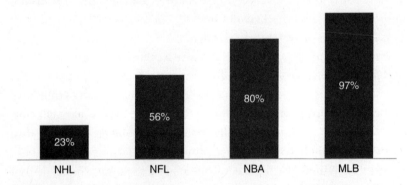

Exhibit 11.02 Percentage of Teams That Employ Analytics Professionals

NFL, 80 percent for the NBA and 97 percent for MLB, as shown in Exhibit 11.02.

Moneyball completely shifted the power and team performance from star players to the executives and Sabermetric-inclined general managers. It has disrupted the demography and profile of the new generation of general managers. Before Epstein got into the executive ranks of the Red Sox, they were dominated by former players, like Billy Beane, and ex-scouts, like Pat Gillick of the Seattle Mariners and later of the Philadelphia Phillies. Today, they all follow Epstein's tracks. Out of the thirty MLB general managers, 26 got their jobs after Epstein. They are all under fifty, and very few of them played professional baseball at any level.

Despite tangible success from teams such as the Oakland A's, there are still some owners, general managers, and coaches who are not comfortable with the use of analytics for their team. While some sports, such as hockey, basketball, and professional soccer, have been very fast to adopt analytics, other associations like the NFL are straggling. In the next section, we will discuss and provide actionable facts to support the impact of UDA in sports.

WHY SHOULD YOU CARE ABOUT UDA IN SPORTS?

As was the case in other industries, Big Data and computing power enabled data processing in real or near-real time, which was a game changer in sports. It can help teams and associations with their finance and marketing decisions, optimize player development, optimize game training and practice techniques and strategies. The sports industry represents a great market opportunity that is constantly growing; according to a report from PricewaterhouseCoopers, annual global sports revenues ballooned to $145 billion in 2015.[7]

The use of data analytics (structured and unstructured) can contribute to success on the field, on the court, and on the ice; improve player safety, health, and performance; and contribute to ticket sales and fan engagement. It does so by providing actionable insight to players, coaches, managers, and front office executives.

Specifically, UDA can have an impact on player evaluation, player health and injuries, contract negotiation, roster construction, draft analysis, training and preparation, games and training data visualization, game strategies, and coaching evaluation.

UDA's Impact for Players

UDA of player data and field data can help players with:

- *Performance tracking*, by helping to track strengths and weaknesses during practices and games, thereby highlighting areas for improvement as well as best practices.

- *Player practice and game review*, through videos and clips that harness all the training and game data, collected via GPS and accelerometers.

- *Biometric data*.

- *Improved health and safety*, by tracking and analyzing player health conditions on the field. In the NFL, for instance, sensors in helmets record contact hits to anticipate accidents and concussions.

In tennis, during major tournaments such as US Open, where tennis is played simultaneously on 19 courts for two weeks, all action during the two-week tournament is captured and broadcasted worldwide. UDA, powered with technologies such as multiple cameras, replays that captured action, and computers that analyze in near-real time can help players dispute bad calls and help fans see every point, game, and set, as well as the speed of a serve and the trajectories of the balls.

UDA Impact for Coaches and Managers

By analyzing a player's past and present performance data, UDA can help coaches and managers to best determine:

- Whom to select
- Whom to align in the field, on the court, or on the ice
- Overall team game-planning, as well as in-game decision making
- What the best roster is to ensure success against an opponent
- What strategy to put in place for the game
- Lessons learned during game review after a win or a loss.
- Adjustments required for an upcoming opponent
- Roster construction

UDA provides target performance analysis, which is fundamental to player evaluation. Additionally, it can provide injury analysis of players and a personalized tactical analysis for each player during practice and games.

There are several reasons for sports teams to use analytics. The following represents some of them:

- Enhancc the team performance
- Select the best players and create an optimal roster
- Field the best possible team to ensure victory
- Make the best possible game strategy on the court, the field, or the ice
- Explore dynamic pricing of sports tickets

Analytics could also provide the following actionable insights to coaches and managers:

- Performance analyses that a coach can share with his/her players, his/her team, and an opponent team to reinforce messaging and empower the players to take ownership of their overall performance
- Insights on player performance to provide specific statistics and knowledge on conditioning
- Player development and physical training
- Modeling of the pattern of player injuries, with the optimal goal of prediction and prevention
- Support for individual game strategy, including tactical options and competitive intelligence
- Deep-dive analysis of the team overvlew: individual performance, sleep monitoring, and player heart monitoring

Evidence-based coaching is presented to players, including analysis of GPS data captured during games and practices and data from other wearable devices.

Harnessed effectively, this data allows teams to monitor the return times of injured athletes and more efficiently manage player placement and substitution patterns in games. Coaches can use this information strategically to implement game substitution schemes.

For example, the Toronto Raptors optimize their roster building when they do their draft selection; they look at stats that you would expect. According to Paul Zikopoulos, vice president of Big Data and cognitive computing at IBM, the Raptors team management "leverages unstructured data solutions such as social media analytics by capturing all of their players and athletes' Twitter posts, all of the Facebook posts, all of their video interviews, and all their press interviews, then converts them into text and runs them through IBM personality analyzer to see if their personality fits with the team."

UDA Impact on Fans

Getting technologies and 360-degree views of the game and player movements makes fans smarter and more passionate about the game. Using UDA to analyze fans data can provide managers and owners with actionable insights regarding their fanbase including:

- The voice of the fans:
    - Fan sentiment analysis (what do fans think about the team, the players, the coach, and the infrastructure such as the stadium location and amenities?)
    - Fan engagement and motivation to support the team and attend games
    - Fan conveniences, such as ordering food and drinks, returning home without traffic, or viewing an instant replay of the game
- Fan needs:
    - Statistically inclined fans now have a tremendous number of websites, such as BrookBaseball.net, that provide compiled historical data on teams and players. Fans can visit those sites to see statistical breakdown for their favorite players and deep dive on specific games and plays.
    - Fans can track player performance before, during, and after the game. In tennis, for example, the IBM Slam Tracker application provides fans with ball and player position data, depth of return, speed of the ball, and player distance run. Using historical performance data and data of previous matchups between the players, Slam Tracker also provides insight into pressure situations, revealing underling patterns in match dynamics.

▪ Digitize the game and bring a new fan experience.

▪ IBM Watson Visual Recognition API is used in some tennis open tournaments. It analyzes photos taken by official photographers and uses metatagging capabilities to quickly identify players and celebrities in the crowd. It also significantly streamlines the production process for the open digital and social media teams. Fans also have access, via cloud technology, to real-time data.

UDA can help governing bodies optimize scheduling, optimize resource allocation, and examine the legal environment within their organizations:

▪ Help sports media providers study relevant markets from fantasy sports to sponsorships.

▪ Improve officiating; according to an article by Shawn Krest, technology has helped revolutionize tennis officiating.[8] For the last ten years, the US Open has used Hawk-Eye tennis system cameras to automate line-judging. Prior to that, human judges had to determine, in real time, whether a ball was in or out, leading to some epic player meltdowns (such as John McEnroe). Those live challenges and uncomfortable exchanges are over with instant live review of the player challenge. Technology such as Hawk-Eye can track the ball and take the objective decision out of human perception.

Team Ticket Sales

By better understanding the needs, wants, and characteristics of their fan base, owners can perform sentiment analysis to organize game schedules, game locations, ticket prices, players on the field, and fan engagement to support the team. UDA also helps in dynamic ticket pricing.

UDA helped small market teams such as the Oakland A's and the Green Bay Packers compete against large market teams such as New York Yankees.

Analytics will never replace star player talent and great coaching, but it will definitely provide actionable key success factors to coaches, owners, and players, to drive performance, compete, and win.

WHAT IS UDA IN SPORTS?

UDA in sports is about leveraging player and game data to drive performance, including individual player performance, team performance, ticket sales performance, fan engagement and satisfaction, and net promoter score.[9]

UDA leverages both structured and unstructured sports data to address the following:

- What happened?
- What's happening now, and why?
- What will happen? And what should we do to prepare for it?

As for any analytics, the goal of UDA for an organization is to anticipate future performance of a team and its players by capturing and understanding relevant past and present data. It involves gathering the right performance and conditions data from players and, for ball sports, ball information (captured via embedded sensors) to create actionable values for the team, players, and fans.

With players wearing biometric devices, teams can capture their condition, distance run, ball touches, and overall motion path to help track real-time player paths on the field, player actions, and player graphs. Data usually collected includes:

- Player height
- Player weight
- Player hits
- Distance run
- Ball touches
- Player movement
- Player time on the field
- Player position
- Player passes
- Player graph before scoring

- Team motion graph before scoring
- Team motion graph before a bad action or conceding a goal to the opponent

The data collected from the ball usually includes:

- Ball size
- Ball weight
- Ball velocity
- Inflate rate
- Sensor information (speed/rotations)

Weather conditions are tracked too, such as whether it is windy, cold, humid, or the like.

Leading sport organizations are now gathering this data to understand their team's and athletes' past performance, improve game strategy, and answer: What went wrong? Is there a correlation and causation between distance run and player performance? Is there a correlation between player motion graphs and number of goals scored, or between player position and number of points scored?

In baseball, there are now bats that can record the motion of the bat angle and the power of the swing. Video analysis of the game, as well as deep-dive analysis of strengths and weaknesses, can identify opportunities for improvement.

With past behavioral data at their disposal, teams can create player and team dashboards and other key performance indicators (KPIs) and set up strategic alerts to apply based upon game conditions and trends.

Video analytics in basketball, powered by deep learning algorithms, has been empowering leading organizations to keep track of descriptive analytics such as:

- Ball touches
- Rebounds (won lost)
- Time run
- Three point versus two point shot success

- Actions before a goal
- Graph motion leading to a goal

Analytics can provide actionable insights and guide players when driving toward the basket. In baseball, video analytics enables getting usable data, for example, for base stealing:

- Initial lead
- Secondary lead
- Pitcher windup
- Pitch time
- The pop times
- The time it takes the catcher to throw to second base

Locational and biometric devices, including GPS radio frequencies, accelerometers, and other types of biometrics, are mostly used to access total activity, such as distance run and average player speed in a game or practice.

This data also helps to understand the interaction between players: the distance a player has run during a game or a practice, the distance a player has run before scoring a goal, and positions before shooting and succeeding on a three-point shot.

What's Happening? And Why?

UDA helps to capture real-time data to understand how the team or a specific player is performing and make necessary adjustments. During the Olympic Winter Games in Sochi, Russia, Canadian jumper Justine Dufour Lapointe received real-time advice during practice from her team based in Montreal, thanks to a sensor embedded on her clothes. The Olympian wore Hexoskin shirts, which track G-forces experienced by the body as well as heart and breathing rates,[10] while she was training. She won the gold medal.

Formula One cars have hundreds of sensors that provide race data such as speed, tire condition and adherence, weather conditions, and engine conditions. This usually generates 10 TB of data that is sent to engineer teams in real time to be analyzed. The "what's happening" data helps the team to make adjustments while the race is underway, ensuring all the winning conditions are in place, so that drivers have the success factors that they can execute.

Baseball and Football

NFL footballs can have hundreds of sensors that capture a variety of data. This data, mined properly, provides insight of player touchdown performance. You have probably heard of Deflategate, when Tom Brady of the New England Patriots was accused of deflating the football prior to a playoff game leading to the Super Bowl. A report determined that a Patriots staff member probably deflated balls in the Patriots' 45–7 win over the Indianapolis Colts.[11] The balls were reportedly underinflated by about two pounds per square inch, consequently giving Brady more grip in the cold and wet conditions. Some leading organizations are leveraging UDA to create tactical strategies that they can implement based on weather conditions such as rain or snow to optimize player performance and results.

What Will Happen? And What Should We Do?

Using video replay data, past game data, player motion data, and player graphs, coaches can analyze specific issues, weaknesses, or opportunities to play a better offensive game. They can share simulations of winning motions to achieve success against an opposing team. Motion graph simulations, thanks to Big Data and visualization, can also help players better understand optimal motions to execute, how to move, and where to be on the field while knowing what the overall outcome of the move could be. It helps to better understand what impact passes, dribbles, or 3-point shots will have on the overall results. It also helps to identify adjustments a team should make to address weaknesses and issues and to improve its performance and results.

A significant number of sports teams such as New England Patriots are trying to predict the needs and wants of their fans with team-specific mobile apps that provide specific content, such as live play-by-play, access to compilations of scoring plays from games around the league, concessions and food ordering, bathroom wait times, parking availability, traffic updates, and seat concessions.[12]

Take a tennis player like Serena Williams, for instance. IBM Watson Cognitive Analytics found, while analyzing her game, that her strength was her serve. Each time she trails in her service game, she is 5.8 times more likely to serve an ace than other top players, thereby improving her chance to win. These actionable insights help her maximize her performance and results, leveraging her serve when appropriate. I truly believe that in the near future, players and coaches will turn to cognitive analytics software and artificial intelligence solutions for on-court strategy advice.

HOW IT WORKS

The process outlined in this section (and illustrated in Exhibit 11.03) encompasses the main type of sports data where UDA is used to optimize an outcome, whether for fans, players, teams, general managers, or opponents.

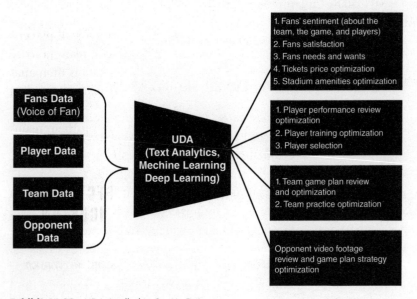

Exhibit 11.03 UDA Applied to Sports Data

Fan Data

Unstructured fan data generally includes fan opinion and feedback regarding teams, games, players, managers, opponents, and amenities. These will be usually gathered via social media, such as Twitter, Facebook, Instagram, or from open-ended questions in fan satisfaction surveys. This text-heavy data is then analyzed using text analytics techniques such as content categorization or sentiment analysis to derive fan sentiments regarding the team, the game, fan satisfaction, fan net promote score, or fan needs and wants. Machine learning is used for ticket price optimization and stadium amenities optimization.

Player Data

Unstructured player data generally includes biometrics data and other data from wearable devices, as well as player performance evaluation forms, rosters, and social media data. This data is then analyzed using UDA to derive optimal training plans, identify player strengths and weaknesses, and enhance player selection.

Team Data

Unstructured team data generally includes biometrics for all players, performance evaluation forms, team wearable devices, team practice and game video footage and social media data. This data is then analyzed leveraging UDA techniques to optimize practice plans, game plan strategy, and player lineup selection.

Opponent video footage is reviewed and analyzed to help teams determine the best lineup and the best game strategy.

INTERVIEW WITH WINSTON LIN, DIRECTOR OF STRATEGY AND ANALYTICS FOR THE HOUSTON ROCKETS

I had the opportunity to discuss the impact of analytics in sports with Winston Lin, Director of Strategy and Analytics at Houston Rockets

Isson: What made your organization decide to invest in sports analytics?

Lin: There are two fundamental philosophies behind our organization decision to invest in analytics:

- *Player evaluation: We use data analytics insights to support our decisions in regards to player evaluation trading and our in-house player moves.*

- *Business operations: We have built an analytics center of expertise to help assist the organization with our business operations, such as ticket-selling optimization, customer segmentation, fan engagement, fan base knowledge, fan satisfaction, and fan loyalty and retention.*

It would be impossible to get all that knowledge without tapping into data intelligence that analytics provides us with.

Isson: The majority of organizations I've spoken with have told me they are being inundated with disparate data and reports, and not enough understanding of what that data and those reports mean. Would you agree and, if so, how is your organization working to leverage its player, team, and fan data that leads to a better understanding and insight? (Such as player selection, roster building, fan satisfaction, and team performance?)

Lin: Yes I agree we have a lot of data. But we have started building our master data management as a foundation to clean, integrate, govern, and build analytics. We use analytics insights for player selection and a lot of internal moves. For instance, we have some players, like Ryan Anderson, Eric Gordon, and Dwight Howard, who were somehow undervalued on the market. Eric Gordon and Ryan Anderson were two players that came from injuries. We were able to sign them, and they became free agents. They were very successful before the injuries that affected their seasons and their market value. The market was very low on them, but we decided thanks to our analytics insights to go against the market regarding these players. We signed them, and they ended up having great seasons. Of course, we did not make the playoffs the first year, but the year after, we made the playoffs and finished third in the NBA Western Conference behind the Golden State Warriors (1) and San Antonio Spurs (2). Eric Gordon, our "shooting man," finished in the top six list of the best shooting players for the season; he had a great year. And Ryan Anderson did a decent job. Analytics insights really helped us to find and trade for undervalued talents who ended up having great performance. Analytics helped us to identify undervalued talent who outperformed their market value. We also leveraged analytics as one of the key components during our roster-building salary packages; we even use it to review our contracts through some legal analytics.

Isson: Can you give me examples of challenges your team has addressed with analytics or UDA in the past? What solutions did you leverage, and what were the benefits of your investment?

Lin: When I started back in 2010, most of our data was in spreadsheet. We have been able to implement master data management and build enterprise data warehouse and data marts, so we can now aggregate data from variety of sources, do predictive models for retention, or simply plug the data into *visualization tools like Tableau. We still use Excel, but along the way we use tools like Tableau, Python, and R. We have a very gradual approach. Contrary to other teams we are very lean; we have leveraged analytics for player evaluation, our core business operation, and we leverage analytics for our customer retention. We have now opportunities to enrich our predictive models for customer retention with instructed data such as social media, fan engagement, site traffic, and customer satisfaction surveys.*

Isson: In this Big Data era, what advice would you give to an organization trying leverage Big Data, such as social media data, text data, images, and video data to get the most out of their sports analytics capabilities? What are the dos and don'ts of this undertaking? What strategies are important to make the project successful?

Lin: My admonition will be you adapt to your own situation. First, you need to identify what is the most pressing business challenge you would like to address with Big Data analytics.

Do your homework in terms of tools; what tools are available to solve the problem?

Talents: What talents do you need to build and deliver your analytics insights to the business? And techniques; what techniques should you use to address your key business challenges? Keep in mind that today there are a lot of open sources that could you could use.

For some small to medium-sized businesses, I would also recommend you figure out what is the minimum valuable project you can deliver to build the momentum from.

Think big, start small, and try to have some quick wins. And move gradually.

For our organization, our focus was initially our ticket database and customer relationship management (CRM) database. And then we were able to append some advanced analytics to it and build predictive models, such as propensity to buy and retention models.

Isson: What is the number one benefit or top reason to invest in sports analytics? What is the biggest hurdle you will face when implementing it?

Lin: I can tackle that from the standpoint of why I am in sports in general? The sports industry itself is very unique. You have a catholic audience that is very strong.

In sports, you also have one of the attributes that every brand really wants. Every brand wants to display that their customer is right in creating emotional moments of connection. The connection between your customer, your brand, and your product ultimately drives affinity to that brand or product, and that ultimately drives loyalty and evangelism. In sports, all that is already built, while if you look at other industries, much of the analytics they do is about quantifying the campaign, for instance, that helped to move your customers down to the bottom of that sales and marketing funnel. They are trying to build it. Sports are inverse; they already have that, you already have great brand and product. The number-one benefit will be to take our catholic audience, digitize their identity, and be able to analyze how to build relationships with them.

Isson: How do you see UDA such as video analytics being used now and in the future in sports?

Lin: Video analytics, for instance, is something that the league has spearheaded. By installing sportview cameras in all arenas for every game. NBA has licensed birdseye views of players' performances to every team. And I think they even have made it open to fans as well, because there are a lot of people playing fantasy sports who leverage that raw data and in some cases transform it into actionable intelligence. For our organization, the team is definitely leveraging video analytics for player performance and preparation. And I think this will have tremendous value when organizations will start harnessing new opportunities such as image recognition and deep learning to prepare and refine practices, game lineup strategies and even game outcomes based upon historical analysis of videos.

With video analysis, organizations will gain competitive edge by discovering weaknesses and strengths of their teams as well as their opponents. They will be able to tap into advanced scouting by deeply learning what their teams will be up against, be able to avoid and prevent injuries, and ultimately be able to optimize their team performance and results.

Sports Analytics by Catapult provides performance analysis, injury analysis, and tactical analysis. These devices can measure the relative speed of players, their placement and movements on the court, and their interactions.

KEY TAKEAWAYS

■ Sabermetrics and the book *Moneyball*, detailing the success of the Oakland A's, were the catalysts that led to a broader adoption of analytics in MLB and other sports. Today, every leading sports organization has its own analytics team to support the team decision-making process.

■ The advent of technology such as wearable devices and embedded sensors has changed the way coaches, players, and general managers approach practices and games and has enabled them to optimize their outcomes, to better compete and win. Embedded sensors, biometrics data and UDA, analyzing and reviewing all the data collected, help leading athletes, players, and teams optimize their practices, performance, and game results, and can prevent injuries.

■ The use of text analytics and natural language processing techniques provides actionable information to general managers and teams that helps them better understand the voice of their fans, and, using social media, to ultimately meet and exceed fan expectations.

■ Leading organizations are leveraging UDA powered by machine learning and deep learning for ticket price optimization, to determine fan needs and wants, and ultimately to optimize the overall game experience.

NOTES

1. Sabermetrics refers to the Society for American Baseball Research (SABR).

2. "Hawk-Eye," Wikipedia: https://en.wikipedia.org/wiki/Hawk-Eye

3. Joris Drayer and Joel Maxcey, "Sports Analytics: Advancing Decision Making through Technology and Data," Institute for Business and Information Technology, Temple University, April 13, 2014: http://ibit.temple.edu/blog/2014/04/13/sports-analytics-advancing-decision-making-through-technology-and-data-2/

4. Inderpal Bhandari, Edward Colet, Jennifer Parker, Zachary Pines, Rajiv Pratap, and Krishnakumar Ramanujam, "Advanced Scout: Data Mining and Knowledge Discovery in NBA Data," *Data Mining and Knowledge Discovery* 1, no. 1 (1997): 122–125: https://link.springer.com/article/10.1023/A:1009782106822

5. ESPN, *The Great Analytics Rankings*: www.espn.com/espn/feature/story/_/id/12331388/the-great-analytics-rankings

6. Drayer and Maxcey, "Sports Analytics."

7. PricewaterhouseCoopers, "Changing the Game: Outlook for the Global Sports Market to 2015," December 2011: www.pwc.com/gx/en/industries/hospitality-leisure/changing-the-game-outlook-for-the-global-sports-market-to-2015.html

8. Shawn Krest, "Pro Tennis Serves Fans Riveting Real-Time Data," iQ (Intel), September 16, 2016: https://iq.intel.com.au/pro-tennis-serves-fans-riveting-real-time-data/

9. Net Promoter or Net Promoter Score (NPS) is a management tool that can be used to gauge the loyalty of a firm's customer relationships. It serves as an alternative to traditional customer satisfaction research and claims to be correlated with revenue growth.

10. David Common, "Hexoskin Wearable Technology Helps Elite Athletes, Astronauts," CBC, April 11, 2014: www.cbc.ca/beta/news/canada/hexoskin-wearable-technology-helps-elite-athletes-astronauts-1.2607846

11. "Deflategate Timeline: After 544 Days, Tom Brady Gives In," ESPN.com, July 15, 2016: www.espn.com/blog/new-england-patriots/post/_/id/4782561/timeline-of-events-for-deflategate-tom-brady

12. Lauren Brousell, "Patriots Deploy Stadium Wi-Fi to Compete with the Comforts of Home," *CIO Journal*, August 28, 2013: www.cio.com/article/2383142/mobile/patriots-deploy--stadium-wi-fi-to-compete-with-the-comforts-of-home.html

FURTHER READING

"Big Data Is Changing the Nature of Sports Sciences," *MIT Technology Review*, March 7, 2016: www.technologyreview.com/s/600957/big-data-analysis-is-changing-the-nature-of-sports-science/

Trevir Nath, "How Big Data Has Changed Sports," *Investopedia*, April 27, 2015: www.investopedia.com/articles/investing/042715/how-big-data-has-changed-sports.asp

"NBA Teams That Have Analytics Departments," Analytics 101. NBAstuffer: www.nbastuffer.com/component/option,com_glossary/Itemid,0/catid,44/func,view/term,NBA%20Teams%20That%20Have%20Analytics%20Department/

Alexis Wright-Whitley, "The Importance of Sports Analytics, Both in the Game and off the Field," *Fox School of Business Catapult Case Study*: www.fox.temple.edu/cms/wp-content/uploads/2014/04/final-MaxcyDrayerIBITReport.pdf

CHAPTER 12

The Future of Analytics

*Imagination is the beginning of creation. You imagine
what you desire, you will what you imagine, and at last
you create what you will.*

—George Bernard Shaw

n the past years we all witnessed a lot of blandishments around
artificial intelligence (AI). The phenomenon of advanced analytics
and artificial intelligence is not new, but the pace of recent development is. The main factors driving this acceleration are:

- The progression of machine learning, deep learning, and cognitive analytics algorithms.

- The enhanced computing capacity, enabling fast training of
large and complex models.

  - Graphics processing units (GPUs), originally designed for
video games, have been repurposed for high-speed data
and algorithms crunching at speeds many times faster than
traditional processor chips.

- Silicon-level advances beyond GPUs are emerging, such as tensor processing units (TPUs), which are now aggregated in scalable data centers and are accessible through the cloud. Leading tech giants like Google are rethinking their computational architecture to run on TPUs, which are 15 to 30 times faster and 30 to 80 percent more power efficient than CPUs and GPUs.

- The access to massive amounts of data generated in billions through daily creation of images, online click streams, voice and video, mobile locations, wearables, sensors, and smart machines, embedded in the Internet of Things and clouds.

The combination of these breakthroughs led to the creation of Google DeepMind's AlphaGo and IBM Watson, which were not only capable of mastering complex games and defeating human champions but were also able to master diagnostics, in the case of Watson, and lip-reading, in the case of DeepMind.

Significant technological challenges must still be overcome before computers can match human performance across the range of cognitive skills. Perhaps the biggest challenge is for computers to understand and generate natural languages and humanlike intuition, and describe and interpret what they see. Such capabilities are indispensable for work applications and leisure activities. Digital personal assistants such as Apple's Siri, Amazon's Alexa, Microsoft Cortana and Google Assistant are still in development, and avatars and humanoids are being tested in healthcare situations that require sensitivity, tact, and empathy.

HARNESSING THESE EVOLVING TECHNOLOGIES WILL GENERATE BENEFITS

For companies and organizations, successful adoption of these evolving technologies will significantly enhance performance and perhaps define survival. The gains will be seen in enhanced productivity, by 50 percent according to experts. This will be seen in raised throughput, improved predictions, outcomes, accuracy, and optimization. These technologies will also lead to new solutions of complex problems in areas such as synthetic biology, material, and even social science. Due to automation, some of the gains will come from labor substitution, as seen today:

▪ Rio Tinto deployed automated haul trucks and drilling machines at its mines in Pilbara, Australia, and claims a 10 to 20 percent increase in utilization.

▪ Google applied AI from its DeepMind machine learning to its data centers and cut its energy use by 40 percent. In Dec 2017 NASA's Kepler spacecraft discovered an eight planet Kepler 90 - I with the help of Google neural network technology.

▪ Financial services are using straight-through processing (digitized end-to-end transaction workflows) to increase transaction throughput by 80 percent while reducing errors by half. JPMorgan Chase uses AI tech solution called COIN (Contract Intelligence) to save 360,000 hours of annual work by lawyers and loan officers.

Furthermore, a plethora of cases are emerging in which advanced analytics and AI are successfully used across sectors like:

▪ Telecommunication

▪ Finance (personalized financial products, identification of fraudulent transactions)

▪ Insurance (fraud detection and prevention)

▪ Human capital management (optimize recruitment, retention, and wellness)

▪ Energy (real-time predictive maintenance)

▪ Media (personalized advertising)

▪ Travel, transport, and logistics (optimize pricing and scheduling)

▪ Manufacturing (predictive maintenance)

▪ Consumer (discover new consumer trends, optimize merchandizing strategy)

▪ Public and social

▪ Healthcare and medical research (diagnose diseases, predict health outcomes)

▪ Automotive (driverless vehicles identify and navigate roads)

▪ Pharmaceutical (optimize clinical trials)

▪ Agriculture (align crops with individual conditions)

Overall, I foresee a bright future for advanced analytics. It will become the new normal for government, businesses, corporations and individuals. Soon the merits and criticality of Big Data, processed by advanced analytics, will be a given for all businesses, along with a coherent data strategy and appropriate analytical tools and know-how. In short, the operationalization of analytics within organizations will become as ubiquitous as the data itself. In the same way that companies have strategies for human capital, marketing, products, services, and technology, they will also have a formal strategy for advanced analytics and UDA.

Another influence of data and analytics ubiquity will be the emergence of an analytical mind-set across modern cultures: a move from industrial thinking. As more analytical tools develop, people will rely more heavily on them, so their perceived necessity will increase. For example, 25 years ago there was no consumer Internet, so people relied primarily on their impressions, word of mouth from their entourage, or sales representatives when making a purchase decision for a product or a service. Today, most consumers use the Internet to research the quality and price of a product or a service, gathering information from professional reviewers, consumer reviews, news stories, and comparison tools. As a result, consumers have become more analytical in their acquisition approach for products and services. I believe the continued proliferation of data and analytical tools will strengthen this trend. As a result, consumers will have an ever-increasing reliance on the analytics that surrounds them, as well as on the technology that enables it. A wide range of technological trends is just beginning to pave the way for advanced business analytics, including UDA, people analytics, social computing, artificial intelligence, machine learning and deep learning, cognitive computing, Internet of Things (IoT) and Analytics of Things, the use of blockchain models in non-financial industries, and human-centered computing. These trends are making computational analytics possible, a reality not envisaged even five years ago.

In this chapter, I will discuss technology-related trends that will enable a future state of analytics. I will also address ways in which advanced analytics will help facilitate the improvement for some of the world's critical social, economic, and health challenges. I will provide examples of these advances and allude to the future to come.

A strong future of advanced analytics and UDA will mean:

- Data becomes less valuable and analytics becomes mainstream
- Predictive analytics (AI, machine learning, deep learning) becomes the new standard
- People analytics becomes a standard department in businesses
- UDA becomes more prevalent in corporations and businesses
- Cognitive analytics expands
- The IoT evolves to the Analytics of Things
- Massive online open courses (MOOCs) and open source software and applications will continue to explode
- Blockchain and analytics will solve social problems
- Human-centered computing will be normalized
- Data governance and security will remain the number-one risk and threat

DATA BECOMES LESS VALUABLE AND ANALYTICS BECOMES MAINSTREAM

Data Becomes Less Valuable

This may seem counterintuitive, but I believe data will become less valuable in the future. Basic economic theory dictates that when something is widely available, it becomes less valuable, and when something is scarce, it becomes more valuable. Currently, people and organizations are overwhelmed by data. In the future, having a treasure trove of data will not, by itself, hold much value. However, the companies that can create actionable, knowledge-based tools from data, either using their own data or using someone else's data, will see the benefits of the expected analytical economy. This will take many forms: everything from applications that sift through data for nuggets of insight to personalized algorithms that allow individual users to analyze their own data to understand something about themselves and take action.

To illustrate why I think data will become less valuable, consider the early days of the commercial Internet, in the late 1990s. At that time, as it is today, almost anyone could create Internet content for others to view. At first, this was a novelty, and consumers were happy to view new Internet information as it came online. Early users of the commercial Internet used a Gopher protocol, a model rooted in traditional library science, to organize content into logical categories. With Gopher, every Internet document had a defined format and type, and the typical user navigated through a single server-defined menu system to get to a document. This worked well for several years. However, soon the amount of data on the Internet began to expand exponentially. As a result, the amount of data and documents available quickly became overwhelming, and navigating through using Gopher became inefficient. Web-based Internet search engines that allowed for unstructured content soon emerged. These analytical tools served as a gateway to the Internet. This is where people eventually found the most value. Can you imagine trying to make sense of the 1.3 billion websites without the analytical help of sites such as Google or Bing? Without them, would there be any value in adding another one million websites to the worldwide total? This logic applies to data as well: It will become less valuable over time while effective analytical techniques will become very valuable.

Analytics Will Become Mainstream

Today, advanced analytics is still mainly adopted by major businesses and corporations. However, we have recently seen an increase of small to medium-sized businesses (SMBs) injecting analytics into their business decision-making processes. Decreased costs, advances in computing power, automation, cognitive analytics and democratization of AI, machine learning, and deep learning will dramatically increase SMB analytics funding and its subsequent adoption. In the past years, we have witnessed advanced analytics success stories in several aspects of our lives. In politics, advanced analytics helped with the 2012 re-election of U.S. President Obama. In healthcare, sensors and wearables, along with advanced analytics, help to delocalize healthcare and create smart hospitals. In medical research, advanced analytics helps with genomic, cancer, brain, and other research. In population health, Google algorithms predicted the spread of the swine flu. In e-commerce, Netflix, Spotify, and Amazon developed successful recommendation engines. Other examples can be found in sports, with athlete performance and fan-enhanced experiences, and in businesses, customer acquisition, and retention. Advanced analytics helped with prospect conversion, up-sell, and win-back models. Marketing has been successfully promoting the benefits and the power of analytics. In human capital management, advanced analytics helped with talent life cycle management (acquire develop and retain talent).

Companies today can copy each other on product development. However, the real differentiator between leaders and laggards resides in their capacity to attract talent and innovate from actionable business value derived from their data, both internal and external. Winning companies will be those making analytics central by using their talent to compete and win through harnessing all customer and consumer data and feedback to meet and exceed expectations.

PREDICTIVE ANALYTICS, AI, MACHINE LEARNING, AND DEEP LEARNING BECOME THE NEW STANDARD

In previous chapters, I provided comprehensive examples of the power of predictive analytics in customer acquisition and retention, talent life cycle management, sports, product development, national security, and fraud detection. As we progress in the future, predictive analytics will become more widespread and evolve as a norm along with UDA and text mining. Analytical techniques will require a predictive component to be considered business relevant or effective. This will rely on more sophisticated statistical and machine-learning techniques and more computational power; both are now a reality. It will also require the expertise of people who can develop predictive models effectively using an arsenal of advanced analytical techniques. There are certainly many examples of predictive analytics applied to the business world, especially across Internet-based businesses, and I expect this to spread across all industries in the future. Recent advances in computing power supported by GPUs and TPUs led to breakthroughs in AI, machine learning, and deep learning. From the automation of customer service interaction to self-driving cars, the emergence of digital personal assistants to machine-mastering games and healthcare avatars or humanoid assistants, we have been witnessing how AI, machine learning, and deep learning are changing the way we live, think, sell, buy, commute, and even access and use the healthcare system and medical services.

The democratization of AI will lead to more knowledge sharing and accelerated advanced analytics breakthroughs. At first, AI will be used to solve specific, narrow problems. An example of this is Google's DeepMind AlphaGo, which used deep learning, Monte Carlo tree search, and deep reinforcement learning to solve the ancient game of Go (a game where progress toward more advanced play is akin to reaching a higher level of consciousness) and beat Go champion Lee Sedol. In late 2017 OpenAi an AI start-up owned by Elon Musk defeated the world's best DOTA 2 players; DOTA 2 is an on-line game.

This optimized intelligence path will develop automation that works well in highly complex domains. We can expect to see many new applications that combine conventional computer science algorithms with deep learning to achieve sophisticated narrow intelligence applications like:

- Self-driving cars
- Search engines
- Detecting credit card fraud
- Stock market analysis
- Speech and handwriting recognition
- Lip-reading recognition
- Robot locomotion
- Aircraft autopilot
- Computational finance
- Sentiment analysis
- Recommender systems
- Legal assistant AI app

Along with advances in machine learning and deep learning, the digitization of medical records and smart machines (that correlate data from different sources, including sensor equipped digital devices) will improve healthcare access and delivery. This trend will mostly impact:

- Medical diagnosis
- Bioinformatics

- Cheminformatics (or chemo-informatics)
- Classifying DNA sequences
- Diseases detection, treatment, and management
- Diagnostic radiology
- Patient engagement, patient monitoring, and wellness management
- Drug discovery with faster go-to-market
- Personal genetics with personalized diagnostics and treatment

Another example of specific narrow problems solved with the expansion of machine learning and deep learning is the development of negotiator apps. These apps will be able to replicate humanlike intelligence, like intuition to negotiate and close deals such as:

- Purchasing a travel ticket at the lowest price; the app could bargain to get the best price
- Help a job seeker find a new job; unlike a traditional job alert, this virtual job agent app will perform interactive negotiation for salary, vacation, conditions, and job requirements
- Paying bills and negotiating terms
- Buy or sell a house at the best price
- Bid for the best search engine optimization (SEO) or pay per click (PPC)
- Perform a variety of interactive online transactions, including bluffing or lying if necessary to get deals closed; as per Facebook's new algorithm that uses reinforced learning to learn from mistakes, it will learn to bluff to get to the final outcome

As Google rightly pointed out, machine learning is the future. Machine learning is a rapidly evolving field that has the potential to impact experiences in human lives. However, to solve complex social or societal problems, artificial general intelligence (AGI) or self-aware intelligence will be required, which goes beyond the narrow intelligence applications just described.

It is not clear how future advances in machine learning will affect the need for human resources such as trained analysts.

As machine-learning models and techniques improve over the long term, it is possible that there will be a reduction in demand for people with that specialized skillset. In addition, as sophisticated applications are developed, it will be easier to run larger, more complex organizations with fewer people, possibly leading to corporate consolidation, new alliances and consortiums, and the ability to do more with a smaller workforce. I also foresee resources being relocated in more strategic, less repetitive and high volume jobs.

PEOPLE ANALYTICS BECOMES A STANDARD DEPARTMENT IN BUSINESSES

In human capital management, there will be a proliferation of advanced analytics. Human capital businesses will leverage more unstructured data from social media network and niche-sites to better understand and predict talent behavior, talent needs and wants, and their next moves. With the change in workforce demographic, where by 2030 all Baby Boomers will retire, the Millennials will represent the largest group in the workforce and the job market. To be successful, companies will have to inject advanced analytics at every stage of their human capital management including:

- Workforce planning
- Talent sourcing
- Talent acquisition
- Talent onboarding
- Culture fit
- Talent retention
- Talent performance management and lifetime value
- Employee wellness and safety

I foresee significant increase in analytics adoption in the human resources (HR) departments that will trigger the transformation of HR and human capital perception from cost center to strategic advisers and partners in talent life cycle management. HR will help the business address Who, When, Why, and more importantly, What should be done to attract, keep, protect, and grow the best talent.

UDA BECOMES MORE PREVALENT IN CORPORATIONS AND BUSINESSES

Advances in UDA will enable more breakthrough analyses of unstructured data, with image recognition, video recognition, and classification analysis leading the way in employer and business decisions. Computer vision will impact many aspects of our lives, predominantly in national security to predict and prevent risks such as terror threats or attacks and fraud. Fraud analytics will become central for most government organizations to offer safe and secure environments to citizens without jeopardizing their privacy rights and their overall experience.

COGNITIVE ANALYTICS EXPANSION

As analytical techniques become more accessible to the general business user, users will become more analytical in their approach to business questions. With general knowledge of analytics spreading in the business world, software providers will simplify the use of techniques such as data modeling, text analytics, Web analytics, and segmentation through automation, thereby making the steps involved in data analytics hidden to the users. This approach will enable people with little or no analytical background to run models and take appropriate business actions. We can already see instances of this occurring in certain analytical disciplines. For example, the rise of automated online survey tools during the last fifteen years has empowered people in all departments of organizations to create and analyze their own customer surveys. While this might frustrate the marketing research experts because at times the survey questions are ill-conceived or poorly worded, or margins of error are not considered, I believe this trend will be net-positive in the long run. The famous saying, "to the man with a hammer, everything looks like a nail," has relevance here. At first, laymen are likely to apply analytical techniques improperly or with incorrectly prepared data. As a result, there will be confusion and frustration as analytics resources try to intervene. However, over time, analytics will be used more effectively across organizations.

Recall the *Harvard Business Review* article that stated, "Data scientist is the sexiest job in the 21st century." I foresee an increase in cognitive analytics that will permit nontechnical people to communicate with the computer via a natural language app. The barrier of learning and mastering a programming language will be lifted. More service providers of computer algorithms will understand and process natural language requests to provide the users with meaningful insight delivered through natural language.

One company that greatly raised awareness about cognitive analytics is IBM, whose Watson wowed the technology and pop world in 2011 with its win against two of *Jeopardy*'s greatest champions, Brad Rutter and Ken Jennings. Now it is impossible to talk about cognitive analytics without referring to Watson. IBM has been training Watson in other areas such as healthcare, where it will assist physicians in detecting some cancers and serious diseases. Watson will also help democratize access to healthcare information, enabling citizens to get answers and take action regarding their health using recommendations from millions of physicians and caregivers around the world. This innovation will enable healthcare to become location independent.

There will be a significant increase of legal analytics tools and solutions, such as AI apps that will assist law firms in the e-discovery phase, in building arguments for their cases, and in developing the overall defense strategy for large cases by capturing all available legal documents and legal information related to their cases and determining the best optimal legal defense strategy using machine learning and deep learning.

THE INTERNET OF THINGS EVOLVES TO THE ANALYTICS OF THINGS

Most estimates predict there will be more than 50 billion connected devices by 2030. Businesses and corporations will be able to easily get access to that tsunami of Internet Protocol (IP) data and, more importantly, will be able to analyze and create actionable insights from that data. The impact of the Analytics of Things will be seen in:

- Smart grid
- Smart road

- Smart airports
- Smart community services
- Smart hospitals, clinics, and health apps.

These smart systems will be based on the integration of multiple types of intelligence, such as: energy data, travel and transport data, nutrition data, biometrics, medical records data, fitness data, work data, and medical research data. The Internet of Things will create a centralized global database or knowledge base that can be used by several apps in all industries.

While this will optimize productivity, it will also come with more security risks from hackers accessing highly sensitive and strategic data, such as personal data, financial data, power supply data, national security data, airline security data, and the like.

MOOCS AND OPEN SOURCE SOFTWARE AND APPLICATIONS WILL CONTINUE TO EXPLODE

The advent of MOOCs and the expansion of open source software and applications will be more prevalent. Knowledge, when easily accessible, will lead to breakthroughs and huge enhancements of open source software with more organizations turning online to train and equip their workforce.

Software such as R, Python, and Spark will continue to provide easy access to technical resources to support organizations and businesses, share knowledge, and jointly work on solutions to address unresolved problems.

Crowdsourcing companies such as Kaggle by Google will continue to help organizations address challenging business questions by leveraging the worldwide horsepower of a pool of highly qualified resources without boundaries or borders. There will be a proliferation of data science and analytics communities and social networks eager to participate and contribute in problem solving, thereby reducing the cost to access knowledge and analytics support. Enterprises, universities, and individuals will all benefit from it.

BLOCKCHAIN AND ANALYTICS WILL SOLVE
SOCIAL PROBLEMS

Blockchain is the world's leading software platform for digital assets. From a mathematical perspective, blockchain is a publicly available ledger in which participants enter data and certify their acceptance via an elliptic curve digital signature algorithm (ECDSA). This distributed transparent consensus-based peer-to-peer network has shown to be extremely resilient against adversarial attacks.

Blockchain will become more prevalent and will impact the investment world, as well as financial and nonfinancial services. People around the world will leverage this new disruptive and decentralized digital technology using Internet and their mobile phones. Numerous firms, including several start-up organizations, are pursuing blockchain to facilitate and streamline many types of financial transactions. One of the key value propositions of blockchain is to solve social problems. As indicated on the Blockchain company website:

> We are on a mission to build a more open, accessible, and fair financial future, one piece of software at a time. Our technology is revolutionizing the financial services industry by empowering millions across the globe to authenticate and transact immediately and without costly intermediaries.[1]

Beyond exciting applications for blockchain in financial and investment world, I foresee the proliferation of this model in a notary public role (for notarization of documents as well as verification of the authenticity of documents). This will be enhanced by UDA to analyze the text and images imbedded in these documents.

In the music industry, blockchain will provide decentralized royalties distribution. The advent of the Internet and new ways of distributing music such as streaming has been detrimental to the distribution of royalties. The blockchain model will leverage the smart contract and a distributed database of music rights and ownership information to distribute royalties between songwriters, labels publishers, and streaming service providers and music artists.

The second major nonfinancial impact will be on the decentralized IoT. As discussed in a previous section, there is a tremendous opportunity for the IoT to become mainstream in the enterprise and consumer world. However, the main challenge lies in the centralized model of the IoT system. Centralization becomes problematic when billions of interactive devices need to share data between themselves autonomously. To address this issue, leading organizations are turning to decentralized IoT using the blockchain model. Yes, one of the biggest impacts of blockchain will be decentralized IoT platforms, such as secured and trusted data exchange and recordkeeping. A whitepaper written for the University of California Berkeley's Sutardja Center for Entrepreneurship & Technology describes how IBM worked with Samsung to develop a blockchain platform:

> ADEPT (for Autonomous Decentralized Peer-To-Peer Telemetry) . . . uses elements of the bitcoin's underlying design to build a distributed network of devices: a decentralized Internet of Things (IoT). ADEPT uses three protocols—BitTorrent (file sharing), Etherreum (Smart Contracts) and TeleHash (Peer To-Peer Messaging)—in the platform.[2]

One of the great promises of the future of analytics is its ability to help solve large-scale social problems. For example, will distributed analytics someday lead to a rapid cure for a new virus or diseases, as people begin to share more health analytics with one another? Will it be possible to provide early warning systems ahead of natural disasters using analytics that will save thousands of lives? Will data from sensors in the Earth help us effectively manage and maintain our natural resources and provide for a fairer distribution of resources around the world? Will learnings from space exploration accelerate and help us solve problems on Earth?

These types of applications may sound a bit farfetched; however, the reality is that similar applications are already happening today. For example, a study by medical researchers at Harvard showed that data from Internet-based news and Twitter feeds was faster than traditional sources for detecting the onset and progression of the cholera epidemic in post-earthquake Haiti, which sickened almost half a million people.[3]

"When we analyzed news and Twitter feeds from the early days of the epidemic in 2010, we found that they could be mined for valuable information on the cholera outbreak that was available up to two weeks ahead of surveillance reports issued by the government health ministry," said Dr. Rumi Chunara of the Informatics Program at Children's Hospital Boston, a research fellow at Harvard Medical School, and the lead author of the study. "The techniques we employed eventually could be used around the world as an affordable and efficient way to quickly detect the onset of an epidemic and then intervene with such things as vaccines and antibiotics."[4]

Earlier, the research group from the Children's Hospital in Boston had launched www.healthmap.org in 2006 based on the same ideology: to provide "real-time surveillance of emerging public health threats." This site is designed to automatically capture any coverage or mention of health issues from a variety of information sources.

HUMAN-CENTERED COMPUTING WILL BE NORMALIZED

Another future analytics trend will be the proliferation of various forms of human-centered computing, the application of computer science, information technology, and psychology to enable computers to interact with humans effectively. Human-centered computing deals with human–technology interaction issues, such as algorithms, databases and information systems, AI, information theory, software engineering, data mining, image processing, modeling and simulation, signal processing, discrete mathematics, control and system theory, circuit theory, and psychological states and motivations. Human-centered computing generates new knowledge on how humans can effectively interact with technology and on the tools to create that knowledge. Eye-tracking technology is one form of human-centered computing, whereby a camera tracks the eye movement of someone viewing a computer screen, recording data on the location and frequency of sighting different areas of the screen. This technology has been applied in areas as diverse as website usability testing, sports medicine, automobile testing, geriatric research, training simulators, and infant research.

As we look to the future, I expect that more devices will interact directly with the human body and, as a result, generate data from those interactions that will need to be analyzed. In terms of the future applications of human-centered computing, I think the following applications will be relevant for the field of analytics:

- Wearable computing/smart fabrics
- Consumer health informatics
- Brainwave measurement
- Facial recognition
- Emotional recognition
- Exercise informatics
- Body scan technologies
- Gesture-based interfaces
- Virtual reality
- Augmented reality
- Motion-detection devices
- Molecular computing

DATA GOVERNANCE AND DATA SECURITY WILL REMAIN THE NUMBER-ONE RISK AND THREAT

While advanced analytics will have a positive impact on every aspect of our lives, if this knowledge or intelligence falls into the wrong hands—fraud perpetrators, terrorist groups, and the like—a lot of damage and harm can ensue. Every week, we witness new security breaches from hackers or even from government-sponsored hackers. The goal of protecting citizen, customer, and consumer data has become paramount. The same protection extends to analytics and algorithms. We have all witnessed different threats from cybercrime, and identity theft is experiencing a sharp increase (see Chapter 5).

When 50 billion connected devices will be interacting using algorithms, the number-one priority for government and organizations will be data and algorithm security and proper governance, making sure that you can protect your data as a customer, a consumer, and a citizen. Organizations will need to obtain proper authorization or consent to share part of their information in a way that will not jeopardize the user experience by adhering to overly stringent fraud or hacking business rules that detect and prevent fraudulent behavior.

Data and analytics privacy will be a hot topic in the future, as consumers continue to grapple with the notion that many of their activities are being tracked by multiple organizations around the world and by many popular sites such as Google, Twitter, Amazon, and Facebook. Also, as analytics becomes more sophisticated and human-like, consumers may get an uncomfortable feeling when they are given realistic insights or advice that is unsolicited, unexpected, or intrusive.

As we progress into the future, and data and analytics become mainstream in our daily lives, there will be a data privacy backlash in which consumers will demand more aggressive government involvement in consumer data privacy standards and protection. I do not know what form this will take: whether it will be a credit agency model, whereby all information is centralized in a few organizations, or whether it will be distributed across each data provider, whereby users can decide which information about them is shared, hidden, or permanently deleted. Either way, the field of analytics must take note and engage in the conversation, because it will be directly affected by any change in data privacy policies and standards.

KEY TAKEAWAYS

- Overall, I foresee the analytics future to be bright. The practice of unstructured data analytics is still in its relative infancy; however, technology advances in computer power, artificial intelligence, and the proliferation of data will begin to fulfill the promise of improving lives.
- I foresee the following in the world of analytics:
  - Data becomes less valuable and analytics becomes mainstream
  - Predictive analytics (AI, machine learning, deep learning) becomes the new standard
  - People analytics becomes a standard department in businesses
  - UDA becomes more prevalent in corporations and businesses
  - Cognitive analytics expands

- The IoT evolves to the Analytics of Things
- Massive online open courses (MOOCs) and open source software and applications will continue to explode
- Blockchain and analytics will solve social problems
- Human-centered computing will be normalized
- Data governance and security will remain the number-one risk and threat

NOTES

1. Blockchain.com website.

2. Michael Crosby, Nachiappan, Pradhan Pattanayak, Sanjeev Verma, and Vignesh Kalyanaraman, "BlockChain Technology: Beyond Bitcoin," whitepaper developed for the Sutardja Center for Entrepreneurship & Technology, University of California Berkley Engineering, October 16, 2015: http://scet.berkeley.edu/wp-content/uploads/BlockchainPaper.pdf

3. Rumi Chunara, Jason R. Andrews, and John S. Brownstein, "Social and News Media Enable Estimation of Epidemiological Patterns Early in the 2010 Haitian Cholera Outbreak," *The American Journal of Tropical Medicine and Hygiene* 86, no. 1 (January 2012): 39–45. www.ajtmh.org/content/journals/10.4269/ajtmh.2012.11-0597

4. "Internet-based Newsfeeds Found to Be Faster at Determining Disease Progression," *Vaccine News Daily*, January 11, 2012: https://vaccinenewsdaily.com/stories/510532665-internet-based-news-feeds-found-to-be-faster-at-determining-disease-progression

FURTHER READING

Kangkan Acharyya, "Big Data Analytics in Healthcare: Fuelled by Wearables and Apps, Medical Research Takes Giant Leap Forward," *Firstpost*, July 9, 2017: www.firstpost.com/india/big-data-in-healthcare-fuelled-by-wearables-and-apps-medical-research-takes-giant-leap-forward-3793155.html

Doug Adamson, "Big Data in Healthcare Made Simple: Where It Stands Today and Where It's Going," *HealthCatalyst*, www.healthcatalyst.com/big-data-in-healthcare-made-simple

Tech Corner
Details

his Tech Corner section is for readers who are interested in getting more details regarding some linear algebra techniques commonly used in text analysis to reduce document-by-terms matrices and for information retrieval and computer vision. If you are not interested to learn more about these linear algebra techniques feel free to give this entire appendix section a skim. This chapter provides some useful details about linear algebra techniques we recalled throughout the book.

The three powerful techniques we will discuss here for matrices factorization and reduction include:

- Singular value decomposition (SVD)

- Principal component analysis (PCA)

- QR factorization

For each technique we will provide a description of the technique along with a step-by-step example on how to apply the technique throughout an example.

SVD and QR are both matrix decomposition techniques. SVD and QR help to produce a reduced rank approximation of the document matrix, as we need to identify the dependence between rows (documents) and columns (terms).

To easily navigate through some technical details of this section, readers require basic knowledge of linear algebra and matrix calculations are prerequisites, including:

- Space point
- Scalars
- Vectors
- Matrices
- Matrix reduction, matrix decomposition
- Matrix diagonalization
- Inverse matrices
- Characteristic equations
- Eigen-decomposition, eigenvalues, and eigenvectors
- Orthogonal and orthonormal vectors
- Gram–Schmidt orthonormalization process

SINGULAR VALUE DECOMPOSITION (SVD) ALGORITHM AND APPLICATIONS

Why SVD?

You have probably come across experiments for which you have to record and keep more data than you need just for the sake of not missing anything. Experimenters are always trying to balance quantity and quality while removing redundancies and noise from their data, especially when it is impossible to know what measurements would best capture the information needed in the future.

Most experimenters usually take several measures of the same event to ensure they are not missing any useful information. By doing so, they systematically add redundancies, since several measures will be correlated to each other, on top of the noise that comes with every measurement. Just imagine processing millions of correlated measurements to distill some meaning. It would not only require a lot of computing power, but would also be extremely cumbersome to process.

Today most of the data comes in a high-dimensional space with a lot of information being generated every second. SVD-like PCA enables us to apply linear algebra technique to the data to derive a subset of factors or vectors that encompass the most useful or most important information from the original high-dimensional data.

Those useful new factors are represented in a new subspace or basis that provides more efficiency to process and analyze the data and to find key meaning.

Imagine you are a marketing manager for Amazon Prime. Amazon has more than 85 million subscribers who can watch each of the 18,405+ movies on its streaming video service. As a marketing manager, you wonder if there is a subset of Amazon Prime customers who would best represent the 85 million users and help you derive the types of movies or genre of movies that you should recommend to some new and existing members. SVD helps to achieve that goal through dimension reduction. By applying matrix reduction on the 85 million Prime subscribers and 18,405 movies, you would get, let's say, one hundred key subscriber-groups and twenty-five movie types. SVD helps group customers and movies into segments of customers and type of movies, respectively. This reduction improves movie recommendations for customer acquisition and customer retention efforts.

The output of the reduction provides customer grouped by movies by type or genre, such as: action, adventure, comedy, crime, drama, horror, political, fantasy, romance, mystery, science fiction, thriller, saga, urban, and Western, just to name a few.

The end result? SVD reduced 18,405 movies and 85 million customers to 25 types of movies to recommend to 100 customer groups.

Likewise Spotify covered in chapter 2 leverages linear algebra matrices factorization models to create its personalized playlist that best match our musical tastes. From its Big Dataset of Users by Artists ranking, the company applies latent factor models to its Users-Artists matrix to create micro-genres by customer segments.

What Is SVD?

SVD is an extremely important linear algebra technique used for dimension reduction. The goal of SVD is to represent the data from a high-dimensional space in a reduced low-dimensional space, keeping the most important information from the data.

SVD is useful in many tasks across several industries. For text analytics, SVD provides the mathematical foundation for text mining and classification techniques generally known as *latent semantic indexing*. In SVD, the matrix is an entity of documents matrix; a way to represent documents and texts to be mined in a high-dimension vector space model, generally known as hyperspace document representation. By reducing the dimensional space, SVD helps to reduce redundancies and noise in the data.

It then provides new dimensions that capture the essence of the existing relationship in the data. SVD defines a small number of concepts that connect the rows and columns of the matrix. The trade-off for having fewer dimensions is the accuracy of the approximation.

SVD Theorem

SVD is based on a powerful theorem in linear algebra which states the following: Every rectangular matrix A can be represented as a product of three matrices: an orthogonal matrix U, a diagonal matrix Σ, and the transpose of an orthogonal matrix V^T. Therefore, the SDV of the matrix A could be presented by the product of three matrices:

$$U * \Sigma * V^T$$

Thus, any given rectangular matrix A_{mn} (*m rows and n columns*) has a singular decomposition that could be written as following:

$$A_{mn} = U_{mr} * \Sigma_{rr} * V^T_{rn}$$

where:

A_{mn} is m by n matrix: for instance, document to terms matrix with m documents and n terms

U_{mr} is m by r matrix: for instance, m documents and r concepts

Σ_{rr} is r by r diagonal matrix: r is the rank of the matrix and represents the strength of each concept

V^T_{rn} is r by n matrix and represents the r terms and n concepts matrix

$$A_{mn} = U_{mr} * \Sigma_{rr} * V^T_{rn}$$

How SVD Works

In the following section we will discuss how to build an SDV of any given matrix.

For several applications, the data matrix A is close to a matrix of low rank, and it is useful to find a low-rank matrix that is a good approximation to the data matrix. In 1965, Golub and Kahan published a paper that presented a comprehensive algorithm for SVD.[1] They provided an algorithm to decompose any rectangular matrix and its pseudo-inverse.

Methodology to Compute SVD

Using Golub and Kahan's SVD algorithm, below are the five major steps we use to compute an SVD for any given rectangular matrix. An example will be provided, as well as a straightforward R code and outputs so the reader can practice and vet results using any text analytics software.

The five-step methodology to build the SVD of any matrix includes:

1. Compute A^T and A^TA

2. Determine eigenvalues of A^TA and sort them in descending order in the absolute sense. To obtain the singular values of A, square root A^TA eigenvalues

3. Construct diagonal matrix Σ by placing singular values in descending order along its diagonal; then compute Σ^{-1}

4. Compute eigenvectors of A^TA eigenvalues. Place these eigenvectors along columns of V and compute its transpose V^T

5. Compute U as $U = A * V * \Sigma^{-1}$

Then compute the singular decomposition of A:

$$A_{mn} = U_{mr} * \Sigma_{rr} * V^T_{rn}$$

Important to note: After calculations $U_{mr} * \Sigma_{rr} * V^T_{rn}$ should be approximately equal to A.

We will start by providing an example of a 2×2 SVD calculation using Golub and Kahan's method and follow with a 7×5 matrix. We will discuss how eliminating the least important concepts gives us a smaller representation that closely approximates the original matrix.

SVD through an Example: A 2 × 2 Matrix

Using the algorithm described above, let's compute the full SVD of the following matrix A that represents rating of customer food choice between fruits and vegetarian salad from the airline customer satisfaction survey.

For simplicity, matrix A is just a 2 × 2 sample extracted from a broader list of respondents to the airline food satisfaction survey.

$$A = \begin{bmatrix} 3 & -1 \\ -1 & 3 \end{bmatrix}$$

Let's compute SVD by using the five-step algorithm:

Step 1

Compute A^T and $A^T A$

$$A^T = \begin{bmatrix} 3 & -1 \\ -1 & 3 \end{bmatrix} . \text{ For this example } A^T = A$$

$$A^T A = \begin{bmatrix} 3 & -1 \\ -1 & 3 \end{bmatrix} \begin{bmatrix} 3 & -1 \\ -1 & 3 \end{bmatrix}$$

$$= \begin{bmatrix} 10 & -6 \\ -6 & 10 \end{bmatrix}$$

Step 2

Determine eigenvalues of $A^T A$ and sort these in descending order in the absolute sense. Square root these to obtain the singular values of A.

To determine eigenvalues of $A^T A$, we have to solve the characteristic equation of $A^T A - \lambda I = 0$; $A^T A - \lambda I = \begin{bmatrix} 10 - \lambda & -6 \\ -6 & 10 - \lambda \end{bmatrix}$

$$A^T A - \lambda I = (10 - \lambda)(10 - \lambda) - (-6)(-6)$$

$$= (10 - \lambda)^2 - (-6)^2$$

$$= (10 - \lambda - 6)(10 - \lambda + 6)$$

The equation $(10 - \lambda - 6)(10 - \lambda + 6) = 0$ gives two values:

$$\lambda = 4 \text{ and } \lambda = 16$$

In descending order, we then obtain:

Eigenvalues $\lambda_1 = 16$ and $\lambda_2 = 4$ and

Singular values:

$$s_1 = \sqrt{16} = 4 \text{ and } s_2 = \sqrt{4} = 2$$

Step 3

Construct diagonal matrix Σ by placing singular values in descending order along its diagonal:

$$\Sigma = \begin{bmatrix} 4 & 0 \\ 0 & 2 \end{bmatrix}$$

Compute Σ^{-1}

$$\Sigma^{-1} = \frac{1}{8} \begin{bmatrix} 2 & 0 \\ 0 & 4 \end{bmatrix}$$

$$= \frac{1}{4} \begin{bmatrix} 1 & 0 \\ 0 & 2 \end{bmatrix}$$

Step 4

Compute eigenvectors of $A^T A$ using $A^T A$ ordered eigenvalues from step 2.

For $\lambda_1 = 16$:

$$A^T A - \lambda_1 I = \begin{bmatrix} 10-16 & -6 \\ -6 & 10-16 \end{bmatrix} = \begin{bmatrix} -6 & -6 \\ -6 & -6 \end{bmatrix}$$

$$(A^T A - \lambda_1 I)X_1 = 0$$

$$\begin{bmatrix} -6 & -6 \\ -6 & -6 \end{bmatrix} \begin{bmatrix} x_1 \\ x_2 \end{bmatrix} = 0$$

$$-6x_1 - 6x_2 = 0$$

Solving $x_2 = -x_1$

$$X_1 = \begin{bmatrix} x_1 \\ x_2 \end{bmatrix} = \begin{bmatrix} x_1 \\ -x_1 \end{bmatrix}$$

Compute the length (L) of X_1

$$L = \sqrt{(x_1^2 + x_2^2)}$$

$$= x_1 \sqrt{2}$$

Dividing X_1 by its length

$$c = (1/L) \begin{bmatrix} x_1 \\ -x_1 \end{bmatrix}$$

$$= \begin{bmatrix} 1/\sqrt{2} \\ -1/\sqrt{2} \end{bmatrix}$$

For $\lambda_2 = 4$:

$$A^T A - \lambda_2 I = \begin{bmatrix} 10-4 & -6 \\ -6 & 10-4 \end{bmatrix} = \begin{bmatrix} 6 & -6 \\ -6 & 6 \end{bmatrix}$$

$$(A^T A - \lambda_2 I)X_2 = 0$$

$$\begin{bmatrix} 6 & -6 \\ -6 & 6 \end{bmatrix} \begin{bmatrix} x_1 \\ x_2 \end{bmatrix} = 0$$

$$6x_1 - 6x_2 = 0$$

Solving $x_1 = x_2$

$$X_2 = \begin{bmatrix} x_1 \\ x_2 \end{bmatrix} = \begin{bmatrix} x_1 \\ x_1 \end{bmatrix}$$

Compute the length (L) of X_2

$$L = \sqrt{(x_1{}^2 + x_2{}^2)}$$

$$= x_1 \sqrt{2}$$

Dividing X_2 by its length

$$c = (1/L) \begin{bmatrix} x_1 \\ x_1 \end{bmatrix}$$

$$= \begin{bmatrix} 1/\sqrt{2} \\ 1/\sqrt{2} \end{bmatrix}$$

Place these eigenvectors along column of V and compute its transpose V^T:

$$V = [X_1\ X_2]$$

$$= \begin{bmatrix} 1/\sqrt{2} & 1/\sqrt{2} \\ -1/\sqrt{2} & 1/\sqrt{2} \end{bmatrix}$$

$$V^T = \begin{bmatrix} 1/\sqrt{2} & -1/\sqrt{2} \\ 1/\sqrt{2} & 1/\sqrt{2} \end{bmatrix}$$

Step 5

Compute U as $U = A * V * \Sigma^{-1}$ and then the decomposition of A as:

$$A = U * \Sigma * V^T$$

$$U = A * V * \Sigma^{-1}$$

$$= \begin{bmatrix} 3 & -1 \\ -1 & 3 \end{bmatrix} \begin{bmatrix} \frac{1}{\sqrt{2}} & \frac{1}{\sqrt{2}} \\ -\frac{1}{\sqrt{2}} & \frac{1}{\sqrt{2}} \end{bmatrix} \frac{1}{4} \begin{bmatrix} 1 & 0 \\ 0 & 2 \end{bmatrix}$$

$$= \begin{bmatrix} 3 & -1 \\ -1 & 3 \end{bmatrix} \frac{1}{4} \begin{bmatrix} \frac{1}{\sqrt{2}} & \frac{2}{\sqrt{2}} \\ -\frac{1}{\sqrt{2}} & \frac{2}{\sqrt{2}} \end{bmatrix}$$

$$= \frac{1}{4\sqrt{2}} \begin{bmatrix} 3 & -1 \\ -1 & 3 \end{bmatrix} \begin{bmatrix} 1 & 2 \\ -1 & 2 \end{bmatrix}$$

$$= \frac{1}{4\sqrt{2}} \begin{bmatrix} 4 & 4 \\ -4 & 4 \end{bmatrix}$$

$$= \frac{1}{\sqrt{2}} \begin{bmatrix} 1 & 1 \\ -1 & 1 \end{bmatrix}$$

And compute the full decomposition of A:

$$A = U * \Sigma * V^T$$

$$= \frac{1}{\sqrt{2}} \begin{bmatrix} 1 & 1 \\ -1 & 1 \end{bmatrix} \begin{bmatrix} 4 & 0 \\ 0 & 2 \end{bmatrix} \begin{bmatrix} 1/\sqrt{2} & -1/\sqrt{2} \\ 1/\sqrt{2} & 1/\sqrt{2} \end{bmatrix}$$

$$= \begin{bmatrix} 1/\sqrt{2} & 1/\sqrt{2} \\ -1/\sqrt{2} & 1/\sqrt{2} \end{bmatrix} \begin{bmatrix} 4 & 0 \\ 0 & 2 \end{bmatrix} \begin{bmatrix} 1/\sqrt{2} & -1/\sqrt{2} \\ 1/\sqrt{2} & 1/\sqrt{2} \end{bmatrix}$$

The result of the product of the previous three matrices is exactly the matrix $\begin{bmatrix} 3 & -1 \\ -1 & 3 \end{bmatrix}$ that is basically our matrix A.

SVD Interpretation

From the matrix $A = U * \Sigma * V^T$:

If A is a document-to-terms matrix, $A^T A$ is term-to-term similarity matrix while AA^T is document-to-document similarity matrix.

U is the document-to-concept similarity matrix

Σ is strength of the concept

V^T is the term to concept similarity matrix

So, applying this to our previous example, where $A = \begin{bmatrix} 3 & -1 \\ -1 & 3 \end{bmatrix}$, U represents the document concept matrix; the first column of $U \begin{bmatrix} \frac{1}{\sqrt{2}} \\ -\frac{1}{\sqrt{2}} \end{bmatrix}$ therefore represents the concept (here the first concept is fruit and the second column represents vegetables).

The diagonal elements of $\Sigma = \begin{bmatrix} 4 & 0 \\ 0 & 2 \end{bmatrix}$ represent the strength of each concept. The strength of the first concept (fruit) is 4 while the second concept (vegetable) has strength of 2.

Elements of the matrix $V = \begin{bmatrix} 1/\sqrt{2} & -1/\sqrt{2} \\ 1/\sqrt{2} & 1/\sqrt{2} \end{bmatrix}$ include terms to concepts similarity matrix, in this example element fruit $\frac{1}{\sqrt{2}}$ is the value of fruit and the first concept.

In this example, we started with a 2 × 2 matrix and ended up with a rank 2 matrix.

Using SVD for a 2 × 2 matrix was only illustrative, since it does not really exhibit the power of matrix reduction conferred by SVD when working with high-dimensional document-by-terms matrices.

Getting a piece of code in R:

```
> A = matrix(c (3, −1, −1, 3), nrow = 2, ncol = 2)
> svd(A)
```

The R command *svd(A)* produces the three factorization matrices of A.

First it produces singular values of the diagonal matrix Σ:

$d [1]4 2

$$\$u = \begin{bmatrix} -0.70710683 & -0.70710683 \\ 0.70710683 & 0.70710683 \end{bmatrix}$$

$$\$v = \begin{bmatrix} -0.70710683 & -0.70710683 \\ 0.70710683 & 0.70710683 \end{bmatrix}$$

We have used a 2 × 2 matrix to showcase how to calculate full SVD, but to really see the power of SVD in finding concept and strength of the concept and more importantly dimension reduction, let's take a matrix with seven rows and five columns, also called a 7 × 5 matrix. The matrix represents a sample of customer response from the airline food satisfaction survey.

We will use R code to get the SVD; however, SVD could be obtained from many statistical packages. Below is the vector space that includes a sample of customers and their rating of fruits and vegetables:

Customer/Choice	Mango	Blueberry	Kiwi	Broccoli	Cauliflower
Customer_1	2	2	2	0	0
Customer_2	3	3	3	0	0
Customer_3	2	2	2	0	0
Customer_4	5	5	5	0	0
Customer_5	0	0	0	2	2
Customer_6	0	0	0	3	3
Customer_7	0	0	0	1	1

Let's call A the representation of the above table vector space:

$$A = \begin{bmatrix} 2 & 2 & 2 & 0 & 0 \\ 3 & 3 & 3 & 0 & 0 \\ 2 & 2 & 2 & 0 & 0 \\ 5 & 5 & 5 & 0 & 0 \\ 0 & 0 & 0 & 2 & 2 \\ 0 & 0 & 0 & 3 & 3 \\ 0 & 0 & 0 & 1 & 1 \end{bmatrix} \left. \begin{array}{c} \\ \\ \\ \\ \end{array} \right\} \text{Fruits choice} \quad \left. \begin{array}{c} \\ \\ \\ \end{array} \right\} \text{Vegetables choice}$$

By applying SVD to A, we will see how it helps to determine the two concepts from customer choice along with the strength of each concept. Though we can apply the same algorithm we have used with our 2 × 2 matrix to compute SVD, for simplicity we will use R code to generate SVD because calculating manually a 7 × 5 matrix can become quickly cumbersome and confusing. You can use any other statistical software to get the SVD.

There are a lot of statistical packages built in R that can be used to solve linear algebra equations such as SVD. To get SVD of the matrix A is pretty straightforward; it just requires two lines of code:

1. Set up the matrix in R

```
> A=matrix(c(2,3,2,5,0,0,0,
    2,3,2,5,0,0,0,2,3,2,5,0,0,0,0,0,0,0,2,3,1,
    0,0,0,0,2,3,1),7,5)
```

2. Calculate SVD of the matrix A using R svd(A)

```
> svd(A)
```

This second line of code provides three sets of outputs elements of the matrices Σ, U, V.

The first outputs are singular values: diagonal elements of the matrix Σ.

Note in this case the matrix Σ has only two singular values, since three of its five eigenvalues are equal to zero.

$$\lambda_3 = \lambda_4 = \lambda_5 = 0$$

Therefore, the diagonal matrix

$$\Sigma = \begin{bmatrix} 11.22 & 0 \\ 0 & 5.29 \end{bmatrix}$$

since $\lambda_3 = \lambda_4 = \lambda_5 = 0$ and

$$U = \begin{bmatrix}
-0.31 & +0.00 & +0.41 & +0.31 & +0.46 \\
-0.46 & +0.00 & +0.15 & -0.11 & +0.83 \\
-0.31 & +0.00 & +0.10 & +0.92 & -0.11 \\
-0.77 & +0.00 & -0.29 & -0.18 & -0.27 \\
+0.00 & -0.53 & +0.71 & +0.00 & +0.00 \\
+0.00 & -0.80 & -0.43 & +0.00 & +0.00 \\
+0.00 & -0.27 & -0.14 & +0.00 & +0.00
\end{bmatrix}$$

$$V = \begin{bmatrix}
-0.58 & +0.00 & +0.00 & +0.00 & +0.82 \\
-0.58 & +0.00 & +0.00 & -0.71 & -0.41 \\
-0.57 & +0.00 & +0.00 & +0.71 & -0.41 \\
+0.00 & -0.71 & +0.71 & +0.00 & +0.00 \\
+0.00 & -0.71 & -0.71 & +0.00 & +0.00
\end{bmatrix}$$

Since Σ only has two singular values, matrix U is therefore reduced to a 7 × 2 matrix. We can eliminate the last three columns without losing any significant portion of information.

Matrix V likewise is reduced to a 2 × 5 matrix, where we can also eliminate the last three rows. The reduced matrices U, Σ, and V contain the most meaningful information from the original high rank matrix A.

We can derive two concepts from the survey responses (in this case, fruit and vegetables) After getting rid of nonmeaningful columns and rows, U and V are as follows:

$$U = \begin{bmatrix} -0.31 & +0.00 \\ -0.46 & +0.00 \\ -0.31 & +0.00 \\ -0.77 & +0.00 \\ +0.00 & -0.53 \\ +0.00 & -0.80 \\ +0.00 & -0.27 \end{bmatrix} \quad V = \begin{bmatrix} -0.58 & +0.00 & +0.00 & +0.00 & +0.82 \\ -0.58 & +0.00 & +0.00 & -0.71 & -0.41 \end{bmatrix}$$

Therefore

$$A = U * \Sigma * V$$

Recalling U is the document-by-concepts matrix, we can see that we have two concepts. The first concept, represented by the first column of the matrix U, is fruit; vegetables is the second concept, represented by the second column of the matrix U.

The strength of the first concept fruit is 11.22, almost twice the strength of vegetables, which is 5.29.

And V represents the terms (mango, blueberry, kiwi, broccoli, cauliflower)-by-concepts similarity matrix.

It is easy to use the same approach and apply the same algorithm to our 85 million Prime subscribers against 18,405 movies to derive both the movie types based on a tiny subset of one hundred segments of customers that represent the 85 million subscribers.

Why Matrix Decomposition?

When performing text analyses of documents, we need to identify the dependence between column and rows, meaning documents and terms. Matrix decomposition such as SVD, PCA, or QR factorization are then used to produce a reduced rank approximation of the document matrix. As discussed earlier, the decomposition produces several similarity matrices (document-to-document similarity matrix, document-to-concept similarity matrix, and term-to-concept similarity matrix) and the strength of concept matrix.

Those matrices are used to categorize or define concepts from the documents and text. For instance, SVD is used to reduce the customer food choices, their type of salad preferences, or their movie reviews.

QR factorization is mostly used for information retrieval, such as search engine query.

PRINCIPAL COMPONENT ANALYSIS (PCA) AND APPLICATIONS

Why PCA?

PCA is the most valuable output of applied linear algebra. It has a broad range of applications from computer vision to neuroscience, including:

- Taxonomy
- Healthcare (detection of certain disease and genetics pathology)
- Biology
- Pharmacy
- Finance
- Agriculture
- Ecology
- Architecture

Even if there are more recent powerful algorithms, such as deep learning, for facial recognition, PCA has been broadly used for face recognition with the notion of eigenface, which was introduced in 1987 before the recent advent of deep learning applications. The principle is to use PCA to classify faces by finding average face and eigenfaces.

PCA is a nonparametric method of extracting relevant information from confusing datasets. It reduces a complex dataset into a lower dimension to showcase the underlying hidden, simplified dynamics in the data.

PCA is fundamentally related to the mathematical technique of SVD that we have covered in the previous section.

We often do not know what measurements best reflect the dynamics in a given system. As previously discussed, we sometimes record more dimensions than we actually need.

The goal of PCA is to compute the most meaningful low-dimension basis to re-express a noisy, high-dimensional dataset. The hope is that this new basis will filter out the noise and reveal key hidden dynamics in the data.

What Is Principal Component Analysis?

PCA, as its name implies, finds principal components in data. Invented in 1901 by Karl Pearson, PCA is a statistical technique that uses orthogonal transformation to convert potential highly correlated variables into a set of values of linearly uncorrelated variables called principal components. Like SVD, PCA is a dimension reduction procedure in which the first principal components account for the majority of the variability (or variance) in the data. Principal components are the directions where there is the most variance, the directions where the data is most spread out in a hyperdimensional space.

Each component is defined to encompass the most useful information from the data. PCA helps to exhibit the internal structure of the data in a way that best describes the variance in the data. You can think of PCA as a synthesized way to re-express the data as a linear combination of its basis vectors.

With PCA, we go from a large number of features (or measurements) to a small number of components, which still contain a sufficient proportion of the information.

Let's go over PCA using linear algebra transformations.

Let's assume that $X = [X1, X2, \ldots Xm]$ represent some measurements of some type of x_i. So, each column of X is a measurement from a particular trial. The covariance matrix of X is defined as:

$$S_X = \frac{1}{(n-1)} X X^T$$

The covariance matrix explains all the relationships between pairs of measurements in our dataset. So, to reduce noise and redundancy, we need to have low correlations between all x_i.

To solve the PCA: Eigenvectors of covariance are needed to perform eigenvectors decomposition.

With X, an m by n matrix, where m is the number of measurements and n is the number of data trials, we need to find an orthonormal matrix P with:

$$Y = PX$$

P is the new basis where we will represent X.

Therefore:

$$S_Y = \frac{1}{(n-1)} Y Y^T$$

The rows of P are the principal components of X.

By replacing Y in the above equation, we get:

$$S_Y = \frac{1}{(n-1)}(PX)(PX)^T$$

$$= \frac{1}{(n-1)}(PX)(X^T P^T)$$

$$= \frac{1}{(n-1)}(PX)X^T P^T$$

$$= \frac{1}{(n-1)}PX X^T P^T$$

$$A = X X^T$$

$$S_Y = \frac{1}{(n-1)}PA P^T$$

A is diagonalized by an orthogonal matrix of its eigenvectors.

$$A = E\Sigma E^T$$

E is the matrix of eigenvectors of A.

Therefore,

$$P = E^T$$

$$A = E\Sigma E^T \text{ meaning } A = P^T \Sigma P$$

$$S_Y = \frac{1}{(n-1)}PA P^T$$

$$= \frac{1}{(n-1)}D$$

The principal component of X is the eigenvectors of $X X^T$.

And with this latest transformation we notice that SVD is a more generalized method in describing and understanding change of basis.

How PCA Works

In this section, we will see how to do PCA manually, and then how to use R's built-in function. In practice, you'll usually use the built-in function, but doing it manually is a great way to understand this powerful linear algebra technique.

There are six main steps involved in PCA:

1. Data: Get the data in a rows-and-columns matrix format
2. Normalize: Subtract the mean (average) from each of the data dimensions, so that each column has a mean of zero and a standard deviation of 1
3. Calculate the covariance matrix
4. Calculate the components (eigenvectors) and eigenvalues of the covariance matrix
5. Choose components and form a feature vector or reduced matrix of vectors

    Once eigenvectors (components) are found from the covariance matrix, they are ordered by eigenvalues, highest to lowest, in order of significance. The components of lesser significance can be ignored. Some information is lost, but if the eigenvalues are small, very little information is lost. By removing eigenvectors, the final dataset (reduced matrix or feature vector) will have fewer dimensions than the original one.
6. Derive the new transformed data: Multiply the transpose of the feature vector and the transpose of matrix containing the original data.

Let's showcase how PCA is applied to real data using the above steps:

PCA through an Example

Let's assume that in the following we have two variables X1 and X2 that represent 11 recordings of door ring duration.

$$X1 = (0.6, 3.3, 1.8, 2.5, 1, 2.2, 3.4, 2.7, 1.3, 2.1, 0.8)$$
$$X2 = (0.9, 3.9, 2.7, 2.9, 1.5, 1.9, 3, 3.1, 1.8, 2.8, 1.1)$$

Step 1

Get the data in row-and-column format. This step we simply transform our datasets into a vector/matrix representation.

X1	X2
0.6	0.9
3.3	3.9
1.8	2.7
2.5	2.9
1	1.5
2.2	1.9
3.4	3
2.7	3.1
1.3	1.8
2.1	2.8
0.8	1.1

Step 2

At this step, we normalize our data by subtracting the mean (average) from each of the data dimensions, so that each standardized column has a mean of zero.

$$mean(X_1) = (0.6 + 3.3 + 1.8 + 2.5 + 1 + 2.2 + 3.4$$
$$+ 2.7 + 1.3 + 2.1 + 0.8)/11$$
$$= 1.972727273$$

Likewise,

$$mean(X_2) = 2.3272727247$$

The normalized datasets look like the following

X1 − μ(X1)	X2 − μ(X2)
−1.372727273	−1.427272727
1.327272727	1.572727273
−0.172727273	0.372727273
0.527272727	0.572727273
−0.972727273	−0.827272727
0.227272727	−0.427272727
1.427272727	0.672727273
0.727272727	0.772727273
−0.672727273	−0.527272727
0.127272727	0.472727273
−1.172727273	−1.227272727

Where:

$$\mu(X_1) = \text{mean}(X_1) \text{ and } \mu(X_2) = \text{mean}(X_2)$$

Step 3

Build the covariance matrix. Covariance matrix C for our two datasets vectors X1 and X2 is a 2 × 2 matrix defined as the following:

$$C = \begin{bmatrix} Cov(X1, X1) & Cov(X1, X2) \\ Cov(X2, X1) & Cov(X2, X2) \end{bmatrix}$$

since Cov(X1,X2) = Cov(X2,X1) we will only compute Cov(X1,X2)

$$C = \begin{bmatrix} Cov(X1, X1) & Cov(X1, X2) \\ Cov(X1, X2) & Cov(X2, X2) \end{bmatrix}$$

$$Cov(X1, X1) = \frac{1}{(n-1)} \Sigma_1^n [(X1j - \mu(X1))^2] \text{ here we have } n = 11$$

$$Cov(X2, X2) = \frac{1}{(n-1)} \Sigma_1^n [(X2j - \mu(X2))^2] \text{ here we have } n = 11$$

$$Cov(X1, X2) = \frac{1}{(n-1)} \Sigma_1^n [(X1j - \mu(X1)(X2j - \mu(X2))]$$

here we have $n = 11$

X1 − μ(X1)	X2 − μ(X2)	[X1 − μ(X1)]²	[X2 − μ(X2)]²	[X1 − μ(X1)] [X2 − μ(X2)]
−1.372727273	−1.427272727	1.8843802	2.037107438	1.959256198
1.327272727	1.572727273	1.7616529	2.473471074	2.087438017
−0.172727273	0.372727273	0.0298347	0.13892562	−0.064380165
0.527272727	0.572727273	0.2780165	0.328016529	0.301983471
−0.972727273	−0.827272727	0.9461983	0.684380165	0.804710744
0.227272727	−0.427272727	0.0516529	0.182561983	−0.097107438
1.427272727	0.672727273	2.0371074	0.452561983	0.960165289
0.727272727	0.772727273	0.5289256	0.597107438	0.561983471
−0.672727273	−0.527272727	0.452562	0.278016529	0.354710744
0.127272727	0.472727273	0.0161983	0.223471074	0.060165289
−1.172727273	−1.227272727	1.3752893	1.506198347	1.439256198
Sum:		9.3618182	8.901818182	8.368181818

From the sum obtained, we can now easily calculate all elements of C to obtain elements of the covariance matrix Cov(X1, X2) by dividing the sum by $(n - 1) = 11 - 1 = 10$.

Therefore:

$$\text{Cov}(X1, X1) = \frac{1}{(n-1)} \Sigma_1^n [(X1j - \mu(X1))^2]$$

$$= \frac{1}{(11-1)} (9.3618182)$$

$$= 0.93618182$$

$$\text{Cov}(X2, X2) = \frac{1}{(n-1)} \Sigma_1^n [(X2 - \mu(X2))^2]$$

$$= \frac{1}{(11-1)} (8.901818182)$$

$$= 0.8901818182$$

$$\text{Cov}(X1, X2) = \frac{1}{(n-1)} \Sigma_1^n [(X1j - \mu(X1))(X2 - \mu(X2))]$$

$$= \frac{1}{(11-1)} (8.368181818)$$

$$= 0.8368181818$$

$$C = \begin{bmatrix} 0.9361818182 & 0.8368181818 \\ 0.8368181818 & 0.8901818182 \end{bmatrix}$$

We can notice that the nondiagonal elements of our covariance matrix are positive; therefore, X1 and X2 should increase together.

Step 4

Calculate eigenvectors (principal components) and eigenvalues of the covariance matrix C.

Our covariance is a 2 × 2 square matrix so we can easily get eigenvalues and eigenvectors of C. Eigenvalues and eigenvectors entail the pattern and features that could be derived from the data.

Let's get eigenvalues of the covariance matrix C.

As we have seen with the singular value decomposition, eigenvalues of C are the solutions of the characteristic equation of

$$C - \lambda I = 0$$

where I is a 2 × 2 identity matrix:

$$C - \lambda I = \begin{bmatrix} 0.9361818182 - \lambda & 0.8368181818 \\ 0.8368181818 & 0.8901818182 - \lambda \end{bmatrix} = 0$$

The equation

$$(0.9361818182 - \lambda)(0.8901818182 - \lambda) - (0.8368181818)^2 = 0$$

gives two values:

$$\lambda = 1.75031603 \text{ and } \lambda = 0.07604762$$

In descending order, we then obtain:

eigenvalues $\lambda_1 = 1.75031603$ and $\lambda_2 = 0.07604762$

and following the same methodology we used in the SVD section above we therefore get eigenvectors with unit length as is required for principal component analysis:

$$V = \begin{bmatrix} -0.7167547 & 0.6973254 \\ -0.693254 & -0.7167547 \end{bmatrix}$$
$$\quad\quad V_1 \quad\quad V_2$$

Eigenvectors provide us with very useful information regarding the data pattern and dispersion. It provides the relationships between elements in the datasets as well as the strength of these relationships. The largest eigenvalue here is $\lambda 1 = 1.75031603$

We have derived the eigenvector V1, which entails the largest portion of the variance and information in our datasets. We can decide to keep V1 and represent the data on the new system with one vector instead of two, since the second eigenvalue is too small to contain any significant information about the data.

V1 helps us to achieve what PCA is meant to do: get a representation of a large noisy dataset into reduced dimensional vectors; eigenvectors that encompass the most important information of the original dataset.

Graphically

If we plot the normalized dataset against the eigenvectors as in Exhibit A.01, we can see that V1, our first eigenvector, carries the largest portion of the data variability in the new eigenvector space

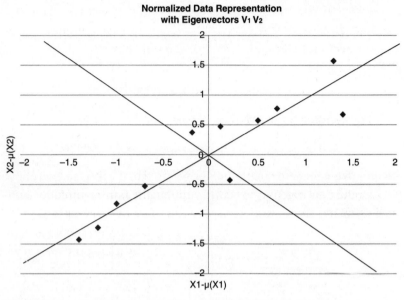

Exhibit A.01   Normalized Data Representation with Eigenvectors V1, V2

representation. V1 and V2 are perpendicular and V2 does not add much information, just two data points along its line. This graphical representation supports the notion of eliminating V2 as it provides less important information from our data. The eigenvector of the covariance matrix C enables us to extract the most important vector that characterizes our data.

Step 5

Derive the principal components. Once we get our eigenvalues and eigenvectors, we order them in decreasing order so that the largest eigenvalue provides the first eigenvector. That first eigenvector entails the most useful information regarding our original data and therefore represents the first principal component.

We can easily obtain the principal components by looking at the eigenvectors. They are also called feature vectors of the original data:

Eigenvector V = Feature Vector

$$V = \begin{bmatrix} -0.7167547 & 0.6973254 \\ -0.6973254 & -0.7167547 \end{bmatrix} = (\text{Feature 1, feature 2}) \text{ from our data.}$$
$$\quad\quad V_1 \quad\quad\quad V_2$$

As discussed in the previous section, the second eigenvector accounts for less information; therefore, we can leave it out.

Consequently, from our data we can only have:

$$V = V1 = \begin{bmatrix} -0.7167547 \\ -0.6973254 \end{bmatrix}$$

This eigenvector feature vector encompasses the most useful information from our data.

Step 6

Derive the new transformed data. Multiply the transpose of the feature vector and the transpose of matrix containing the original data.

We will derive the new transformed data by first using the two eigenvectors components and then secondly by taking the most useful eigenvector/component.

Let's start with the eigenvectors with the two components:

$$V = \begin{bmatrix} -0.7167547 & 0.6973254 \\ -0.6973254 & -0.7167547 \end{bmatrix}$$

We need to transpose V and then multiply V by the transpose of normalized covariance matrix.

$$V \text{ transpose} = V^T = \begin{bmatrix} -0.7167547 & -0.6973254 \\ 0.6973254 & -0.7167547 \end{bmatrix}$$

$$= \begin{bmatrix} -0.72 & -0.70 \\ 0.70 & -0.72 \end{bmatrix}$$

$$M = \begin{bmatrix} -1.37 & -1.43 \\ +1.33 & +1.57 \\ -0.17 & +0.37 \\ +0.53 & +0.57 \\ -0.97 & -0.83 \\ +0.23 & -0.43 \\ +1.43 & +0.67 \\ +0.73 & +0.77 \\ -0.67 & -0.53 \\ +0.13 & +0.47 \\ -1.17 & -1.23 \end{bmatrix}$$

$$M^T = \begin{bmatrix} -1.37 & +1.33 & -0.17 & +0.53 & -0.97 & +0.23 & +1.43 & 0.73 & -0.67 & +0.13 & -1.17 \\ -1.43 & +1.57 & +0.37 & +0.57 & -0.83 & -0.43 & +0.67 & 0.77 & -0.53 & +0.47 & -1.23 \end{bmatrix}$$

$V^T * M^T$

$$= \begin{bmatrix} -0.72 & -0.70 \\ 0.70 & -0.72 \end{bmatrix}$$

$$\times \begin{bmatrix} -1.37 & +1.33 & -0.17 & +0.53 & -0.97 & +0.23 & +1.43 & 0.73 & -0.67 & +0.13 & -1.17 \\ -1.43 & +1.57 & +0.37 & +0.57 & -0.83 & -0.43 & +0.67 & 0.77 & -0.53 & +0.47 & -1.23 \end{bmatrix}$$

$$= \begin{bmatrix} 1.99 & 0.07 \\ -2.06 & -0.20 \\ -0.14 & -0.39 \\ -0.78 & -0.04 \\ 1.28 & -0.08 \\ 0.14 & 0.47 \\ -1.50 & 0.52 \\ -1.06 & -0.04 \\ 0.85 & -0.09 \\ -0.42 & -0.25 \\ 1.70 & 0.07 \end{bmatrix}$$

As mentioned earlier we can remove the second vector as it does not provide any significant information. The first eigenvector with the largest eigenvalue best characterizes the data. And by keeping this vector and living out the second eigenvector we assume the dimension reduction. This vector represents the principal component of our dataset.

PCA APPLICATION TO FACIAL RECOGNITION: EIGENFACES

PCA is an effective technique that has been used to recognize and classify images of faces. Eigenfaces are simply eigenvectors that are derived from human facial recognition method using PCA. The method originally developed by Sirovich and Kirby was first used by Matthew Turk and Alex Pentland for facial recognition in 1991. Turk and Pentland EigenFaces algorithm uses PCA steps described in the section above for facial recognition.

How it Works?

Let's assume you want to build a facial recognition algorithm based upon a training dataset of 50 x 50 grayscale images. Meaning you will have 30 faces images with 2,500 features, where each feature corresponds to the intensity of each pixel. After importing your training dataset of 30 Faces Images following are PCA steps that you need to apply:

Convert your 30 Faces Images into 30 Faces Vectors (30 columns and 2500 rows)

Compute the Average Face Image: Average Face Image is the average face vector of 30 faces vectors that is usually called Mean Face

Compute Normalized Faces Vectors by subtracting the Mean Face from each Face Vector. For instance Normalize Face Vector1 (for the first image) is: Face Vector1 - Mean Face

Compute the Covariance matrix of the Normalized Faces Vectors that we call C

Compute the Eigenvectors of the covariance matrix .Eigenvectors are also called :principal components, principal features or features vectors; for instance if we have 20 principal components that represent 97 percent of 2,500 original features every face image in the dataset can now be represented with 20 components or eigenvectors not 2,500 features. And representations of these normalized faces vectors as weighted combinations of 20 eigenvectors are called Eigenfaces.

At this stage we can see that the algorithm helped to perform dimension reduction and has also removed redundancy by getting 20 principal components that account for the most variance of the 2,500 features.

How to classify a new face image?

If we have a new image and want to know if that image belongs to a person in our training dataset, we just have to calculate the Euclidian distance between our new image weights vectors based on the 20 eigenvectors and the weights vectors of images in our training dataset.

If the distance is below our acceptance threshold then we conclude that there is a match; the new image belongs to a person in our training dataset. If the distance is above the threshold then the new image is not recognized.

Eigenfaces is an effective facial recognition algorithm that has been around for quite some time. It is extremely straightforward and the simplest facial recognition method to implement. EigenFaces method works well and helps to better understand how facial recognition and dimension reduction are used. The method is fairly easy to implement using any currently available programming languages.

QR FACTORIZATION ALGORITHM AND APPLICATIONS

Why QR Factorization?

The QR matrix decomposition can solve linear systems of equations. It produces a reduced rank approximation of document matrix that enables an easier identification of the dependence between the rows (the terms) and the columns (the documents). QR decomposition is implemented in several programming languages as *QR Decomposition*.

What Is QR Factorization?

QR factorization is another useful dimension reduction and matrix decomposition technique that is used for text mining information retrieval, such as responding to a search engine query.

The term QR stands for the product of two matrices, Q and R. QR factorization stipulates that for any given document matrix M, the QR decomposition or matrix decomposition is the product of two matrices Q and R: M = QR

The QR factorization, also called QR decomposition, is a decomposition of a matrix into an orthogonal matrix and a triangular matrix.

The QR decomposition of a real square matrix A is a decomposition of A. For instance, a document matrix A can be decomposed as A= QR:

Where Q is $m \times m$ orthogonal matrix (i.e., $Q^T Q = I$)

Where R is $m \times m$ upper triangular matrix

If A is nonsingular, then this factorization is unique.

The factorization can be used to determine the basis vectors of any matrix A.

In information retrieval, for instance, the factorization can be used to describe the semantic content of the corresponding text collection. When you submit a search query, the text collection that you type in is transformed into a vector and matrices so that factorization, like QR factorization, can then be performed by indexing and assessing the vector of your submitted text against the basis vectors that exist in the knowledge base of the search engine you are using.

The process will then look at the similarity distance between your vector and the search engine knowledge base vectors to return only vectors (results) that are the closest to your query.

There are several methods for computing the QR decomposition. For the scope of this tech corner, we will use the Gram–Schmidt process, which is a straightforward algorithm to decompose any matrix A into QR factors.

How QR Factorization Algorithm Works

We will provide a high-level overview of the algorithm leveraging Gram-Schmidt matrices factorization process.

Gram–Schmidt Process Overview

Let's consider the Gram–Schmidt procedure, with the vectors as columns of the matrix M:

$$M = [m_1 \ m_2 \ m_3 \ \ldots m_n] \text{ then,}$$

$$v_1 = m_1,$$

$$e_1 = v_1 / \|v_1\|$$

$$v_2 = m_2 - (m_2 \cdot e_1)e_1,$$

$$e_2 = v_2 / \|v_2\|$$

$$v_3 = m_3 - (m_3 \cdot e_1)e_1 - (m_3 \cdot e_2)e_2$$

$$e_3 = v_3 / \|v_3\|$$

$$v_{k+1} = m_{k+1} - (m_{k+1} \cdot e_1)e_1 - \cdots - (m_{k+1} \cdot e_k)e_k,$$

$$e_{k+1} = v_{k+1} / \|v_{k+1}\|$$

Note if $X = (x_1, x_2, x_3 \ldots x_n)$ $\|X\| = \sqrt{x_1^2 + x_2^2 + \ldots x_n^2}$ is the norm of X.

And the resulting QR factorization is:

$$M = [m_1 \; m_2 \; m_3 \ldots m_n]$$

$$= [e_1 \, e_2 \, e_3 \ldots e_n] \begin{bmatrix} m_1 e_1 & \cdots & m_n e_1 \\ 0 & m_2 e_2 & m_n e_2 \\ 0 & 0 \cdots & m_n e_n \end{bmatrix}$$

$$= QR$$

QR Factorization through an Example

Let's consider the following document term matrix:

$$\mathbf{M} = \begin{bmatrix} 1 & 1 & 0 \\ 1 & 0 & 1 \\ 0 & 1 & 1 \end{bmatrix}$$

M represents a recommendation to movies: 1 means recommend and 0 do not recommend

The rows of the matrix M represent the feedback of the three moviegoers while the columns represent their ranking.

The first column was for Action movies.

The second column was for Horror movies.

The third column was for Comedy movies.

From the matrix M, we have three vectors:

$$m_1 = \begin{bmatrix} 1 \\ 1 \\ 0 \end{bmatrix} \qquad m_2 = \begin{bmatrix} 1 \\ 0 \\ 1 \end{bmatrix} \qquad m_3 = \begin{bmatrix} 0 \\ 1 \\ 1 \end{bmatrix}$$

Applying the Gram–Schmidt process to the matrix M, we have:

$$v_1 = m_1 = \begin{bmatrix} 1 \\ 1 \\ 0 \end{bmatrix}$$

$$e_1 = v_1 / \|v_1\|$$

$$\|v_1\| = \sqrt{1^2 + 1^2 + 0^2} = \sqrt{2}$$

$$e_1 = \begin{bmatrix} 1/\sqrt{2} \\ 1/\sqrt{2} \\ 0 \end{bmatrix}$$

$$v_2 = m_2 - (m_2 \cdot e_1)e_1$$

$$= \begin{bmatrix} 1 \\ 0 \\ 1 \end{bmatrix} - \begin{bmatrix} 1 \\ 0 \\ 1 \end{bmatrix} \begin{bmatrix} 1/\sqrt{2} \\ 1/\sqrt{2} \\ 0 \end{bmatrix} \begin{bmatrix} 1/\sqrt{2} \\ 1/\sqrt{2} \\ 0 \end{bmatrix}$$

$$= \begin{bmatrix} 1/2 \\ -1/2 \\ 1 \end{bmatrix}$$

$$e_2 = v_2/\|v_2\|$$

$$= \begin{bmatrix} 1/2 \\ -1/2 \\ 1 \end{bmatrix} (1/\sqrt{3/2})$$

$$= \begin{bmatrix} 1/\sqrt{6} \\ -1/\sqrt{6} \\ 2/\sqrt{6} \end{bmatrix}$$

$$v_3 = m_3 - (m_3 \cdot e_1)e_1 - (m_3 \cdot e_2)e_2$$

$$= \begin{bmatrix} 0 \\ 1 \\ 1 \end{bmatrix} - \begin{bmatrix} 0 \\ 1 \\ 1 \end{bmatrix} \begin{bmatrix} 1/\sqrt{2} \\ 1/\sqrt{2} \\ 0 \end{bmatrix} \begin{bmatrix} 1/\sqrt{2} \\ 1/\sqrt{2} \\ 0 \end{bmatrix} - \begin{bmatrix} 0 \\ 1 \\ 1 \end{bmatrix} \begin{bmatrix} 1/\sqrt{6} \\ -1/\sqrt{6} \\ 2/\sqrt{6} \end{bmatrix} \begin{bmatrix} 1/\sqrt{6} \\ -1/\sqrt{6} \\ 2/\sqrt{6} \end{bmatrix}$$

$$= \begin{bmatrix} -1/\sqrt{3} \\ 1/\sqrt{3} \\ 1/\sqrt{3} \end{bmatrix}$$

Since $\|v_3\| = 1$

$$e_3 = \begin{bmatrix} -1/\sqrt{3} \\ 1/\sqrt{3} \\ 1/\sqrt{3} \end{bmatrix}$$

Since:

$$QR = [e_1 \ e_2 \ e_3 \ \ldots e_n] \begin{bmatrix} m_1 e_1 & \cdots & m_n e_1 \\ 0 \ \vdots & m_2 e_2 & \ddots & m_n e_2 \\ 0 & 0 \cdots & m_n e_n \end{bmatrix}$$

$$Q = [e_1 \ e_2 \ e_3] = \begin{bmatrix} 1/\sqrt{2} & 1/\sqrt{6} & -1/\sqrt{3} \\ 1/\sqrt{2} & -1/\sqrt{6} & 1/\sqrt{3} \\ 0 & 2/\sqrt{6} & 1/\sqrt{3} \end{bmatrix}$$

$$R = \begin{bmatrix} 2/\sqrt{2} & 1/\sqrt{2} & 1/\sqrt{2} \\ 0 & 3/\sqrt{6} & 1/\sqrt{6} \\ 0 & 0 & 2/\sqrt{3} \end{bmatrix}$$

and $A = QR$

$$= \begin{bmatrix} 1/\sqrt{2} & 1/\sqrt{6} & -1/\sqrt{3} \\ 1/\sqrt{2} & -1/\sqrt{6} & 1/\sqrt{3} \\ 0 & 2/\sqrt{6} & 1/\sqrt{3} \end{bmatrix} \begin{bmatrix} 2/\sqrt{2} & 1/\sqrt{2} & 1/\sqrt{2} \\ 0 & 3/\sqrt{6} & 1/\sqrt{6} \\ 0 & 0 & 2/\sqrt{3} \end{bmatrix}$$

Application in Information Retrieval

To retrieve a document from a search query, for instance, search engine using QR Factorization will usually perform the following:

- Transform the query to a vector space model.
- Find the most similar document vector to the query, using cosine distance that provides similarity measure between vectors.

- In the information retrieval, assuming that φ is the angle between vectors, the cosine between vector is defined as

$$\cos(\varphi_j) = [[\ (a_j^T)q/(||a_j||^2(||q||^2)]$$
$$= [(Q_1 r_j)^T]/[||Q_1 r_j||^2(||q||^2)]$$
$$= [(r_j^T)(Q_1)^T q]/[(||r_j||^2(||q||^2)]$$

Important to Note

Two vectors with the same orientation have a cosine similarity of 1 while two vectors at 90° have a similarity of 0.

Examples and details provided here were to showcase how SVD PCA and QR Factorization work for readers eager to have a better understanding, willing to put their linear algebra knowledge to action. Today all major statistical and data science software and packages can be used to get SVD PCA and QR Factorization. Open sources such as R and Python provide everything you need to get the job done. So you don't have to do everything manually. With the UDA framework, Tools and techniques discussed and the frontline stories, don't wait to start your UDA journey or bring your current state to the next level. UDA will definitely help your organization to compete and win with this untapped data intelligence.

NOTE

1. G. Golub and W. Kahan, "Calculating the Singular Values and Pseudo-inverse of a Matrix," *J. Soc. Indust. Appl. Math. Ser. B Numer. Anal.* 2 (1965): 205–224. http://web .stanford.edu/class/cme324/classics/golub-kahan.pdf

FURTHER READING

Parinya Sanguansat (Editor), *Principal Component Analysis* (InTech, 2012): www .intechopen.com/books/principal-component-analysis-multidisciplinary-applications

About The Author

JEAN PAUL ISSON is a recognized worldwide expert and evangelist in Advanced Business Analytics and Big Data Analytics with over 22 years of experience. He is an internationally acclaimed speaker and an analytics professional thought leader who specializes in helping organizations create business value from their big or little data. Mathematician and Statistician by training, he loves helping executives to leverage data science to address business challenges to tell the data story and was named among the 180 leading data science, big data and analytics bloggers in the world by *Data Science Central*.

As Global Vice President of Predictive Analytics & BI at Monster Worldwide Inc. he has built his team from the ground up and successfully conceived and implemented global customer scoring, predictive models and segmentation, machine learning and deep learning solutions, web mining applications, and people analytics solutions for Monster across North America, Europe, and Asia/Pacific. He is also the Founder of the People Analytics Institute. Prior to joining Monster, Mr. Isson led the global customer behavior modeling team at Rogers Wireless, a Canadian Leading Telecommunication company implementing, churn predictive models and pioneering customer life time value segmentation to optimize services marketing and sales activities.

Mr. Isson frequently keynotes at international executive events on advanced business analytics, big data analytics, data science, artificial intelligence, human capital management, people analytics and innovation in United States, Canada, the United Kingdom, Germany, France, Belgium, Switzerland Denmark, the Netherlands, Poland, the Czech Republic, Australia and China. He has proven track record of 22 years of experience and research in advanced business analytics focusing on data science, machine and deep learning, big data analytics, predictive analytics, customer behavior modeling, market segmentation and sales coverage optimization. He is regularly invited by larger banks and economic organizations to share his People Analytics and Big Data Analytics Expertise. And recently spoke at OECD New Approaches to Economic Challenges Seminars front of Ambassadors from multiple countries members of OECD. He teaches the Executive Certificate in Advanced Business Analytics at Concordia University. He has delivered advanced business analytics workshops at executive program in United States, Canada, Europe, Asia and Australia.

He is the author (with Jesse Harriott) of Win with Advanced Business Analytics(John Wiley & sons, 2012) an People Analytics in the Era of Big Data (John Wiley & sons, 2016) reference books in business analytics and talent analytics that were translated in several languages including Chinese. He is also a contributor to several local and international newspapers and online magazine including the *Journal of American Management Association, MIT Sloan Management Review, The Wall Street Journal, Forbes Magazine, The Guardian, Financial Post, National Post, Staffing Industry Magazine, Which-50(Australia), Challenges Magazine, Liberation, Le Monde, Le Figaro, The Gazette and The Globe & Mail*. Mr. Isson has appeared in various media outlets including TV to cover Big Data Analytics, Data Science, people analytics and Employment Conditions.

Index

Page references followed by *e* indicate an Exhibit